Homo Mimeticus II

RE-TURNS TO MIMESIS

Homo Mimeticus II

RE-TURNS TO MIMESIS

Edited by
Nidesh Lawtoo
and
Marina Garcia-Granero

Leuven University Press

This project has received funding from the European Research Council (ERC) under the European Union's Horizon 2020 research and innovation programme (grant agreement n°716181: Homo Mimeticus, www.homomimeticus.eu)

erc

European Research Council
Established by the European Commission

Published with the support of the KU Leuven Fund for Fair Open Access

Published in 2024 by Leuven University Press / Presses Universitaires de Louvain / Universitaire Pers Leuven. Minderbroedersstraat 4, B-3000 Leuven (Belgium).

ISBN 978 94 6270 441 1 (Paperback)
ISBN 978 94 6166 594 2 (ePDF)
ISBN 978 94 6166 595 9 (ePUB)
https://doi.org/10.11116/9789461665942
D/2024/1869/53
NUR: 730

Layout: Crius Group
Cover design: Anton Lecock
Cover illustration: *Discus Thrower*, ink and acrylic on aquarelle paper, 2024.
© Michaela Lawtoo.

GPRC
Guaranteed
Peer Reviewed
Content
www.gprc.be

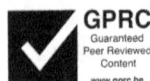

The stone went humming.

Homer, *The Odyssey*

CONTENTS

MAPPING MIMETIC STUDIES

Nidesh Lawtoo and Marina Garcia-Granero

> Mimesis is integrated in the complex vision of humanity.
> It is thus true that to the notions of
> *homo sapiens, demens, faber*, or *economicus*,
> we can add the term *homo mimeticus*.
>
> —Edgar Morin in *Homo Mimeticus*

With this epigrammatic affirmation reintegrating mimesis in the complex genealogy of *Homo sapiens*, the transdisciplinary thinker Edgar Morin (1921–) joined hands to bring the first volume of *Homo Mimeticus* to an end. This ending marked, in fact, a new beginning. Launching a new theory of imitation vital to facing the contemporary manifestations of mimesis that, under different masks, cast a long material shadow on the present and future, the goal of the first volume was to set new theoretical foundations for an emerging field we called mimetic studies, a transdisciplinary field now furthered in a planned trilogy on *Homo Mimeticus.*

As the subtitle of the second volume already indicates, our goal is to promote a mimetic turn or, rather, a plurality of *re*-turns to a different, more plastic and protean conception of mimesis that is already informing different strands in continental philosophy, literary theory, and social and political theory, stretching to include the neurosciences as well. A re-turn is not quite the same as a turn, but includes it in a movement of repetition with a multiplicity of differences. Hence re-turns. Going beyond stable binaries that simply oppose innovation to imitation, originality to reproduction, the re-turns to mimesis compose a spiraling figure that turns back, genealogically, to one of the most influential, resilient, and longstanding concepts in western thought in order to propel it further into the present and future metamorphoses of homo mimeticus that will continue to occupy us in volume three as well.

From a variety of contemporary perspectives that cut across the two-cultures divide, it is in fact clear now that mimesis can no longer be restricted to a realist copy, imitation, or representation of nature predicated on the logic of the same. Rather, mimesis turns out to be constitutive of the birth of a protean, embodied, relational, and eminently innovative species caught in an ongoing process of becoming other. From the affective turn to the ethical turn, the cognitive turn to the new materialist turn, the neuro turn to the posthuman turn to the nonhuman turn, some of the most influential turns in critical theory over the last decades have in fact been re-turning to the ancient realization that humans are thoroughly imitative animals. This confirmation, however, was often implicit, as mimesis appeared under different conceptual masks or personae constitutive of homo mimeticus' protean identity. They go from identification to simulation, affective contagion to performativity, influence to inclinations, animal mimicry to biomimicry, plasticity to mirror neurons, to name but a few contemporary avatars of mimesis we now explicitly pursue.

In the process, one of the general ambitions of mimetic studies is to redraw nothing less than the ever-changing contours of who humans are and can potentially become. *Homo sapiens sapiens* can, in fact, no longer be solely defined as a maker of tools (*homo faber*) or maker of profits (*economicus*), as a player of games (*homo ludens*) or a player of god (*homo deus*)—though humans continue to impersonate these roles with disconcerting efficacy in the digital age (*homo digitalis*). Nor is the qualifier "*mimeticus*" simply one more adjectival attribute in a long chain of qualifications of the genus *homo* that already include *religiosus* and *aestheticus*, *academicus* and *empathicus*, *bellicus* and *ecologicus*, among other masks adopted by a protean species—though we shall see that masks remain constitutive of mimetic personalities (from Latin, *persona*, mask worn in the theater). Rather, the overarching hypothesis internal to the *Homo Mimeticus* trilogy is much more radical and fundamental: it suggests that humans' longstanding inclination for plastic transformations, chameleon-like adaptations, and technological innovations that allowed us to become, in a relative short time, the dominant species on Earth with the power to change not only ourselves but also the geology of the planet itself in an epoch many call Anthropocene—this striking power, or as we call it, *pathos*—stems, somewhat paradoxically, from an all too human capacity to imitate others, be they human or nonhuman, real or artificial, offline or online.

As we set out to further map the fast-expanding field of mimetic studies in view of opening up new paths for interdisciplinary exploration, it is thus important to briefly glance back to the ground covered thus far in order to go further.[1] Despite a longstanding restriction of mimesis to the realistic logic of sameness, or its most recent attachment to a chain of linguistic differences, let us recall that the theory of homo mimeticus goes beyond sameness and difference. Its genealogy, in fact, originates in a long chain of Dionysian thinkers who, from Plato to Nietzsche into the present, were sensitive to the magnetic, contagious, and in this sense mimetic properties of a concept that originates in dramatic performances (*mimēsis*, from *mîmos*, performance or actor). Reframed from an immanent, embodied, and intersubjective perspective, it becomes quickly clear that mimesis, already for the ancient Greeks, went beyond visual representations to affect all the senses. It does so in a plurality of ways, both individually and collectively, consciously and unconsciously, rationally and irrationally, empathically and violently, and we should now add, analogically and digitally, online and offline, via human and artificial intelligence.

This also means that mimesis does not simply generate phantoms or shadows of reality to be critiqued as illusory appearances from the idealist distance of the *vita contemplativa*. On the contrary, once animated by actors, phantoms have the power to *spell*-bind the audience: that is, to bind them via a hypnotic spell, generating phantoms of the ego living what we proposed to call a "*vita mimetica*" (Lawtoo 2022, 69–92). In the process, mimesis also generates contagious phenomena that go beyond good and evil in the ethical, political, but also diagnostic sense that it produces both life-negating pathologies—fascist movements, viral pandemics, escalating wars, and climate catastrophes being obvious examples—and, at the same time, and without contradiction, promotes life-affirmative diagnostics of the contagious logic of mimetic pathos, or as we call them, patho-*logies*.

This overturning of perspectives that turns a pathology into a diagnostic *logos* on contagious affects is of modernist, Nietzschean inspiration. Its genealogy, however, harkens back to Plato's insight that physicians "would prove most skilled [...] if they themselves had suffered all diseases and were not of very healthy constitution" (Plato 1963, 3.408d). It also finds in the Renaissance philosopher Michel de Montaigne a key genealogical link between the ancients and the moderns. As he puts it in his final essay, "On Experience:"

> Certainly medicine professes always to have experience as the touchstone of its performance [*intervention*]. Plato was therefore right to say that to be a true doctor [*vrai médecin*] would require that anyone who would practice as such should have recovered from all the illnesses which he [*sic*] claimed to cure and have gone through all the symptoms and conditions on which he [*sic*] would seek to give an opinion [*juger*]. (2003, III.13, 1225)

Whether Nietzsche inherited this diagnostic insight from Plato or Montaigne is not the point, for he had read both. What matters for us is that for a tradition that goes from Plato to Montaigne, Nietzsche to mimetic studies, what applies to bodily sicknesses in general continues to apply to contagious sicknesses that affect the soul in particular: a first-person experience of imitative illnesses with one's body is a first step vital to developing a diagnostic with one's mind—if only because for these philosophical physicians the mind or, to use a more recent term, the brain, remains rooted in the body. As recent returns to affect, embodiment, and the brain suggest, this is a good moment to keep turning mimetic pathologies into patho-*logies*. As the conjunction between pathos and logos also indicates, this diagnostic method relies on the dynamic interplay between the *logos* of critical distance and inner experiences of mimetic *pathos* to diagnose what neuroscientist Vittorio Gallese, in the Coda to this volume, calls "brain-body."

Returning to the dawn of mimetic studies in classical antiquity, as the Prelude that follows will also show, remains a necessary step back that will allow contributors to leap ahead to modern and contemporary manifestations of homo mimeticus. As Plato was the first to notice, and a number of contemporary philosophers and classicists will confirm in part 1, mimesis is a Janus-faced concept with the (im)properties of a *pharmakon*—both poison and cure. We classify the duplicity of mimesis not only as pharmacological but, rather, as *patho(-)logical*, for a reason that is at least double. First to propose a theory of imitation that includes but is not limited to desire or writing, if only because it finds in an all too human vulnerability to what we call *mimetic pathos* a more general, immanent, and embodied starting point. And, second, to stress that the pathological aspects of mimesis that infect and affect homo mimeticus do not simply oppose pathos and logos, affect and reason, bodies and minds, let alone brains. Rather, they generate a complex spiraling loop in which an all too human vulnerability to mimesis can be put to both pathological and patho-*logical* uses, generating diagnostic *logoi* on mimetic *pathos*.

The pluralist focus on different *logoi* informing mimetic studies, then, marks an open, flexible, and dynamic epistemological orientation that is not reducible to a single, totalizing, and universal theory of culture. As Morin reminds us, a "complex" (from *complexus*, weaving together) vision of humanity entails interweaving a multiplicity of disciplinary perspectives—what Nietzsche also calls perspectivism. If these perspectives tend to be split in an increasingly hyperspecialized academic world, they need to be joined in order to face the complex challenges of the present and future. Mimetic studies opens up a middle path: it aims to sail past the Scylla of universalizing theories of imitation with the ambition to propose a single, universal, and totalizing solution to a protean problem on one side, and the Charybdis of fragmentary hyperspecialization that splits the protean masks of mimesis in disconnected rivalrous fields, on the other. Instead, it proposes a perspectival approach that brings different disciplinary threads together. The goal is to weave a complex tapestry in which each thread contributes to delineating the changing faces of homo mimeticus from distinct, innovative, yet interwoven perspectives qua patho-*logies*: from philosophy to psychology, sociology to anthropology, literary studies to media studies, political theory to environmental studies, posthuman studies to the neurosciences, among other emerging fields. Indeed, the re-turns to mimesis are currently gaining speed and momentum as mimetic studies enters in productive transdisciplinary exchanges with some of the most exciting areas of investigation in the humanities, social sciences, the neurosciences, and the earth sciences.

This is a brief and partial genealogical reminder of methodological principles mapped in more detail in volume 1. Still, it should suffice to confirm that Morin's concluding phrase was actually not an end; nor is he alone in thinking that mimesis needs to be integrated in a complex vision of humanity today. On the contrary, this conceptual affirmation from one of the most influential thinkers who spanned the entirety of the past century, reaching well into the present century, entails an open invitation; it also provides mimetic studies with a *coup d'envoi* that already set in motion a plurality of scholars across disciplines. Morin quite literally joined hands at the end of *Homo Mimeticus* to declare the field of mimetic studies officially open, for new generations of thinkers to follow up. This also means that the epigraph with which we started is not simply mimetic in the restricted traditional sense of constative, reproductive, and realistically descriptive of a pre-existing reality; rather, it is mimetic in our general sense that it is performative, productive, and geared to generating contagious effects. No wonder, then, that a second volume promptly emerged assembling a plurality of perspectives with the shared intention to *re*-turn to homo mimeticus to expand the growing field of mimetic studies.

As a complex, neuro-bio-psycho-anthropo-political phenomenon, mimesis is constitutive of the birth of *Homo sapiens*, manifests itself differently across periods and cultures, and is endowed with powers of adaptation that require each generation to keep up with its protean metamorphoses. These hypermimetic metamorphoses are now also intensified by a plurality of new digital media and artificial intelligence (AI) simulations that reload homo mimeticus with a 2.0 vengeance.[2] Assembling an international network of scholars of mimesis who increasingly feel the need to build diagonal bridges across different disciplines and perspectives, this second volume affirms new beginnings in the never-ending processes of understanding who we are—and can potentially become.

Mimetic Re-Turns

Conceived as a sequel to further the mimetic turn, then, *Homo Mimeticus II: Re-Turns to Mimesis* is not deprived of methodological advantages that are at least double, or rather, multiple: first, coming second, scholars are now in a position to build on concepts, genealogies, and methods of analysis constitutive of mimetic studies that are already in place so as to go further and focus on new territories and unresolved problems; second, this advantage is multiplied by the collective nature of a volume that includes a plurality of thinkers working in different areas of specialization, including classics, continental philosophy, media studies, performance studies, literary theory, political theory, environmental humanities among other perspectives now informing mimetic studies.

While volume 1 was primarily focused on the philosophical, aesthetic, and political manifestations of homo mimeticus, it cast as wide a net as possible for a single author. The goal was not so much to map the whole field in advance according to a predefined plan, model, or idea. Rather, it aimed high to open up a new field of investigation and invite supplements by scholars working on other areas. The aspiration was thus to pursue the "diagonal science" of mimesis pioneering figures like Roger Caillois already called for.

Many responded to the call; more voices joined a chorus on homo mimeticus than we could possibly accommodate here, including figures who played a pioneering role in the re-turn of attention to mimesis across two-culture divides.[3]

Mimesis, in fact, turned out to be central in building new bridges between "art, philosophy and science" (Gebauer and Wulf 1995, 2) as Gunter Gebauer and Christoph Wulf's magisterial study first published in 1992, *Mimesis*, had already anticipated at the twilight of the past century.[4] In fact, if a genealogist of the future were to date when the mimetic turn starts, one could do worse than pointing to the early 1990s as the period in which the re-turns to mimesis started to pick up speed.[5] A discovery was in the air, promising new connections that would cut across art, philosophy, and science.

In a striking synchronicity, a team of neuroscientists in Parma led by Giacomo Rizzolatti made a revolutionary discovery, first in macaque monkeys, and later in humans as well, that provided empirical foundations to the hypothesis of homo mimeticus: namely, that the drive to imitate others, including affects like empathy that generate a shared pathos, or *sym-pathos* (feeling with) might be rooted in "mirrors in the brain" (Rizzolatti and Sinigaglia 2008) that do not simply mirror or represent reality but, rather, mirror other people. How? On the basis of what Vittorio Gallese calls an "embodied simulation" that gives "birth to intersubjectivity" (Ammaniti and Gallese 2014) along phenomenological and unconscious principles, which, as we saw in volume 1, are resonant with the birth of homo mimeticus.[6] We shall return to clarifying the genealogical continuities between the theory of homo mimeticus and the one of mirror neurons in both the Prelude and, in the company of Gallese, in the Coda as well.

As any book on a subject as longstanding, influential, and above all resilient—for it spans nothing less than the entire history of culture—what applied to volume 1 equally applies to volume 2: although we aimed to cover as many areas as possible in terms of disciplinary perspectives, historical periods, and cultural as well as scientific manifestations of mimesis, our ambition was never to be exhaustive—obviously so, since mimetic studies is an emerging area of studies with fast-expanding, plastic, and porous borders. The aim was rather to provide new theoretical perspectives, conceptual tools, and critical discourses, or *logoi,* that both establish foundations for mimetic studies and serve as inspiration for further studies on homo mimeticus and the hypermimetic patho(-)logies it entails. Thus, if part 1 gives significant attention to re-framings of classical figures in mimetic studies such as Aristotle and, especially, Plato, it is for genealogical reasons in line with the re-turns to a *vita mimetica* that was well-known at the dawn of philosophy and is worth reconsidering in the digital age.

Historical philosophizing, as Nietzsche understood it, is not the same as antiquarian history for it keeps a focus on problems vital for the present. It also calls for a type of modesty that leads genealogists of mimesis to acknowledge influential precursors. To be sure, Plato and Aristotle are often considered re-sponsible for framing mimesis in a stabilizing metaphysical mirror or aesthet-ic representation mimetic studies aims to go beyond. In the case of Plato, "he," under the mask of Socrates, even dismissed mimesis as an illusory shadow or phantom without reality thereby staging "the programming of *non-mimetic* discourse" (Lacoue-Labarthe 1998, 123) that reached up to the past century.[7] And yet, a careful re-reading of founding texts about mimesis like *Republic*, *Ion*, and the *Poetics* central to part 1, shows a more complex picture: Plato and Aristotle, in fact, set theoretical foundations for a more nuanced understanding of "technai," as Henry Staten argues, as well as of "contagious" affects, as Mikkel Borch-Jacobsen stresses—both of which are central to a genealogy of homo mi-meticus that is rediscovered today. These classical figures also staged an agon between a *critique* of mimetic pathos and the pathologies it generates (Plato), on the one hand, and a *defense* of mimesis for the philosophical logos it entails (Aristotle), on the other. And yet, their drawing hands are not simply opposed via the violent logic of mimetic rivalry. Rather, they set in motion a mimetic agonism that, as we shall see, informs the genealogy of mimesis from antiquity to modernity and continues to inform the patho(-)logical tendencies of homo mimeticus in the present.

More recent precursors of mimetic studies need to be acknowledged as well. As we move into the twentieth century, critical theorists like Walter Benjamin, Roger Caillois, and Theodor Adorno agreed that "the mimetic fac-ulty" (Benjamin's term) is central to the evolutionary development of *Homo sa-piens*. Here, too, Nietzsche is a key influence, for he traced the birth of homo mimeticus back to animal mimicry, as we saw in volume 1.[8] In *Minima Moralia*, Adorno is thus missing Nietzsche's complex patho-*logical* diagnostic of the birth of consciousness as a social network as he unilaterally aligns his influential pre-cursor with a celebration of "authenticity" and "genuineness" (Adorno 2005, 154). Nietzsche would have been the first to agree with Adorno, and thus with a long tradition in mimetic studies that goes back to Plato, that "[t]he human is indissolubly linked with imitation: a human being only becomes human at all by imitating other human beings" (154). The agon between Adorno and Nietzsche is thus a mimetic one, if only because they both agree in tracing the birth of *Homo sapiens* back to an all too imitative principle.[9] Beyond ancient and mod-ern quarrels that, for a long time, simply opposed *les anciens* and *les modernes*, realists and modernists, this is, indeed, the fundamental hypothesis this volume continues to reevaluate and promote.

Closer to us, mimetic studies is fully informed by precursors sensitive to the imitative nature of human desire and the destabilizing improperties of writing; yet it should not hastily be confused with neither mimetic theory nor deconstruction. There is, in fact, a genealogical sense in which perspectival patho-logies drive a wedge between mimetic theory and poststructuralism, mimetic desire and the mime of nothing, scapegoating (*pharmakos*) and writing (*pharmakon*), as was also shown in volume 1. It does so to account for the immanent, material, and embodied manifestations of a homo mimeticus in need of supplementary theoretical foundations sensitive to both logical and patho-logical perspectives.

Mimetic studies both draws on previous theories of mimesis while developing new concepts in order to promote a more encompassing, transdisciplinary, and collaborative field of investigation. Suffice it to recall that on one side, René Girard rightly stresses the anthropological foundations of mimesis by rooting them in triangles of mimetic desires and rivalry; yet the narrow focus on quasi-Oedipal triangulations that unilaterally lead to violence and scapegoating neglects the anthropological fact that mimetic pathos goes beyond good and evil in the sense that it operates for good and ill, generating pathologies and patho-logies. Hence the suggestion to incorporate mimetic desire in the more generalized concept of mimetic pathos, and the patho(-)logies it entails, a move that as was shown elsewhere is productively entangled with affect theory.[10]

On the other side, a poststructuralist tradition that finds in Jacques Derrida, Jean-Luc Nancy, J. Hillis Miller,[11] and even more acutely, Philippe Lacoue-Labarthe, its major representatives, was very sensitive to the troubling and destabilizing pharmacological "improprieties" of mimetic subjectivity crucial to the critique of rising (new) fascist movements, for instance. Lacoue-Labarthe, for one, already announced that "mimesis returns to regain its powers" (1998, 138). Supplemented by feminist, decolonial, and posthumanist theorists like Luce Irigaray, Homi Bhabha, and Katherine Hayles, among other thinkers internal to this volume like Mikkel Borch-Jacobsen and William E. Connolly, a number of influential figures have been contributing to launching mimetic studies on the international scene.[12] This tradition also denounced ethnocentric and phallocentric tendencies that tend to project the troubling (im)proprieties of mimesis onto gendered, racial, and queer others via a move characteristic of what we call mimetic racism and mimetic sexism qua transphobia. While attention to the feminist implications of what we call, with Adriana Cavarero, "mimetic inclinations," is already informing the re-turn to mimesis,[13] there is still much to be done on the front of gender equality. Hence, we aim to return to this subject in *Homo Mimeticus III* in the company of Catherine Malabou.[14]

Since the general commitment to the linguistic turn dominant from the 1970s to the 1990s did not sufficiently emphasize the embodied, relational, affective, and mirroring qualities of subjects embedded in what an immanent tradition calls a "world of becoming" (Connolly 2011), a supplement to mimetic studies is needed. A theory of homo mimeticus is, in fact, not exclusively limited to humans—though it finds in our species distinctive features of mimesis; it also troubles a set of binaries that dominated rationalist accounts of *Homo sapiens* in the past, such as brain/body, pathos/logos but also human/nonhuman, mimicry/biomimicry among others, in view of propelling mimesis beyond nature and culture in the present and future.

All contributing to the same forward-oriented gesture beyond aesthetic realism, the chapters that follow draw sustenance from a variety of disciplines that go from classical philosophy to the neurosciences, literary studies to the social sciences, new materialism to environmental studies, among other perspectives informing and transforming the mimetic turn via a plurality of re-turns. Let us thus outline the general trajectory of this gesture animating *Homo Mimeticus II* by paying attention to the plurality of voices that compose its tune in more detail.

Program

Given the genealogical orientation of the book, we shall follow a trajectory that draws selectively from a tradition in mimetic studies from antiquity (part 1) to modernity (part 2) into the present (part 3). In a way, Nidesh Lawtoo's Prelude titled "The Discus and the Bow" condenses this threefold approach by following a mimetic agon that goes from Homer to Machiavelli, reaching, via *grandissimi esempli*, present generations as well. Its general goal is to flesh out new conceptual arrows for mimetic studies that will inform many of the chapters that follow. It also sounds the initial tune to launch the plurality of voices re-turning to an ancient mimetic agon reframed in light of modern and contemporary preoccupations.

And yet, despite its threefold temporal division, we hasten to add that the volume does not aim to develop a linear historical argument based on a grand narrative of progress. On the contrary, each essay provides a different perspective on the spiraling patho(-)logies of homo mimeticus that keep turning and re-turning in a kaleidoscope of changing masks. We shall thus consider phenomena as diverse as poetic inspiration and technical craft, coercion and domestication, mimetic nihilism and heterology, violence and theatricality, empathy and pedagogy, hysteria and the mimetic unconscious, the Anthropocene and biomimicry, among other concepts and perspectives that, once again, do not aim to map the entirety of a fast-expanding field; rather, they open up transdisciplinary paths for new mimetic studies to come.[15]

Across the shifts of emphasis and perspectives, all the chapters contribute to the re-turns to mimesis. They do so by shifting the focus from the dominant definition of this longstanding concept restricted to a visual representation or copy of reality, toward the immanent, embodied, and material foundations of a homo mimeticus who imitates with all the senses. This overturning of perspective proposes an alternative to what Adriana Cavarero calls a "videocentric" (2005, 40) tradition whose roots stem from ancient thought and will be subjected to a rigorous reconsideration in part 1. It also overturns the idealist privilege given to ideal Forms over and against base material copies by focusing on modern materialist theories that reveal how bodily drives are at the origins of thought. Lastly, the focus on mimetic pathos unmoors mimesis from Oedipal triangles restricted to mimetic desire and rivalry to affirm a pre-Freudian conception of the unconscious that was marginalized in the past century for it was untimely but, as genealogical lenses make clear, finds timely empirical confirmations in the neuroscience of the present post-Freudian century.

The general aim of part 1, "Re-Framings of Classical Mimesis," is to return to the Greek origins of mimesis to find the means to understand our present. Prominent and emerging classicists, philosophers and theorists join forces to display the still-standing strength of the Greek concept of *mimēsis* by relying on technical bows whose conceptual arrows—techne, enthusiasm, pathos, among others—reach into the present.

In "Plato on Facebook," Mikkel Borch-Jacobsen goes back to the problematic of the mimetic subject that already preoccupied him at the dawn of his career;[16] he does so by inscribing this subject at the dawn of philosophy itself while showing its relevance for the present. In particular, he takes the Arendtian injunction to "think the present" as a starting point to diagnose our phantom-like condition in the digital age. To that end, he re-turns to a founding text for mimetic studies: namely, Plato's *Ion*—a dialogue we already encountered in volume 1 now interpreted from the angle of psychic dispossessions reloaded by new media. This genealogical move allows Borch-Jacobsen to diagnose multiple variants of infectious mimesis and psychic dispossessions currently at the heart of today's populisms, post-truth, and spell-binding social networks. In particular, via the protean figure of the rhapsode, Borch-Jacobsen reminds us that already in Plato mimesis troubles the philosopher for its disquieting malleability—or, as we shall call it in volume 3, troubling plasticity. The magnetic chain of the *Ion* that goes from Apollo to the Muses, Homer to rhapsodes, reaching via new magnetizing media into the present, turns out to be a contagious and viral chain, or network; it includes digital networks where each one joins in turn in the dance to become *other*, the same as another. Rather than simply banishing mimesis, Borch-Jacobsen shows that Plato's strategy consists in using "*mimesis* against *mimesis*." In a paradoxical, patho(-)logical move the antidote (*pharmakon*) against the mimetic poison of mimesis—namely philosophy—turns out to be implicated in this very same poison (*pharmakon*, again) it attempts to cure.

Furthering a reevaluation of mimesis as both poison and remedy, in "Techne vs. Mimesis in Plato's *Republic*: What Socrates Really Says against Homer," Henry Staten overturns the metaphysical foundations of the most influential text for idealist theories of mimesis—namely, Book 10 of the *Republic*—via an immanent techne theory that goes beyond the mirroring logic of representation. In particular, Staten shows that the notorious *Platonic* "imitation of a copy" schema is quickly left behind by *Socrates* in favor of an entirely new three-level schema of techne in which the concept of artisanal "use" replaces the level of abstract ideas. Showcasing an agon between Socratic techne contra Platonic mimesis, the chapter proceeds to uncover a Socratic theory of techne (or "techne theory") sensitive to the immanent power of technai to give material *form* not only to artisanal *objects* but also to ethical *subjects* in the Greek polis. Rigorously focused on the tensions and aporias in Plato's text, which is re-framed in the context of a consistent Socratic concern with techne haunting a plurality of Platonic dialogues, this chapter has far-reaching consequences for classicist and philosophy more generally. It shows that the Platonic metaphysics of ideal Forms that dismisses art as an "imitation of an imitation" rests on nothing more, but also nothing less, than the history of an interpretative error. In the process, Staten contributes to contemporary re-turns to different, more embodied, and immanent, Socratic-Nietzschean crafts of imitation that benefit from a down-to-earth technical supplement.

Acting as a counterpoint to one-sided interpretations of Platonic mimesis as a dangerous pathology, in chapter 3, "Coercion and Mimesis in Plato: Compelling Someone to Change their Nature," Carlos Carvalhar focuses on Plato's diagnostic of the power of dramatic mimesis to form and transform subjectivity, a question known by classicists as "second nature" shaped by mimetic experiences. The chapter contributes to the mimetic turn by displaying Plato's ethical and pedagogical concerns with plastic subjects formed by mythic and literary models for both good and ill—a point central to mimetic studies in general that will re-turn in *Homo Mimeticus III* as well. In particular, Carvalhar foregrounds Plato's patho-*logical* evaluation of mimesis geared toward "becoming-god" via a mimetic reenactment of positive models discussed in less-known dialogues such as *Protagoras* and *Theaetetus*. He also suggests ways in which this "becoming-god" impulse can manifest itself in today's secular societies, for instance, as a striving for perfection, or as a pursuit of elevated virtues.

In chapter 4, "Mimetic Resistance," Teresa Casas Hernández offers a comparison between Plato's and Aristotle's foundational accounts of mimesis that does not focus on their often-repeated opposition but on their continuity instead. Caught in the paradoxical logic of mimetic agonism, Casas Hernández shows that the founding fathers of antithetical traditions in philosophy shared, across their opposed evaluations, a similar concern to move away from an oral tradition of mimesis rooted in *mimos* and performance. Since the *telos* of mimetic studies is to recover an oral tradition sensitive to the contagious powers of pathos, the chapter contributes to the mimetic turn by tracing the hidden reasons that lead Plato and Aristotle to replace oral mimesis via the visual trope of painting. The chapter ends with a return to the present, suggesting that oral mimesis is a potentially political and epistemic tool for social resistance, as shown by contemporary performative manifestations of passive forms of imitation that stress its power to steal, re-appropriate, and subvert.

Mark Pizzato concludes this first part with a chapter arguing that Plato's allegory of the cave can be reframed in light of the problematic of media violence. In "Behind Plato's Shadows and Today's Media Monsters," he shows that the distinction between a visual mimesis based on representation and a bodily mimesis based on (imaginary) identification—both of which are present in the cave *dispositif*—helps understand the power of images to cast a spell on the ego generating what mimetic studies calls phantom egos. Drawing on a wide range of theories that go from anthropology to evolutionary psychology to the neurosciences Pizzato furthers a transdisciplinary re-turn to homo mimeticus that shows how ritual aesthetic experiences are not opposed to the findings of science, even on a topic as contested as media violence. In line with neuroscientists like Vittorio Gallese who engage with cave paintings from the dawn of *Homo sapiens* (Gallese and Guerra 2020, xv–xvii), Pizzato goes from Plato's cave to prehistoric cave art to foreground an "inner theater" generated by neuronal networks that intersect patho(-)logically with media networks with the potential to trigger mass-shootings in the United States and elsewhere. In the process, Pizzato emphasizes transdisciplinary genealogical continuities across nature/culture divides that support the hypothesis that our *vita mimetica* is born out of ancient caves. Be they prehistoric, philosophical, or mediatized, these caves set the stage for theatrical spectacles that are not only visual and exterior but affective and interior. This also means that they do not simply generate visual phantoms but phantom egos instead.

Overall, these five chapters in part 1 mark a shift from a predominantly visual and realistic mimesis that cast a shadow on most theories of mimesis in the past toward a more embodied, relational, and theatrical mimesis, which provides the driving telos of the mimetic return oriented toward the present and future. Together, the chapters demonstrate that the Greek philosophical origins of mimetic studies do not merely serve as subjects of antiquarian interest. Instead, they open up philosophical genealogies and wellsprings of ideas to diagnose a plurality of problems, including viral mimesis in modern media, education, plasticity, performativity, and violence, among many others.

Part 2 furthers the "Theorethical Re-Turns to Homo Mimeticus" by focusing on genealogical precursors of mimetic studies in modern and contemporary philosophy. In particular, they deepen our understanding of mimesis pathos and the multiple patho(-)logies of mimesis internal to contemporary preoccupations, including the modern nihilism first diagnosed by Friedrich Nietzsche, René Girard's account of escalation of violence during war, George Bataille's heterology as a science of the excluded or accursed share, an account of the mimetic unconscious via a reframing of hysteric women at play in dramatic spectacles, and a reevaluation of Philippe Lacoue-Labarthe's and Luce Irigaray's sensuous, theatrical mimesis which is not one.

Given Nietzsche's centrality in our genealogy of homo mimeticus, in chapter 6, "Nietzsche's Nihilism and Mimetic Studies," Marina Garcia-Granero studies the birth of nihilism out of mimetic relations. After contextualizing Nietzsche's account of the different layers of nihilism, she argues that, like mimesis, nihilism has a Janus-faced nature, manifesting both as salvation and threat. As a mimetic affect, nihilism produces a crisis of difference and loss of the ego that Nietzsche himself conceptualized via the mimetic trope of the "shadows of God." Garcia-Granero furthers an agonistic confrontation with Girard's mimetic theory to show that its theological solution to the death of God reveals itself as a nihilistic "shadow of God." Indeed, different strands of contemporary philosophy have focused on either side of nihilism: as a threat, like mimetic theory, or as a liberation, such as the hermeneutic school. Instead, mimetic studies fosters a pluralist, comprehensive understanding of the patho(-)logical character of nihilism as a *pharmakon*.

Picking up the discussion on Girard, in chapter 7, "Essential Violence and René Girard's Mimetic Theory," William Johnsen presents Girard's theory of essential violence as a precursor of the mimetic turn for he shifted attention from mimetic realism to an anthropology of mimetic desire and violence. While Girard's theory of desire, violence, and the scapegoat is well-attested in the scholarship, his early interest in cybernetics is not. Consequently, an entire area of research has been left unexplored. Johnsen begins to close this important gap. Thus, he recalls Girard's alarms concerning radical violence and viral contagion in *Battling to the End (Achever Clausewitz)* to show that violence is a single subject for Girard, wherever it starts. He argues that competition over scarce resources is not the focal point of Girard's own thinking—rather, the way violence spreads once fighting starts. To stop the reciprocal and escalating violence of the war—regrettably, a timely question—it is thus crucial to understand the logic of bifurcation that turns pathology into patho-*logy*. Demystifying the logic of contagion and polarization, Johnsen generates productive connections between mimetic theory (via Girard and Dupuy) and mimetic studies (via Morin, Lawtoo, and Gallese), furthering the productive dialogue between the two transdisciplinary fields.

After Nietzsche and before Girard, Nidesh Lawtoo argues that it is Georges Bataille who went furthest in recognizing the centrality of mimesis in intersubjective forms of non-verbal communication mediated by affective contagion. Hence, in chapter 8, "Bataille on Mimetic Heterology," he shows how multiple concepts now internal to mimetic studies emerge, phantom-like, from Bataille's early and little-known theory of heterology he developed in the 1930s and the well-known later concerns with the sacred, eroticism, and affective contagion it foregrounds. Supplementing Durkheim, Plato, and Freud, Lawtoo presents Bataille as a transdisciplinary thinker *avant la lettre* who paves the way for mimetic studies. He does so by proposing heterology as a materialist science of troubling subject matters—from (new) fascism to ecstatic experiences internal to death and love—an idealist tradition tended to exclude in the past but are currently resurfacing via new turns to affect, materialism, and mimesis. Following the transgressive dynamic of "mimetic communication" that has been neglected during the linguistic turn allows Lawtoo to show that Bataille remains a powerful transdisciplinary ally to account for both the affective and hetero-logical foundations of the mimetic turn.

In "A New Logic of Pathos: The Anti-Oedipal Unconscious and Hysterical Mimesis," María del Carmen Molina Barea further unravels the thread of a theatrical mimesis that cannot be restricted to realism but destabilizes the very notion of a proper subject. In particular, she develops a genealogy of the mimetic unconscious from an anti-Oedipal perspective on desiring mimesis that turns the dominant pathological view of hysteria into a patho-*logical* dramatization that escapes representation. Gilles Deleuze's and Félix Guattari's well-known anti-Oedipal theories of desiring production, in fact, cannot be dissociated from their less-known interest in "microimitation" that flows contagiously between self and others. Drawing on theories of hypnosis internal to both anti-Oedipal and mimetic accounts of the unconscious as well as on Antonin Artaud's theater of cruelty, Molina Barea turns to Robert Wilson's theater as well as paintings and photographs to provide dramatic specificity to her diagnostic. In the process, she reframes the pathological stereotype of hysteric women as an active mimetic subject that explodes Oedipal schemas and goes beyond psychoanalytical theaters of the unconscious. What emerges in the end is an account of the mimetic unconscious driven by an anti-Oedipal desiring pathos that transgresses representational forms and opens up immanent possibilities for becoming other.

In chapter 10, "Exhibition/Exposition: Irigaray and Lacoue-Labarthe on the Theater of Mimesis," Niki Hadikoesoemo connects two prominent precursors of the mimetic turn, namely the French philosopher and critic Philippe Lacoue-Labarthe and the feminist philosopher Luce Irigaray, thus providing a feminist and gendered supplement to our mapping of mimetic studies. Hadikoesoemo argues that the double sidedness of Lacoue-Labarthe's theatrical conception of mimesis bears the traces of Irigaray's deconstruction of "two mimeses" already staged in Plato. Both thinkers join hands in this chapter to affirm a corporeal philosophy of theatrical/feminine mimesis that anticipates the rise of performativity. They also pave the way for a feminist theory of gendered mimesis that is internal to mimetic studies. In the process, Hadikoesoemo links femininity to theatrical mimesis thereby troubling the binary logic of theater (re-presentation of reality) and the feminine (re-creation of a masculine imaginary) in favor of a more sensuous, relational, and process-oriented display of mimeses.

Part 3, "New Mimetic Studies from Aesthetics to Biomimicry," provides present and future-oriented lines of inquiry for mimetic studies: a genealogy of negative empathy overcoming the *aporias* of current debates in post-critique; two patho(-)logical accounts of fiction—one on Fernando Pessoa, the other on Maylis de Kerangal; a revolutionary perspective on how technology can imitate nature—or biomimicry—to face the impeding ecological crisis; and, finally, a call for a radical reassessment of our experience of time via a planetary mimesis in the epoch of the Anthropocene by one of the most influential political theorists writing today. Across their innovative perspectives central to new mimetic studies, these chapters also *re*-connect with the original, etymological understanding of aesthetics, that is, the science of sensation and feeling. Together, they confirm that the mimetic turn goes beyond autonomous conceptions of artistic representation that dominated the past century. They do so by engaging with the affective, bodily, technological, and immanent powers of art to break the wall of representation via a sym-pathos that reconnects, on new foundations, homo mimeticus to homo aestheticus.[17]

In chapter 11, "Negative Empathy in Fiction: Mimesis, Contagion, Catharsis," Carmen Bonasera frames the concept of negative empathy as a mimetic, immanent, and contagious human behavior. By drawing on reevaluations of empathy central to Fyodor Dostoevsky's *Crime and Punishment* (1866) and *Demons* (1873), this chapter defines negative empathy as a form of emotional contagion constitutive of complex aesthetic experience. Negative empathy encourages readers to oscillate back and forth between emotional identification and moral detachment toward/away from certain works and characters disturbingly portrayed as immoral and seductive. This oscillation between humans' openness to pathos and the ability to set up a critical distance from it, parallels the Nietzschean concept of pathos of distance that set the theory of homo mimeticus in motion. Thus reframed, empathy is put back in touch with its aesthetic origins first theorized by the nineteenth-century aesthetic theorist Theodor Lipps, now reclaimed as a precursor of mimetic studies, affect theory, and the discovery of mirror neurons. Bonasera supplements current debates in post-critique that tend to privilege positive empathy with fictional characters generative of negative empathy instead.

In chapter 12, "Fernando Pessoa and the ([P]Re)Birth of Homo Mimeticus," Kieran Keohane and Carmen Kuhling show that Fernando Pessoa's poetic and philosophical fascination with protean identities and multiple personalities make him an important precursor of the mimetic turn. Pessoa's literary language and multiple heteronyms give poetic and experiential lifeform to a *vita mimetica* that is constitutive of artistic creation, including the emulation of artistic models. Rather than generating envious rivalries that develop into sacrificial crisis and scapegoating, Keohane and Kuhling show that Pessoa and his multiple heteronyms imitate and emulate diverse models—from Shakespeare to Walt Whitman to Oscar Wilde—that resonate with one another joyfully, playfully, and above all, creatively. Located at the productive intersection of the Oedipal and the mimetic unconscious, the chapter ultimately shows how Pessoa's *personas* are not simply pathological; rather, they support the patho-*logical* embodied and phenomenological foundations of mimetic studies.

In line with a diagnostic streak that started in modernism, in chapter 13, "Literature, Pedagogy, and the Power of Mimesis: On Teaching Maylis de Kerangal's *The Heart*," Evelyne Ender reflects on the pedagogical powers of mimesis via stories that shape new generations of readers in the classroom. Given the origins of mimetic studies with Plato's pedagogical concerns with the power of narratives to form and transform subjects, it is a welcome move to bring mimesis back in touch with the effects of a contemporary text in the classroom. Drawing on her teaching experiences at Johns Hopkins University with students exposed to the *pathos* internal to Maylis de Kerangal's *The Heart*, Ender argues for the cultivation of a mimetic, literary education. Her strategy is to progressively move from the pathos generated by the experience of reading to a type of patho-*logy* articulated on the delicate pharmacological balance between emotion and thought. More generally, establishing productive continuities between phenomenology, deconstruction, and mimetic studies, Ender argues that the rise of the novel and its influence on our modern sensibilities involves both a historical and an epistemic awareness that fiction triggers a resistance conducive to critical thought, providing its own antidotes and remedies in the reading process.

The two final chapters complete the volume by opening up new mimetic studies to two major areas of investigation that take mimesis beyond nature and culture: biomimicry and planetary mimesis. In chapter 14, "The Biomimicry Revolution: Contributions to Mimetic Studies," Henry Dicks unfolds the relevance of mimetic studies for the environmental crisis via the concept of biomimicry and the new philosophy it entails. Supplementing Janine Benyus's *Biomimicry* (1997), Dicks proposes a "biomimicry revolution" (2023) that challenges the dominant conception of mimesis restricted to aesthetic creation in favor of a theory of techne based on the imitation of nature. His goal is to find points of convergence between biomimicry and mimetic studies while also broadening the reach of both fields. In particular, engaging mimesis from the angle of the object rather than the mimetic subject allows Dicks to expand the genealogy of mimetic studies beyond Plato and Aristotle (via Democritus of instance), to account for the shift to the imitation of God in the Medieval period (or theomimicry), while also reaching into the anti-mimetic foundations of modernism and hypermimetic inclinations of postmodernism central to mimetic studies as well. In the process, Dicks develops new patho-logical insights on how technology and its contemporary re-turns to the imitation of nature not only goes beyond anthropocentrism; it can also help mitigate impending eco-logical crises and environmental catastrophes in the Anthropocene.

In the concluding chapter, "Arks at Sea and Arcs of Time," political theorist William E. Connolly re-turns to the myth of Noah and the Ark, as portrayed in the *Book of J*, to explore dicey relations between events of nature and mimetic relays in cultural life, where temporal interruptions periodically occur. Connolly considers the "evental register of time" as a fundamental feature of time itself, and, as a result, points to some necessary philosophical and cultural adjustments concerning the character of time, culture and nature relations, as well as mimetic processes. To that end, Connolly establishes a dialogue with Michel Serres, Joseph Conrad, and Nidesh Lawtoo, all drawn upon to help explore time as a multiplicity and think of time as composed of multiple temporalities moving at different speeds and tra-jectories. Each evental turn in an old trajectory carries pressure to adjust and revise old extrapolations misinforming our understanding and experience of time, tra-ditionally influenced by both Christian religion and sociocentric tendencies that run deep in western culture. Such an exploration contributes to overcoming what Connolly calls "climate casualism." It also gauges the relations between evental time and mimesis during the period of the Anthropocene, in line with mimetic studies' environmental sensibilities underscored by previous chapters.

Acting as a Coda to the volume, in "Beyond Brain and Body: A Dialogue with Vittorio Gallese," Vittorio Gallese and Nidesh Lawtoo show that the mi-metic turn finds in contemporary neuroscience a timely empirical supplement to promote a re-turn to homo mimeticus that cuts across the brain and body divide. Part of the original Parma team led by Giacomo Rizzolatti that discov-ered mirror neurons in the early 1990s, Gallese contributed to the (re)discov-ery that we are mimetic animals. He is thus a strong ally for the mimetic turn: he develops a theory of "embodied simulation" relevant for imitation, but also empathy, theory of mind, aesthetics, film studies, and emerging hypermimetic subjects central to mimetic studies as well. Thirty years after the discovery of mirror neurons, Lawtoo travelled to Parma in 2023 to meet Gallese and deepen the genealogical connections between neuroscience and mimetic studies. They first discuss untimely philosophical physicians like Nietzsche, Charles Féré, and Pierre Janet, who anticipated the contemporary association between "move-ment and sensation" (Féré's phrase) via the insight that humans are embodied, relational, and intersubjectively attuned to the mind of others. As the dialogue unfolds ranging from phenomenology to mimetic theory, from critics of mir-ror neurons to the most recent experiments in the neurosciences on aesthetic experiences, Gallese provides new empirical evidence to support the mimetic hypothesis that we are embodied, social, and relational creatures whose behavior is shaped by mimesis, for good and ill. In conclusion, Gallese and Lawtoo join voices across old-fashioned two-cultures divides to call for new interdisciplinary bridges to tackle multiple social and technological challenges transecting new mimetic studies in the years to come, such as hypermimesis in the digital age.

As the chorus of voices in this volume confirms, mimetic studies arises with force and attention to confront pressing social issues and challenges that require the awareness that we are, for good and ill, mimetic creatures. This ancient realization calls for new perspectives to reevaluate the patho(-)logical manifestations of mimesis in the past, present, and future. We are confident this further mapping of mimetic studies by a plurality of international scholars will provide coordinates to navigate this fast-moving field while also encouraging transdisciplinary and innovative diagnostics of homo mimeticus to come.

Notes

1   In addition to vol 1 of *Homo Mimeticus*, mimetic studies has so far been the subject of special issues on "Poetics and Politics: with Lacoue-Labarthe," *MLN* 132.5 (2017), "The Mimetic Condition," *CounterText* 8.1 (2022), "Posthuman Mimesis," *Journal of Posthumanism* 2.2 (2022), "Mimetic Inclinations with Adriana Cavarero," *Critical Horizons* 24.2 (2023), and "The Mimetic Turn" *MLN* 138.5 (2023). For further mapping of "mimetic studies" see also Lawtoo 2023a, 1–34, 2023b, and www.homomimeticus.eu.

2   For a collective volume on "homo mimeticus 2.0" exploring "posthuman mimesis," see Lawtoo (ed.) 2024.

3   This volume assembles only a small selection of more than 60 papers presented at an international conference titled "The Mimetic Turn" held at KU Leuven in 2022 to mark the conclusion of the *Homo Mimeticus* project and the beginning of mimetic studies. Other essays emerging from the same conference were published in a special issue of *MLN* on *The Mimetic Turn* (2023). Chapter 1, "Plato on Facebook" by Mikkel Borch-Jacobsen was first published in *MLN* 138.5 (2023); chapter 7, "Bataille on Heterology," is a revised version of an article that first appeared in a special issue of *Theory, Culture, & Society* 35.4–5 (2018) devoted to "Bataille & Heterology." We are grateful to both journals for allowing us to reproduce them. All the other chapters are original works that have not appeared in print before.

4   Wulf's and Gebauer's contributions to mimetic studies appeared in *CounterText* 8.1. For other excellent introductions to mimesis in line with mimetic studies by contributors to the conference see Borch-Jacobsen 1993, Potolsky 2006 and Borch (ed.) 2019. For an informed praise of copying as essential to humans see Boon 2013. For a more recent study on the way "mimetic processes" at play in rituals, dance, play, performance, and gesture contribute to the transmission of "cultural heritage" and "identity formation" see Wulf 2022, 11. On the role of mimesis during the Covid-19 crisis, see also Gebauer 2022.

5   As indicated in volume 1, signs of a re-turn of mimesis were already emerging in the twentieth century, paving the way for the mimetic turn. For an informed overview see Spariosu (ed.) 1984.

6   As Ammaniti and Gallese put it: "the mirror mechanism may play a role in imitative behavior, even perhaps in unconscious mimicry of body postures, facial expressions, and behaviors of social partners" (2014, xi). Despite some psychoanalytical assumptions in productive tension with mimetic studies, the overall focus on maternal forms of empathic communication that foster "cooperation" more than rivalry and violence is perfectly in line with Nietzsche's genealogy of homo mimeticus (see Lawtoo 2022, 51–67).

7   Lacoue-Labarthe shows that Plato's "refusal of mimesis" predicated on a "psychology of desire (*epithumia*) and aggressivity (*thumos*)" (1998, 98) leading up to the sacrificial "expulsion of the pharmakos" (103) qua sacrificial poet not only anticipates the fundamental building blocks of René Girard's theory; it also entails a dramatization in which "'he', he who is named Plato, loses 'himself'," thereby anticipating a problematic central to mimetic studies.

8   See Lawtoo 2022, 43–67.

9   For a Benjamin-inspired account of mimesis understood as "the nature that culture uses to make second nature" (the latter being a concept as old as Plato) see Taussig 1993, 70 and Boon 2013. For recent accounts of Benjamin's and Adorno's critical theories in line with the mimetic turn see also Wolf 2022 and Durrant 2023.

10 On the links between mimetic studies and affect theory see Lawtoo 2023a, 19–34.

11 For Nancy and Miller direct contributions to mimetic studies see Nancy and Lawtoo 2022, and Miller and Lawtoo 2020.

12 For dialogues on imitation including William E. Connolly, J. Hillis Miller, Jean-Luc Nancy, Katherine Hayles, Christoph Wulf, Gunter Gebauer, Vittorio Gallese, Adriana Cavarero, Mikkel Borch-Jacobsen, and Edgar Morin, see HOM Videos, https://www.youtube.com/@homvideosercprojecthomomim971/videos

13 See Cavarero and Lawtoo 2021. For a special issue on mimetic inclinations see also Lawtoo and Verkerk (eds.) 2023.

14 Provisional title: *Homo Mimeticus III: Plasticity, Mimesis, Metamorphoses with Catherine Malabou.*

15 Mimetic studies has been from the beginning sensitive to the "mimetic racism" and "mimetic sexism" (Lawtoo 2013, 101–130) projected onto gendered, sexual, and racial others. For readers interested in the relation between gender and mimesis from the angles of feminist philosophy, queer theory, and lesbian, gay, bisexual, transgender, queer/questioning, and others (LGBTQ+) studies see "Gendered Mimesis Project," https://genderedmimesis.com/. While the link between mimesis and racist images of Africa has been investigated from the angle of "postcolonial mimesis" (Lawtoo 2016, 173–209) and influential studies on "mimesis and alterity" have helpfully revaluated the powers of "sympathetic magic" (Taussig 1993), a project on contemporary decolonial mimesis is still missing and would greatly benefit (from) mimetic studies.

16 Borch-Jacobsen's early work on the psychoanalytical subject was informed by deconstruction (Lacoue-Labarthe), mimetic theory (Girard), and a pre-Freudian tradition attentive to hypnosis, all of which are now internal to mimetic studies. For a good starting point into his early work on mimesis see Borch-Jacobsen 1993.

17   For an account of homo aestheticus that revisits "empathy theory" from a transdisciplinary
      perspective that resonates with our theory of homo mimeticus, see Dissanayake 1992, 140–
      193.

Bibliography

Adorno, Theodor (2005). *Minima Moralia: Reflections on a Damaged Life.* London: Verso.
Ammaniti, Massimo, and Vittorio Gallese (2014). *The Birth of Intersubjectivity: Psychodynamics,
      Neurobiology, and the Self.* New York: W. W. Norton & Company.
Boon, Marcus (2013). *In Praise of Copying.* Cambridge, MA: Harvard University Press.
Borch, Christian (ed.) (2019). *Imitation, Contagion, Suggestion: On Mimesis and Society.* New
      York: Routledge, 2019.
Borch-Jacobsen, Mikkel (1993). *The Emotional Tie: Psychoanalysis, Mimesis, Affect,* trans. Douglas
      Brick et al. Stanford: Stanford University Press.
Cavarero, Adriana (2005). *For More than One Voice: Toward a Philosophy of Vocal Expression,*
      trans. Paul A. Kottman. Stanford: Stanford University Press.
Cavarero, Adriana, and Nidesh Lawtoo (2021). "Mimetic Inclinations: A Dialogue with Adriana
      Cavarero," in *Contemporary Italian Women Philosophes: Stretching the Art of Thinking,* eds.
      Silvia Benso and Elvira Roncalli. Albany: State University of New York Press, 183–199.
Connolly, William E. (2011). *A World of Becoming.* Durham, NC: Duke University Press.
Dicks, Henry (2023). *The Biomimicry Revolution: Learning from Nature How to Inhabit the Earth.*
      New York: Columbia University Press.
Dissanayake, Ellen (1992). *Homo Aestheticus: Where Art Comes from and Why.* Toronto: The Free
      Press.
Durrant, Sam (2023). "Homo Ecologicus: Animism, Historical Materialism and Planetary Mi-
      mesis." *MLN* 138.5, 1520–1544.
Gallese, Vittorio, and Michele Guerra (2019). *The Empathic Screen: Cinema and Neuroscience,*
      trans. Frances Anderson. Oxford: Oxford University Press.
Gebauer, Günter (2022). "The Undifferentiation of Mimetic Violence: From Oedipus to COV-
      ID-19." *CounterText* 8.1, 88–102.
Gebauer, Gunter, and Christoph Wulf (1995). *Mimesis: Culture, Art, Society,* trans. Don Reneau.
      Berkeley: University of California Press.
Lacoue-Labarthe, Philippe (1998). *Typography: Mimesis, Philosophy, Politics.* Stanford: Stanford
      University Press.
Lawtoo, Nidesh (2013). *The Phantom of the Ego: Modernism and the Mimetic Unconscious.* East
      Lansing: Michigan State University Press.
——— (2016). *Conrad's Shadow: Catastrophe, Mimesis, Theory.* East Lansing: Michigan State
      University Press.
——— (2022). *Homo Mimeticus: A New Theory of Imitation.* Leuven: Leuven University Press.
——— (2023a). *Violence and the Mimetic Unconscious: vol. 2 The Affective Hypothesis.* East Lan-
      sing: Michigan State University Press.
——— (2023b). "Introducing Mimetic Studies." *MLN* 138.5, 1379–1391.
Lawtoo, Nidesh (ed.) (2017). *Poetics and Politics: with Lacoue-Labarthe. Modern Language Notes*
      132.5.
——— (2022a). *The Mimetic Condition. CounterText* 8.1.
——— (2022b). *Posthuman Mimesis. Journal of Posthumanism* 2.2.

——— (2024). *Mimetic Posthumanism: Homo Mimeticus 2.0 in Arts, Society and Technics*. Leiden: Brill.

Lawtoo, Nidesh, and Willow Verkerk (eds.) (2023). *Mimetic Inclinations with Adriana Cavarero*, *Critical Horizons* 24.2.

Miller, Hillis J., and Nidesh Lawtoo (2020). "The Critic and the Mime: J. Hillis Miller in Dialogue with Nidesh Lawtoo." *Minnesota Review* 95, 93–119.

Montaigne, Michel de (2003). *The Complete Essays*, trans. M. A. Screech. London: Penguin Classics.

Nancy, Jean-Luc, and Nidesh Lawtoo (2022). "The CounterText Interview: Jean-Luc Nancy. Mimesis: A Singular Plural Concept." *CounterText* 8.1, 23–45.

Plato (1963). "Republic," in *The Collected Dialogues of Plato*, trans. Paul Shorey, eds. E. Hamilton and H. Cairns. Princeton, NJ: Princeton University Press, 575–853.

Potolsky, Matthew (2006). *Mimesis*. New York: Routledge.

Rizzolatti, Giacomo, and Corrado Sinigaglia (2008). *Mirrors in the Brain—How Our Minds Share Actions and Emotions,* trans. Frances Anderson. Oxford: Oxford University Press.

Spariosu, Mihai (ed.) (1984). *Mimesis in Contemporary Theory: An Interdisciplinary Approach. Vol. 1, The Literary and Philosophical Debate*. Philadelphia: John Benjamins Publishing Company.

Taussig, Michael (1993). *Mimesis and Alterity: A Particular History of the Senses*. New York: Routledge.

Wolf, Philipp (2022). "Posthuman Mimétisme: Caillois, Adorno and an Aesthetics of Mimesis." *Journal of Posthumanism* 2.2, 125–137.

Wulf, Christopher (2022). *Human Beings and their Images: Imagination, Mimesis, Performativity*. London: Bloomsbury.

THE DISCUS AND THE BOW

Homer, Machiavelli, and the *Grandissimi Esempli*

Nidesh Lawtoo

> From time to time, opposition to Homer
> rose up from the deepest foundations of Hellenism;
> but he always remained victorious.
>
> —Friedrich Nietzsche, *Human, All Too Human I*

Mimetic studies creates new concepts to diagnose the immanent patho(-)logies of homo mimeticus in the twenty-first century. Concepts, just like theories, do not come down ready-made from the sky of ideas; nor do they emerge from the solipsistic head of *Homo sapiens* considered in isolation. Rather, concepts emerge genealogically from logical and affective encounters with a long chain of thinkers generative of a productive interplay between pathos and logos. Often, in fact, new concepts emerge via agonistic intellectual confrontations with influential predecessors that are not simply antagonists or rivals but, rather, serve as models on whose shoulders younger generations can push against—with agonistic gratitude in view of going further. Over time, and not without efforts and good doses of perseverance, if a diagonal field is opened up, concepts sometimes become interwoven to form a longer chain, or conceptual network, which allows for innovative communications moving back and forth across periods, disciplines, and traditions of thought.

Following up on volume 1, the present volume connects genealogically a long chain of untimely thinkers to form precisely such a theoretical network. To broaden its ramifications, in guise of Prelude, I flesh out three additional conceptual rings in a chain that is not meant to constrain movement or imprison, as in Plato's cave but, rather, to channel pathos and set new patho-*logies* in motion. Re-turning to the dawn of western myth to a foundational scene that gives birth to the concept of mimetic agonism in Homer's *Odyssey* (ca. 8th C. BC) will allow us to pick up a conceptual discus and propel it further in time, toward the Renaissance that started the re-turns to mimesis in the first place. Not without Homeric echoes, Machiavelli's *The Prince* (1513) will then provide us with a theoretical bow that fleshes out new conceptual arrows that reach into the present. But let us proceed in order by stepping back to a Homeric contest, or agon, that set mimetic studies into motion in the first place.

Conceptual Arrows for Mimetic Studies

We have already seen in volume 1 how a conceptual trilogy—namely, "mimetic pathos," "pathos of distance," and "patho(-)logy"—provide a theoretical matrix, or womb, out of which mimetic studies is born. These three concepts, let us stress it again, do not form an a-historical structure or universal system aimed to be mechanically applied to cultural, aesthetic, or political phenomena from the origins of culture to the present. On the contrary, they set in motion a complex contradictory double movement between attraction to pathos and critical distance to mimetic pathologies. This movement, in turn, is endowed with the theoretical power, or *dunamis*, to keep up with the spiraling transformations of homo mimeticus in its multiple and often paradoxical patho(-)logical manifestations.

What we now need to further specify in guise of Prelude is that the next conceptual trilogy informing volume 2—namely, "mimetic agonism," "hypermimesis," and the "mimetic unconscious"—provides three additional conceptual arrows that allow contributors to further extend the network of mimetic studies to new areas of investigation. Let us introduce these arrows individually first, before foregrounding the conceptual discus that gives them a direction, providing a resounding note that resonates throughout the volume more generally.

First Arrow: Mimetic Agonism

This is a performative concept in the sense that it itself emerges out of the agonistic dynamic it accounts for. Mimetic agonism is, in fact, meant as a productive supplement to the Girardian concept of mimetic rivalry. If the latter's theory of desire leads inevitably to a rivalry with a model in view of possessing the same object of desire, our focus on mimetic pathos is neither deterministic nor unilateral in its diagnostic evaluation. On the contrary, it opens up a type of competitive yet creative and productive intellectual confrontation, or contest (*agon*), with predecessors that is not simply generative of pathological violence but, rather, of new creative insights and theoretical patho-*logies* instead.

First described in the context of Nietzsche's philosophical agon with his intellectual models qua educators, the beginnings of mimetic agonism go way back to pre-Platonic, and thus Homeric times.[1] A genealogical starting point can be traced back to an ancient Greek culture dominated by what Nietzsche's colleague at Basel, the Swiss historian Jacob Burckhardt, calls "agonal age" (1998, 160–213), a period spanning from the twelfth to the sixth century BC. Part of a noble spirit of competition at play in a plurality of contests, from gymnastic to chariot racing, dance to music, epic poetry to tragedy, stretching to include philosophy as well,[2] the agon was central to the education and formation of the Greeks. It informs the history of culture, and might continue to transform our education today.

One must turn to myth to find, if not an origin, at least a starting point to push the mimetic turn further. The *dunamis* or power of mimetic agonism is perhaps most famously dramatized in Book 8 of Homer's *Odyssey*, a pivotal book where Odysseus, invited at the court of King Alcinous, asks a blind rhapsode called Demodocus if he "can sing the story about the Wooden Horse" and show that he is truly "blessed with inspiration" (Homer 2020, 8.499).[3] This is a mise en abyme if there is one. The scene is thus not deprived of mirroring effects and affects that reach—via a chain of listeners and readers—into the present: if the blind rhapsode alludes to Homer, the song also leads Odysseus to be moved to tears by pathos—though "no one noticed that his eyes were wet with tears, except Alcinous" (8.532–533). Wrapped in his purple robe, he is moved to reveal his identity that is no(t) one.

Odysseus is not only *polymētis* (cunning), but also *polytropos* (of many turns), for he twists and turns assuming different roles: he is King and warrior, pirate and lover, husband and friend, carpenter and thief, sailor and liar, father and beggar, rhetorician and trickster, among other protean masks of a homo mimeticus that is both vulnerable to contagious pathologies such as violence and revenge and, at the same time, and without contradiction, is able to rely on his cunning logos to generate life-affirmative patho-*logies*. How does this mythic figure, then, reveal a paradoxical identity that is no(t) one for he is presumably everyone? By narrating "himself," in mimetic speech, who he "is." Thus, he tells the journey that now bears "his" name. "I am Odysseus, Laertes's son / known for my many clever tricks and lies" (9.21), and so on, you know the myth of that self-proclaimed "lord of lies" (21.73). Another designation would be, of course, lord of mimesis.

But the pathos of the mimetic agon does not concern only poetry and the "lies" it presumably dramatizes. During the day, in fact, the Phaeacian had organized games, which, to this day, provide the mythic model for the Olympic games. Challenged to prove his athletic skills by youngsters, Odysseus initially refuses. He does so by taking some distance from the competitive pathos internal to the challenge. As he puts it: "now I only want to get back home" (Homer 2020, 8.157). But as the agon turns rivalrous and offensive and a youngster accuses Odysseus to be "no athlete" (8.165), his agonistic strife or *Eris* is awakened. This does not mean that rivalry turns into violence. On the contrary, it turns into a contest (*agon*) to prove both his skill (*technē*) and excellence (*arēte*) as he says: "you have challenged me and stung my heart. / Despite my suffering, I will compete" (8.185–186). Odysseus does so by seizing what Homer describes as "a massive discus, heavier than that used by the others." And then, dramatizing this athletic turn, the poet adds:

> He spun around, drew back
> his arm and from his brawny hand he hurled.
> The stone went humming [*bombēsen*] (8.188–191)

Athena is mimetically disguised in the crowd via a mimicry she shares with the owl that bears her name (Minerva) and makes her—and sometimes Odysseus as well—imperceptible during the day. We are told that she "marked the spot," and concludes: "A blind man, stranger, could discern this mark by groping. It is far ahead than all the others" (8.197–198). A pioneering practitioner of the agon, we find in this nomadic character without a proper identity on the way home an exemplary model who, in his best agonistic moments, is perhaps still worthy of imitation today—not simply physically but intellectually as well. In any case, Athena joyfully concludes: "You can celebrate!" (8.198).

Striving to reach his natal home, in this founding scene of mimetic agonism, Odysseus' strife (*Eris*) is, in fact, not driven by envy, "jealousy," and "resentment" characteristic of what Jacob Burckhardt, following Hesiod's *Works and Days*, calls "bad *Eris*" (1998, 165)—that will only reappear toward the end of the *Odyssey* in Odysseus's violent confrontation with the suitors occupying his home, which leads to a brutal escalation.[4] Here, during the games organized by the Phaeacians, Odysseus' agon is animated by a noble spirit of competition driven by bad *Eris*' positive counterpart: namely, "good *Eris*," which as Burckhardt reminds us "was the first to be born" and was placed by Cronos at "the very root of the earth" (165). Indeed, if bad Eris is characterized by sad passions central to mimetic rivalry and violence that threaten more than ever to escalate today, mimetic agonism finds in good Eris its genealogical starting point to promote life-affirmative possibilities and festive celebrations rooted here on earth.

What was true in Johan Huizinga's account of "homo ludens" (Huizinga 2016) remains true for our account of homo mimeticus: the separate space of games, including intellectual games, has the quasi-magical power to contain all too human violence in order to channel it, via measured confrontations between worthy contenders, toward agonistic, productive, and ultimately creative use. That massive discus—you will have understood the mise en abyme—has a mirroring counterpart...in a massive concept: namely, mimesis. Collectively, contributors to this volume picked it up from our mythic past; we then used the (will to) power of the ancient agon to hurl it into the future. Titled "Discus Thrower" the image on the cover of this book outlines precisely this gesture. Michaela Lawtoo does so by not simply representing a discobolus from a stabilizing visual distance; on the contrary, she captures the destabilizing power, or pathos of throwing the discus itself via a dynamic, spiraling brushstroke that artistically performs the *re*-turns to mimesis.[5]

Still central to classical quarrels between philosophy and poetry (Plato contra Homer comes to mind), the re-*productive* dynamic of mimetic agonism continues to silently inform intellectual and creative confrontations from ancient to modern quarrels (*les anciens contre les modernes* come to mind); it resurfaces in the modernist period and, we contend, it continues to inform mimetic studies in the present period as well. After mimetic theory's obsessive focus on the jealousy, rivalry, and resentment of bad *Eris*, it seems indeed vital to recuperate its positive and forgotten counterpart: namely, the productive, generous, yet still competitive spirt of good *Eris*, which, as Burckhardt puts it, "awakens even the indolent and unskilled to industry" (1998, 165). This turn from bad *Eris* to good *Eris*, from the violence of mimetic rivalry to the creation of mimetic agonism is more urgent than ever. In times of planetary crises that include the re-turn of escalating wars, we already have ample manifestations of bad Eris. No scapegoating mechanisms are likely to put an end to them—on the contrary, these mechanisms are constitutive of the escalating logic of violence itself. Alternative diagnostics and therapies are thus needed. Philosophical physicians, in fact, remember that crisis (from *krino*) indicate a medical judgment or diagnostic marking the critical decision in which a patient will live or die.

Without ignoring the violence of bad or pathological Eris, mimetic studies strives to turn to good or patho-logical Eris for vital inspiration. It is perhaps no genealogical accident that in order to "face the planetary" (Connolly 2017, 4), as William E. Connolly urges us to do, chapters in this volume turn to a type of strife rooted in the materiality of the earth. This entails, among other things, furthering a vibrant conception of mimesis that goes beyond nature–culture binaries, as Jane Bennett's contributions to the mimetic turn also suggest.[6] In the process, we shall propose a return to nature as a "model" to imitate, perhaps even as a "mentor" who can teach us the virtue of "measure," as Henry Dicks's account of "biomimicry" as a revolutionary philosophy (Dicks 2023) indicates. There are thus performative properties built in mimetic agonism to be pursued further, which leads us to the next conceptual arrow.

Second Arrow: Hypermimesis

If mimetic agonism looks back, genealogically, to better look forward to the creation of new concepts, *hypermimesis* provides its mirroring counterpart. It takes as a starting point the future-oriented concept of "hyperreality," defined by Jean Baudrillard as a type of "simulation" that no longer rests on the logic of "imitation" or "doubling" for it entails a "generation by models of a real without origins or reality: a hyperreal" (1981, 11, 10). Defined at the dawn of the digital revolution, this world of hyperreal simulations prefigures the replacement of reality by digital simulacra that do not simply represent an external reference that would serve as a model, along the traditional lines of aesthetic realism. On the contrary, as Guy Debord was quick to note, it is the "spectacle that constitutes the contemporary model for the dominant form of social life" (Debord 1992, 17; my transl.). The implications of this overturning move are far-reaching not only for mimetic studies but for the entire history of metaphysics. As Nietzsche would say, such an overturning dissolves the very distinction between copy and original, the "true world" and what he called, in an ironic overturning of Platonism, the "*apparent one*" (Nietzsche 1982b, 486). We now live, or attempt to live, in what Morpheus, echoing Baudrillard in *The Matrix*, calls the "desert of the real."

What we must add in this echo chamber is that an immanent philosophical tradition encourages not only to dismiss the ideal world as a fable; it also urges homo mimeticus not to forget its embodied, relational, and all too imitative nature rooted in the earth—lest we lose sight of the earthly cave in which we are bound to live. This also means that hyperreal simulations no longer rest on the logic of mimesis understood as simple copy or representation of a pre-existing world; and yet, these simulations continue to generate all too real performative effects that operate on the brain-bodies of homo mimetics—and quite contagiously so. In the wake of artificial intelligence (AI) revolutions in which chatbots effectively simulate human language (GPT-4 being the latest version as I write), the risk that *homo mimeticus 2.0* will be increasingly dispossessed of its already limited agentic control over an ego that is not one but is a phantom ego instead will increase exponentially in the years to follow: from deepfakes to digital avatars, chatbots simulating human logos to simulacra generating all too human pathos, it should be clear to all by now that mimesis, understood in its plural manifestations that go beyond realism, is back—with a hypermimetic vengeance.

It is thus urgent to open up a new transdisciplinary field to study the insidious ways in which new AI phantoms driven by increasingly effective algorithms will take advantage of humans' all too mimetic tendency to believe phantoms that dispossess them of an already limited agentic control over a phantom ego. The proliferation of AI simulations that increasingly assume human roles, from the workspace to education, entertainment to politics is thus calling for new diagnostics of "posthuman mimesis" that are already underway animating homo mimeticus 2.0.[7] They shall also continue to inform the plastic metamorphoses of *Homo Mimeticus III*, both consciously and, more often, unconsciously so. This leads us to the third and, for the moment, last conceptual ring in the chain we inscribe in the network of mimetic studies.

Third Arrow: The Mimetic Unconscious

For a long time, the unconscious has been limited to Freud's discovery. Still, historians of psychoanalysis have now confirmed that this concept has a long-neglected history that intersects productively with mimetic studies. Genealogical lenses reveal, in fact, that well before Freud, a number of philosophical physicians were sensitive to the involuntary nature of imitation rooted in an unconscious that is physiological, embodied, relational, and thus social in orientation. If this immanent unconscious has been mostly forgotten in the past Freudian century, under different names—be it cognitive, cerebral, or as we call, it mimetic—it is currently returning to the forefront of post-Freudian theoretical discussions in the present century.

This re-turn is, in many ways, long overdue. In the wake of influential critiques of the "repressive hypothesis" (Foucault 1976, 23-67) redoubled by equally influential "anti-Oedipal" critiques of the unconscious staged within a familial and rather "classical order of representation" (Deleuze and Guattari 2008, 62), the mimetic unconscious has been waiting to reemerge from the shadow of Oedipus for quite some time. This is especially evident in theorists like Gilles Deleuze and Félix Guattari who rightly critique Freud for not seeing what a previous pre-Freudian tradition saw very well: namely, that "the unconscious itself is essentially a crowd" (2008, 33) traversed by what they call, following pioneer of mimetic studies Gabriel Tarde, "flows of microimitation" (241). Hence their claim that "*imitation is the propagation of a flow*" (241). In the wake of these and other feminist, queer, post-feminist critiques, it is somewhat surprising that whenever the question of the unconscious is concerned, scholars in the humanities tend to routinely rely on Oedipal or quasi-Oedipal models rooted in patriarchal myths or repressive legends.

The problem with legends is that they do not need to be historically true to continue informing or disinforming the public imagination. As the historian of psychology Henry Ellenberger has shown, the mythic appeal of the "Freudian Legend" (1970, 547) rests on the romantic myth of a single heroic figure that overcomes insurmountable resistances to access the repressed truth of his Oedipal desires. This is a legend that had the power to impress many in the past century. Its mimetic effect was subsequently redoubled as influential successors generated influential repetitions with linguistic differences that cast an imaginary spell on generations spell-bound by the linguistic turn. As Mikkel Borch-Jacobsen has convincingly shown in a series of books genealogically entangled with mimetic studies, psychoanalysis—in both its Freudian and Lacanian variants—was born out of the initial fascination with and subsequent foreclosure of "affective mimesis" (1991, 70).[8] While not repressed in the Freudian sense, it is this affective-hypnotic-suggestive—and we should now add—neuronal mimesis that now *re*-turns onto the theoretical scene. The mimetic turn, in many ways, entails a genealogical re-turn to the hypnotic-affective-contagious tradition of the mimetic unconscious that does not have dreams but mirroring reflexes as a *via regia*. While the Oedipal/repressive hypothesis has come under severe attacks in recent years, untimely theoretical figures now allow us to leap ahead to recent discoveries, or rather, rediscoveries of mirroring principles they had anticipated in the first place.

Such serendipitous genealogical connections will be pursued in more detail in the Coda to this volume. A brief anecdote will suffice here. We were honored to have the neuroscientist Vittorio Gallese as a keynote speaker for the conference at the origins of this volume. Along with Giacomo Rizzolatti, Gallese was part of the team in Parma who discovered mirror neurons in the early 1990s. He has since developed a theory of "embodied simulation" (Gallese 2017) with significant implications for aesthetics, the phenomenology of intersubjectivity, and the humanities in general.[9] The talk, titled "Narrative as Body," was a success. It drew a large virtual public eager for new dialogic connections between the neurosciences and the humanities that go beyond ossified nature–culture divides.

Right after his presentation, I sent Gallese a personal email of thanks and took the occasion to mention why I got interested in mirror neurons in the first place.[10] Genealogical lenses reveal that Nietzsche, in aphorism 142 of *Daybreak* titled "Empathy [*Mitempfindung*]," had actually anticipated the theory of embodied simulation. As I showed in *The Phantom of the Ego*, he did so via a phenomenological account of unconscious mirroring reflexes that blur the boundaries between self and other generating a sym-*pathos* (feeling with) at play in empathy and other shared affective experiences, including aesthetic experiences (Lawtoo 2013, 38–43). This was thus the ideal occasion to hear the response from one of the participants in what many consider a revolutionary scientific discovery.

The response was genealogically illuminating. Revealing his philosophical knowledge, Gallese not only confirmed he was familiar with that specific section of *Daybreak*; he was also happy to confirm that it describes "something similar to embodied simulation" as he specified: "it prefigures the inner imitation [*innere Nachahmung*] of [Theodor] Lipps." Lipps had indeed been the figure that, along with Nietzsche, had been originally convoked to account for this mimetic reflex.[11] The mirroring effects of this genealogical connection were striking. A scholar of mimesis can only dream of such a specific intellectual correspondence. Gallese himself concluded: "Impressive! There is nothing that is really new!" [*Non c'è mai nulla di veramente nuovo*!].

For those afraid that the neurosciences are anxious to replace the humanities, this genealogical anecdote suggests that there is no need to worry. In this case, the opposite is true: science can draw sustenance from the long tradition in the humanities that precedes it, paves the way for it, and, sometimes, anticipates revolutionary discoveries. Independently of the controversies mirror neurons generated and will continue to generate, it is becoming uncontroversial to claim that humans are eminently social creatures who resonate with other humans and nonhumans. As sociologist Hartmut Rosa puts it, the discovery of mirror neurons "does not necessarily lead to a kind of scientific neuro-reductionism that traces all consciousness, communication, and social processes back to neurological processes" (2019, 150). On the contrary, these processes introduce intersubjective resonances that arguably gave birth to *Homo sapiens*, are not deterministic in their reciprocal orientatidn, and can both be "obstructed" from a critical distance and "amplified" (151) with pathos to generate broader societal transformations. The new relational concept of resonance, in other words, is not only a new conceptual mask of mimesis; it also rests on similar intersubjective, affective, and mirroring presuppositions that will have to be explored in more detail in *Homo Mimeticus III*.[12]

Hence the need for mimetic studies to deepen genealogical connections between philosophy and neuroscience, untimely discoveries and timely (re)discoveries in order to go beyond body–brain dualisms we shall return to in the dialogue with Gallese that concludes the volume. In the end, what Gallese suggests is an insight valuable for mimetic studies more generally: rather than making radical claims about one's originality in a way characteristic of previous mimetic theories, it is more productive to step back to untimely predecessors who may have been marginalized, yet open up paths on the long journey of homo mimeticus that deserve to be pursed in the present. In the process, contributors pick up conceptual arrows from the past in order to propel them further into the future. Let us take a look at the virtues internal to these paths and arrows.

Virtues for Homo Mimeticus

The mimetic turn aims to be innovative and forward oriented. Still, a modesty in genealogical matters cautions us against claiming that the re-turns to homo mimeticus operate a full-blown paradigm shift in theorizations of mimesis—at least not in Thomas Kuhn's sense of "scientific revolution" (Kuhn 1996). In fact, for Kuhn, who theorized the latter in the first place, such a shift entails a radical break with previous theories that are "replaced" and rendered "incommensurable" with the new theory. Such epistemic breaks characteristic of scientific revolutions, for Kuhn, find in figures like Kepler, Newton, and Einstein their paradigmatic examples in the hard sciences. These are of course exemplary thinkers still worthy of imitation. Already for the moderns, they generated imitations that went beyond nature and culture oppositions.

Given the imitative tendencies of *Homo sapiens*, we can thus understand that it has been tempting for humanists of the past to align themselves with grand paradigmatic shifts operated by the like of Kepler and Darwin—the case of Freud as the self-proclaimed "Darwin of psychology" comes to mind.[13] More recently, among mimetic theorists, René Girard played with the same *topos* as he considered that despite his theological focus on Christ as the ultimate scapegoat he operated, paradoxically, within a "Darwinian perspective" (2007, 96). This led him to accept Michel Serres' denomination of "Darwin of the human sciences" with an immodest, "why not?" (2007, 96)—perhaps unsurprisingly so, given the numerous affinities between Girard and Freud.[14]

Renaissance of *Grandissimi Esempli*

Mimetic studies is rooted in a-theological foundations very much in line with both evolutionary theory and more recent epigenetic developments in the biological sciences we shall return to in volume 3; yet it chooses an alternative path in line with a different attitude and *ethos*. In fact, genealogical lenses on the long and complex history of mimesis urge theorists of the present to cultivate "the virtue of modesty" (Nietzsche 1997, 17)—Nietzsche's advice in volume 1 comes to mind. For this reason, we opted for stressing *re*-turns to mimesis that propose not so much a *paradigm* shift but, rather, a paradigmatic *shift of emphasis* or, better, of *perspective*. If a revolutionary break might sometimes (very rarely) take place in the hard sciences, we argue that the humanities benefit from shifts of emphasis that retain selective continuities with the past to foreground perspectival changes—sometimes quite radical ones—in the present and future.

There is much to be learned from the past, but there is also much to add to it. While shifting perspective from dominant accounts of aesthetic realism to the fundamental philosophical, but also anthropo-logical, psycho-logical, neuro-logical realization that humans imitate with their brains as much as with their bodies, individually as well as collectively, subjectively as well as technologically, contributors trace genealogical continuities with exemplary theories of mimesis of the past that serve not only as models to passively imitate. Rather, they can inspire contemporary practitioners of good *Eris* to go further than they did in a spirit of agonistic gratitude—what William Connolly also calls "agonistic respect" informing relations of "affective modes of communication" with "Double[s]" (2022, 123, 112) not far from home. Hence the importance of stepping back, selectively, to influential precursors in view of pushing against their shoulders to provide new conceptual foundations, reorient the field, and open up new areas of inquiry to be pursued in the future.

A field called mimetic studies could not fail to realize the importance of imitation, not only as an *object* of study but also as a problematic that informs the all too human *subject* of study. While a romantic anxiety of influence made it sometimes difficult for modern and contemporary theorists to acknowledge influential models, or precursors, whose traces are erased via what we call romantic agonism, the chapters that follow recuperate a pre-Romantic awareness of the importance of models to imitate with an agonistic difference characteristic of mimetic agonism. After the Greek agonal period recuperated by Burckhardt and Nietzsche, this agonistic culture finds, perhaps, in the Renaissance some of its most influential representatives. This was already suggested in the reference to Montaigne in the Introduction as a key genealogical link between the ancients and the moderns in matters of patho(-)logies.

After the Greeks, it is arguably in the Renaissance that key figures in mimetic studies find the theoretical *élan* that propels this field into the future. This should not come as a surprise. After all, it is in the Renaissance that the Greek immanent spirit was reborn as philosophical and literary texts were rediscovered, including the Homeric poem with which we started. As Henry Dicks also notes in his contribution to this volume, in this period we witness a shift from a "theomimetic" conception of mimesis based on the imitation of God that dominated the medieval period toward an "anthropomimetic" tradition predicated on the "imitation of the 'most excellent' being in nature, namely man". This does not mean we should limit mimetic studies to anthropocentrism for nature will become a source of imitation as well. To confirm this genealogical shift of perspective that, in different, often imperceptible ways, informs many essays that follow, paving the way for "posthumanist," "planetary" and "biomimetic revolutions" already underway,[15] let us thus engage with another renaissance thinker of mimesis who is deeply aware of the virtue of imitating what he called the "greatest examples" (Machiavelli 2020, 17), including, of course, Homeric examples.[16]

That Machiavelli has Homer in mind is clear, but what hero should be taken as example to imitate is less so. In chapter 18 of *The Prince,* in fact, Machiavelli outlines two methods of fighting that go beyond human and animal qualities. Ideally, if all men were "good," properly human means of fighting should operate by "law," but since humans are a "sad lot" for Machiavelli, he advises the prince that it is necessary to fight by "force" (2020, 55) as well. The explicit example of this duality is, indeed, Achilles who "was sent to be reared by Chiron, the centaur," a mythic figure whose human–animal duality embodies Machiavelli's principle that "the prince must know how to make a good use of the beast as well as the man" (55).

The beast, however, is already double and opens up an ambivalence in the Homeric example in question. Thus, Machiavelli famously specifies that the prince must choose to imitate both "the fox and the lion" for it is "necessary to be a fox to recognize traps and a lion to frighten off the wolfs" (55). Both qualities, he later specifies, the prince "must imitate [*necessarie imitare*]" (62). This is an indication that not only foregrounds the centrality of mimesis in learning and education along classical humanistic lines; it also anticipates a type of mimesis that goes beyond culture and nature. The examples of the fox and the lion, in fact, trouble the binary dividing human from non-human animals; they also place the latter as models endowed with animal instincts for humans to imitate culturally, but also by drawing on the "beast" in them.[17] Now, if the force of the lion is an attribute characteristic of wrathful Achilles that is not deprived of violent pathological implications, it seems that it is the patho-*logical* cunning of Odysseus Machiavelli has in mind as he speaks of the cunning of the fox.[18]

Interestingly for Machiavelli, the fox's cunning method of deception is explicitly based on chameleon-like qualities of "pretense" that are partially lost in translation; yet, once they are rendered in the original color of "simulation," they turn out to be well known to mimetic studies. As Machiavelli puts it: "The man who enjoyed the greatest success was the one who knew best how to use the fox. But it is necessary to know how to do a good job of coloring [*colorire*] over this character, and to be good pretender and dissembler [*gran simulatore e dissimulatore*]" (56). Simulation and dissimulation are indeed not only the specialty of a mythic hero who is "no one [*outis*]" and is thus endowed with "cunning" [*mètis*]—an intentional and playful homophony that performs the cunning of a *grand simulatore* also called Odysseus we shall return to.[19] Both simulation and dissimulation that color this character are also, and above all, eminent mimetic qualities Machiavelli considers worthy of emulation. Mimesis of mimesis via a paradigmatic mimetic example: this is, in a nutshell, the formula that emerges from the patho(-)logical examples Machiavelli convokes from antiquity. Which also means that if we further their paths from antiquity to the Renaissance into the present a discerning evaluation of both the pathos and the logos still worthy of imitation today is required.

If these mythic examples come from the past, with some caution, we can still pick up their conceptual arrows of knowledge in the present to shoot them further into the future. Here is how Niccolò Machiavelli describes the process of creation based on the imitation of *grandissimi esempli* in chapter 6 of *The Prince* that paves the way for the examples we have just discussed:

> Since men almost always walk along the paths beaten by others and proceed to act by imitating them [*e procedendo con le azioni loro nelle imitazioni*] and since they cannot always stay on others' paths or attain the level of skill [*virtù*] of those you imitate [*tu imiti*], a prudent man

[*sic*] should always enter the paths beaten by great men [*sic*] and imitate those who were the very best, so that, if his [*sic*] own talent (*virtù*) does not measure up to theirs, at least it will give off something of its odor. (2020, 17)

Prudence is indeed an underrated quality of the mimetic fox with the power to supplement the brute force of the lion. What was true of theoretical virtue for a Renaissance theorist like Machiavelli who imitated ancient models to address modern transformations, might still hold true for theoretical virtue in mimetic studies prudently addressing contemporary metamorphoses—provided we understand what the connection between "imitation" and "virtue" actually entails. As Nietzsche reminds us via an interrogation that finds inspiration in past virtues while being aimed, like an arrow, toward future readers: "how to nourish yourself so as to attain your maximum of strength, of *virtù* in the Renaissance style, of moraline-free virtue?" (1980, 52). Let us find out by considering the mimetic paths re-turning to Renaissance virtues.

Paths for Renaissance Virtues

With the untranslatable concept of *virtù* (Italian translation of the Greek *aretē*) Machiavelli certainly does not mean a moral virtue predicated on the imitation of Christian figures. Neither does he suggest imitating the character or soul of these models themselves, via what a Roman and later Romantic tradition called "sublimity" understood as "the echo of a great soul" (Pseudo-Longinus 2005, IX: 98). Rather, the focus of imitation is directed at the "actions" [*azioni*] of exemplary models endowed with a type of excellence, strength, or skill [*virtù*] trained via a plurality of crafts or, as Henry Staten calls them, "*technai*."[20]

Not unlike techne, *virtù* as Machiavelli understands it, is immanent, embodied, practical, and material in its orientation. It is thus the technical excellence internal to the actions of exemplary figures that is the object of imitation, not the moral character or soul of the exemplar. If we apply technical virtue to the art of reading central to the theory we pursue, we can already see that the metaphor of walking along a path opened up by predecessors remains down to earth, allows for movement, and provides the *re*-turns to mimesis with an immanent goal or telos; it also strays from passive notions of imitation, for following up on a path presupposes an ability to walk with one's own legs in order to travel further. As Nietzsche will later put it in *Thus Spoke Zarathustra*, "'One repays a teacher poorly if one always remains only a student'" (2008, 68).

What is the relation then, between imitation, *virtù*, and the type of future-oriented innovation that mimetic studies aims to foster? Again, let us be ambitiously modest and follow up on the paths opened up by worthy predecessors. This entails looking for secret passages that have been left untrodden for decades, or perhaps centuries, yet might provide shortcuts that allow long-distance runners to leap ahead into the present. In the process, we might even open up new paths of our own—or, to switch metaphor, pick up arrows of predecessors and shoot them high up in order to reach distant targets.

The Sweet Note of an Ancient Bow

This is, indeed, what Machiavelli also suggests, albeit between metaphoric lines in need of strong interpretations. In fact, he abruptly shifts metaphor from a "path" to a "bow" to give speed and intensity to a conceptual arrow. He does so in view of describing the action of what he calls a "prudent archer" whose exemplary virtue worthy of imitation might help us propel the re-turns to homo mimeticus further into the future. Here is how the passage continues:

> And he [*sic*] will do what prudent archers do when the spot they want to hit seems too far away: knowing the strength [*virtù*] of their bow, they aim much higher than the target they have chosen, not because they expect their arrow to reach such a height, but to be able to hit their target by aiming above it. (Machiavelli 2020, 17)

Prudent archers must imitate the prudence of the fox if they expect their arrow to reach a distant target in space and, perhaps, in time as well. In its future-oriented trajectory, this image captures nothing less than the gesture we aspire to reproduce: if we aimed high in mapping the new transdisciplinary field of mimetic studies, we also adopted a modest position by prudently following ancient paths first breached by exemplary predecessors that traverse the history of culture. This also means that from different angles, contributors to this volume, by training and exercise, "know the *virtù* of their bow." From excellence to skill, techne to strength, power to will to power, the *virtù* we imitate actively from exemplary theoretical actions of the past rests on the intimate "knowledge" of how far we can stretch the bow of knowledge.

Inspired by fox-like figures whose journey home (*nostos*) already oriented volume 1, Machiavelli's double metaphors of the path and the bow account for the virtue of an imitation that is already yours. Notice, in fact, the narrative shift from the diegetic and gendered-biased "he" to the mimetic and gender-balanced "you" [*tu imiti*], perhaps to performatively induce a virtuoso imitation in the Prince he is addressing and, at one further remove, in you, the reader, as well. What is certain is that this Renaissance spirit will continue to animate the actions promoted in the *Homo Mimeticus* trilogy. The conceptual arrows that follow are thus shot high, not to reach the world of ideas located in imaginary worlds behind the world. Rather, they are shot high for the practice of mimetic agon re-turns to *grandissimi esempli* to further their thoughts and reach new targets down to earth. Our goal, as the double metaphor suggests, is thus both modest and ambitious: modest because we follow up on the paths of exemplary models; ambitious because we shoot high to explore new paths for mimetic studies to come.

In the end, having picked up the arrow of mimesis, we needed a strong bow to shoot it further. And what bow could be stronger than an ancient mythic bow central to a long journey home with which we started? Remember that in the *Odyssey,* after the Phaeacians ship Odysseus back to Ithaca overnight, having (almost) re-turned home, he engages in what his son Telemachus calls the "contest of the bow" (Homer 2020, 21.112). Penelope, in fact, challenges the suitors to string Odysseus's old bow and shoot an arrow through twelve axles. A final agon is thus staged at the end of a long journey home. All the suitors engaged in the agon naturally fail to even string the bow. Only Telemachus comes rather close, paving the way for the protean "Foreigner," "dressed as a beggar," lord of camouflage tricks who espoused prudence as a virtue. The colors changed by the prudent simulation; the agonistic spirit remains unchanged.

To narrate this special dramatic moment, Homer convokes a musical language that is inspired by Apollo. That is, the god of archery, but also, as we know, the god of music. Here is how an inspiring voice tied to a long chain that goes from Apollo to the Muses, reaching via Homeric rhapsodes to a magnetized audience and readership tells, or rather sings, the story:

> So he had tricked [*polymētis*] them all.
> After examining the mighty bow
> Carefully, inch by inch—as easily
> As an experienced musician [*aoidēs*] stretches
> A sheep-gut string around a lyre's peg
> And makes it fast—Odysseus, with ease,
> Strung the great bow. He held it in his right hand
> And plucked the string, which sang like a swallow-song [*chelidoni eikelē audēn*],
> A clear sweet note. (21.406–413)[21]

The final trick of this figure of many turns who is no(t) one is, of course, a mimetic trick: it consists in turning the bow into a lyre, and, conversely, the lyre into a bow. The string of the lyre inspired by the Muse is thus entangled with the string of the bow at play in the agon, just as the fox cannot be entirely dissociated from the lion, or the discus from the bow. Together, they generate patho(-)logies that still need to be disentangled, for the pathos of the bow and the violence it generates is not the same as the pathos of the lyre and the agonistic contest of which it is part. And yet, at the instant in which Odysseus' destiny, after twenty years of navigation, is about to turn, they are paradoxically joined in a single string. And it is this double string that strikes the note of a return home. For is it an accident that this "singing" (*aiese*) marks precisely the *re*-turns of "swallows" (*chelidoni*)? That is, migratory birds par excellence whose collective journey always leads them back home, in the end.

And so, from different perspectives, in a virtuoso reenactment of an ancient agon, contributors joined forces, drew back their arms, and aimed high. The arrow, not unlike the discus that preceded it , went humming on its course, from antiquity to modernity, reaching into the present—and mimesis re-turned to regain its ancient power, or pathos. If you listen carefully in the pages that follow, perhaps you can still hear the distant echo of this humming resounding—in the chorus of voices singing swallow-songs, propelling homo mimeticus toward the future.

A strong bow,
A virtuous string,
A clear sweet note.

Notes

1   In "Homer's Contest" Nietzsche specifies that the focus of the agon is not on the individual genius who creates in (romantic) isolation. Rather, the focus is on "several geniuses, who incite each other to reciprocal action as they keep each other within the limits of measure" (1996, 5). For a detailed and penetrating discussion of agonism in Nietzsche see Siemens 2021; for the difference between mimetic rivalry and mimetic agonism see Lawtoo 2023, 45–57.

2   As Emily Wilson notes, by 566 BC the civic/religious festival of the Panathenaia was instituted "which included a poetic competition featuring performances of the Homeric poems" (2020, xviii). For an account of Plato's quarrel with Homer in the context of an agonistic "oral culture" see Havelock 1963, 61–86, 134–164. See also Borch-Jacobsen's chapter in this volume.

3   For a compelling reading of this Homeric scene by an ally in mimetic studies see also Cavarero 2000, 17–31.

4   See also Kehoane and Kuling who pursue the patho(-)logical diagnostic of homo mimeticus in this volume.

5   The editors warmly thank Michaela for using her inimitable *techne* to perform this spiraling gesture.

6   For Jane Bennett's first engagement with mimesis via the mediation of Lacoue-Labarthe and Lawtoo, see Bennett 2017; in her more recent work, Bennett develops a conception of the "porous I" or ego open to a "mimetic" sympathy (Bennett 2020) that is genealogically and productively entangled with mimetic studies (see Lawtoo 2022, 255–275).

7   See Lawtoo ed. 2024 as well as Hayles and Lawtoo 2022.

8   Furthering insights internal to key rings in the chain of mimetic studies (most notably, Girard and Lacoue-Labarthe), Borch-Jacobsen also supplements a psychological tradition attentive to hypnosis to the mimetic turn. See Borch-Jabcobsen 1992. For a further genealogical link between Nietzsche, Freud, and Girard, see Lawtoo 2023, 81 –100, 129–135. For a return of attention to identification as central to both the feeling (or pathos) of attachment in art "which is not the opposite of critical or reflective thought" (or distance) see Felski 2020, 83, 79–120.

9   For a rich study on the role of embodied simulation in film, see Gallese and Guerra.

10 The following quotes are from an email communication between Gallese and Lawtoo, 22 April 2022.

11 See Lawtoo 2013, 257. For a re-evaluation of Lipps' theory of empathy from a perspective on homo aestheticus that resonates productively both with homo mimeticus and embodied simulation, see Dissanayake 1992, 140–157.

12 While the connections between mimetic studies and resonance theory are many a point of divergence could be the following: for Rosa "resonance" is the "solution" to the pathologies of modernity and the "acceleration" it entails (Rosa 2019, 1); a long genealogy in mimetic studies reminds us that there are pathological resonances just as there are mimetic pathologies. For a chapter that pursues the links between resonance and mimesis see Mathijs Peters' contribution in *Homo Mimeticus III*.

13 For an informed historical reframing of Freud's "self-canonization" as the "Darwin of psychology," see Borch-Jacobsen and Shamdasani 2021, 1–24.

14 See Lawtoo 2023a, 33–80.

15 See Lawtoo ed. 2024; Connolly 2017; and Dicks 2023.

16 As Peter Ahrensdorf notes: "even though Machiavelli never explicitly mentions Homer in the *Prince*, he unmistakably singles out Homer for praise as a fellow, effective, teacher of princes" (2016, 15); specifically "through the example of Achilles" he stresses "the importance of imitating the harsher qualities of beasts and not simply the finer qualities of men" (15–16). Let us take a closer look.

17 In *Homo Mimeticus III* we shall return to a mimesis that goes beyond nature and culture via contemporary developments in epigenetics.

18 Registering this implicit shift of examples to "imitate," Ahrensdorf also notes that "the Homeric hero who excels at deception is Odysseus himself" (2016, 22) and proceeds to indicate that "Odysseus also exhibits a leonine ferocity against his enemies" (22), a point that confirms the patho(-)logical double sides of *homo mimeticus*. See also Ahrensdorf 2016, 23–29.

19 As Jean-Pierre Vernant points out: "the two syllables *ou-tis* can be replaced as another way of saying *mètis*. In Greek *ou* and *mè* are the two forms for negation, but if *outis* means no one, mètis designates deception [*ruse*]" (2007, 80; my transl.).

20   See chapter 2 in this volume. For a more general account of the way a "mimetic tradition" can store technical skills learned by "pure imitation" across generations, from tool making onward, informing a techne theory that goes from Plato to Kafka, see also Staten 2019, 77.

21   The editors thank Carlos Carvalhar for his assistance in checking Wilson's excellent but free translation of *The Odyssey* against the Greek original version for this crucial passage.

Bibliography

Ahrensdorf, Peter J. (2016). "Machiavelli and Homer on the Man and the Beast," in *Principle and Prudence in Western Political Thought*, eds. Christopher Lynch and Jonathan Marks. Albany: State University of New York Press, 15–31.

Baudrillard, Jean (1981). *Simulacres et simulation*. Paris: Galilée.

Bennett, Jane (2017). "Mimesis: Paradox or Encounter." *MLN* 132.5, 1186–1200.

—— (2020). *Influx & Efflux: Writing Up with Whitman*. Durham, NC: Duke University Press.

Borch-Jacobsen, Mikkel (1991). *Lacan: The Absolute Master*, trans. Douglas Brick. Stanford: Stanford University Press.

—— (1992). *The Emotional Tie: Psychoanalysis, Mimesis, Affect*, trans. Douglas Brick. Stanford: Stanford University Press.

Borch-Jacobsen, Mikkel, and Sonu Shamdasani (2012). *The Freud Files: An Inquiry into the History of Psychoanalysis*. Cambridge: Cambridge University Press.

Burckhardt, Jacob (1998). *The Greeks and Civilization*, trans. Sheila Stern, ed. Oswyn Murray. New York: St. Martin's Griffin.

Cavarero, Adriana (2000). *Relating Narratives: Storytelling and Selfhood*, trans. Paul A. Kottman. New York: Routledge.

Connolly, William E. (2017). *Facing the Planetary: Entangled Humanism and the Politics of Swarming*. Durham, NC: Duke University Press.

—— (2022). *Resounding Events: Adventures of an Academic from the Working Class*. New York: Fordham University Press.

Debord, Guy (1992). *La Societé du spectacle*. Paris: Gallimard.

Deleuze, Gilles, and Félix Guattari (2008). *A Thousand Plateaus: Capitalism and Schizophrenia*, trans. Brian Massumi. London: Continuum.

Dicks, Henry (2023). *The Biomimicry Revolution: Learning from Nature how to Inhabit the Earth*. New York: Columbia University Press.

Dissanayake, Ellen (1992). *Homo Aestheticus: Where Art Comes from and Why*. Toronto: The Free Press.

Ellenberger, Henri F. (1970). *The Discovery of the Unconscious: The History and Evolution of Dynamic Psychiatry*. New York: Basic Books.

Felski, Rita (2020). *Hooked: Art and Attachment.* Chicago: University of Chicago Press.

Foucault, Michel (1976). *Histoire de la sexualité I: la volonté de savoir*. Paris: Gallimard.

Gallese, Vittorio (2017). "Mirroring, a Liberated Embodied Simulation and Aesthetic Experience," in *Mirror Images: Reflection in Art and Medicine,* eds. Helen Hirsch and Alessandra Pace. Thun: Verlag für moderne Kunst, 27–37.

Girard, René (2007). *Evolution and Conversion: Dialogues on the Origins of Culture* (with Pierpaolo Antonello and João Cezar de Castro Rocha). London: Continuum.

Havelock, Eric A. (1963). *Preface to Plato*. Cambridge, MA: Harvard University Press.

Hayles, Katherine N., and Nidesh Lawtoo (2022). "Posthuman Mimesis II – Connections: A Dialogue Between Nidesh Lawtoo and Katherine Hayles." *Journal of Posthumanism* 2.2, 181–189.

Homer (2020). *The Odyssey,* trans. and ed. Emily Wilson. New York: W. W. Norton & Company.

Huizinga, Johan (2016). *Homo Ludens: A Study of the Play-Element in Culture.* Kettering, OH: Angelico Press.

Kuhn, Thomas S. (1996). *The Structure of Scientific Revolutions.* Chicago: The University of Chicago Press.

Lawtoo, Nidesh (2013). *The Phantom of the Ego: Modernism and the Mimetic Unconscious.* East Lansing: Michigan State University Press.

—— (2022). *Homo Mimeticus: A New Theory of Imitation.* Leuven: Leuven University Press.

—— (2023). *Violence and the Oedipal Unconscious: vol. 1, The Catharsis Hypothesis.* East Lansing: Michigan State University Press.

Lawtoo, Nidesh (ed.) (2024). *Mimetic Posthumanism: Homo Mimeticus 2.0 in Arts, Society and Technics.* Leiden: Brill.

Machiavelli, Niccolò (2020). *The Prince,* 3rd ed., trans. and ed. Wayne A. Rebhorn. New York. W.W. Norton & Company.

—— (2021). *Il Principe,* ed. Ugo Dotti. Milan: Feltrinelli Editore.

Nietzsche, Friedrich (1980). *Ecce Homo,* trans. R. J. Hollingdale. London: Penguin.

—— (1982a). *Daybreak,* trans. R. J. Hollingdale. Cambridge: Cambridge University Press.

—— (1982b). "Twilight of the Idols," in *The Portable Nietzsche,* ed. Walter Kaufman. New York: Penguin Books, 464–563.

—— (1996). "Homer's Contest," trans. and ed. Christa Davis Acampora. *Nietzscheana* 5, 1–8.

—— (1997). *Human, All Too Human I,* trans. Gary Handwerk. Stanford: Stanford University Press.

—— (2008). *Thus Spoke Zarathustra,* trans. Graham Parkes. Oxford: Oxford University Press.

Pseudo-Longinus (2005). "On the Sublime," in *Critical Theory since Plato,* eds. Hazard Adams and Leroy Searle. Boston: Thomson Wadsworth, 95–118.

Rosa, Hartmut (2019). *Resonance: A Sociology of Our Relationship to the World,* trans. Hames C. Wagner. Cambridge: Polity.

Siemens, Herman (2021). *Agonal Perspectives of Nietzsche's Philosophy of Transvaluation.* Berlin: De Gruyter.

Staten, Henry (2019). *Techne Theory: A New Language for Art.* New York: Bloomsbury.

Vernant, Jean-Pierre (2007). "L'Univers, les dieux, les hommes: récits grecs de l'origine, " in *Œuvres I.* Paris: Seuil, 11–151.

Wilson, Emily (2020). "Introduction," in *The Odyssey,* ed. and trans. Emily Wilson. New York: W. W. Norton & Company, 1–79.

PART 1

RE-FRAMINGS OF CLASSICAL MIMESIS

CHAPTER 1

PLATO ON FACEBOOK

Mikkel Borch-Jacobsen

Socrates: Of the many excellences which I perceive in the order of our state, there is none which upon reflection pleases me better than the rule about Internet.
Glaucon: To what do you refer?
Socrates: To our refusal to admit the memetic kind of media, for it certainly ought not to be received ... Speaking in confidence, for you will not denounce me to Facebook and the rest of the memetic networks, all memes are made to contaminate the thinking (*dianoia*) of the hearers, unless as an antidote (*pharmakon*) they possess the knowledge of their true nature.

We must think the present, Hannah Arendt (1961) admonished in the preface to her collection of exercises in political thought, *Between Past and Future*. We must think the present because thought is born of the event, of what happens to us here and now.

Her present was, of course, totalitarianism, which she defined as a totally new political regime, different as much from the various forms of tyranny as from democracy. No regime until then had completely abolished the differences around which the *Polis* is organized and articulated. Democracy, in particular, rests on the explicit recognition of the division of society—horizontal division between parties, classes, and opinions, vertical division between the people, *demos*, and its representatives. In contrast, totalitarianism, whether Nazi or Stalinist, was characterized according to Arendt by a unification and homogenization of society through the imposition of an ideology, by which she meant the logical coherence of an idea, of a grand omni-explicative narrative that was made real, literally, through terror. Anything that contradicted the cohesion of the Germanic *Volksgemeinschaft* or of the classless society was physically eliminated, whether it be "inferior races" or "moribund classes." It did not matter whether this ideological narrative corresponded to reality or not, since reality itself could be shaped in the image of the narrative, with death or re-education camps, autos-da-fe, or cultural revolution. Minds, likewise, were formed and informed by a centralized and omnipresent propaganda that disseminated the narrative to the masses using all the means of mass communication available at the time—press, radio, cinema, not to mention art and literature.

Our present is no longer that one, even if truly totalitarian regimes have appeared since the time of Hannah Arendt, such as Maoist China, the Khmer Rouge, or the Islamic State. What we are witnessing today is the rise of populisms. They too are characterized by a will to abolish the division of society in favor of a people that is one, united, unanimous, except that this will, unlike what happened in totalitarian regimes, arises from within democracy itself. Populism is often seen as a threat to democracy, but we forget that it is its staunch defender. Populism, whether of the right or the left, does not want less, but *more* democracy, and a more direct one, more referendum-based, more representative of the *demos*: "Stop the steal!" "Take back control!" Populism wants to get rid of all the mediations that separate the people from itself—political or trade union representatives, governmental institutions, media outlets, experts, lobbies, Eurocrats, all accused of deciding in place of the people, without the people, and behind its back: "Drain the swamp!" Hence the propensity of populist movements to give credence to the most outlandish conspiracy theories, insofar as any official discourse or narrative necessarily becomes suspect since it is distant and therefore opaque, non-transparent. The criterion of truth is no longer the consensus of experts on a "matter of fact," but the proximity of the people to itself: "It's true because my neighbor or my cousin told me so, and I believe it precisely because the elites say the opposite and see it as a baseless fiction." In a dizzying reversal, the rumor becomes truer than the best-established fact because that fact has been established by witnesses who cannot be trusted. Welcome to the world of "alternative facts" and "post-truth."

We see the difference with totalitarianism and its regime of truth: whereas totalitarian propaganda formed unanimous masses by imposing on them a top-down Single Narrative that was supposed to be truer than reality, populisms achieve the same result by the proliferation of narratives and rumors that spread from one person to another, in a rhizomatic and horizontal way. And if they achieve this so easily, it is because proximity has taken on a whole new meaning with these novel forms of mass communication that are electronic social networks, Facebook, Twitter/X, TikTok, and so on. In the past, rumors were limited to small, word-of-mouth social networks, such as congregations, neighborhoods, or professional circles. Today, they are shared "virally" by millions of people who are all "friends" or "followers" of one another, all united in a single rejection of the lies that are the official truths. That these rumors are sometimes launched or retweeted by the head of state himself does not change anything, insofar as he presents himself as the first and closest "friend" of his millions of "followers" and denounces the actions of the "deep state" and the cabal of pedophiles of which he is both the victim and the slayer. The populist demagogue, unlike the charismatic leader of totalitarian regimes, is a deconstructor of state and truth, a clown who ridicules his office to be closer to us, his "base." He is like us, and we are like him, "We the people."

So, this is what we need to think through, this electronic sociality and this politics of "post-truth" that seem to us to destroy at its base the social and epistemic contract on which democratic life is based. How is this reversal of truth into falsehood and falsehood into truth even possible? How can enlightened and law-abiding citizens be transformed overnight into an irrational, emotional, violent, insurrectional mob? Obviously, it is not on the side of modern philosophies of the social contract that one should look for an answer since it is precisely this contract that populisms shatter. I propose therefore to go back to the past, as Hannah Arendt always did, and more particularly to Plato, the father of political philosophy, to find the means to understand our present.

***

Plato's great text on social networks is the *Ion*. Ion, in the dialogue that bears his name, is a rhapsode, that is, a professional reciter of Homeric poetry. Rhapsodes, dressed in sumptuous red costumes, would recite or, better, *perform*, mime passages from Homer, Hesiod, or Archilochus (these being often in the direct style, the recitation of rhapsodes came necessarily close to acting). Rhapsodes often contended for prizes at the rhapsodic contests held during the religious festivities of Greek cities, such as the Athenian Panathenaic Games. For context, let's recall that these festivals, like the Great Dionysias during which tragic contests were held in Athens, were civic events which gathered all the residents, male and female, except for the slaves (Plato, in the *Ion*, speaks of an audience of 20,000 people). The citizens communed there in the ritual recall of the great stories (*muthoi*) in which the poets, in particular Homer, the "father of Greece," told the divine and human origins of Hellas. In this still largely oral culture that was Greece of the fifth century, rhapsody and the tragic theater were, literally, the means of mass communication of the time, just like the recitation and memorization of poetry was the essential instrument of education (*paideia*).[1]

So, one day Socrates meets Ion in the street. Ion has just returned from the festival of Epidaurus where he has won the first prize by reciting Homer. For Ion is specialized in the interpretation (*hermeneia*) of Homer, a bit like Laurence Olivier was specialized in the interpretation of Shakespeare or Glenn Gould in that of Bach. Socrates admits to him that he envies his profession (*technê*), which allows him to wear such beautiful clothes and especially to be the "interpreter of the poet's thought to those who listen," which is "impossible unless one knows just what the poet is saying (*oti legei*)" (*Ion* 530c). *Technê*, which is translated here as "profession" and elsewhere as "art," "craft" or "skill," means more precisely the know-how of a specialist, the knowledge that allows someone to do or make something, and only *one* thing.[2] Socrates insists on this point, both in the *Ion* and in the *Republic*: "The deity has assigned to each separate profession the power of knowing a particular occupation" (537c), so that the pilot does not have the same *technê* as the doctor, the doctor does not have the same *technê* as the carpenter, and so forth.

So how is it, Socrates then asks, that Ion can only interpret what Homer says, his *logos*, and not what other poets say? Archilochus and Hesiod also talk about divination and war, just like Homer, but Ion only knows how to talk about it as Homer talks about it, by adopting his *lexis*. Ion is obliged to admit, he poetizes and rhapsodizes well only when it's Homer who is in play. So, his art is not the "*technê* of poetry taken as a whole" (532c) and it is not, Socrates explains to him at some length, a *technê* at all:

> This gift you have of speaking well on Homer is not a *technê*; it is a divine force (*theia dunamis*), impelling you like the power in the stone Euripides called the magnet [...] This stone does not simply attract the iron rings, just by themselves; it also imparts to the rings a force enabling them to do the same thing as the stone itself, that is, to attract another ring, so that sometimes a chain is formed, quite a long one, of iron rings, suspended from one another. For all of them, however, their force depends on that loadstone. Just so the Muse. She first makes men inspired [*entheous*, enthusiasts], and then through the inspired ones others share in the enthusiasm, and a chain is formed, for the epic

poets, all the good ones, have their excellences, not from *technê*, but are inspired and possessed (*katechômenoi*). So it is also with the good lyric poets; as the participants in the Corybantic rites are not in their senses when they dance, so the lyric poets are not in their senses when they make these lovely poems [...] they are seized with the Bacchic transport and are possessed. (*Ion* 533d–534a)

The poets, Socrates continues, are only "interpreters of the gods, each one possessed by the divinity to whom he is in bondage," and the rhapsodes in their turn are "interpreters of interpreters" (534e–535a), each one held by the poet by whom they are possessed, before transmitting this enthusiasm to their public (*hermeneia*, interpretation, also means transmission): "Well, do you see that the spectator is the last of the rings I spoke of, which receives their force from one another by virtue of the loadstone? You the rhapsode and actor (*hupocrités*), are the middle ring, and the first one is the poet himself" (535e–536a).[3]

Here is a chain, a social network through which a "divine force" is transmitted from one person to the other, attaching them to each other. Now, what is thus transmitted is not a content, a message, a divine *logos*; it is a very specific state that allows the transmission, the magnetic contagion. Plato calls it enthusiasm (*enthusiasmos*), in other words the trance of possession (*katokôchê*). The poet, then the "rhapsode and actor," then the public are all *entheous*, that is literally "en-godded": they become the god (*theos*), each one in its turn.

The reference to the Corybants and the Bacchants will help us understand what Plato is talking about. The Corybants, or, more accurately, those who "act like Corybants," celebrated rites (*teletai*) intended to relieve people affected by what Plato calls in *Phaedrus* the ritual or "telestic" madness (*Phaedrus* 265b). Phrygian melodies attributed to the Silene Marsyas and his disciple Olympos, two figures of the Dionysian pantheon, were played on the *aulos*, at which point the celebrants, recognizing the god's signal, would go into a trance and perform a furious dance during which they imitated the behavior of the particular *daimôn* they were possessed by. In *Laws*, Plato thus mentions "the Bacchic dance and those who engage in these dances that they mime (*mimounthai*) by evoking, it is claimed, Nymphs, Pans, Silenes and drunken Satyrs, in certain rituals of purification (*katharmoi*) and initiation (*teletai*)" (*Laws* 815c). The corybantic ritual to which Plato compares the enthusiasm of poets, rhapsodes, actors and their audiences consisted therefore in a spectacular *mimêsis* during which the celebrants literally, identified with the divine force that agitated them and thus found a "cathartic" deliverance and purification—this is the term used by Aristotle in an identical context (*Politics* 1342a).

The magnetic chain or network of the *Ion* is a *mimetic* chain or network where each one joins in turn in the dance to become an *other*, the *same* as another. Hence its contagious, viral character: behind the dances of the Corybants loom the ritual choreas of the Bacchants, these ecstatic orgies of women of which poor Pentheus, in the tragedy of Euripides, say that they spread "like a fire" (*Bacchae* 778). The mimetic pull of the dance/trance of possession is properly irresistible (one is reminded of the medieval dances of Saint Vitus in which Nietzsche and his friend Erwin Rhode saw a return of the Dionysiac, or again of the epidemics of demonic possession of Loudun, Louviers, and Morzine). What Plato describes here is exactly what others, at the turn of the 19th and 20th centuries, would call variously "psychic contagion," "collective hysteria," or "crowd psychology," all phenomena characterized by a subjective malleability and a contamination—"imitative" in nature said Gabriel Tarde, "identificatory" said Sigmund Freud—between individuals. Needless to say, these phenomena are now the affective/infective subject matter of mimetic studies as well.

As a matter of fact, the enthusiasm that is communicated from one to another is not something that would be communicated; it is communication itself, the receptivity to the other. Mimetic enthusiasm is communicative. When Ion interprets, that is to say "transmits" Homer, it is not so much Homer who possesses him, it is the state of enthusiasm that had allowed Homer to be possessed, inspired by his characters and that now allows him too, Ion, to play the roles of Andromache, Hecuba, or Priam by experiencing all their emotions before having them be experienced in turn by his listeners: "Whenever I recite a tale of pity (*eleinon*)," Ion explains, "my eyes are filled with tears, and when it is one of terror (*phoberon*) or dismay, my hair stands up on end with fear and my heart goes leaping" (*Ion* 535c). (One will have recognized in passing the effect proper to tragedy according to Aristotle, the famous *katharsis* of fear, *phobos*, and pity, *eleos*.)

***

In *Ion*, Plato is content to describe this contagious force of poetic *mimêsis*, even qualifying it as divine. In the *Republic*, on the other hand, he firmly condemns it. This is even, Socrates tells Glaucon at the very beginning of Book 10, the reason why mimetic poetry had to be solemnly banned from the City: "Why, between ourselves—for you will not betray me to the tragic poets and all other mimeticians (*mimetikous*)—that kind seems to be a corruption of the minds of all the listeners who do not have as an antidote (*pharmakon*) the knowledge of its real nature" (*Republic* 595b). Socrates comes back to this a bit later:

But we have not yet brought our chief accusation against poetry. Its power to take possession (*lambasthai*),[4] with rare exceptions, of even the better sort is surely the chief cause for alarm. [...] When we hear Homer or some other of the makers of tragedy imitating one of the heroes who is in grief and is delivering a long tirade in his lamentations or chanting and beating his breast, you know that even the very best of us feel pleasure and abandon ourselves. We follow him in genuine sympathy, and we praise as an excellent poet the one who so to speak puts us in the same state as his hero. (605c–605d)

Notice that this *sum-patheia*, the feeling-with or com-passion, takes place when we *listen* to "Homer or some other of the makers of tragedy imitating one of the heroes who is in grief," and so on. Not only does Plato quite simply identify the epic poet and the tragic one (which in fact was common at the time: Aeschylus was often quoted as saying that his tragedies were "slices of Homer's banquet"), but he stages them, literally, as rhapsodes or tragic actors playing roles in front of us, the listeners. A little earlier, Plato had also used the verb "rhapsodize" (*rhapsôdein*) to describe Homer and Hesiod reciting their verses (600d). The reason for this crushing of all differences between poets and performers is of course that for him they are all interpreters, *hermeneis*, that is, enthused and enthusing, magnetized and magnetizing, inspired and inspiring mimeticians.

Socrates then warns against this "sympathetic" contagion that makes the passionate part of the soul (*psuchê*) escape from the control of its rational part, thus upsetting the hierarchical division of the soul, which echoes the hierarchical division of the City into distinct professions and skills (*technai*):

That part which is by nature best in us [...] relaxes its guard over this plaintive part under the pretext that it is the spectator of another man's sufferings and there is no disgrace in praising and pitying someone else who [...] abandons himself to excessive grief. Few people, I think, are capable of reasoning that the enjoyment we derive from other people's experiences inevitably affect our own. For it's not easy to restrain pity in our own sufferings when we have nurtured it and made it strong in those of others [...] And poetic *mimêsis* has the same effect on us with regard to sex and anger and all the other appetites and pains and pleasures of the soul [...] For it nourishes and waters them when they ought to be dried up. (606a–606d)

Poetic *mimêsis* is an accelerator of passions, just like the modern algorithms of Facebook or Twitter/X. It impassions us, affects us, infects us, and as such it has a real power over us. Under its influence, we espouse the passions of others and become properly irresponsible, uncontrollable, since we are no longer ourselves. We should not believe therefore, Plato tells us, that it is a mere simulacrum, a copy without reality that we could watch unharmed.

Yet this is what he had just stated a little earlier, when defining *mimêsis* not as "the imitation of what is as it is," but as "the imitation of what appears (*phainomenon*) as it appears," that is to say as a mere semblance or simulacrum (*phantasma*) (598b). The passage is well known:

1. The God produces the Idea or Form (*idea, eidos*) of the bed, which is unique and solely real.
2. The bed-maker (*demiourgos klinês*) "does not make anything real but something that is similar to what is without really being it" (597a); this is what Plato calls elsewhere the image or copy (*eikôn*), which is a resembling, "eikastic" imitation (*mimêsis*) of the original (*Sophist* 235d–236a).
3. The painter produces an "appearance," a "semblance" of the manufactured bed, that is what Plato calls here simply a *mimêsis* and more specifically, in the *Sophist*, a "phantastic" imitation (*mimêsis*). (236b)

The painter, like "the maker of tragedies (*tragôdopoios*) [...] is in his nature three removes from the king and truth, as are all other mimeticians" (*Republic* 597e). Thus, the Model, the copy, and the copy of the copy. Or, as Gilles Deleuze put it in a famous essay on Plato: the Same, the Similar, and the Simulacrum.[5]

It is at this ontological hierarchy that commentators usually stop, even when they want to overturn it in a Nietzschean or Baudrillardian fashion: the mimetic simulacrum or phantasm would have less being, it is said, than the Idea and its exact copy, the good eikastic imitation. But why then would this pale phantom be so dangerous, so *politically* dangerous that Socrates sees in the banishment of mimetic poets the essential achievement of his plan for the *Polis* (595a)? In fact, the passage on the three beds is not so much about the being of imitations, good or bad, as about the being, or better said, the identity of the imitator. Either the craftsman, the *demiourgos*, always imitates the same model to always make or do the same thing, in which case he has a *technê* of his own that defines, *identifies* him as a bed maker, a pilot, or a doctor. Or he is like the fantastic *demiourgos* Socrates imagines, who can create anything by holding up a mirror to the world, in which case he is a mimetician, that is, a polytechnician who has no *technê* of his own. "The painter," says Socrates, "will paint us a cobbler, a carpenter, and other craftsmen (*demiourgous*), though he himself has no knowledge of any of these professions" (598c). Likewise for the makers of tragedy and their "father, Homer," of whom "some people tell us that these poets know all kinds of crafts (*technas*)" (598d).

This is the reason why mimeticians are so dangerous: they imitate everyone, thus destabilizing the strict division of roles and identities on which Socrates, in Book 2, had founded the just City: "One man, one *technê*." Worse still, the mimeticians invite us to imitate their mimicry, to enter the dance of enthusiasm and to become in our turn a ring in the mimetic chain or network. As Socrates said, mimetic poetry corrupts "the minds of all the listeners who do not have as an antidote (*pharmakon*) the knowledge of its real nature."

***

This antidote is of course none other than the theory of Ideas, which allows here to tie each *technê*, and thus also each craftsman to the unique and invariable model to which they must conform (which they must imitate, in other words). Platonic ontology is a *politics* of Ideas, a way to stabilize the division of society by rigidly distributing skills and identities, and thus prevent the viral proliferation of ideas, stories, and memes: "One Idea, one man, one *technê*." But it should be noted that this ontology had first to be created, made (*poietos*) and even, very literally, fictionalized, since it is presented in Book 7 in the form of a story (*muthos*), that of the Cave, and this within the larger narrative or myth that is the *Republic* itself. It should be borne in mind that Socrates, in this dialogue, "maps out," as Glaucon puts it, "a City that is founded only in our words (*logois*), for I think that it can be found nowhere on earth" (592a). Having "laid the foundation of a city by words (*tô logô*)" (369c), namely the "true principle" according to which "it is impossible for one man to do the work of many professions (*technas*)" (374a), Socrates proposes in Book 2 to create a body of "guardians" to protect the City against internal as well as external violence. It will therefore be necessary to train, that is, to educate, men having a character corresponding to this *technê* that will be, as we will learn subsequently, the *technê* of the philosopher-kings: "Come, then, just as if we were telling stories or myths (*muthologountes*) [...] let us educate these men in our discourse (*logô*)" (376d).

It turns out that this pedagogical *logos* is a discourse about the pedagogical power of *logos*, more precisely of the stories (*muthoi*) that one tells children. The Greek *paideia* was based on gymnastics for the body and *mousikê*, the art of the Muses, for the mind, the latter of which consisting largely in the oral, sung, and sometimes danced recitation of the deeds of the Greek gods and heroes as narrated by the poets. Now, Socrates explains, these stories told to children may well be a fiction or a lie (*pseudos*), but they still form their *psuchê*, that is, their mind and character (or soul, as *psuchê* can also be translated): "That is the time when they are easily molded and take the impression [or model, *tupos*] that one wishes to stamp upon them" (377b).[6] This is of course the very principle of *paideia*, but it is also its danger: the *psuchê* of children and more generally of men is mimetic, it models itself on everything it is told, whether it be a true or a false *logos* (377a). The mimetic regime is the regime of post-truth, which it would actually be better to call pre-truth since it predates the very distinction of truth from fiction and fake news: we become—better, we *are*—the stories we are told, beyond truth and falsity, beyond good and evil.

Since such is our mimetic condition,[7] it is therefore necessary to control the *logos* of poets and storytellers in order to propose to the future guardians only models or types that will form their mind and character in the desired direction. This is the age-old logic of censorship, which we still find today in discussions around media and social networks. Note that Socrates defends himself from forging myths here, even though this is obviously what he is doing: "Adeimantes, you and I are not poets but founders of a city; and founders need to know the models (*tupous*) on which poets are to compose their stories [...] but they don't need to compose the stories themselves" (378e). Socrates consequently enjoins poets to depict gods and heroes that are virtuous, honest, temperate, courageous, and so forth, so that the future guardians model themselves on them. In particular, poets should not represent a god who changes form like Proteus (380d–381e), for the guardians must follow only *one* role-model, a model who "remains in his own form without variation for ever" (381c), lest they follow a mimetician fit for all kinds of roles and *technai*.

Indeed, this would pose a grave threat to the stability of the social differences on which Socrates founded the City, which is why Socrates goes on to censor not only the poets' *logos*, what they say, but also their *lexis*, their way of saying it. For the storyteller must not set the bad example (the bad model) of someone who speaks "as if he were someone else" (393e). This is the well-known distinction between simple narration (*haplê diêgêsis*), where the poet uses indirect speech without confusing himself with the one he is talking about, and mimetic narration (*mimêsis*), where he uses direct speech—imitating, therefore, the characters he is having speak. This idea of the poet imitating his characters may of course seem strange to us who associate poetry with literature, that is to say with writing, but it was in fact self-evident in a culture that was still largely oral and for which the arch-poet, Homer, was a bard (*aoidos*) who would sing and perform the stories he composed. Still in *Poetics* 1455a, Aristotle recommends that the poet "carry out the appropriate gestures as he composes his speeches," as if he were on stage. The young Nietzsche will later remember: "Aeschylus composed as he played, as an actor."[8] The poet, as soon as he gives the floor to gods and heroes, is necessarily a mime, a *mimos* who assumes all kinds of roles.[9]

But in our City, Socrates declares, "there is no twofold or manifold man among us, since every man does one thing" (397e). We must therefore banish all the mimetic storytellers—epic poets and rhapsodes, tragic poets and actors—and retain only the more austere storyteller who proposes distinct and invariable role-models while remaining himself invariable. Only in this way will it be possible to form and mold guardians who will remain in their turn invariable, each one in his place, before they become philosophers by turning their gaze toward the immutable Ideas of the Beautiful, the Just, and the Good, this conversion of the soul being the ultimate goal of *paideia* (518b–518d).

This, in a nutshell, is *what* Plato says in his story about the education of the guardians-philosophers. But *how* does he say it? He says it in a story where he speaks through a general narrator, Socrates, who himself oscillates between narrative passages and mimetic ones in which he speaks "under the name" of Glaucon, Adeimantus, Thrasymachus, and others. So Plato does, as has often been pointed out, the very thing he reproaches the poets and rhapsodes for doing. This is all the truer since Plato, as Pierre Hadot reminds us, used to read his dialogues aloud in public readings that were at the time the most efficient way to spread one's ideas.[10] Plato must therefore have been "interpreting," miming Socrates and the other characters, just like any old rhapsode or actor. The reason for this, Hadot explains, is that Plato viewed his dialogues as a means to change people. They were not written, Hadot says, to "inform" his listeners, but to "form" (118) and transform them: "The dialogues can be considered as propaganda works, [...] intended to convert to philosophy" (Hadot 1995, 116) and their aim was therefore eminently political (124).

More precisely, it was a matter of forming, shaping, and fictionalizing citizen-philosophers with the help of appropriate myths, all the while making them believe that they were *born* and not *made* such. Socrates, in the *Republic*, thus recommends committing a pious lie (*pseudos*), a "useful remedy" (*pharmakon chresimon*, 382c, 389b) reserved for rulers (and even more so for city-founders-who-are-not-poets). The guardians will be told the ancient "Phoenician" fable of the founding of Thebes, how Cadmos, "as the poets have said and made believe," had sown dragon's teeth in the earth from which the hoplites who were to defend the new city had emerged fully armed, and so on:

> I will try to persuade first the rulers, then the guardians, and then the rest of the citizens, that this education and instruction which they received from us and of which they believed they had the feeling and experience, all that was only a dream; that in reality they were fashioned and raised in the bosom of the earth, they, their weapons and all their equipment; that after having fully formed them, the earth, their mother, brought them into the world; that from then on, they must regard the land they inhabit as their mother and nurse, defend it against anyone who attacks it, and treat the other citizens as brothers, as sons of the mother earth like themselves. (414d–e).

But will we manage, Socrates asks, "to make people believe this *muthos*"? No, answers Glaucon, at least "to those of whom you speak, but it seems to me that it can be persuaded to their sons, their descendants and all those who will be born in their wake." Well, then, Socrates concludes, "let this," our myth, "make its way as rumor pleases" (415c–d). No one disputes the rumor, *phêmê*, that spreads by word of mouth, for it is ageless and without creator—without *poiêtês*.

We see that what Plato tells *in* the story that is the *Republic* is exactly what he *does* with us, his captive and captivated audience. He educates and trains us by telling us the myth of a City where everyone stays in place, keeping to oneself and minding his own *technê*, without being carried away in the mimetic chain of storytellers and rumormongers. But he does this by using *mimêsis* against *mimêsis*, the power of myth and story-telling against myth, philosophical enthusiasm against the enthusiasm of crowds and social networks. In the end, the antidote (*pharmakon*) against the poison of viral *mimêsis* is this very same poison (*pharmakon*, again). It is called philosophy, useful rumor.

Notes

1   See Havelock's seminal work, *Preface to Plato* (1963). Editors' note: all the translations of Plato and Aristotle are the author's and follow the standard numeration by line number (Stephanus for Plato and Brekker for Aristotle).

2   On Plato and *technê* in the *Republic* see ch. 2 in this volume [editors' note].

3   On mimesis and Dionysian contagion in *Ion* see also Lawtoo 2022, 74–80.

4   As Rouget points out, the verb *lambanô*, "to take," "to seize," was part of the vocabulary of possession: one was "seized" by the deity, just as nowadays one can still be "seized" by the demon (1980, 272).

5   See Deleuze 1969, 292–306.

6   See Lacoue-Labarthe 1989 and Roux 1961.

7   See also a special issue of *CounterText* 8.1 (2022), titled *The Mimetic Condition,* which started to disseminate mimetic studies [editors' note].

8   Nietzsche, unpublished fragment 5[69] from Autumn 1870 (Nietzsche 1978, 112).

9   This is why Aristotle added that "poetry implies a happy gift of nature or a strain of madness. In the one case a man is able to easily take the mold (*euplastoi*) of any character; in the other, he is lifted out of his proper self (*ekstatikoi*)" (*Poetics* 1455a). Also, Agathon, in Aristophanes' *Thesmophoriazusae,* 149–156: "To be a poet a man must fashion his way of being (*tous tropous*) to the requirements of his plays. [...] But qualities we do not possess must be sought by *mimêsis*."

10   See Hadot 1995, 116. See also Detienne 1981, 71–72.

Bibliography

Arendt, Hannah (1961). *Between Past and Future.* New York: Viking Press.

Aristophanes (1971). *Complete Plays,* ed. Moses Hadas. New York: Bantam Books.

Deleuze, Gilles (1969). *Logique du sens.* Paris: Les Éditions de Minuit.

Detienne, Marcel (1981). *L'Invention de la mythologie.* Paris: Gallimard.

Euripides (1913). "The Bacchae," in *Euripidis Fabulae,* vol. 3, ed. Gilbert Murray. Oxford: Clarendon Press.

Hadot, Pierre (1995). *Qu'est-ce que la philosophie antique?* Paris: Gallimard.

Havelock, Eric A. (1963). *Preface to Plato.* Cambridge, MA: Harvard University Press.

Lacoue-Labarthe, Philippe (1989). "Typography," in *Typography: Mimesis, Philosophy, Politics,* ed. Christopher Fynsk. Cambridge, MA: Harvard University Press, 43–138.

Lawtoo, Nidesh (2022). *Homo Mimeticus: A New Theory of Imitation.* Leuven: Leuven University Press.

Nietzsche, Friedrich (1978). *Nietzsche Werke. Kritische Gesamtausgabe. Abteilung III. Band 3,* eds. Giorgio Colli and Mazzino Montinari. Berlin: De Gruyter.

Rouget, Gilbert (1980). *La musique et la transe.* Paris: Gallimard.

Roux, Georges (1961). "Le sens de TUPOS." *Revue des études anciennes* 63, 5–1.

CHAPTER 2

TECHNE VS. MIMESIS IN
PLATO'S *REPUBLIC*

What Socrates Really Says Against Homer

Henry Staten

I

At the beginning of *Republic* 10 Socrates expresses satisfaction with the
now-completed design of his optimal polity, and in particular with the ban on
tragic poetry. Evidently unsatisfied with his previous justification for the ban,
however, he returns to the attack. Mimetic poetry is a peril for a just society
because it "corrupts the soul" of those who don't possess the "antidote" to its
toxicity: a knowledge of its "true nature"; and so, apparently to provide this an-
tidotal knowledge, he initiates a final confrontation with tragic poetry and its
master, Homer.

What does Socrates identify as this antidote? How does he define the "true
nature" of imitation? The answer is not as clear as has often been presumed. It
isn't that poetry is an "imitation of an imitation."

He begins via the customary Socratic route, the positing of a single Idea
(*idea*) or Form (*eidos*) in the case of any empirical multiplicity; for example, a
unique Idea/Form of couch, which a *demiourgos* "artisan" can "look to" in order
to make multiple physical copies (Plato 1988, 596ab).[1] However, Socrates adds,
there is also a sort of artisan who can make anything without consulting the
Form, simply by reflecting it in a mirror. This "imitator," as opposed to the genuine artisan, Glaucon observes, creates only the *phainomena* "appearances," not

onta, "realities" (596e), and Socrates then gets him to agree that the painter is the same kind of *demiourgos* as the mirror-holder—a mere imitator. Since Glaucon's point is to deny that the imitator is a genuine artisan, the implication is that the genuine *demiourgos* does indeed produce *onta* "realities." But this implication is for the moment lost as Socrates launches into his famous "imitation of an imitation" allegory. The *eidos* "Form" of couch, he suggests, has, so to speak, been made by god; the physical couch by an artisan; and the image or appearance of a couch in a painting, by an imitator, the painter, who is introduced as analogous to the mirror-holder. The god-made Form is truly, completely (*teleos*) real, whereas the couch made by the artisan and the imitation made by the painter are only *amudron* "dimly, obscurely" real (597a). Socrates never calls the artisanal work an imitation, and it's apparently this single reference to the dimness of its reality that has authorized the phrase "imitation of an imitation."

The three couchmakers/three couches allegory has been represented for centuries as the epitome of Platonic art theory; yet it is both obscure in its relation to the standard Platonic "Theory of Forms," and a deviation from the line of argumentation indicated by the immediately preceding mirror analogy and the associated distinction between appearances and realities.[2]

The super-worldly Platonic Forms are of abstractions like the Good, the True, the Beautiful, and the One, not of empirical objects, and Socrates makes no attempt to explain how Forms of artifacts would be possible.[3] Recognizably misguided though it be in its application to artifacts, most readers have assumed the ontology of Form to be in some vague way the basis for the entire critique of mimesis, including the culminating critique of Homer. Yet when Socrates finally gets to Homer, he doesn't (except by dubious implication) convict him of failing to imitate Forms; rather, he argues that Homer, like the mirror-holder and painter, lacks the knowledge of a techne and is thus not a real demiourgos. Demiourgos just means "artisan," but, as numerous dialogues show, Socrates always thinks a demiourgos as *one who knows a techne,* and we miss the underlying thrust of his thinking here if we do not keep in mind the sustained exploration of the nature of techne that he mounts in the early and early middle dialogues.[4] Throughout, from the first evocation of the mirror holder, the true demiourgos is conceived as maker of *onta* "realities" on the basis of authentic proficiency in a techne. Only passingly, and in a way that is obscurely connected to the trajectory of his argument, when the dubious notion of the god-made Form pops up, does Socrates class the artisanal work with the imitation as deficient in reality (596e).

An important clue to the real focus of Socrates' critique of mimesis is the fact that when he introduces the mirror-holder as paradigm of the imitator at

596de he says that such an imitator can make *everything* and repeats five times that he can make it *quickly (taxu)*. The significance of this emphasis doesn't emerge until after the digression into the allegory of the three couchmakers, when the argument finally (at 598) starts turning away from painting and toward poetry. At that point Socrates says that the mimetic techne can (like the earlier mirror) produce everything because it imitates only a phantasm, and then (at 599a) explains that the poet's own ease of creation, like that of other imitators, results from the fact that he gets by without the techne-knowledge that a real artisan would possess. The absolute reality of the Forms is at best a peripheral issue in this argument, even if we overlook the logical difficulties involved in trying to adapt it to the ontology of artifacts.

The notion that the Form of couch is made by a god rhetorically underlines the gap between the reality of the Form and the reality of the artisanal copy, thereby creating the misleading sense that the artifact's deficiency of reality is the fundamental issue for Socrates' critique of mimesis. Socrates himself wavers on this point when he momentarily disparages the reality of the artisanal product as *amudron,* a characterization that corresponds to the popular concept of "Platonism," the sense that this whole world is a world of appearances, some more substantial than others, but all mere appearance. Yet, immediately after characterizing artisanal products as sharing the ontological deficiency of mere appearances, he begins turning back toward his essential concern with techne by sharply distinguishing both god and the carpenter from the imitator as true makers, god as the couch's source in nature and the carpenter as *demiourgos* "maker, through the exercise of techne" (597d); and from this point on there is no more talk of the ontological poverty of artifacts.[5] From this point on Socrates throws the relation between objects and transcendent Forms into the background and focuses on the question of the maker qua artisan, therefore as knower of a techne, as opposed to the mere imitator, who only pretends to techne-knowledge.

Only after he concludes his indictment of Homer, however, does Socrates fully clear his argument of its shady relation to absolutely real Form, in the three-techne hierarchy that he articulates at 601c–602a, and that, because of its disconnection from the ontology of Form, scholars have found either puzzling or inconsequential.[6] When he identifies the technai of use, based on practical experience with artifacts, as the highest level of his new hierarchy and as the true locus of *episteme,* Socrates finally rids his argument of the distracting reference to a god-made Form. The new three-level hierarchy of technai, which makes clear what it is that makes true techne different from quick-and-easy imitation, looks very much like a direct replacement of the earlier Form-copy-imitation hierarchy, yet it is a replacement that without comment boots the transcendent Form from the top spot.

It may be that, as Anders Wedberg suggested, Plato himself did not clearly make the distinctions in the meaning of *eidos* "form" that we make.[7] The word-concept *eidos* has three commonly recognized senses in Plato. The first, ordinary-language sense of eidos is the visual shape of an entity; from this sense Platonic Socrates developed the notion of an intellectual form, a concept or "idea" in our sense of the term; and then he raised these forms to a metaphysical, eternal, transworldly status. In *Republic* 10 it's sometimes hard to see which of these latter two senses Plato intended.[8]

But there's also a fourth, more complex sense of *eidos* that scholars have largely ignored, and that is central to the present interpretation. David Wolfsdorf has recently focused attention on this fourth sense of *eidos*: that of artisanally shaped form. Wolfsdorf suggests that Socrates' own intuitions of the principles of intellectual form were initially derived from observation of artisans imparting form in their various crafts.[9] On this reading, Socrates initially understood intellectual form in terms of the "organized work or structure" that the artisan creates by skilled practice of a *techne,* a systematic form of knowledge of how to do something, such as carpentry or mathematics or battlefield strategy. The notion of transcendent Form magnetizes our attention on the relative degrees of reality possessed by a material artisanal product such as a couch or table and its visual imitation, but, seen from the techne-perspective, what Socrates is primarily illustrating, even in the Form–copy–imitation allegory, is not the ontological nature of the three couches, but the nature of the productive powers of the two earthly couchmakers, the *demiourgos* "artisan" and the imitator. The posited artisan-god, who is explicitly evoked only as a manner of speaking to underline the transworldly nature of the Form, is nothing to this point, since he, like the imitator, creates without need of a techne. Hence, he quickly recedes into the background of Socrates' discourse. The reference to the god is a back-formation from the divine nature of the absolutely real Form, and the only productive powers that are actually in play here are the ones Socrates is concerned with—those of the artisan and the imitator.

The obscurities in the critique of mimesis in Book 10 make most sense if we see them as products of the growing pains of the Platonic theory of transcendent forms out of the artisanal background from which Socrates began. The Socratic line is intensely concerned with the model of the technai, from cookery to rhetoric to mathematics; in the *Republic,* the Platonic ontology of Form or "theory of Ideas"—which emerges in the dialogues of the middle period, beginning with the *Phaedo,* and gradually becomes dominant in subsequent dialogues—co-exists with the Socratic line. But this co-existence creates a muddle in the critique of mimesis of *Republic* 10, a muddle that it is possible to untangle.

II

In Section IV I will begin tracing the path by which Socrates slides from his initial to his final three-level hierarchy, but this section and the next briefly summarize the way in which the concept of techne ties together every aspect of Socrates' thinking in the *Republic.* This dialogue can be described as fundamentally a treatise on education, as Eric Havelock masterfully did; but we might equally describe it as a treatise on techne.[10] (Both immanent perspectives are central to mimetic studies as developed in these volumes on *homo mimeticus.*)

The danger of mimetic illusionism is not, for Socrates, that the audience will mistake an image for a real object, but that the image will mold their own psyches into the unstable, self-divided forms of irrational, unmeasured types, and the pre-eminent counterforce to such disruption is the devoted, soul-unifying practice of a techne; hence the most insidious mimetic illusion of all is that which counterfeits the knowledge of techne. This—counterfeiting the knowledge not just of a techne, but of all technai—is the charge that Socrates ultimately makes against Homer.

It's notable that Socrates in his assessment of the role of techne in his imagined city doesn't acknowledge the essential role that imitation plays in education. As Havelock says, all the practical details of techne-knowledge that Homer leaves out of his formulaic descriptions of traditional procedures (such as sailing a ship or piloting a chariot) are, in the training of an artisan, "communicated by example and habituation *and imitation*" (1963, 82–83; italics added). Socrates briefly suggests this kind of imitation when he says that if one is going to imitate, one should imitate the good man, but he doesn't connect such imitation to practical training, in which apprentices take skilled artisans as "role models" in a way that transcends merely following their lead.[11]

Techne is so important to Socrates because it's fundamental to his pursuit of a reliable definition of *arete* "excellence, virtue" and of a reliable way of teaching it.[12] Unlike the transcendent Forms, the forms created by the technai are ineluctably *functional,* definable only in relation to the material exigencies of the practical tasks of human existence. All the fundamental, worldly technai—carpentry, farming, horsemanship, military strategy, politics—are concerned with the forms of objects or states of affairs that belong to the world perceived by the senses, and they exist, as Socrates says specifically of medicine in *Republic* 1, in order to fulfill a need of the human body (341e). Socrates explains there that medicine has been discovered "because our bodies are deficient rather than self-sufficient," and the same can be said of all the technai: the kind of knowledge they involve is tied to the needs of the body, thus as far removed as possible from the static perfection of the transcendent Forms. Unlike animals, which can survive using only their bodies and their instincts, human beings require tools and techniques optimally adapted to the performance of specific practical functions.

Yet, while Socrates speaks respectfully of techne most of the time, he demeans it when discussing it in the vicinity of the transcendent Forms. Thus in Book 1, where there's no reference to such Forms, he says that every techne is "perfect in itself;"[13] but in Book 7, where he introduces the Form of the Good, he says that the technai are *banausoi,* menial or vulgar.[14] Similarly, as we've seen, in the allegory of the three couches, where he floats the notion of a god-made Form of couch, Socrates demeans the reality of the carpenter-made couch, and of the techne of carpentry itself, along with that of the painter-made imitation and the techne of painting. He agrees with Glaucon that the painter doesn't make things that really exist (*onta*), and then adds that the carpenter too doesn't make "that which is" (*ho esti*) but only something "resembling" that which is, hence its "dim" or "obscure" reality (596e–597a). Most strikingly, he says that compared with the higher reality of the Form of the Good human affairs in general "aren't worth taking very seriously" (604b–c)—not even the pursuit of justice in the law courts, which he describes as contention over mere "shadows" of justice (517d). This, even though in the entire *Republic* he labors to design an earthly polity that could instantiate the virtue of justice.

Nevertheless, after his flights into the ideal Socrates always comes back down to earth to grapple with the problems of ethics—and of the enabling condition of ethics, the constitution of the polis, the central problem of the *Republic.* Even in Book 7, where he describes how dialectic leads the mind from the darkness of the cave up to the vision of the intelligible sun—and emphasizes how paltry our worldly doings are by comparison—Socrates ends by treating the ascent to the vision of the Form as *instrumental* to the cause of earthly justice. He reminds Glaucon that the polis educates the guardians up to the vision of the Good-in-itself "not in order to turn in whatever direction they want, but *to make use of them (katachraomai)* to bind the city together" (520a; emphasis added). I leave it to the reader to decide how much significance there is in the invocation of the notion of *use* here, where it is the vision of the Good itself that is being turned to practical account.[15] However much the philosopher-guardians might desire to spend their lives rapt in intellectual vision, they are obligated to put their knowledge to use because they *owe a debt* to the city for educating them, a debt they must pay by coming back down "to the common dwelling place" where they must "grow accustomed to seeing in the dark" (519–520), so that, *using* the Good itself as a model (*paradeigmati chromenous*), they can bring good order to the city and its citizens (540a–b; emphasis added).[16] The life of the polis is notionally of little importance, yet it's the supreme value that drives Socrates' pursuit of philosophy, as it was, apparently, the main purpose of his own life—he who spent his entire life trying to make the citizens of Athens better, and who drank the hemlock rather than be exiled. If the struggle for justice in the law courts were really just contention about shadows, there would be no compelling reason for the dialecticians to sacrifice their ecstatic vision for the aggravation of governing, or for Socrates to expend so much effort in designing the polis that would educate them.[17]

III

The fundamental way in which the guardians would bind together the optimal polity is through the new pedagogy that Socrates proposes as a replacement for the Homeric pedagogy. One can act wisely only by learning to see the Form of the Good, which Socrates describes as the *aitia* "source" of all that is correct and beautiful, *orthos* and *kalos*, and of all truth and understanding (517c). The most elite guardians who became philosopher-rulers would get their own intuitions of graceful Form, which would give them the power to govern wisely, from the direct vision of this Form. *Aitia* is usually translated into English as "cause," but, as Gregory Vlastos pointed out, this is misleading, because *aitia* has a much broader meaning than cause does, and Plato never treats the Forms as causal in the usual English sense.[18] In the *Phaedo*, where the transcendent Forms are first introduced, Socrates says the real cause of all things is Mind, to which he attributes the power to direct everything in the best possible way; mind is the *aitia* of a *dynamis* in each thing with the "divine power" *daimonian iskhun* to be in the best possible arrangement (97c, 99c). But Socrates confesses that he doesn't know how Mind carries through this causality; and a similar problem arises with respect to the Form of the Good in *Republic*. How is the influence of the Form supposed to translate into guidelines for correct action? The only rational, reliable guide for action that Socrates knows is techne; and he tries to bridge the gap between the Form and the technai through "number and calculation." The vision of the Good can only be attained by those who follow the mathematical path of abstraction all the way up, but something of the benefits of mathematics accrues to any technites, no matter how lowly—the carpenter and the cook as well as the general and the statesman—because all the technai must measure and calculate things in their true proportions, undeceived by the illusions of perspective (a point to which he returns in Book 10, after the discussion of mimesis, to explain how the soul-distorting effects of mimetic pathos are to be resisted).[19] Dialectic is the highest of the technai because it raises the arts of calculation to the highest level of abstraction, treating pure numbers detached from any "visible or tangible" realities (525d). By doing this, dialectic teaches the soul to look "upward" to the realm of the invisible, while remaining linked to the lower technai by the reliance on number. There is thus a sort of techne-pyramid, with the most material, least abstractly mathematical, of the technai at the bottom, and dialectic at the apex from which the Forms can be viewed in their purity. What links them all, from the highest to the lowest, is their foundation in the arts of objective measurement. They are all part of a complete system of *paideia,* all of which is essential to the order and perpetuation of the community.

For the Socrates of Book 7, then, the transcendent Form of the Good is not only real but also, in principle at least, *effectual* (although not as direct cause): it is the source of all that is orthos and kalos, correct and beautiful, but its power remains merely potential unless actualized by human action, via the formative power of the technai. As long as the minds of human beings are fixated on the shadows of the cave, the Form itself has no power to turn them toward itself; the *paideia* "techne of education" is required to actually *turn* the soul from darkness to light (518b–d), and the paideia to be instituted by the guardians must mobilize every aspect of the city so that the souls of the citizens can be properly molded from earliest childhood, so that they will be inclined to turn toward the good. To begin with, the citizens must be exposed to "harmony, grace, and rhythm" on all sides, through the technai of music and poetry and the forms represented in weaving, embroidery, pictures, or architecture (400–401). Such works, when properly crafted, will "permeate the inner part of the soul," endowing it with *euskemosune* "grace" (3.401a–402a); such a soul will "sense it acutely" when it encounters something that has not been *kalos demiourgothenton,* "finely crafted," intuiting the lack of grace not only in poor craftsmanship but in shameful be-havior, even before it achieves the age of reason (401d–402a). The soul will then finish its process of formation through the practice of one, and only one, techne as a lifelong discipline.

Childhood paideia would be followed by apprenticeship in a techne that would render each of the citizens capable of organizing some specific corner of reality in a kalos "optimal, therefore fine, graceful" way, whether that be a couch, a performance of music, or the fighting of a battle. Each techne has its specific *dynamis* "power, mode of effectuality" (346a), and one who acts in accord with this dynamis practices it in a way that is kalos (347a), so that such practice brings graceful form to the soul of the artisan (a soul already oriented toward such gracefulness, as a consequence of childhood exposure to graceful forms) at the same time as it shapes the artifact. But graceful form would be nothing without the *unity* that practice of a techne brings to the soul; "No one in our city is dou-ble or multiple because each practices only one thing" (397e), and it's the unity of the soul that throws up the prime boundary against mimetic contamination (370, 374). The guardians, who are responsible for the harmonious order of the city as a whole, above all others must make their souls unitary, avoiding the dan-ger of imitating unworthy people; it would be intolerable for them to "mold" *ekmattein* and "fix" *enistanai* their souls in the shape of an inferior *tupos*, "type, pattern" (396d–e). And what is true of the entire soul is true also of its three parts. Each part has its own proper techne; when each part practices its own techne correctly the soul is harmonious, with a harmony that adumbrates the justice of the entire city (443).

The entire *Republic* tries to work out in as much detail as possible the organ-ization and teaching of the technai—from farming and carpentry to gymnastics, warfare, and dialectic—by which they would be able to actualize the ordering influence of the supreme Form of the Good.[20] The specific political techne of the guardian-dialecticians would be that of organizing the entire hierarchy of technai in the polis, and of doing so in the most orthos and kalos way.

Thus, Socrates tries in the *Republic* as a whole to devise a bridge between the mysterious influence of the Forms and the practicalities of techne, which is supposed to implement this influence.

IV

The mirror analogy with which Socrates launches his attack on mimesis implies that images are reflections of realities, from which they are once removed, and that artisanal products, even of a humble kind, are among the realities that can be imitated; but in the three-level ontology images are at two removes from the only kind of reality that is really real, and artisanal objects (like all other merely physical objects) are, like mere appearances, deficient in their reality. So painted imitations of such deficient *onta,* are not at one but two removes from the only full reality; and, by analogy, Socrates eventually concludes that tragic poets too—even though they imitate, not objects like couches that have a transcendent Form, but the world-shaping activities of generals, statesmen, and educators—are, like painters, at two removes from the truth.

However, immediately after the initial statement of the "two removes" argument in connection with the three-couches ontology, perhaps sensing that this ontology has muddied the waters, Socrates returns to the reality–appearance distinction that Glaucon had articulated in relation to mirror-images. They have left this distinction insufficiently examined, he says, and now "need to get clear about that" (598b). To effect this clarification, he now distinguishes between the physical couch and its *phainomenon* "appearance," saying that the phainomenon, not the actual couch, is what the imitator imitates; and he uses the terms *ho esti* and *to on,* previously used to name the reality of the Forms, to name the reality of the couch.

This new distinction between the physical couch and its phainomenon introduces a new level of unreality separating imitations from Forms. Socrates is now saying that imitations not only don't imitate Forms, they do not even imitate physical objects, only the perspectival appearances of such objects. Since the perspectival appearance is itself already ghostly, the imitation of the perspectival appearance would be, it now seems, the ghost of a ghost. The individual three-dimensional couch, by contrast, is now evoked without qualification as a unitary reality, referred to as *ho esti* that remains hidden and unchanging behind its multiple appearances. It thus replicates, at a lower level of reality, the unity and unchangingness that Socrates had previously attributed to the Form in relation to its multiple copies; and when Socrates then asks again whether the painter imitates the real, *to on,* or whether he imitates "what appears as it appears" (598b), the reference of *to on* is clearly to the reality of the couch that remains hidden behind its appearances, and no longer to the Form that is *to on* in a higher sense; "what appears as it appears" isn't the couch itself but a *phantasma* that intervenes between the bed's reality and the perceiving eye.[21]

The notion of the image, *phantasma* or *eidolon,* that is reproducible without techne-knowledge finally fills out the analogy of imitator with mirror-holder toward which Socrates had pointed at the beginning of his discourse on mimesis. He can now explain that the mimetic art, like the earlier mirror, can "make" everything because it produces only images of this kind (598bc), and he can now set up the transition to Homer by declaring the reported existence of "a man who knows all the technai"—that is, the imitator, the maker of mere images—to be a fraud.

But Socrates concludes his indictment of paintings of artifacts with the remark that imitations are "at the second remove from *onta,*" "real things," and "easy to make without knowledge of the truth" (599a). The "two removes" formula indicates that he is still thinking in terms of the Form evoked in the three-couches ontology, ignoring his recent reference to physical artifacts as *onta,* as well as the further distancing of imitation from Form that he has introduced by denying that it is the reality of the artisanal couch that the imitator imitates. Here we see how the "theory of Ideas" intermittently pulls on the artisanal conception of form described by Wolfsdorf, a tendency that will continue through the remarks on Homer, and that will only be completely absent when Socrates finally articulates the three-techne hierarchy.

On the present reading, Socrates has now gotten three sets of distinctions tangled together in his argument: reality/appearance, transcendent reality/artisanal copy/imitation, and, now just beginning to make its full emergence, making easily/making with knowledge. The reality–appearance distinction (which digressed into the ontological hierarchy) is rooted in the realm of perception, but the making easily/making with knowledge distinction comes from the realm of techne. Socrates is trying to navigate from appearance–reality to the question of making, which would be straightforward in itself (those who make with knowledge make realities; those who don't, make appearances), but the notion of the transcendent Form has obscured what would otherwise be a clear logical path.

That would explain why at 598bc, immediately after establishing his new phantasm-of-the-empirically real account of the object of imitation, Socrates so abruptly shifts his critique of painting from representations of phantasms of artifacts to representations of phantasms of *artisans.* It's really artisans and their techne-knowledge that Socrates has aimed at from the beginning of his discourse on mimesis, and techne-knowledge not of the type that makes artifacts, but of executive practices of the type with which the guardians are charged.

Now, artisans are physical realities just as much as artifacts are, and their images can be similarly reproduced in painting. But even paintings of artisans won't get Socrates where he needs to go, because the physical reality of the artisans whose image is reproduced is the basis of the analogy of painted artisans with painted artifacts, and the counterfeiting of physical realities is not the point of Socrates' new argument; the point is the counterfeiting of the reality *behind* the image, the techne-knowledge that real artisans possess. This reality, which lay behind his earlier complaint that the mirror-holder could reproduce everything quickly (and so, easily), and that is the reality that Socrates is most urgently concerned with, can't be pictorially represented at all. That's why the whole three-couches ontology and its introduction of the analogy with painting is such a serious misstep. Socrates can't get to where he wants to go by proceeding logically from this analogy; so in the end he's forced to brazenly smuggle the reality of techne-knowledge into his analogy.[22] A good painter, he says, can make a painting of a carpenter that at a distance "would deceive children and foolish men, and make them believe it to be a real carpenter"; but the sin of which he convicts the painter isn't making people think this is a real *technites* (the way they might mistake a painted couch for a real one). This mistake is only the basis for the real sin, which is that these ignorant and foolish viewers would attribute to the illusory artisan the techne-knowledge that corresponds to the kind of artisan imaged, and would, thus, be further deceived into thinking that the painter himself knows what the supposedly real artisan in the picture knows, even though the painter "has no expertness in any of these technai" (598bc).[23]

So, when Socrates finally concludes at 605b that poetry "sets up in each individual soul a vicious constitution by fashioning phantoms far removed from reality," the most pernicious phantoms will be, not of objects with a heavenly original, but of techne practice.

V

With the turn to imitations of artisans, and the far-fetched notion that the artisanal knowledge of the imaged artisans will be attributed to the painter, Socrates is at last in position for his direct assault on tragedy and its leader, Homer—all of it based on the notion that Homer did not possess the genuine knowledge (*gignoskein*) (600c) of those who have successfully practiced the executive technai of war, civic life, and teaching (599d). Some people think that "these poets know all the technai," because in order to make poems well, they must do so "knowing what they do" (598ce); these people, then, don't see that the works of the poets produce *phantasmata,* not *onta,* and so are "two removes from reality" (599a), and therefore easy (*hraidia*) to make. Because Socrates has defined the artisanal object as the reality that the painter fails to imitate, and phantasmal appearance as what he does actually imitate, the implied reasoning is that the poetic imitation of techne-practice is, analogously, at one remove from the phantasm of techne-practice that it doubles in painted form, and at two removes from the empirical reality of the actions whose phantasm it doubles. But Socrates apparently doesn't see, or doesn't yet see, the way his new *phantasmata-onta* distinction has muddied the "two removes" terminology, because he will shortly say that if Homer had possessed the genuine techne-knowledge to make other humans better he would have been at one remove from truth and reality (599d). This implies that techne-knowledge is, like the physical objects that painters imitate, a defective, *amudron* reality, a mere copy of a transcendent Form, ignoring the difficulty in assimilating highly stochastic technai like those he names (statecraft, generalship, and pedagogy), technai possessed by those who do make men better, to mere artisanal objects.

Nevertheless, he points toward what is really at stake when at the end of his tirade he concludes that "all the poetic tribe" are "imitators of images of excellence (*arete*)" who do not "lay hold on (*haptesthai*) truth," and makes clear that arete and techne are essentially related, if not identical, by immediately rephrasing "images of arete" as "colored pictures of the various technai" (601a). He then culminates his indictment of imitators at 601c by saying that they know only appearance, not reality, and says that he and Glaucon *still* have not fully explicated the appearance–reality distinction. This, at last, leads into the exposition of the three-techne hierarchy.

Whereas *poiesis* "making" in the three-couches ontology had been the only kind of techne mentioned by Socrates, and knowledge glossed as knowledge of the Form, or at least the ability to "look to" the Form, those who *use* the artifacts produced by makers—a class of demiourgoi not previously evoked—are now introduced as the supreme knowers of the real. For each thing there are three technai, "one that uses it, one that makes it, and one that imitates it" (601c–d), and only the user possesses actual *episteme* about the excellence of the artifact, because only the user knows whether the artifact functions well in actual use, and can instruct the maker as to what is and what is not *chreston,* optimally functional or usable, about the artifact (601e). Whereas in Book 7 he says that the correctness and beauty of all things derive from the Form, now, apparently in direct contradiction, he says that "the arête, the kallos, and the orthotes of each implement, living creature, and *praxis*" are "related to *nothing but the chreian* 'use' (*ou pros allo ti e ten chreian*) for which each is made or naturally adapted" (601d; emphasis added).[24] The bit-and-bridle maker, or the flute maker, has only "right opinion" about their products, since they don't know first-hand how well the artifact functions in use; but the user has *episteme* about it, because he has the most *empeiria* "experience" (is *empeirotaton*) working with the implement.[25]

We might still read Socrates as silently taking for granted the three-level ontology, with the transcendent Form at the top, as the background for these remarks, and now simply addressing a lower level of reality. Yet this supposition has been making less and less sense since the introduction of the empirical reality/phantasm distinction—the distinction that Socrates says he left half-stated and that he now claims to be articulating in full. Nor can the supposition that he still has the Forms in mind account for the categorical nature of his declaration that *all* the ruling values of Form (*arête, kallos, orthotes*) are related to *nothing but* (*ou pros allo ti*) the friction with empirical reality involved in the artisanal use of implements. The doctrine of use opens the eidos "form" of both implement and practice to all the contingencies of experience. On one side there is a maker who has to try out different materials, tools, and procedures until the right ones are found; on the other side, the skilled user who must try out the finished artifact to see if it will perform excellently in the exercise of the superordinate techne for which the artifact has been designed, and sends it back to the maker for revision as needed. On this account, function determines form, not as itself a form to which the demiourgos can simply look, as a painter looks to his or her model, but as something the nature of which is gradually discovered in the interaction among user, maker, tool, and world.[26]

It remains true, as Socrates says several times, that the carpenter does not make the unique eidos/idea of the bed, but for a more profound reason than its failure of ideality. The new hierarchy implies that the artisanal eidos is not *made* at all, not even by a divine maker; it emerges as a set of functional principles from the intersection of human purposes with the conditions set by the material realities of tools, materials, and the uses to which the resultant products are put.[27] It is still *form* that the user discovers, but not by consulting a pre-existing, intellectually apprehensible Form. For Platonic Socrates, however, these implications are not fully thinkable, as the thought that drives these pages is pulled in two incompatible directions.

This, then, is Socrates' full account of the knowledge of *to on* of which the imitator is ignorant. Homer possesses neither the true opinion of the maker, nor the episteme of the user; his techne belongs to the third and lowest level in the hierarchy of technai—if, that is, imitation is to be called a techne at all.

VI

The new hierarchy, with its three levels of techne—user, maker, and imitator—bends the discussion of imitation back toward the central concern of the entire dialogue, the organization of the polis, in which the supreme "use," according to Book 7, would be that which the philosopher-guardians make of the Idea of the Good in order to properly organize and govern it (see section II, above).

The technai themselves contain no guidance regarding the moral value of their goals, and in the earlier dialogues Socrates repeatedly arrived at a dead end when he tried to conceive what a techne of virtue would be like. In the *Republic,* by contrast, he seems to take for granted that virtue cannot be taught as a techne-knowledge communicated by a teacher to a pupil. Instead, in the well-formed polis all the technai must function as an ensemble to shape the souls of its citizens in a way that immunizes them from the soul-distorting influences of mimesis—a process that, if it is to succeed in at least some measure in turning the eyes of the soul toward the intellectual Sun, must begin in earliest childhood.

The works of poets, unlike those of true demiourgoi, because they are "mere appearance" (601c), are "easily produced without knowledge of the truth" (598e–599a)—a truth that starts out being identified with the Form but has by now modulated into the truth of use, as known by a master user-artisan. But images of this sort can only fool "children and foolish people" (598b); the normal adult in the optimally organized polis would be a skilled technites raised in a milieu of harmonious aesthetic forms who knows that real things are not "easily produced," but require deep and protracted discipline, and who have put "the part of the soul that puts its trust in measurement and calculation" in charge of their souls (603a). Such persons would be secure against the seductions of unmeasured emotion as represented in poetry, and minimally susceptible to the allure of mimetic identifications.

This, then, would be the knowledge of the true nature of mimesis that Socrates calls its "antidote" at the outset of Book 10.

Socrates' best clue to what he calls arete—and we call virtue, which is far from the same thing—is the skilled exercise of these highly stochastic technai.

Hence, as I've noted, what he first calls Homer's imitations of "images of arete" (600e) he quickly restates as "colored pictures of each of the technai" (601a). The higher stochastic technai on which he focuses represent the conceptually obscure area in which strictly techne-guided action shades off into the larger field of the ethical conduct of life, with all its uncertainty—the field evoked in 603ff, where Socrates talks about the disorderly emotions that poetry stimulates.

Socrates doesn't try to model moral knowledge on techne, but he does his best to extend the insight into the nature of well-formed action that he gleans from observation of techne-practice from the level of the lowest technai, where the *kalos* form of action is easily discernible, and therefore reliably teachable and practicable, to that of the highest practical technai, where the intuitive part becomes more prominent, and from that to gain some insight into how one can shape an entire life in an ethically correct and graceful way. In this attempt he navigates as close as he can, as long as he can, to the shoreline of purposeful, well-formed action in the subordinate technai, then tries to extend the insights gained from the lower technai into the area of the higher, but still practical, technai. The higher a techne is in the hierarchy of practical technai, the more its practice depends on chance and on the character and judgment of the demiourgos; hence, the practitioner of the fundamental technai, who, in principle at least, acts at each moment with the assurance of one who intuitively knows the correct next move because he has been rigorously trained in his techne, remains Socrates' best clue regarding what it would be like to know how to live rightly.

The actions strictly associated with the performance of one's techne are not the whole of virtuous behavior; but, on Socrates' account, they manifest the stable sub-structure of personality that provides a ground for the rest of virtuous behavior, and thus the most solid ground he knows from which to negotiate the relation to mimesis of both the impersonative and the mirroring type.

VII

But Socrates was conceptually unequipped to address the fact that learning a techne, becoming a professional, especially in the case of the higher stochastic technai, requires imitation of excellent "role models"—which is even truer about learning to become an ethical subject. Even within the realm of techne narrowly defined, apprentices don't only imitate the specific craft-performances of an artisan, they're also subjected to mimetic contamination by the role model's personal mood, manner, and attitude.

The concept of mimesis with which Socrates works in the *Republic* doesn't extend as far as this socio-psychological concept of imitation,[28] perhaps because the idea that mimetic identification is fundamental to learning a techne is abhorrent to him, but also because his conception of mimetic identification remains tied to the notion of theatrical representation. In Book 3 he says that the guardians must neither "do nor imitate anything else" than their own techne of guardianship, "lest from the imitation they come to enjoy the reality," and that "such imitations are most dangerous when practiced from youth"; but even here he is clearly not thinking of unmediated imitation of *demiourgoi* and their actions, the kind an apprentice in a workshop practices. Socrates is evoking imitation of fictional or imagined representations of persons—their phantasms—in make-believe play or on the stage.[29] (This could, perhaps, truly be called an "imitation of an imitation.")

Thus, when he says the guardians shouldn't imitate those in lowly occupations, we could take this to mean they shouldn't imitate the practice of those occupations; but in Book 3 he clearly means they must not play-act at being *the kind of person* that performs them. As Janaway notes, Plato is thinking in terms of someone *kalos kagathos,* "a superior person of noble class" or "gentleman," and the limits of allowable imitation are being defined in a way that follows from this class distinction. Obviously, no "gentleman" would take a woman or slave or lowly workman as a role model in the sociological sense, much less those of persons who display obviously pernicious and shameful behavior, and least of all madmen; but he might do so in theatrical play.

Notes

1   Unless indicated otherwise, all line references are to the *Republic*. Other Platonic dialogues are drawn from the Perseus Collection and quoted via standard Stephanus pagination: https://www.perseus.tufts.edu/hopper/collection%3Fcollection%3DPerseus:collection:Greco-Roman [editors' note].

2   Cf. Nehamas, who writes that, while "it's important for [Socrates] to show that imitation is at two removes from reality," showing this "does not clearly require" Forms of artifacts, or a god, or even the one-over-many argument that opens the door to the three-couches hierarchy (Nehamas 1999, 257). But Nehamas doesn't explain exactly how the "two removes" terminology works without transcendent Forms (for which, see below).

3   Christopher Janaway summarizes the problems with the notion of Forms of artifacts in Janaway 1995, 112. Plato never formalized his list of Forms, which are a mixed bag that shifts from dialogue to dialogue. See the concise and comprehensive list of types of Forms in Wedberg 1971, 35–36.

4   The *Ion,* in particular, shows this aspect of Socrates's thought in a way that is directly linked to *Republic* 10. Editors' note: see also chapter 1 in this volume and chapter 2 in volume 1 of *Homo Mimeticus,* both focusing on the affective powers of mimetic impersonation linking *Ion* and the *Republic.*

5   I use "artisan" as the name for every kind of practitioner of a techne, from carpenters to musicians, rulers, and mathematicians. A person skilled in a techne was called by various names, including *technites,* "one skilled in a techne," and, more commonly, *demiourgos,* "one who works for the people." The point is that all of these must have expert knowledge of the "art" or "craft" (techne) that they practice if they are to perform their functions well. See the survey of the ancient Greek conception of techne in Roochnick 1996, 17–88. Editors' note: see also Staten 2019, 47–83.

6   Halliwell says that the second, pragmatic hierarchy is merely "unintegrated" with the first, metaphysical hierarchy. The "most economical" explanation for the discrepancy is, according to Halliwell, that Plato was earlier addressing knowledge of "things as such" but is now addressing "knowledge of 'how to'" (Halliwell in Plato 1998, 129). This explanation skips over difficulties that I address below. Nikolas Pappas thinks the new hierarchy is "hard to make sense of," but suggests that the association of flutes and bridles with Athena might give the category of use a divine reference, therefore linking it somehow to the divine couch-maker (Pappas 2020, n.p.). Alexander Nehamas simply ignores it (1999, 251–278). See also Janaway 1995, 140–142.

7   Wedberg 1971, 31n. 4.

8   Halliwell, for example, thinks the form in question in *Republic* X can't be "simply logical," but concedes that "it remains opaque...what the transcendent reality associated with 'couch' is supposed to be" (Halliwell in Plato 1988, 112–113).

9   Thus, according to Wolfsdorf, in the early dialogues Socrates understands *eidos* not as a universal of any kind but as "an idealization of the *ergon* [work or product] of a craftsman" (2008, 117). As I read it, Plato, having idealized the form that results from artisanal work, in the Theory of Forms reversed the derivation, making metaphysical Form the cause of the artisanal work's being correct in the first place.

10   See Havelock 1963.

11   Havelock explained how Homer and the tragedians promulgated a model of pedagogical mimesis that operated at a physiological level, entraining the entire psyche-soma of the viewer or listener in traditional models of behavior that were far from completely rational and measured. This traditional mode of socialization was to be replaced by the visual-intellectual model of knowledge Plato developed in the wake of Socrates, but this could only happen if the grip of poetry on the city could be broken (see Lawtoo 2022, 74–92). The identification of mimetic psychic formation with the seductive power of poetry, however, appears to have made the whole notion of mimetic identification so noxious to Plato that he ignores its fundamental role in the transmission of technai from one generation to another in the process of paideia. Yet, as Roochnick points out, the pre-Socratic writings on techne of the Hippocratic authors on medicine and Isocrates on rhetoric stress that "the relationship between student and teacher must be intimate; in order to convey the kind of sensitivity to the medical version of the *kairos* [the particular occasion, with its unpredictable demands] the student must spend time with the master." And he adds: "A human paradigm replaces the purely abstract and formal one" (Roochnick 1996, 80, 78).

12 See Roochnik's lucid overview of the complex debate over whether Plato considered "moral knowledge" to be "analogous to a techne" (Roochnik 1996, 1–15). His own view that it is not follows from his definition of a true techne on the model of mathematics, which he calls "techne1"; technai like medicine and rhetoric that don't always provide results, and that require constant adaptation to circumstances by the technites, he defines as "stochastic technai" or "technai2," which, in Roochnik's view, aren't true technai. His conclusion, that Plato conceives moral knowledge as at best a techne2, is surely correct; but in my view the terms of this debate (technical or non-technical?) are somewhat ossified, and I don't frame my own reading in these terms. I find more useful Roochnik's vaguer conclusion that Plato is "ever exploring, through the lens of techne, the nature of the extraordinary moral knowledge that he seeks" (176).

13 Book 1 is presumed to have been written earlier than the last 9 books of the *Republic*, and the notion that each techne is self-sufficient is repudiated by the argument in Book 10 that the technai of making require direction from the techne of use, but it nonetheless indicates the respect that Socrates has for the technai.

14 When he says the technai are *banousoi*, he must mean the more menial technai, not mathematics and dialectic, which are also technai, and probably also not the higher practical technai that he discusses: generalship, government, paideia.

15 Techne is knowledge of how to accomplish the end that is intrinsic to a given techne; but techne-knowledge says nothing about how this end is to be fitted into the larger realm of human ends. This larger realm, Roochnik argues, is that of *chrestos* "use," which "means not only 'useful' but also 'good;'" "...it is in the use of the techne, not simply in the techne itself, that ethical value resides. This importation of ethical weight into 'use' is reflected in the Greek Word *chrestos*. A verbal adjective derived from *chraomai*, 'to use,' it means not only 'useful' but also 'good'" (Roochnik 1996, 31). Ethical evaluation in general takes place within the realm of "use" (31); but of course not all use is necessarily good in an ethical sense. Hence the problem of how to get from the practical good of techne to the good of ethical virtue.

16 Socrates passingly suggests that it's possible for men like his philosopher-guardians to grow up spontaneously in other, less well-ordered cities (520b); and Socrates himself, of course, was such a spontaneously grown lover of Truth. But clearly such random growths could not be counted on to keep the polis on its proper course.

17 Nehamas suggests that, given that contemplation is the highest way of life, it's unjust to make the philosophers become rulers (1999, 327, 316–328).

18 See Vlastos 1981, 78–102. Plato recognized that there is a variety of different ways in which X can be the *aitia* of Y, and we have to look to context to see which sense is intended in each case.

19 Plato writes in *Philebus*: "If someone were to take away all counting, measuring, and weighing from the technai, the rest might be said to be worthless" (55e).

20 In Book 7, Socrates says dialectic uses "the crafts we described" to turn the soul around, apparently meaning the crafts of number; but only the philosopher-guardians will learn higher mathematics, whereas all the crafts are necessary for the well-ordering of the souls of the ordinary citizens. The overall architecture of Socrates's argument in the *Republic* implies something like a trickle-down effect, via proper deployment of the technai in the polity as a whole, as guided by the illuminated guardians, of the ordering effects of the Idea of the Good.

21   Nehamas shrewdly remarks that Socrates's use of the terms *phantasma* and *eidolon* for both what is imitated and the imitation itself makes it seem Socrates "believes that the painter lifts the surface off the subject and transplants it onto the painting" (1999, 263). But Nehamas rejects the notion that this appearance has "its own ontological status," and deduces from this denial, and Socrates's assertion that imitation *touches* (ephaptesthai) a small part of the object, that the object itself (though only a small part of it) appears in its appearance. But Socrates has explicitly said that what appears and is imitated is not the object, but its phenomenon, phantasm, or image: an illusory, non-existing object of perception. We need not attribute any distinct ontological status to the image for it to serve in this role, otherwise than to note that it belongs to the realm of appearances, which are far removed from the truth, yet capable of bedeviling perception. As for *ephaptesthai,* Liddell and Scott translate this middle voice of *ephapto,* "to touch," when used with genitive (as it is here), as "to lay hold of with the mind" (cf. 601a). So, when Socrates concludes that the painter *ephaptetai* only a small part of each object, he adds "and that part a mere *eidolon,*" an image or phantasm of the object. An image cannot literally be touched, nor through touching it can any small part of the object of which it is the image be touched. It is the appearance itself (to phainomenon), not the appearing object (to on), that is mentally laid hold of by the imitator.

22   Actually, it is not even techne-episteme per se that will be the reality of which Homer falls short, but the skilled actions or practice that are given their kalos and effectual form by that knowledge. But Plato does not distinguish these two.

23   This is the same indictment of poets that was already brewing in the *Ion.* See the detailed unpacking of this leap from painting to epic in Janaway 1995.

24   The addition of living creatures and praxeis to the list is intriguing, because, whereas the mention of implements follows directly from the examples just given, it would take some unpacking to explain how the forms of organisms or those of actions would be honed by use.

25   Socrates doesn't here bridge the gap between practices like horsemanship and flute playing and the higher technai of government and so forth. But the notion of a hierarchy of technai, in which each level submits its product for use by a higher level, is more fully imagined at *Euthydemus* 290a–292e, where Socrates decides that the highest level of use is kingship, and that its product should be "to make all men good, and good in all respects" by imparting the knowledge that will make other men both good and happy (292de).

26   I have delved deeper into these matters in Staten 2019, ch. 4 and 5.

27   Cf. Annas 1981, 230.

28   That is, the concept of imitation that is now re-turning via mimetic studies [editors' note].

29   Cf. Aristotle's *Politics*, where he writes that tales and stories, told to children, as well as the games they play, "are designed to prepare the way for the business of later life, and all such childish amusements (*paidias*) should be for the most part imitations (*mimeseis*) of the occupations which they will hereafter pursue in earnest" (1336a30–4).

Bibliography

Annas, Julia (1981). *Plato's Republic*. Oxford: Oxford University Press.

Havelock, Eric A. (1963). *Preface to Plato*. Cambridge, MA: Harvard University Press.

Janaway, Christopher (1995). *Images of Excellence: Plato's Critique of the Arts*. Oxford: Clarendon Press.

Lawtoo, Nidesh (2022). *Homo Mimeticus: A New Theory of Imitation*. Leuven: Leuven University Press.

Nehamas, Alexander (1999). *Virtues of Authenticity*. Princeton, NJ: Princeton University Press.

Pappas, Nickolas (2020). "Plato's Aesthetics," in *The Stanford Encyclopedia of Philosophy* (Fall 2020 Edition), ed. Edward N. Zalta. https://plato.stanford.edu/archives/fall2020/entries/plato-aesthetics/.

Plato (1988). *Republic 10*, trans. and commentary by S. Halliwell. Warminster, UK: Aris & Phillips.

Roochnick, David (1996). *Of Art and Wisdom: Plato's Understanding of Techne*. University Park, PA: Pennsylvania State University Press.

Staten, Henry (2019). *Techne Theory: A New Language for Art*. London: Bloomsbury.

Vlastos, Gregory (1981). "Reasons and Causes in the *Phaedo*," in *Platonic Studies*. Princeton, NJ: Princeton University Press, 78–102.

Wedberg, Anders (1971). "The Theory of Ideas," in *Plato: A Collection of Critical Essays, I: Metaphysics and Epistemology*, ed. Gregory Vlastos, London: Palgrave Macmillan, 28–52.

Wolfsdorf, David (2008). *Trials of Reason: Plato and the Crafting of Philosophy*. New York: Oxford University Press.

CHAPTER 3

COERCION AND MIMESIS IN PLATO

Compelling Someone to Change their Nature

Carlos Carvalhar

This chapter examines Plato's criticism of the power of dramatic mimesis to form and transform subjectivity via the interpretative lens of the mimetic turn. It will emphasize his ethical and pedagogical concerns about plastic and mimetic subjects formed by traditional mythical and literary models instead of the prevalent concept of mimesis as mere imitation. This approach allows us to examine a more positive and active aspect of mimetic actions in Plato: the assimilation to an ideal of perfection, powerful enough to change someone's nature. Detaching from the simplistic understanding of mimesis as imitation and reframing it from a visual and external representation to a dramatic impersonation and reenactment, this chapter will focus on the ethical and political use of *mímēsis* through education.

The argument will explore passages from *Republic* and *Protagoras* to clarify how the mimetic power to change one's subjectivity (a question known in Platonic discussion as "second nature") might be beneficial or harmful in education. Since this process in Greek society traditionally involves imprinting models through mimetic pedagogy and poetry, Plato must evaluate these paradigms due to their consequences. It also shows how the artistic vocabulary entangles with philosophical discussion and how the philosopher king should coerce or persuade the citizens, in order to lead them to the most perfect level of human development. The combination of two Platonic concepts, *mímēsis* and *homotōsis theōi* (from *Theaetetus*), allows us to explore a positive and active side of mimesis: the will to assimilate to a model of perfection via its mimetic reenactment.

With this argumentative scheme, this chapter highlights the political aspect involved in the discussion of mimesis, which is directly related to the ethical development achieved through education. The fundamental point is that mimetic affections can induce behavior, especially in children and youngsters, because their temperament is plastic, and they are more easily conformable to society's ideals. In fact, the selection of these paradigms is the main point in Plato's philosophy. After all, they shape how poets can create myths and arouse emotions (*páthos*) through their work, thus embodying the potential for mimetic actions, whether good or bad.

Although this discussion focuses on the Platonic dialogues, and therefore, Greek society, none of these arguments are limited to that period. In our contemporary society, mimetic models still have the same potential to influence behavior, especially among young people—just remember the impact of social media's influencers.[1] Hence this chapter contributes to the mimetic turn or returns, proving that the concept of mimesis, already in Plato, should not be restricted to its ontological and epistemic concerns regarding copies, as it is a vital force strong enough even to create a second nature in homo mimeticus.[2]

The first point to examine is how mimesis has the power to reconfigure a second nature, as Plato explicitly admits in Book 3 of the *Republic*, but also indirectly in *Protagoras*. After this acknowledgment, the powerful capacity for mimetic action creates the need to be controlled by the ruling class, which then selects the models found in the works of poets. Since ancient education centered on copying poetry, the young generation would be raised with moral models derived from these myths. As a result, for Plato, the suppression of any artistic movement that could lead to the reinforcement of future citizens' vices was necessary. Hence, some poets had to be expelled from the city at the end of the *Republic*. In sum, the moralist interpretation of Plato is that myths in poetry act like role models, and because of this, rulers must control how poets influence education. Therefore, mimesis becomes political.

Contrary to the most common reading, the aim here is to interpret mimesis as an instrument of political strategy capable of coercing people to modify their own nature, rather than merely as aesthetic imitation, a copy of a copy. This persuasive and subtle mimesis would be promoted by the ruling class from an early age, whether through education, laws, or even moral sanctions, and it would adhere to their original nature (albeit through coercion), leading them to transform themselves and be consonant with the ideal city. Consequently, it is no longer a problem of imitation because a well-educated person can rationally recognize a higher paradigm and act toward the assimilation with it. This process is a philosophical type of mimesis, that is closely related to the concept of becoming like god, as expounded in *Theaetetus*, and understood here, in our contemporary world that has lost faith in divine beings, as the pursuit of perfection.

A Problem of Nature

What we are, our characteristics and behavior, could be understood in Greek as *phýsis*, our own nature. This concept was often opposed to *nómos*, law, and custom, thus creating a dichotomy between what was considered natural, given by birth, and what was conquered through training and education. As a symbol of aristocratic thinking, some ancient authors regarded innate talent as superior to that acquired through study, such as the poet Pindar, who exalts natural qualities and associates them with the ethics and lineage of nobility.[3] In Plato, conversely, this determinism of nature could be defied by the educational process through *mímēsis*,[4] considered here in its broadest sense, also relative to the performative realms of dance and theater.[5] In this sense, it is best translated as "representation" or "enactment" because it is not yet restricted to the meaning of a copy or an imitation from two ontological levels below the form (as specified in Book 10 of Plato's *Republic*). Therefore, in Book 3, Socrates acknowledges the notion of a second nature reconfigured through mimetic experience since the guardians:

> must imitate [*mimeîsthai*] from childhood what is appropriate for them, namely, people who are courageous, self-controlled, pious, and free, and their actions. They mustn't be clever at doing or imitating [*mimḗsasthai*] slavish or shameful actions, lest from enjoying the imitation [*mimḗseōs*], they come to enjoy the reality. Or haven't you noticed that imitations [*mimḗseis*] practiced from youth become part of nature and settle into habits of gesture, voice, and thought? (395c–d)[6]

The passage above indicates how *mímēsis* is able to reorient the nature of a person, especially a child or a youngster (377a–b), inculcating manners and habits to the point that it is powerful enough to transform the original character. Thus, philosophy becomes a tool to transform subjectivities since it concerns the models and paradigms that reinforce desirable traits acquired through mimetic actions, given that the human condition is endowed with plasticity.[7] Alternatively, as Nidesh Lawtoo defines it, the affective drive resembles the *páthos* experienced in mimetic activities, and it is also susceptible to contagion, since poetry presents a contagious power of affection and has a pedagogical effect.[8] Therefore, Plato also implicitly appointed how human nature is mimetic, as we all tend to act according to models in our own *vita mimetica*.

In addition to this well-known example from the *Republic*, Plato, in a passage from the Protagoras' Great Speech, presents the sophist as an antagonist to Socrates; but, in relation to our discussion, he expresses once again the same general view that we have considered above. In the discussion of education and the teaching of virtues, Protagoras (actually a mouthpiece of Plato) states that children are mimetic beings and that they are able to learn by assimilating a moral model reenacted by poetry:

> when the children have learned their letters and are getting to understand writing as well as the spoken language, they are given the works of good poets to read at their desks and have to learn them by heart, works that contain numerous exhortations, many passages describing in glowing terms good men of old, so that the child is inspired to imitate [*mimḗtai*] them and become like them [*toioûtos genésthai*]. (*Protagoras,* 325e–326a)[9]

The main difference between these two passages is that *Protagoras* only claims that a child "is inspired to imitate" models and "become like them." On the other hand, in the *Republic*, there is an additional statement regarding the quality of the models imitated.[10] The latter entails a selection of moral paradigms and an exclusion of those that do not propagate the philosopher's aim. Furthermore, Plato develops a defense of punishment in the educational process.[11] This attitude is not out of pure vengeance but, contrary to Pindar, because "human beings consider virtue to be something acquired through training" (*Protagoras* 324c), a training supervised by the one responsible for disciplining the wrongdoers. In other words, coercion could be used to compel a person onto the right path—at least in Protagoras' view, since the official mouthpiece of Plato, Socrates, left the topic open.

Notwithstanding these differences, Plato's ruling class might exploit the different types of mimetic actions to foster understanding among citizens and to promote the most beneficial ends for them, namely, the enforcement of good values and desires. Consequently, the rulers create a system of mass coercion through customs and behaviors that influence all fellow citizens. In such a society, youngsters would grow up feeling dishonored if their nature does not resemble the ideals promoted by the government. Thus, they would seek to behave appropriately, not by mere imitation, which might be only a superficial agreement with a veiled revolt, but rather by aligning their desires in consonance with the rulers' strategies determined by law and morality. The first method can punish physically or economically, while the second persuades by arousing feelings of shame and guilt. However, note that both possibilities constitute manners of coercion.[12]

In conclusion, both dialogues demonstrate that mimesis plays an educational role powerful enough to change a person's nature and that the teacher or the ruling class should control this potency through the coercion and selection of models. Hence, in the *Republic*, Plato states that the philosopher king must reinforce good paradigms, for "fine ways of living lead one to the possession of virtue, shameful ones to vice" (444e). Put differently, mimetic actions can lead to good or evil characters, depending on which values are reenacted. Most importantly, however, is that both passages emphasize how these educational paradigms can affect people, as they can encourage either helpful or harmful behaviors, since we all have a mimetic tendency. This conception aligns with Nidesh Lawtoo's central claim for mimetic studies that "humans remain, for good and ill, all-too-mimetic creatures" (2022, 13). Since to be human is to engage in mimetic activity, the judgment of homo mimeticus' actions depends on the moral quality of what is being reenacted. Otherwise stated, the value of the mimetic actions is equivalent to the model's worth, which influences and shapes them. For this reason, they are not only evaluated according to the final result (as it could be understood if we limit the meaning merely to imitation) but also conforming to the quality and moral value of their mimetic expression.

Controlling Mimesis

Plato's diagnosis exposes the danger of mimetic actions since they are so powerful that they can transform one's nature, not only physically but also spiritually. As a result, Plato's moral perspective needs to avoid any artistic movement that would reinforce the evil actions of citizens. Instead, he regards philosophy as the master of the educational process and, later, he will need to expel some poets from the city because of their moral deviation (*Republic* 596a–598d). However, this example also shows that the guardians, or in other words, the philosophers, should only reenact (*mimeîsthai*) in the same sense as an actor who portrays the qualities and gestures of the virtuous and avoids at all costs interpreting dishonorable actions. In conclusion, the shift from the pathological mimesis, which Plato condemns, to the patho-*logical* and philosophical mimesis, which he advocates, arises through the rational selection of paradigms.[13] As this patho-*logical* method indicates how affect and reason (*páthos* and *lógos*) are constitutive of homo mimeticus, the Platonic use of mimesis to reenact good qualities and to shape the human being combines both the rational and the affective approach.[14] Due to the effects produced by the power of the mimetic *páthos*, this philosophy rationally selects models that should adhere to a person's subjectivity, helping them to develop such qualities.[15]

Plato is willing to apply virtuous role models (according to his values) to draw the figure of the philosopher, composing how should be his *skhḗma*. This concept is understood as "a codified and crystallized posture that communicates determined and recognizable values" (Celentano et al. 2004, 94; my transl.).[16] It refers not only to the external appearance (influenced by physical training) but also to the mental attitude and manners (through *mousikḗ*, the art of the Muses) and is always correlated with mimesis and education (*paideía*).

The imprinting of models through mimetic education is a process that preferably takes place at a young age, when a child is still tender and unable to resist conformation. To put this another way, as Plato writes, when "it is most malleable [*pláttetai*] and takes on any pattern [*týpos*] one wishes to impress on it" (*Republic* 377b).[17] In this sense, Lacoue-Labarthe emphasizes that this malleability has a potential for mimetic plasticity that requires a subjective base, like wax, and uses this passage from the *Republic* to affirm that the infant soul is plastic and can be fashioned by myths.[18] This point of view is central to mimetic studies as well. For example, Lawtoo states, in agreement with Lacoue-Labarthe, that for Plato the soul "has a plastic [...] side, which is best molded by the formative power of mimetic impressions generated by mythic models," since a myth, "like mimesis, can [...] have both negative or positive formative effects," and every myth functions "as a formative model that has the power to generate not only copies or reproductions of reality, but also copies or productions of subjects" (2017a, 1210; 2017b, 73, 65).[19]

In sum, Plato believes that higher principles must guide the use of myths in poetry since young people are still flexible and impressionable. In addition, ancient poetry was recited collectively with rhythmic verses and music rather than merely read individually, so this emotional and active effect made it easier for people to absorb the content through memorization, increasing the chances of someone imitating the paradigms contained in the poems and reenacting them throughout their lives. Aside from the fact that the impact of these types can mold the human condition, the educational process based on poems provides many opportunities to impress models and make people conform to them, via coercion or a subtle way that they cannot even perceive the persuasion. Although translators often choose "imitation" to translate *mímēsis*, this choice indicates a passive state (as static as drawings or written texts of poetry copied by students) that represents the idea of someone who suffers the action of being molded. It is, therefore, necessary to emphasize that its semantic field also expresses a sense of creative action by consciously reenacting, that is, actively performing, a type that has been constructed as a role model (good or bad), as portrayed in dance or drama (comedies and tragedies). As a result, for Plato, art is not restricted to aesthetics because *mímēsis* can be pedagogically harmful if it is not moderated, thus requiring good models to influence the development of citizens by shaping their ethical character.[20]

Consequently, those natures deemed unsuitable by Plato must be convinced, through arguments or force, to moderate their undesirable qualities and become harmonious with a city ruled by the purpose of becoming as excellent as possible. Admittedly, this sounds like an oppressive purpose for our modern tastes. Nevertheless, this kind of coercion should not be considered a totalitarian imposition, as Karl Popper concluded. In fact, for Plato, the ruling class acts to benefit all citizens and not just to protect itself from the majority (*Republic* 342e–343a). Moreover, Plato recognizes that everyone is different from everyone else (*Republic* 370a–b). Therefore, he still retains a form of autonomy that contradicts the totalitarian mass control experienced in the twentieth century, as a Popperian reading would imply. Furthermore, in political life, a vivid mimetic action can lead to a conformation with an ideal model of community, achieved through a rational agreement among all citizens, regardless of their class. Everyone has the potential to be well-educated in the ideal city, and the virtue of moderation (*sōphrosýnē*) is the same in the city and in the soul (*Republic* 442c–d). In this way, in an ideal model of a just city, all citizens would be in harmony with the one who holds the political power: on the one hand, they were all raised with good paradigms and did not imitate evil deeds; on the other, the ruler strives to promote happiness in the whole city, and not just for himself and his class (*Republic* 420b).

Mimesis as an Active Force

Now that we have recognized the possibility of the active and positive use of
mímēsis[21] and seen that it is powerful enough to change someone's nature, the
problem shifts to the selection of types and models. Thus, words such as *týpos*
and *parádeigma* represent the Platonic appropriation of the vocabulary already
present in the artistic workshops transposed to philosophical concepts. In other
words, Plato applies an analogy to the process of artistic creation while discussing how education can induce human behavior through the mimesis of forms.[22]
Overall, these concepts come from the artistic field, as in the case of the word
týpos (mold), which is related to the verb *týptein* (to stamp and produce a seal,
a coin relief, or a mold for ceramic reproductions), but presenting a philosophical meaning in Plato's dialogues (that is, the model that should conform good
actions). For example, in the following passage, where the verb *apotypóomai* (to
stamp) is employed alongside two other verbs referring to impression and models (*ekmáttō* and *ensēmaínomai*):

> We make impressions upon this of everything we wish to remember
> among the things we have seen or heard or thought of ourselves; we
> hold the wax under our perceptions and thoughts and take a stamp
> [*apotypoûsthai*] from them, in the way in which we take the imprints
> [*ensēmainoménous*] of signet rings. Whatever is impressed [*ekmagêi*]
> upon the wax we remember and know so long as the image remains in
> the wax; whatever is obliterated or cannot be impressed [*ekmagênai*],
> we forget and do not know. (*Theaetetus* 191d–e).[23]

In this passage, Plato explains how memory recovers the imprints stamped on
the soul via the image of the wax block (a malleable material), performing an
action similar to a sculptor. Therefore, this artistic influence establishes a parallel between the craftsmanship of the workshops and education: both processes
work with models, just as a craftsman who reproduces ceramic votive offerings, a
philosopher, as a guardian of the virtues, nourishes and educates the new generation by selecting the good models used to mold their character. The ability to be
influenced by models is, therefore, a characteristic present in our subjectivity, that
demonstrates the plasticity of the soul.[24] This malleability of the human character
allows the philosopher to encourage his fellow citizens to approach the ideal; that
is, it enables the assimilation of a higher order and can serve as a guide for political

conduct and human development. Irmgard Männlein-Robert calls this positive perspective on imitation the philosopher's mimesis: that is, "a process of assimilation, as a dialogical-dialectical, intellectual movement, which is related to and directed toward a very specific goal" (2021, 189; my transl.), and relates it to *homoíōsis theôi*, a concept that means "assimilation to god" or "becoming like god."

This argument is made explicit in *Theaetetus*, exposing a religious motif in Plato and how it is impossible to detach Platonic philosophy from its theological reformism. As Socrates puts it: "a man should make all haste to escape from earth to heaven; and escape means becoming as like god [*homoíōsis theôi*] as possible; and a man becomes like god when he becomes just and pious, with understanding" (*Theaetetus* 176a–b). In this context the word "god" may suggest a kind of biblical monotheism, but, in reality, it expresses a generic use (the collective meaning of a singular word), keeping the polytheism intact.[25] Besides, this concept indicates the idea of divine perfection that characterizes someone trying to achieve their best form. Thus, being like a god entails a form of mimesis: the assimilation to a paradigm shows that the human is trying to "imitate" the behavior and qualities of a model of supreme quality. In other words, this assimilation to an ideal of perfection shares the same intention indicated by Niccolò Machiavelli's "*grandissimi esempli*," as discussed by Nidesh Lawtoo in this volume's Prelude.[26] Therefore, this assimilation entails a purification of wrong deeds by someone who is rationally pursuing the realm of elevated virtues.[27] However, such assimilation cannot be complete since humans do not become gods in Plato's thought, but they are able to strive and resemble, as much as possible, the divine perfectness.[28] This likeness to an ideal paradigm is also expressed in Book 5 of the *Republic*:

> Then it was in order to have a model [*paradeígmatos*] that we were trying to discover what justice itself is like and what the completely just man would be like, if he came into being, and what kind of man he'd be if he did, and likewise [*hoîos*] with regard to injustice and the most unjust man. We thought that, by looking at how their relationship to happiness and its opposite seemed to us, we'd also be compelled to agree [*homologeîn*] about ourselves as well, that the one who was most like [*homoiótatos*] them would have a portion of happiness most like [*homoiotátēn*] theirs. (*Republic* 472c–d)

In the above passage, Socrates refers to the possibility that a just person will be able to assimilate the paradigm of justice, becoming as similar as possible (*homoiótatos*) to its ideal. In other words, he is saying that the plasticity of the soul must be conformed using one model of the highest standard. Lacoue-Labarthe even comments that mimesis is "literally, *in homoiosis*" (1989, 121) when the former is consonant with truth, that is, the perfect paradigm. In fact, the concept of *homoíōsis* (that is, "assimilation") shares some common points with the semantic field of mimetic actions, and its parallel with *mímēsis* becomes more explicit in the *Republic*:[29]

> as he looks at and studies things that are organized and always the same, that neither do injustice to one another nor suffer it, being all in a rational order, he imitates [*mimeîsthai*] them and tries to become as like [*aphomoioûsthai*] them as he can. (*Republic* 500b–c)

Here, we have two verbs used next to each other, *mimeîsthai* (the mimetic action, that is, "to imitate," "to reenact") and *aphomoioûsthai* ("to become like," etymologically linked to *hómoios* and therefore to *homoíōsis*), to express this mimetic assimilation as a process of thinking, which creates an alignment within the immutable paradigm.[30] Both actions refer to a type of mimesis that does not mean just a copy since it makes a person similar to a high model, and because of this, one becomes altered by the result of their own action. Thus, this assimilation configures an active process[31] that entails an understanding toughly acquired by this will to alter one's nature, an endeavor aimed at a higher ideal and a perfect version of oneself. On this account, the desire to improve, an ethical strive for perfection, is thus comprehended as a mimetic action that can be promoted through education and the selection of the best models of conduct.

Conclusion

The approximation between *Theaetetus* and the "second nature" of the *Republic* (echoed in *Protagoras*) facilitates the understanding of assimilation to a model as a mimetic practice with not only individual consequences but also political. Consequently, a conscious philosopher king would prevent the existence of the evil models perpetrated by poets, artists, and sophists. The latter type of people promotes a mimetic pathology with negative consequences since they lack true knowledge. In addition, the philosopher king would encourage, by persuasion or coercion, this positive side of mimesis, considered here as a resignification equal to *homoíōsis*.[32] For it is, in brief, an effort to adapt one's nature to a higher model of virtuous character. Actually, no one suffers coercion anymore because everyone has assimilated all these higher values and is willing to perfect themselves. This selection of mimetic models through education is the actual utopian project Plato envisioned: to trust in every citizen.

Finally, it is necessary to emphasize that, even in the *Republic*, the meaning of mimesis is not reduced solely to copy or imitation. Mimetic action can also be an active performance, where no one is being passively molded by a tyrannical leader but is diligently aiming to perfect oneself, exposing a philosophical nature (even if only partially). This process happens due to a characteristic shared by the ideal philosophers, as they are moderate and well-educated enough to perceive their flaws and can understand the rational consequences of this assimilation to a higher paradigm. In such idealistic circumstances, coercion would not be necessary; at most, persuasion would be required to convince someone already on the right path to act even more orderly. However, suppose the person (or persons) in charge detects the need to be involved in creating or selecting good models. In that case, they will act to ensure the best scenario, banning false paradigms of virtue (the evil models) and even applying punishment by force, by the penalty of law, or by instilling moral feelings of inadequacy—all of these examples configuring instruments of coercion for the bad or not so good natures.

Notes

1   See also ch.1 in this volume [editors' note].

2   See Lawtoo 2022, 75.

3   Shorey 1909, 188. This position is made explicit by Pindar in *Nemean* 3, v. 40–41: "It is by inborn distinction that a man gains authority, | while he who has only been taught is a man of shadows," translated by Anthony Verity (Pindar 2007, 94).

4   In *Airs, Waters, Places* XIV, Hippocrates discussed nature's determinism, exposing how *nómos* (culture) could force different characteristics in the human body (*phýsis*). He exemplifies this issue with the case of the Macrocephali, a people who had elongated heads due to cranial modifications but supposedly began to reproduce this characteristic naturally due to custom. Thus, this sort of ancient Lamarckism also exposes how culture, by mimetic repetition, could be interpreted as something strong enough to alter natures, although different from the Platonic perspective.

5   As an etymological note: "Linguistically, the root word is *mimos*; derived from it are *mimeisthai, mimesis, mimema, mimetes*, and *mimetikos*. '*Mimeisthai*' denotes imitation, representation, or portrayal. '*Mimos*' and '*mimetes*' designate the persons who imitate or represent, whereby '*mimos*' also refers to the context of the dramatic action. '*Mimema*' is the result of mimetic action, and '*mimesis*' the action itself. '*Mimetikos*' refers to something capable of imitation or to that which is subject to imitation" (Gebauer and Wulf 1996, 27).

6   All citations from Plato's *Republic* in this chapter were translated by G.M.A. Grube and revised by C.D.C. Reeve (Plato 1997).

7   See Garcia-Granero 2023, 115.

8   See Lawtoo 2017a, 1211; 2022, 14–21.

9   Citations from Plato's *Protagoras* were translated by Stanley Lombardo and Karen Bell (Plato 1997).

10   Although in the *Republic*, the distinction between good and evil models is made explicit, a similar comprehension is indeed stated in the already cited passage from *Protagoras* because the adjective "good" in the phrase "they are given the works of good [*agathón*] poets to read" is demarcating an artistic curation of the poets, therefore selecting also the models applied in the educational process of the children.

11   In *Laws* VII 793e, Plato specifies that this punishment in relation to education must not be of a degrading kind.

12   In *Laws* IV 718b, the Athenian exposes how the laws should reinforce the correct behavior by coercion or persuasion: "laws' method will be partly persuasion and partly (when they have to deal with characters that defy persuasion) compulsion and chastisement," translated by Trevor J. Saunders (Plato 1997, 1404). Moral values being used for shaming and blaming are more prominent in passages such as *Laws* IX 881c and XII 964b–c.

13   See Lawtoo 2022, 74–85.

14   See Lawtoo 2022, 21.

15   See Garcia-Granero 2023, 139.

16   The concept of *skhéma* is derived from the verb *ékhein* (to have, to hold) and is used in the sense of behaving in a certain way or taking a certain attitude; the suffix *-ma* expresses the result of the action of the verb. See Mugler 1957, 72. Thus, this concept "designates a behavior fixed in the repetition of the same movements or the irrevocable immobility of an attitude" (Mugler 1957, 75; my transl.). It indicates the body's posture and attitude, and there is no discontinuity in this language of poses among athletes, dancers, and speakers. See Celentano et al. 2004, 10.

17   See also the comments by Lawtoo 2017a, 1211–1212 and Blumenthal 1928, 402. Note that the verb *pláttein* is the attic version of *plássō* (to mold or form), etymologically linked to plasticity.

18   See Lacoue-Labarthe 1989, 115.

19   See Lacoue-Labarthe 1989, 126–127.

20   See Carvalhar 2022.

21   On other positive uses of mimesis see Gebauer and Wulf 1996, 32.

22   See Carvalhar 2022.

23   All citations from Plato's *Theaetetus* were translated by M. J. Levett and revised by Myles Burnyeat (Plato 1997).

24   As Lawtoo points out, plasticity is an innovative and recent concept, but it is not original, since it is linked with the ancient Greek concept of mimesis, and possibly they are two sides of the same double concept. See Lawtoo 2017a, 1201–1203.

25   Van Riel concludes that "there is no significant difference between the plural and the singular form of *ho theós*" (2013, 37). See also Männlein-Robert 2021, 176–183.

26   See Lawtoo's Prelude in this volume, pp. 45–49.

27   See Van Riel 2013, 21.

28   There are passages where Plato specifies a limit to this assimilation, that is, the human impossibility of a total assimilation to a paradigm of perfection. See Van Riel 2013, 23.

29   See Männlein-Robert 2021, 172.

30   See Männlein-Robert 2021, 172.

31   In connection with what Männlein-Robert (2021, 185) designates as *"normierende Mimesis"* (normative mimesis), that is, the positive aspect of a mimetic action, even if available only for the few, that is, the philosophers who orient themselves toward god. See also the distinction between passive and active mimesis, as discussed by Lawtoo (2017a, 1212–1213), based on the work of Lacoue-Labarthe.

32   See Männlein-Robert 2021, 168.

Bibliography

Blumenthal, Albrecht (1928). "Τύπος und Παραδειγμα." *Hermes* 63.1, 391–414.

Carvalhar, Carlos (2022). "A crítica ética ao realismo estético em Platão." *Revista Dissertatio de Filosofia* 56.1, 213–241.

Celentano, Maria, Pierre Chiron, and Marie-Pierre Noël (2004). *Skhèma/Figura – Formes et figures chez les Anciens. Rhétorique, philosophie, littérature.* Paris: Éditions Rue d'Ulm.

Garcia-Granero, Marina (2023). "Cómo una segunda naturaleza deviene primera. La filosofía como práctica transformadora (Platón, Nietzsche, Malabou)." *SCIO: Revista de Filosofía* 25, 113–144.

Gebauer, Gunter, and Christoph Wulf (1996). *Mimesis: Culture, Art, Society.* Berkeley: University of California Press.

Hippocrates (2022). *Ancient Medicine. Airs, Waters, Places. Epidemics 1 and 3. The Oath. Precepts. Nutriment*, ed. and trans. by Paul Potter. Loeb Classical Library 147. Cambridge, MA: Harvard University Press.

Lacoue-Labarthe, Philippe (1989). *Typography: Mimesis, Philosophy, Politics.* Cambridge, MA: Harvard University Press.

Lawtoo, Nidesh (2017a). "The Plasticity of Mimesis." *Modern Language Notes* 132.5, 1201–1224.

——— (2017b). "The Power of Myth (Reloaded): From Nazism to New Fascism." *L'Esprit Créateur* 57.4, 64–82.

——— (2022). *Homo Mimeticus: A New Theory of Imitation.* Leuven: Leuven University Press.

Männlein-Robert, Irmgard (2021). "Mit Blick auf das Göttliche oder Mimesis für Philosophen in *Politeia* und *Nomoi*," in *Platonic Mimesis Revisited*, eds. Julia Pfefferkorn and Antonino Spinelli. Baden-Baden: Academia, 167–192.

Mugler, Charles (1957). "Έξις, Σχέσις et Σχῆμα chez Platon." *Revue des Études Grecques* 70.329, 72–92.

Pindar (2007). *The Complete Odes.* Oxford: Oxford University Press.

Plato (1997). *Complete Works.* Indianapolis: Hackett Pub.

Popper, Karl (2012). *The Open Society and Its Enemies.* London: Routledge.

Shorey, Paul (1909). "Φύσις, Μελέτη, Επιστήμη." *Transactions and Proceedings of the American Philological Association* 40.1, 185–201.

Van Riel, Gerd (2013). *Plato's Gods.* London: Routledge.

CHAPTER 4

MIMETIC RESISTANCE

Teresa Casas Hernández

The mimetic turn is the re-turn of orality. As I will show through attention to details of Plato's and Aristotle's mimetic agon, orality is the ontology of mimesis. At the dawn of mimetic studies, the two philosophers recognize that human beings are homo mimeticus, namely, mimetic animals; equally, they tie knowledge, mimesis and human nature as far as the human natural inclination to mimesis is the manifestation of the equally human natural desire for knowledge.[1] In doing so, they discard oral mimesis in favor of abstract mimesis. The mimetic turn entails the recovering of the fundamental aspect of orality in mimesis.

Nidesh Lawtoo defines mimetic agon as a clash, intellectual and creative, that contains an inconspicuous, though fundamental, relation of continuity. As he puts it: "mimetic agonism is a form of intellectual contest" between younger thinkers and their models or educators "that appear at first sight to be simply opponents, antagonists, or rivals, yet, on a closer genealogical investigation, turn out to provide the very conceptual and theoretical tools to establish an opposition in the first place—in a creative, productive yet still creative way" (Lawtoo 2023, 45).[2] Through the lens of mimetic agon, I want to underscore that both Plato and Aristotle target oral mimesis. The reason is that both intend to protect the core object of their theory from the, in their view, pernicious and threatening effects of orality—deformation.

Traditionally, Plato and Aristotle are seen as promoting opposite theories of mimesis. Indeed, each address it differently: Plato circumscribes poetic mimesis to relations of truth, which is made manifest in the particulars; Aristotle instead pays attention to structure resemblance and judges the resemblance of particulars—or the lack of it—as inconsequential. However, attention to their respective views of orality shows that Plato's preoccupation with the particulars matches Aristotle's concern for structure. Indeed, while Plato protects particulars from deformation, Aristotle shields the stability of structure.

Deformation takes a different form in each of their theories. For Plato deformation takes the form of the ghostly, while in Aristotle it manifests as the monstrous. In both cases, deformation epitomizes perilous contagious pathologies that endanger the stability of the city by populating it with ghosts and monsters. Such a city has no future. Ultimately, targeting deformation, both Plato and Aristotle intend to guarantee the stability and continuity of the city. For it, the two philosophers displace oral mimesis in favor of abstract mimesis. The latter allows for a clean and neat outcome that fosters a sort of positive contagion—the spread of virtue. For the same reason, it ensures the future of the city.

Awareness of the ontology of mimesis, I believe, underpins that the mimetic turn brings deformation back with it—the unforeseen, the changeable; most importantly, sheds light into the possibilities of mimesis beyond imitation and reproduction emphasizing its creative, epistemic, and political potential.

Oral Mimesis vs Pictorial Mimesis

Unlike pictorial mimesis, oral mimesis entails a relation between process and process. Three objects compose the structure of mimesis: model, agent, and object resulting from mimesis (from now on, mimetic object). In oral mimesis the three are in constant movement and change. Both model and mimetic object are performances; they are in movement, and thus are both changing and unfinished. Furthermore, the agent is indistinguishable from the mimetic object; think of an actor playing a character, for instance. Consequently, the relation between the three is blurry. By contrast, pictorial mimesis entails a different structure: first, the three are clearly differentiated objects, and second (and consequently) model and mimetic object are stable and unchangeable.

Oral mimesis is essential in the process of transmission, preservation, and acquisition of knowledge proper of an illiterate culture. Studies on orality make manifest the primacy of oral mimesis in the preservation and transmission of knowledge. As Walter J. Ong puts it in oral cultures "you know what you can recall" (1987, 33); namely, what is not remembered, is forgotten. In oral cultures, remembering is tied to performance, to mimicking, and evanescence: listening, bodily and oral repetition, combining and recombining.

By now, there is no doubt that Ancient Greek poetry was an oral art. Milman Parry found proof of the oral composition of Homeric poetry in the structure of epithets.[3] Memorization of formulae allowed for the process described above: combining and recombing through oral and bodily repetition, poets could compose on the spot poems that were different and yet the same. This reveals first, the inherent variability resulting from oral composition and, second, the key role of such composition in the transmission of knowledge.

Eric Havelock's seminal work *Preface to Plato* applies Parry's theory to the whole of Ancient Greek poetry.[4] By thoroughly discussing the relevance of orality in Ancient Greece before literacy he shows how poetry and performance were means to transmit knowledge, by means of repetition and mimicking. His work also serves to point out an inherent tension in Plato's work: he composes his work at a time of transition between orality and literacy. In the advent of written composition, oral composition felt stiff, limited, and dated.[5]

The tension between orality and literacy pierces both Plato's and Aristotle's approach to poetry: both recognize the oral origin of tragedy and comedy and its epistemic possibilities: Plato uses dialogue and fictionality, while Aristotle discusses tragedy's power for the education of the emotions. However, in their discussions of tragedy and comedy, both present pictorial mimesis as the original paradigm of mimesis. It is not an innocent choice: pictorial mimesis is a steppingstone to privilege written over oral composition – and thus, key to the dissociation of oral mimesis from the transmission of knowledge and from the conception of mimesis itself. The result is a notion of mimesis perilously homogenous and homogenizing.

Plato's and Aristotle's overall operation has far-reaching consequences. The *Republic* and the *Poetics*, as foundational texts for mimetic studies, set the basis for future concepts of mimesis up until today. Addressing how both define and solidify the concept of mimesis is vital to avoid perpetuating the restrictive homogenization that lies under Plato's and Aristotle's claims to universalism. By the same token, it is essential to recover the discarded element of deformation, which broadens both the scope and possibilities of mimesis.

Plato's *Republic*: The Antistrophe of Painting

Finding consistency across Plato's dialogues comes close to an impossibility. An irresolvable tension informs Plato's regard of mimesis and oral tradition: while recognizing their virtues and value, he also judges them as problematic. Here I thoroughly examine the arguments of the *Republic* because, in it, he fully exposes the tension that haunts his thought: on the one hand, Plato recognizes the power of mimesis for the transmission of knowledge; on the other, he solely targets oral mimesis in the form of tragedy and comedy insofar as both epitomize the danger of contagion of deformation. Making mimesis a good source of contagion, so to speak, is Plato's goal.

In Book 3, Plato performs the by now foundational ban of the poets. He concludes that only diegesis (third-person narration) should be accepted in the city; by the same token mimetic composition should be banned. The reason is that stories that show the gods behaving viciously "produce in the youth a strong inclination to do bad things" (391e). The virtue of diegesis, says Plato, is that it is not mimetic and, therefore, it allows for a differentiation between story and narrator that prevents deformation and the contagion of pathologies in the souls of the citizens and the city at large.

And yet, Plato's conclusion is confusing. As the myths banned from the city, the ones allowed in it cannot comprehend direct knowledge of the past. For Plato, "we have no knowledge of these things" (427bc) and, as far as—in his view—access to the past is impossible, so is knowledge of the past.[6] Hence, accounts of the past allowed in the city such as the philosophers' noble lie are not faithful accounts of the past in terms of direct knowledge. This suggests that the philosopher's myth entails some sort of mimesis that is not fully elucidated. Therefore, philosophical myths and poetic myths both seem to employ mimesis and lack direct knowledge of the past; and yet, the first is admitted into the city while the latter is banned from it.

I shall suggest that the difference between poetry and philosophical myth is of mimetic origin: their opposed ontologies result from their different structures of mimesis. In Archaic oral tradition poets could transit between afterlife and the world of the living, hence acquiring direct knowledge of the past. In Ancient tradition, poets preserve their privileged access to the past through the whispering of the muses. Poetic recitation, sung speech, were means to make memory live but also, to preserve memory. To it, Plato opposes the philosophers' access to truth. The different means to access the object of mimesis necessarily yield objects with opposed ontologies.

The distinction becomes clear in Book 10, where Plato's comparison between mimesis and a mirror reflection of the world sets the frame for his hierarchy of mimesis aligned in relation to truth:

> If you are willing to take a mirror and carry it around everywhere; quickly you will make the sun and the things in the heaven; quickly, the earth; and quickly, yourself and the other animals and implements and plants and everything else that was just now mentioned. (596d)

This passage sets up a system of mimesis. First is the nature of the object, then the work of the one with knowledge and skills (*techne*) to create an object based on that nature, and, finally, the painter. The latter, metaphorically speaking, holds the mirror: he can make things appear, but unlike the craftsman, he cannot make things as they are. To put it shortly, the relation among the three is from better to worse in relation to truth.

Through a hierarchy of mimesis, Plato explains the origin of the world of becoming and establishes the ghostly nature of mimetic objects. He identifies a vertical chain of transmission articulated by mimesis, which intervenes in all three stages—nature, craftsman, and painter. However, the kinds of mimesis differ in relation to *techne*: the craftsman's mimesis is based on abstract values such as measurement and proportion, yielding, for example, an actual bed. By contrast, the painter's mimesis is based on mere observation of particulars. As a result, his bed is lacking in *techne* and thus a bed that only seems to be a bed but *is* not a bed: it lacks the foundational ontology of a bed (596a–597e). Therefore, the painter's bed is like the ghost of Hamlet's father in Shakespeare's famous tragedy: he looks like his father, but it *is* not his father because the nature of the ghost is different from that of Hamlet's actual father. Similarly, the painter's bed has the appearance of a bed, but it *is* not a bed. It is the ghost of the idea of "bed."[7]

Having established the ghostly nature of mimetic objects, Plato moves onto the tragedians and their mimesis. Plato succinctly informs us that the tragedian, like the painter, is an "imitator" (597e), inviting us to apply the same ontological structure to objects of tragic mimesis. And yet, when Plato makes "the most serious charge against imitation" (605c), he abandons the comparison between the painter and the tragedian; it is leveled entirely against tragedians and comedians

(605c–607d). Accordingly, only the mimesis involved in tragedy and comedy is banned from the city.

Plato's final use of the analogy between painting and poetry is decisive because it confirms the ban of oral mimesis:

> Therefore, it would at last be just for us to seize him [the poet] and set him beside the painter as his antistrophe. For he [the poet] like the painter is making things that are ordinary by the standard of truth; and he [the poet] is also similar in keeping company with a part of the soul that is on the same level and not with the best part. And thus, we should at last be justified in not admitting him [the poet] into a city that is going to be under laws, because he awakens this part of the soul and nourishes it, and, by making it strong, destroys the calculating part, just as in a city when someone by making wicked men mighty, turn the city over to them and corrupts the superior ones. (605ab)[8]

Key to the passage is how Plato constructs the analogy between painter and poet: poetry is the "antistrophe" of painting, writes Plato.[9] In tragic poetry, the three parts of the chorus' ode were presented in the following order of appearance: *strophe*, *antistrophe*, and *epode*. The first and second can be translated as "a turn" and "come back" or "return," respectively. During that first part, a segment of the chorus sang and danced moving from stage right to stage left. During the second part, another segment of the chorus danced and sang moving left to right. The antistrophe constituted a response to the strophe that consists in a repetition of the strophe with variations. Finally, during the closing third part of the ode, both segments of the chorus united in the center of the stage sang and danced the *epode*.

The image of a poetic antistrophe is extraordinarily rich: if poetry is the antistrophe, then painting must be the strophe. This analogy sheds light on how Plato conceives the relation between both arts. As antistrophe, poetry comes after painting, and it is an inexact and changing repetition. As strophe, painting comes before poetry – meaning that painting is above poetry in the hierarchy of mimesis. The reason, I believe, is that painting yields an unchanging object. Thus, because of the unchanging nature of pictorial mimesis, the deformation its mimetic objects represent is constrained within the static nature of painting. By contrast, tragedy (and comedy) is in constant movement—every instance of poetry entails variation thus increasing deformation. To put it bluntly, tragedy gives birth to an unlimited lineage of ghosts that proliferate in the city. Because poetry produces variable and changing objects, its impact becomes dangerously unpredictable.[10] Consequently, concludes Plato, "we would be justified in not admitting him [the poet]" in the city (605ab).

The essential difference between the unchanging and changing nature of both poetry and painting grounds Plato's "most serious charge against imitation" (605c), which is aimed at tragic (and comic) poetry and its effects. Essentially, Plato critiques that poetry's changing nature whet the appetitive part of the soul and steer it toward "sex, spiritedness, too, and for all the desires, pain, and pleasures in the soul" (606d). The poet, says Plato, "puts a bad constitution in the soul of each individual" (605b), meaning that the orality of poetry fosters mimetic pathos "the relational power of human bodies to be unconsciously affected by human and non-human others" (Lawtoo 2022, 37). Shortly after these claims, Plato restates the ban of the poets. Yet, painters may remain in the city.[11]

Plato's distinct treatment of the poets discloses both the hierarchy of his mimesis and the different structures of mimesis at play. Platonic mimesis emerges as a vertical line that articulates the relation between the nature of objects (the Platonic forms) and the objects that we perceive in the world of becoming. A philosophical mimesis concerned with universals and abstracts mediates between these two ontological spaces. Another kind of mimesis mediates between knowledge and the craftsman's objects. Mimesis of particulars is the third kind mediating between objects in the world of becoming and the objects that result from mimesis of particulars. This third kind of mimesis defines painting and poetry. On Plato's views as expressed in the *Republic*, the main difference between the second and third kinds of mimesis is *techne*. The third kind involves no *techne*.[12] Based on mere perception and deceived by the senses the agent is incapable of engaging with the abstract; the result is an object that is a non-being—a ghost.

The key are the different structures of mimesis and the nature of the objects that result from it. Though the nature of their objects might differ,[13] craftsman and the poet share the same structure of mimesis—it allows for a separation among the model, the mimetic object, and the agent of mimesis. By contrast, the mimesis of tragedy (and comedy), merges the three: the agent of mimesis (the poet or actor) presents himself as the model (a god or a hero), and the resulting object is the appearance of the object of mimesis (said god or hero). Agent, model, and mimetic object are all the same. The lack of distance between all three elements of poetic mimesis has a transformative, contagious, and uncontrollable effect.

Oral mimesis, therefore, riddles the city with ghosts. They are perilous because for the untrained eye, the ghostly appears as a truthful being. Thus, with all the power of truth—it steers our desire, our love for knowledge in the wrong direction fostering corruption and ignorance. Consequently, it corrupts the agent turning it into a ghost. A city in which poetry oversees transmitting knowledge is populated by ghosts, by non-living beings. And thus, it has no future. I contend that Plato bans tragedy for these reasons.

The framing of poetic mimesis within the analogy of pictorial mimesis provides a broader context for Plato's critique of mimesis in Books 2 and 3: it is directly related to poetry's oral composition and its ghostly and contagious nature. Its composition—bodily retrospective, repetition, and on-site assembly of repeated formulae—is rooted in orality.[14] Consequently, poetry in orality is a ghost: it appears to be, but it *is* not. And last but not least, this ghostly condition makes it extremely contagious. By addressing mimesis in relation to the education of the guardians, Plato attempts to undo the mimetic pathos of oral mimesis while preserving its educative function. In this double task, the usage of pictorial mimesis to define poetic mimesis is essential.

Plato disregards mimetic poetry in favor of diegesis because it preserves the contagious effect of mimesis without its pernicious effect—it is mimesis without pathos, so to speak. It allows for distinctions among the model, the agent of mimesis, and the mimetic object. The separation between the three orders permits a relation with truth. Under these reformed conditions, poetic mimesis can yield an object similar to painting: a copy with an unchanging nature that freezes the endless stream of ghosts that riddle Plato's *Kallipolis* with pathologies, which endanger the unity, the order, and the stability of the city.

Aristotle's *Poetics*: Teleological Uninterrupted Change

Aristotle's setting for his discussion on mimesis might obscure the mimetic agon that I am developing. For him mimesis articulates relations in the sphere of what today we would call the Fine Arts; he liberates poetry from the mandate of truth and focuses on its structure instead. However, by analyzing his usage of pictorial mimesis, I show how Aristotle, like Plato, is very much concerned with mimetic deformation, which he attributes to the mimesis of orality and, by the same token, of poetry.

The analogy between pictorial and poetic mimesis literally frames Aristotle's treatise.[15] However, the most telling instance takes place in chapter four where Aristotle offers an apparently historical account of tragedy—its origin, evolution, and final form. However, attention to his explanation reveals that his account is markedly teleological. Aristotle presents the coming into being of tragedy as a change between opposites—from improvisation to tragedy.

Underpinning Aristotle's narrative we find a key change between opposites—from oral mimesis to pictorial mimesis. At the outset, Aristotle states that poetry was brought "into being from improvisations" (1448b20–25), which is determined by mimesis, insofar as it "comes naturally to us" (1448b20–25); he concludes that tragedy achieves "its own nature" (1448b15–20), by the hand of the three great tragedians: Aeschylus, Sophocles, and Euripides; namely when it is composed in writing. I contend that at each end of Aristotle's account we find the two mimetic structures that we have just examined in Plato's *Republic*. Surreptitiously, Aristotle replaces the oral bodily performative mimesis of improvisation from the beginning of his account, by the written[16] mimesis that we find at the end. Aristotle's move, I contend, exhibits the Platonic fear to deformation. And the threat is averted by the same means: using pictorial mimesis to displace oral mimesis and its inherent dangers.

In Aristotle's system of thought, the cause determines the end. In the passage below he establishes two causes for the origin of poetry: first, the human species' distinctive mimetic instinct; and second, he points at human understanding:

> For it is an instinct of human beings, from childhood, to engage in mimesis (indeed, this distinguishes them from animals: man is the most mimetic of all, and it is through mimesis that he develops his earliest understanding): and equally natural that everyone enjoys mimetic objects. (1448b1–10)

Aristotle's first move is to establish that the *telos* of tragedy consists in the relation between mimesis and understanding. Aristotle uses pictorial mimesis to explain how this relationship between mimesis and understanding works:

> This is why people enjoy looking at images, because through contemplating them it comes about that they understand and infer what each element means, for instance that "this person is so-and-so." For, if one happens not to have seen the subject before, the image will not give pleasure qua mimesis but because of its execution or color, or for some other such reason. (1448b15–20)

According to Aristotle, it is by contemplating mimetic objects that we come to understand. The basis of this understanding is recognition of "so-and-so" (οἶον ὅτι οὗτος), which simply indicates the capacity to identify one thing with another, even if one of the two is not present. In that process, human understanding makes possible the recognition of objects that are not necessarily presented as they are. Particularly "poetry does not have the same standard of correctness as in politics" (1460b10–15), which is why it allows to show a "horse with both right legs thrown forward" or "the pursuit of Hector" (1460b15–20).[17] For faults in poetry are acceptable "if the poetry achieves its goal" (146015–20) or if at least, it does not interfere with it. Hence, from very early in his theorization of mimesis, first, Aristotle establishes the relation between mimesis and understanding and, second, he subsumes mimesis to plot structure.

Aristotle identifies two forms of mimesis that he presents in terms of development: a rudimentary, childish mimesis and its corresponding object will develop into an abstract mimesis with its corresponding object. However, I argue, what he presents as an evolution, I believe, entails an opposition between oral and written mimesis, both of which entail different structures and different objects. And he articulates this opposition by presenting pictorial mimesis as the paradigm of mimesis that yields an object that leads to understating: a painting.

What constitutes the object of our contemplation is important for Aristotle. On his view, improvisation is the first result of our mimetic impulse, led by our desire to understand. Aristotle adds that the agents of improvisation are not yet poets; thus, the product of improvisation cannot be considered poetry, let alone tragedy. From improvisation, poetry develops into the forms of tragedy and comedy. This development is achieved mainly by means of the poet's intervention. Beginning with Homer, the first poet to compose distinct genres, Aeschylus, Sophocles, and Euripides give tragedy its final form by means of dramatic composition. In this final form, mimesis achieves its *telos*: contemplating it leads to understanding.

Critically, both improvisation and tragedy are mimetic, but in Aristotle's view, only tragedy can lead to understanding. Improvisation cannot lead to understanding because, as the bodily mimesis that it is, first, it does not contribute to the agent's understanding, and second, as far as it lacks the stable structure of plot (or painting) it does not lead the audience to understand. In short, in Aristotle's view, bodily performance can only participate in *logos* as part of a structure of representation. In any case, it contributes to the learning of the audience, never the agent.

On Aristotle's account, improvisation is the result of primary mimesis—oral mimesis. It reproduces previous performances and particulars, and it has the mark of spontaneity. In improvisation, the agent, model, and mimetic object are indistinguishable. Therefore, the final result is a moving, changing object. It is evanescent and unpredictable. Written mimesis is the opposite of oral mimesis: final, stable, and reliable. The object of the plot is the change between opposites, and its three components are each distinguishable: model, agent of mimesis, and mimetic object. And finally, it yields a written text: a static object.[18]

The culmination of Aristotle's account of the coming into being of tragedy, the final form of tragedy, coincides with the moment in which tragedy is composed in writing. The mimesis at play in the latter is busy with universals rather than particulars, is capable of dealing with abstraction, and, overall, yields a static object: a text. Furthermore, the latter emerges as parallel and resembling to painting: the structure of dramatic mimesis is the structure of pictorial mimesis. First, model, agent of mimesis, and mimetic object are distinguishable, and second, the object is a static unchangeable object. And in both, the structure plays a significant role: as in painting tragedy's ontological model is a change between opposites, a universal that rules in nature. Aristotle identifies as determinant of tragedy a mimesis that is far away from bodily performance, particulars, and enactment: abstract mimesis, mimesis done in writing. Under these conditions, poetry can contribute to *logos*.

I believe that Aristotle substituting oral mimesis for mimesis in writing is directly related to the need to avoid interference of *opsis*: the visual aspect of theater. But it involves more, including all the material elements that make theater possible.[19] Aristotle recognizes *opsis* as one of the parts of tragedy, "tragedy [...] must have six components which give it its qualities—namely plot, character, diction, thought, spectacle (*opsis*), and lyric poetry;" he also presents it as inconsequential, for "the plot should be so structured that, even without seeing it performed, the person who hears the event that occur experiences horror and pity;" and yet, it is deeply problematic because "to create this effect [experiencing horror and pity] through spectacle has little do wo with the poet's art" (1453b10–15).[20] In Aristotle's view, the effect of tragedy should be "built into the events," namely good plot composition. By contrast, the pleasure elicited by *opsis* "has little to do with the poet's art" (1453b5–10) and thus, I argue, with *logos*. Therefore, for Aristotle *opsis* jeopardizes the *telos* of the plot and, when used as a condition of possibility for tragedy, it deforms tragedy.

Aristotle's avoidance of *opsis* is very Platonic: he wants to avoid a futureless city of monsters. In Book 3 of the *Physics*, Aristotle argues that when *telos* is disrupted, the result is a monstrous being—a metaphysically flawed being. Such beings, like cows with two heads, are barren by nature and do not reproduce. When *opsis* acts as a cause in tragedy, it deforms its telos and leads to a deformed being. Provided the educative and epistemic role that Aristotle bestows to tragedy, a monstrous tragedy would lead to a city with no future. By replacing the mimesis of orality for written abstract mimesis, Aristotle imprints in tragedy the good qualities that he finds in pictorial mimesis: stability, unchangeability, and universality. Tragedy determined by abstract mimesis becomes a mimetic object suitable for understanding.

Aristotle, therefore, uses pictorial mimesis to profoundly intervene in the conception of mimesis at the origin of poetry. The consequences are significant. First, the mimesis of orality is stripped of any participation in knowledge. Second, oral mimesis is subsumed under abstract mimesis, which is now charged with making manifest a perfectly constructed plot. Third, abstract mimesis entails a tightly knit structure in which the object of mimesis, the mimetic object, and the agent of mimesis are clearly identifiable and separate. As a result of all of the above, the proliferation of deformed monstrosity is avoided and thus tragedy becomes a welcome being in the city.

Mimesis: A Story of Continuation

In Book 10 of the *Republic,* Plato states his famous challenge:

> All the same, let it be said that if poetry directed to pleasure and imitation have any argument to give showing that they should be in a city with good laws, we should be delighted to receive them back from exile, since we are aware that we ourselves are charmed by them. (607cd)

Aristotle's *Poetics* is traditionally read as a reply to it. His reply, however, as mimetic studies has begun to note, has a lot more of Plato's prejudice than is often recognized.[21] In fact, examining the role of pictorial mimesis in both Plato's *Republic* and Aristotle's *Poetics*, it comes to view that both employ pictorial mimesis in their containment projects. For both the variability typical of orality and, by the same token, of tragedy and comedy, is a sign of deformation. From the standpoint of their theories, this makes sense: if the relation between cause and outcome has no order, then anything is possible. It opens up a chaotic scenario, where predictability, order, stability, and a foreseeable future are impossible. Identifying oral mimesis as the cause of poetic variability, the two mend the perils of oral mimesis by means of pictorial mimesis. The latter establishes hierarchy between mimesis of particulars and abstract mimesis. But also, preserves a logical relation of causality. However, the outcomes of these similarities are different: Plato privileges diegesis and bans the remains of oral mimesis from the city. By contrast, Aristotle privileges writing and tames oral mimesis, thereby rendering it inconsequential for understanding and, thus, for transmitting knowledge.

The different results conceal a story of continuation in taming and containing oral mimesis: both their interventions target it, identify it as the problem in tragedy and comedy, and finally strip it from tragedy and comedy. Considering this, Plato's diegesis and Aristotle's writing hold a striking structural resemblance: differentiation between the elements of mimesis—model, mimetic object, and agent—amounts to an object that provides a stable relation to abstracts. As such, it can convey knowledge.

The ultimate consequence of their intervention is the deep transformation in the structure of mimesis: mimesis imprinted with the structure of pictorial mimesis, first, will become a normative concept and, second, will dominate discussions on mimesis and its two major translations, imitation and representation. The two cast a long-lasting shadow upon oral mimesis. The mimetic turn is the recovery of that foundational, ontological, and primary sense of mimesis.

Mimetic Resistance

Pointing at the structure and role of mimesis in orality, I believe, has a political side, which I would like to sketch further, even if briefly. Inadvertently, both Plato and Aristotle reveal that the mimesis of orality played a core role in the transmission of knowledge. Namely it was core to the "epistemic structure" (Broncano 2020, 364)[22] of the city. Such role emerges as indissociable from the oral and indomitable nature of mimesis, that both Plato and Aristotle intend to correct.

Oral mimesis points directly to our mimetic nature, our condition of homo mimeticus: prone to do and engage in mimesis. However, both Plato and Aristotle seem to imply that the human mimetic faculty needs training. Plato assumes that oral mimesis is impossible to train, as it is the expression of a corrupt nature. While for Aristotle it can be trained, it contributes to nothing substantial unless it is directed to the sphere of abstracts. In either case, oral mimesis is dispossessed of any epistemic value or function. Contra them, what resurfaces through their critiques, and lays at the core of their targeting of oral mimesis, is that our mimetic faculty does not require training for it to be an epistemic asset. And its most immediate expression is the mimesis of orality: performative, changing, intuitive, moving, blurry, and with an unstable structure. It is this freedom that made it so essential in illiterate cultures and still today for our human condition as epistemic agents. But, most important, I believe, it is this freedom that makes it so dangerous, in Plato's and Aristotle's eyes.

The inherent freedom and indomitable nature of oral mimesis, I argue, is key to explaining the ways in which mimesis is both subversive and resistant to the domestication intended by Plato's and Aristotle's reshaping of mimesis. As precursors of mimetic studies such as Homi K. Bhabha, Michael Taussig, Judith Butler, or Luce Irigaray have argued, it is by means of mimesis that we can steal, re-appropriate, subvert, and modify forms of being, narratives, and knowledge. Mimetic studies recover mimesis's instrumentality in articulating knowledge, perhaps a knowledge that defies the abstraction hierarchy.

For Plato's and Aristotle's critiques reveal that mimesis is resistant: it resists Plato's ontology and Aristotle's metaphysics. But, as the works mentioned above suggest, mimesis also plays a role in strategies of political and individual resistance to hegemonic orders. Via a process of doing as others do, the result of mimesis is opened into the unforeseen and the unexpected: to the monstrous and the ghostly. Therefore, mimesis is understood as a faculty that allows for an unfinished process of changing re-appropriation with the potential to transform both objects and agents involved, yielding the possibility of other epistemologies and other ways of being.

This chapter focused on the arguments that have cast a shadow on orality for centuries and intends to stress the central role of orality in mimetic studies. Further attention to the key role of orality, I believe, opens the space to identify the ontological common ground to the many heterogeneous forms of the mimetic re-turn such as attention to the performative, contagion, and affects. Furthermore, the mimetic turn is, necessarily, an oral turn. Consequently, future developments in mimetic studies would benefit from focusing on the oral origin of mimesis and its link to deformation. First, because it exceeds the prevailing understanding of mimesis as either representation, copy, or imitation. And, second, because rather than a means for homogeneity and domination, mimesis becomes an essential tool for otherness and heterogeneity.

The oral tradition of ancient theater is now reemerging under different masks such as the performance of postdramatic theater. For that matter, an awareness of both the ontology of mimesis and the prejudices that have grounded for so long prevailing notions of mimesis are fundamental to avoid perpetuating misconceptions against oral mimesis that live right at the core of mimesis *tout court*. On that note, mimetic studies finds in the ontology of oral mimesis and its far-reaching consequences a solid ground to examine the vital role of mimesis in human affairs.

Notes

1   Plato doesn't literally state that the human species is naturally inclined to mimesis, but his whole discussion in the *Republic*, as well as in other works as such as the *Ion* or *Phaedrus,* suggests that mimesis is key in the relation between the world of being and the world of becoming, as well as for education.

2   Examples of mimetic agon include Plato contra Homer, Aristotle contra Plato, Nietzsche contra Wagner, Malabou contra Derrida, among others. For the oral foundations of mimetic studies see also Lawtoo 2022, ch.2 [editors' note].

3   See Parry 1928.

4   See Havelock 1963, 36–60.

5   See Ong 1987, 20–28.

6   Here Plato is challenging a deep-rooted understanding of poetic tradition as a means to access the past. For more on this see Nikulin 2015, Detienne 1999, and Vernant 2006.

7   For a detailed analysis of mimesis and techne in Book 10 of *Republic* see Staten in this volume [editor's note].

8   This passage has been deeply influential. For example, Arieti (1992), Halliwell (2009), and Puchner (2010) all equate mental representation with staging. Their claim is that mental representation constitutes the problem with poetry. However, this position obviates the performative aspect of tragedy and accepts, prima facie, the equivalence that Plato draws between pictorial and poetic mimesis. One could say that philosophers who have accepted at face value Plato's restricted—and restrictive—view of mimesis, have been tricked by Plato.

9   Some editions choose to translate "antistrophe" as counterpart. But this translation obscures the hierarchical relation between both arts.

10 A similar conclusion can be drawn from Plato's *Ion*. There, Plato shows Ion that painters can paint anyone. By contrast, Plato claims, poets know only the words of one poet. Plato's argument is meant to emphasize the opposition between art (*techne*) and divine possession. The latter entails a changing repetition of the divine owing to the poet's lack of knowledge about what they say. Therefore, in the *Ion*, as in the *Republic*, painting and poetry have different status. Painting, though mimetic, is superior to poetry. [Editors' note: for a discussion of *Ion* see Borch-Jacobsen in this volume and Lawtoo 2022, ch. 2.]

11 See Havelock 1963, 25.

12 Plato's discussion in the *Ion* might suggest that he regarded painting as involving *techne*. On techne in Plato see again Staten's contribution to this volume [editors' note].

13   As established above, painter's and craftsman's mimetic object differ in their ontology: the first does not participate of truth, while the latter does. The structure in place, however, remains the same.

14   Of special importance on this matter are the works of Ong 1987 and Parry 1987.

15   This analogy first appears in chapter one, where Aristotle discusses modes of mimetic production (1447a25). He uses the analogy for the last time in the penultimate chapter (1460b5–120) to defend tragedy from possible criticism.

16   Admittedly, neither tragedies nor comedies were written to be read. But emphasis on written composition, as cause of tragedy, shows that Aristotle was in search of an object that could grant stability to tragedy. For more on this, see Kovacs 2005.

17   Aristotle distinguishes between incidental and intrinsic faults (146010–15). Both can be acceptable insofar as they contribute to achieving poetry's goal. In any case, showing a horse as described above would not prevent the audience from recognizing it.

18   Undoubtedly, texts can be deformed by acting. This is Aristotle's concern, which I address later.

19   Today, we would refer to it as the theatrical dispositive, I believe.

20   See also 1461b25–1462a10, where Aristotle blames actors for the critiques to tragedy.

21   See, for instance, Lawtoo 2023, 109–110.

22   Fernando Broncano defines "epistemic structure" as the structure that sustains the distribution, production, preservation, and transmission of knowledge in a determined society.

Bibliography

Arieti, James A. (1991). *Interpreting Plato. The Dialogues as Drama*. Lanham, MD: Rowman & Littlefield Publishers, Inc.

Aristotle (1999). "Poetics," in *Aristotle: Poetics; Longinus: On the Sublime; Demetrius: On Style*, ed. Jeffrey Henderson. Cambridge, MA: Harvard University Press, 28–141.

—— (2008). *Physics*, trans. Robin Waterfield. Oxford: Oxford University Press.

—— (2016). *Metaphysics*, trans. C D. C Reeve. Indianapolis/Cambridge, MA: Hackett Publishing Company, Inc.

Bhabha, Homi (1984). "Of Mimicry and Man: The Ambivalence of Colonial Discourse." *October* 28, 125–133.

Broncano, Fernando (2020). *Conocimiento expropiado. Epistemología política en una democracia radical*. Madrid: Akal.

Butler, Judith (2006). *Gender Trouble*. London: Routledge.

Detienne, Marcel (1999). *The Masters of Truth in Archaic Greece*, trans. Janet Lloyd. New York: Zone Books.

Halliwell, Stephen (2009). *Aristotle's Poetics*. London: Duckworth.

Havelock, Eric A. (1963). *Preface to Plato*. Cambridge, MA: Harvard University Press.

Irigaray, Luce (1985). *Speculum of the Other Woman*, trans. Gillian C. Gill. Ithaca, NY: Cornell University Press.

Kovacs, David (2005). "Text and Transmission," in *A Companion to Greek Tragedy*, ed. Justina Gregory. Malden: Blackwell Publishing, 299–393.

Lawtoo, Nidesh (2022). *Homo Mimeticus. A New Theory of Imitation*. Leuven: Leuven University Press.

—— (2023). *Violence and the Oedipal Unconscious*. Michigan: Michigan University Press.

Lehmann, Hans-Thies (2006). *Postdramatic Theatre*. London: Routledge.

—— (2016). *Tragedy and Dramatic Theatre*. London: Routledge.

Nikulin, Dmitri (2015). "Memory in Ancient Philosophy," in *Memory, a History*, ed. Dmitri Nikulin. Oxford: Oxford University Press, 35–84.

Ong, Walter J. (1987). *Orality and Literacy. The Technologizing of the Word*. New York: Metheun&Co.

Parry, Milman (1987). "Studies in the Epic Technique of Oral Verse-Making. Homer and Homeric Style," in *The Making of Homeric Verse. The Collective Papers of Milman Parry*, ed. Adam Parry. Oxford: Oxford University Press, 325–364.

Plato (1997a). "Ion," in *Plato: Complete Works*, trans. Paul Woodruff, ed. John M. Cooper. Indianapolis/Cambridge, MA: Hackett Publishing Company, 937–949.

—— (1997b). "Phaedrus," in *Plato: Complete Works*, trans. Alexander Nehamas and Paul Woodruff, ed. John M. Cooper, Indianapolis/Cambridge, MA: Hackett Publishing Company, 506–556.

—— (1997c). "Republic," in *Plato Complete Works*, trans. G. M. A. Grube and C. D. C. Reve, ed. John M. Cooper. Indianapolis/Cambridge, MA: Hackett Publishing Company, 971–1223.

—— (2013). *Plato VI. Republic, Books VI–X*. Loeb Classical Library, trans. Chris Emlyn-Jones and William Preddy. Vol. 276. Cambridge, MA: Harvard University Press.

—— (2016). *The Republic of Plato*, trans. Allan Bloom. New York: Basic Books.

Puchner, Martin (2010). *The Drama of Ideas. Platonic Provocation in Theater and Philosophy*. Oxford: Oxford University Press.

Taussig, Michael T. (1993). *Mimesis and Alterity*. New York: Routledge.

Veloso, Claudio William (2004). *Aristóteles Mimético*. Janeiro: Discurso.

Vernant, Jean-Pierre (2006). *Myth and Thought Among the Greeks*. New York: Zone Books.

CHAPTER 5

BEHIND PLATO'S SHADOWS
AND TODAY'S MEDIA MONSTERS

Mark Pizzato

This chapter adds to mimetic studies by exploring Plato's ancient cave allegory through psychology, anthropology, and neuroscience, regarding current screen media and repeated mass shootings in the United States. It considers developmental, ancestral, and "inner theater" sources of ego and group rivalry, involving animal-human emotional drives. Comparing Plato's metaphors with prehistoric cave art and recent brain mapping discoveries, this spelunking expedition finds a dark side to rational idealism in predatory scapegoating, as *homo mimeticus* path or "patho(-)logy" of the "*vita mimetica*" (Lawtoo 2022).[1] The interplay between inner and outer theater networks reveals subconscious Trojan Horse influences and dangerous melodramatic ideals, with violent mimetic effects, and yet a potential for tragic awareness about such repetition compulsions in our mass and social media today.

In the *Republic*, Plato describes, through the voice of Socrates in dialogue with Plato's brother, Glaucon, a cave where people are chained for their entire lives, heads restricted to watching shadow figures on a wall. Puppets parade behind the prisoners, while a flickering firelight produces the cave-wall show and invisible puppeteers give it voices (like Socrates conducting Glaucon's imagining of the scene and like Plato with these characters). Socrates gets Glaucon's agreement that such spectators would take the apparitions and voices as their only reality. If one of them were unchained and forced to turn, seeing the firelight, and then dragged outside the cave, that former prisoner would resist, yet eventually realize the truth through philosophical reasoning.

One might use such sunny idealism, outside the cave, to question the apparent materialism of neuroscience and its brain–mind explorations.[2] But this chapter takes a more interdisciplinary approach. It re(in)spects the ancient Platonic parable, along with various social science and neuroscience views, through theatrical lenses, to explore new media dangers.

In the ancient text, Socrates directs Glaucon's inner mental theater (and the reader's) to imagine how the freed prisoner in the cave, upon turning around, would be pained by the firelight, at first unable to see the objects creating the shadows. If dragged outside the cave, the former prisoner would be even more pained by the sunlight, seeing only shadows and reflections, but eventually perceiving the stars at night and then daytime things. If that person returned to the cave and tried to liberate others, he (or she) might be mocked or killed, according to the character of Socrates, given voice by Plato. Ironically, the real Socrates was sentenced to death in Athens in 399 BC, two decades prior to Plato's *Republic*, for corrupting the youth with such ideas, which he gained through his own higher-order, sunlit consciousness (and daimonic inspiration). But if we go deeper into his cave, exploring our developmental, ancestral, and neural heritage, what can we see regarding current screen habits and copycat monsters? Specifically, how do mass shootings in the United States, now under the lens of mimetic studies,[3] reflect *melodramatic* temptations from such inherited fissures (and tragic flaws) of the human mind? How do they involve paranoid-schizoid and depressive-integrative, mimetic and mythic, inner to outer theater networks, with cave shadows rationalizing violence through predatory, heroic, victim-vengeance projections?

Develop-mental

Each of us is born prematurely, with about half the maturity of other apes, due to our mother's upright stance and our genetically enlarged brains. We experience a fundamental trauma in leaving the warm, wet cave of the womb and being thrust into cold, bright shapes and sounds. Initially, we are unable to perceive and interact with things as recognizable objects. We cry for the comfort of touch, food, and cleanliness—not yet understanding our difference from those who hold, feed, and clean us, or why the shifting sensations are painful or pleasurable. (My first child had colic, so I remember that mystery from the other side.) In Melanie

Klein's psychoanalytic theory, we swing from *paranoid terror*, at being consumed by the womb or breast, to *schizoid ecstasy* at feeding from the maternal body, which seems to be an extension of our own, yet sometimes is lost, eventually developing a *depressive integration* of anxious object relations.

We each develop personal *desires* for lost objects, as psychoanalyst Jacques Lacan theorized, with remnant animal instincts refashioned as human *drives*. This involves *real* losses (and lack of being) with *imaginary* substitutes and *symbolic* meanings, plus fantasies around them. These dimensions are exemplified by the child's "mirror stage," with imaginary self-recognition, yet real alienation (extended by videogames and social media). Eventually, a framework for mirror stage mimesis, the Father's Name/No, produces symbolic separation from the primary caregiver as (m)Other, through mythic meanings and sacrificial orders (also extended by current media). We develop ways of managing the *terrors of mortality*, as existential loss and alienation, with cultural values, group identifications, and self-esteem, or risky behaviors in defensive denial, according to anthropologist Ernest Becker (1973) and "Terror Management Theory." Yet this is set up, early in life, by our *attachment* to primary caregivers, as (1) securely attuned, (2) anxious, (3) avoidant, or (4) a disorganized mix, in the "Attachment Theory" research of psychiatrist John Bowlby and psychologist Mary Ainsworth. Such developments also involve, according to psychoanalyst D. W. Winnicott, *transitional objects* (such as toys or today's screens), which make us feel playfully connected to primal sources of nurturing and creativity, from childhood onward.

Like Plato's unchained prisoner encountering the firelit imaginary and sunlit symbolic realms as initially fragmentary, but eventually coherent, this organizing of a "phantom ego" (Lawtoo 2013) happens gradually in the first year of life. It develops through cultural frameworks of a more interdependent or independent identity, in many mirroring interactions of touch, sound, sight, and other senses with primary caregivers and the family (or screen) environment, as extended cave-womb. Each of us passes through, yet continues to bear the real, imaginary, and symbolic dimensions of Plato's allegory: (1) cave shadows of lost object relations, (2) fragmentary yet reforming fire-illusions in mirror stage reflections, and (3) starry or sunlit ideals as cultural reality frames. With alienated, meaning-seeking identities, *conflicts* arise between people and groups, through mimetic–mythic rivalries about different terror management defenses, ego attachments, and transitional objects or territories. This produces melodramatic, hero–victim–villain projections in religions, politics, and gaming, sometimes with spillover effects of real-life violence.

Ancestral

According to cognitive anthropologist Merlin Donald, our ancestors shifted from the episodic stage of animal awareness to the "mimetic stage" of early
hominins, such as *Homo erectus*, about two million years ago (2001, 260). This
involved a greater kinesthetic awareness, with tonal prosody, "playacting, body
language, precise imitation, and gesture" (261). It is evidenced by increased
brain size, stone tool making, big game hunting, a more group-oriented life, and
thus "a cultural strategy for remembering and problem-solving," unlike earlier
Australopithecines, who were "immersed in a stream of raw experience" (120),
akin to Plato's shadow-play prisoners.

Starting about a half million years ago, *Homo sapiens* developed a further
"mythic stage," building on the prior ones, with oral storytelling, "mimetic ritual," narrative thought, and a "framework of governance" (Donald 2001, 260).
The archeological evidence includes vocal tract changes, more sophisticated
tools, elaborate graves, complex dwellings, "quasi-symbolic artifacts, and simple
musical instruments" (261–262). By 300 to 400 thousand years ago, humans
were using fire to warm themselves and cook food; by 100 to 200 thousand,
they were decorating themselves with pigments and beads (Fuentes 2019, 92).
Thus, our ancestors developed from the apparent real of episodic shadow-stream
immersion to imaginary mimetic playacting (as with Plato's firelight puppetry
awareness) to symbolic languages across the globe (as with the former prisoner's
sunlit, yet starry eyed, ideal truths).

Approximately 40 thousand years ago, humans started the current "theoretic stage," with the "externalization of memory," fantasy, and reality-making
through technological devices (Donald 2001, 262). But with evermore "powerful external symbolic devices to store and retrieve cultural knowledge," a new
danger evolved, especially in recent decades. With our mass and social media
screens, there is a "Trojan Horse" potential, which "invades the innermost personal spaces of the human mind" (316). Thus, Plato's enchanting cave shadows
return (with Lacanian mirrors) in our megaplex cinema, boob-tube TV, laptop
screen, virtual-reality videogame, cellphone fetish, selfie posting, Facebook liking, TikTok bingeing, global streaming culture. This theoretically shared mem-
ory/fantasy field, as external yet internalized cave-womb shadow show, mixing
truthful insights with conspiracy theories, "can play our cognitive instrument,
directing our minds" (316), as Donald put it two decades ago.

Our theoretical culture continues to build on the prior stages, while each of us recapitulates them developmentally. In our body-brains there is an episodic "stream of discrete events," a mimetic matrix as "the theatrical domain of human life," and a linguistic matrix of "knowledge representation, encoding countless stories, myths, and traditions" (Donald 2001, 321). Also, an external matrix between us, with "powerful media for formulating and displaying knowledge," involves "institutions, governments, and formal symbolic systems of thought" (321). As infants, we start in the episodic stage, but soon develop a mimetic stage of mirroring family theatricality, with an awareness of one's image around year one and of others' intentions and knowledge by year four. We build on that with language learning, creating, and sharing (mythic stage), while the theoretic matrix invades the prior primate–human matrices of our brains, especially through today's screen images and ideals.

Early evidence of the theoretic stage appears in prehistoric, Upper Paleolithic cave art, from 45 to 11 thousand years ago, etched in stone walls, drawn with black charcoal, or painted with red and yellow ochre at many sites in Indonesia, Australia, and Europe. (Evidence of a Middle Paleolithic flute in a Slovenian cave, made by Neanderthals from a small bear bone, 50 or 60 thousand years ago, might push the start of the theoretic stage even earlier.) According to anthropologist David Lewis-Williams (2002), the abstract symbols, animal figures, and animal–human hybrids of prehistoric cave art reflect stages of altered consciousness, which lab experiments re-create today as an inner-theater vortex, akin to walking or crawling through the deep passages of such caves. In these hallucinatory stages, we might also see a return to prior ancestral matrices, as if re-entering Plato's cave, from symbolic light to image-making fire and real-loss shadows.

Indeed, Lewis-Williams theorizes that stone walls, in the deep darkness of firelit caves, became "membranes" to a spirit realm for our ancestors, whose brains projected their hallucinations onto the natural shapes and cracks. They then painted what was perceived as real, yet imaginary, and became symbolic, especially when shared with others—akin to African Bushmen more recently, with their rock art as "a stage set awaiting the shamanic actors" (Lewis-Williams 2002, 35). Returning to the surface where they lived, gathering food and hunting, stone age shamans and their tribes brought the cave shadows with them as fiery emotions and sunlight ideals, continuing such communion with animal and ancestral spirits, if they were like today's hunter-gatherers, who inspired Lewis-Williams's comparisons. Thus, the cave shadows of our Ice Age ancestors became a supernatural reality in the sunlight (*contra* Plato), enabling their survival and genetic/cultural reproduction. But a tragic flaw developed with such theoretic (Trojan Horse) projections, which we inherit in our neural and interpersonal theaters, seeking meaningful lives through *heroic* illusions.

Zombie Scene-Setters, Puppeteers, and Mirrors

Cognition involves prediction and recognition, with current situations, past experiences, and future imaginings interacting through our "inner theater" networks. Our brains have billions more neurons at birth than later in life. Circuitry is "pruned" through experiences, with neurons that fire together wiring together and those not used dying off. This organizes each brain uniquely, at the finest level, with neural circuitry as a basic form of unconscious memory. Yet at another level of detail, the structures we have in common, with each brain's 87 billion neurons and 100 trillion connections, derive from the genetic inheritance of our human and animal ancestors, as a much longer, unconscious memory of motivational and functional circuits. They are also shaped by different cultures and subcultures, as we interact in that environment, from family and peers to schools, playgrounds, and workplaces, with current mass and social (Trojan Horse) media "directing" our cognitive instrument.

More than 90 percent of brain activity is unconscious, beyond the one to four distinct items (or framed chunks) of consciousness in the inner theater's "spotlight," and about seven more on its "stage" of working memory, readily accessible as "actors" competing and cooperating for such presence.[4] Conscious processes are serial, consistent, slower, and more error-ridden, with limited capacity, yet with a greater ability to interrelate conscious and unconscious framing contexts (Baars 2019, 205). Unconscious processors operate in parallel, with more diversity, are faster at their distinct tasks, and less error prone. Together, they have greater capacity, yet each has a limited range over time. An "actor" of consciousness "can call out a question to the audience [of unconscious processors], which may then respond with specialized knowledge" (109).

Conscious events include retrieved, newly generated, and automatic yet challenged images in all sensory modalities, plus "inner speech," which also involves "currently rehearsed words" on the stage area of working memory (Baars 2019, 146). Unconscious events include unretrieved memories, automatized images, and unrehearsed words. Indeed, "inner speech maintains a running commentary about our experiences, feelings, and relationships with others," regarding past events and future plans (149).

Revising Plato's allegory through cognitive science, the brain's inner theater involves: (1) unconscious backstage shadows of diverse parallel feelings and other contents, (2) preconscious stage-edge firelight with puppets of working (or "Short Term") memory, and (3) conscious spotlight-focused sunlit actors, which are interrelated through a serial inner-speech narrative. (Notice that Plato's sunny idealism is hereby shadowed and firelit by the brain's evolving, real–imaginary–symbolic, episodic–mimetic–mythic dimensions.) This inner theatricality also includes rehearsed speech on the working memory stage and "feelings of knowing" even without recall (Baars 2019, 613–615). Thus, a "narrative interpreter" in the left frontal cortex, as "observing self," along with an "inarticulate *self*" in the right, forms the "framework for conscious experience" (107).

Exemplifying the unconscious "scene setters" staging a conscious sense of self (Baars 2019, 101), blind-spots in each eye, where it connects to the optic nerve, are continually filled in, as the eyes move in jerky saccades, with only the foveal center of vision in focus—although a full visual field is perceived.[5] The circuitry of vision runs through the optic nerve to the occipital lobe at the back of the brain, where about thirty different areas interpret various aspects of vision, such as spatial edge detection, complex patterns, orientation, color, speed, direction, contour, and the body's own motion. They then project signals along several pathways to further "association areas" in the middle of the brain, which use prediction and recognition circuits from memories, anticipating and checking what is seen (as expected, new, or hallucinatory) and how the body interacts with it.

People with damage in the ventral (lower) "what" pathway can still touch a point of light on a wall, or put a letter in a mailbox slit, through the dorsal (upper) "how" pathway, without being able to see consciously. This phenomenon is called "blindsight" (Ramachandran 2011, 62–64). It demonstrates the unconscious operation of the "how" pathways (and association areas) as scene-setters in all of us, along with the many partial "what" signals, which become organized into conscious perception and action. According to neurologist V. S. Ramachandran, there is also a "salient" pathway for emotionally valuable perceptions, "such as eyes, food, facial expressions, and animate motion" (65), with quick reactions to them, adding to the unconscious staging of conscious awareness and motivations.

Like Plato's initially freed prisoner, at the fire and then in sunlight, confused but becoming used to new perceptions, each of us makes holistic, focal sense of fragmented aspects of perceived images and interactions with the world. But the cave of shadow-play feelings and firelit imagery comes with us into the light, with the unconscious *salient* and *how* circuits staging the *what* of vision, plus other senses. Through sensorimotor stimuli, translated into numerous, partial, neural signals, and then organized into narrative imagery, which is also "reality" tested, our unconscious scene-setters stage a full shadow-puppet, yet apparently sunlit movie in consciousness. According to neuroscientist Antonio Damasio, this involves dispositional "puppeteers" in parietal, temporal, and frontal areas of the brain, producing perceptions and ideas, from deep goal and conceptual contexts to the "image spaces" of occipital, temporal, and sensorimotor association areas.[6] In Plato's allegorical terms, we take the shadow-play with us, but alter it, from the womb (or nightly dreams) to later waking life, through our inherited brain systems and our current cultural environment. This includes mass and social media, with news and fiction (or conspiracy theories)—as the sunlit realm again becomes an episodic, mimetic, mythic, and theoretic Trojan Horse space with cave fire.

The unconscious "zombie" aspect of dispositional puppeteers appears in some of us with blindsight, sleepwalking, or alien hand syndrome.[7] In the latter case, damage to the anterior cingulate cortex (ACC), a gear shifting network between the prefrontal cortex and central subcortical areas, produces the strange effect of the patient's hand reaching out to do things against her will, while the other hand fights to control it. Such problems are extraordinary. Yet zombie circuits, as unconscious scene-setters, influence the staging of a phantom ego consciousness in all of us.

The zombie circuits of our phantom egos can be considered more collectively through literary anthropologist René Girard's theories, from the 1970s, of mimetic desire (related to Lacan's earlier idea that one's desire is the desire of the Other).[8] According to Girard, as clarified late in his career and developed further by others, mimetic desire can sometimes be positive and creative.[9] But Girard emphasized that *rivalry* often emerges through *liking* between people and groups, with attraction, imitation, and bonding, which may twist into the opposite, a desire to *distinguish* one's self, through what Freud called the "narcissism of small differences." With groups, this also relates to what anthropologists call "schismogenesis," as members cooperate through competition against outsiders, distinguishing their identity (Graeber and Wengrow 2021). According to Girard, mimetic desire, admiration, and liking ironically become envy, rivalry, and scapegoating—with the social drama of "reciprocal violence" between groups (or in family and workplace feuds) potentially resolved by focusing enmity on an innocent person, who is not a member of either group.[10]

Research on *mirror neurons* reveals how zombie puppeteers and phantom egos interact, within and between brains, through mimetic desire. These brain cells fire when watching someone perform salient actions, or hearing sounds for them, or seeing objects related to them, or reading about them—and also fire when the viewer/listener/reader performs the same action.[11] The spectator's mirror neuron system thus increases empathy, especially with artworks, "automatically simulating the emotional expression, the movement or even the implied movement within the representation" (Freedberg and Gallese 2007, 197). The brain sends signals to mimic (e)motions seen and heard, as spontaneous, staged, or read, while other neural circuits block the automatic mimicry from being fully acted out.

Experiments find that mirror neuron areas are more active in dancers watching videos of a dance style from their own "motor repertoire" than from others (Calvo-Merino et al. 2005). Mirror neurons also relate to "emotion synchrony" through shared facial and bodily expressions, which involves the power "to *manipulate* the internal states and behavior of others" (Harris 2018, 257–261). Thus, personal memories and physical experiences increase the salient, inner-theater mimicry in all of us and its potential for outward, emotional, shared expressions "in service of social goals." Yet how do such mimetic mechanisms, with zombie circuits, phantom-ego pathologies, and intersubjective mirrors, involve emotional drives and inner/outer theater networks, especially with mass, social media monsters?

Animal-Human Drives of Inner-Theater Shadows, Fire, and Sunlight

Remnant instincts inherited from our animal ancestors and transformed by various human cultures extend from primary to complex social emotions and values, motivating mimetic and mythic, creative and destructive actions, through our inner-theater puppetry and theoretic Trojan Horse technologies. Most basic to all of life are the drives of competition and cooperation, through the genetics of survival and reproduction. The *survival* drive is felt in desires and fears, especially through ego and group pride or conflicts, as courage or anxiety, with moral rewards and punishments. The *reproduction* drive is felt with love and lust, through cooperative legacies even beyond one's lifetime, involving friendship or greed, toward beliefs and rituals, religious and secular.[12]

Building on those basic drives, we share with many animal species: *territoriality* as a form of competition and cooperation, protecting or expanding survival and reproduction. Human extensions of ego and group territoriality involve feelings of security or rage, especially through border trading or wars, with nostalgia for one's homeland and vengeance for historical (yet mythic) victimization, sometimes focused on sacred sites as sanctuaries. Humans also share with mammals the *nurturing-care* drive, building on survival, reproduction, and territoriality. Yet this is reshaped in each person by beneficial and traumatic experiences of mother–infant attachment, through feelings of sympathy—or grief and panic in separation, at the infant's loss of maternal care, with seeking and cries, then depressive withdrawal for safety, as in the related behavior of rat pups when the mother is missing.[13] Later in life, such sympathy or panic may involve self-sacrifice or transitional object attachments (from toys and handheld screens to memorabilia, cars, and collectibles) with complex feelings of kinship, reciprocal altruism, and consumerism—sometimes in the staging of violent acts through group identifications. Care also becomes violent through the western heritage of Roman law, with "family" related to the Latin *famulus* (house slave) and *paterfamilias* (patriarchal head of the house), while "dominate" relates to *domus* (household) and *dominium* (power over property), as anthropologists have pointed out.[14]

Humans share with social animals, especially primates, the *alliance-hierarchy* drive, often felt as mimetic fairness or rivalry, as shown in experiments with capuchin monkeys, who reject cucumber slices by throwing them back if a neighbor is given more delicious grapes for the same task.[15] With humans this extends to laws and rulers, in complex emotions of honor, awe, and envy, plus moral devotion. Throughout the millennia of patriarchal "civilization," males have specialized in the alliance-hierarchy and territoriality drives, although matriarchies existed across the globe, with remnants today, according to some researchers.[16] Females are biologically equipped for the physical care of children, with reproduction in the womb and nurturing at the breast, but in various cultures multiple parents and parenting styles are possible, involving men as nurturers also.[17]

Many mammal species exhibit another drive at a young age, competitive and cooperative *play*, practicing survival, reproduction, territoriality, care, and alliance-hierarchy skills. Yet humans extend playfulness far into adulthood, with emotions of joy-surprise or mischief, through organized sports, creative art-works, and multiple media, involving complex emotions of freedom and rebel-lion, sometimes with a sense of spiritual powers. According to neuro-psychoana-lyst Mark Solms (2021), play "hovers, as it were, between all the other instinctual emotions—trying them out and learning their limits" (119). Play, with its "as if" quality, may thus be a bridge from animal to human consciousness: "a biological precursor of thinking in general (i.e. of all virtual versus real action) and the whole of cultural life" (120, 234). The shadowy figures, fiery passions, and sunlit ideals of play reprogram other drives, especially through theoretic Trojan Horse influences, in our mass social media, virtual and real worlds.

Primates spend as much as 20 percent of their waking hours grooming one another, parting the hair and touching the skin of a fellow troop member, pick-ing out and eating insects. This increases cleanliness, belonging, and reciproca-tion, leading to more food sharing and sex between mutual groomers, some-times using playful trickery to avoid the alpha male's hierarchic and territorial control. Humans, however, have converted such *belonging-grooming* massages (and messages) into culturally legitimate or secretive acts, along with *gossip* as a verbal extension of ingroup identifications and personal bonds.[18] This relates to dramatic news and entertainment media, sometimes focusing mimetic rivalry into scapegoating vengeance. Belonging–grooming–gossip, building on care, alliance, and play, involves trust in comrades or disgust at aliens, with emotions of liking (through endorphin pleasure and oxytocin bonding), shame, or guilt, toward *melodramatic* ideologies of good and evil.

The most distinctive human drive is *seeking immortality*, which transforms animal foraging for survival, with *meaning and purpose* beyond loss, as hope emerges from grief, through stories about the past and future (with dopamine anticipation/reward circuits). Humans find symbolic meaning, despite real and imaginary mourning, through a sense of metaphysical purpose in mortality and other ills, producing optimistic gratitude toward life itself or religious figures. And yet, belonging–grooming–gossip and metaphysical seeking drives can turn into ideologies of mimetic–mythic, sacrificial bonding, with group demands, collective conspiracy theories, and hate-mongering leaders, who increase their power by stressing outgroup threats—in the "melodramatics of the paranoid style" (Melley 2021, 59).

The left cortex of the human brain has developed specialized functions of symbolic narrative verbalizing, abstract analysis, and focal control, with what might be termed, regarding the inner theater's staging of consciousness, *script-writer/critic* networks.[19] These evolved from predatory, objectifying, focused functions of the left hemisphere in many vertebrates, including birds and toads, compared with prey-wary, mating, and broad awareness functions of the right.[20] In humans, left-cortical, symbolic, *scriptwriter/critic* networks *interpret*, through specific cultural frameworks, the emotional drives of territoriality, alliance-hierarchy, play, grooming-gossip, and seeking immortality, which also involve subcortical affect signals and right-cortical imagery. It is not a matter of more left or right "brained" people. But with political melodramas, online conspiracy theories, and related real-life violence, how do *rationalizing* ego/group ideals filter *holistic* world views, between left and right cortical networks, as various inner-theater elements stage self and Otherness through animal–human, mimetic–mythic drives?

Reentering Plato's cave from the sunlit surface of mythic, more left-cortical functions, we can see the puppets in firelight as reflecting mimetic, right-cortical *mime-improviser/scene-designer* networks. Right-cortical (hemispheric) characteristics involve care, cooperation, and more unconscious socio-environmental influences, through intuitive emotions, via limbic and subcortical ties. Thus, the right hemisphere includes a Devil's Advocate anomaly detector, often filtered by left-cortical beliefs, competitiveness, conscious agency, analytical thinking, and rule-based, orthodox ideas.[21] With verbal language hubs in the left-cortex (although new metaphors and prosody involve image circuitry in the right), the *scriptwriter/critic* specializes in self-referential certainty, as thing and machine oriented, even toward the virtual and unrealistic. The right-cortical *mime-improviser/designer* is other-engaged and empathic toward the living world, through responsibility, shame, and guilt. It is also more realistic. Left-cortical aspects of self–other consciousness are more optimistic, but involve anger and *projections* onto others, while right-cortical are more melancholic, yet *sensitive* to change. These characteristics can also be seen in Plato's metaphysical idealism vis-à-vis recent philosophers of "inclination" (Cavarero 2016; Lawtoo 2022, 70–74). But there are subcortical and limbic (temporal-lobe) networks with key theatrical aspects as well.

Baars uses the term "scene setters" for unconscious processors that frame consciousness and "audience" for ones that it asks questions of. Adjusting the first term via affective neuroscience (Panksepp 1998), subcortical drive-emotion circuits could be considered as *stagehands*, with their ties to the right (more so) and left cortex, in the staging of Other and self consciousness. Such *stagehands* are mostly supportive in the homeostatic regulation of bodily systems, yet may also become trickster-like, particularly with allostatic social relations. As Baars suggests, we might consider the temporal lobe memory system (especially the hippocampus) on each side of the brain as a mostly darkened *audience*,[22] with intuitive emotional circuits, particularly disgust (insula) and anger (amygdala) more on the left,[23] plus various other emotions, such as fear and sadness, on the right.

An inner *actor* might be seen in the neural network mapped by Matthew Lieberman (2013), with a key hub in the medial prefrontal cortex (MPFC), when brain-scan subjects were asked to think of aspects about themselves that others do not know. Focusing attention on one's hidden self may shift the spotlight toward this inner *actor*, briefly staging it, even as it involves many unconscious frames, deeply influenced by bottom-up, motivational, emotional *stagehands* and memorial, intuitive *audience* members. Using terms from Plato's allegory, the freed-prisoner awareness of internal fire-puppetry involves an *actor* self, while sunlit performances outside the brain-body cave involve a *character* self. But these still include the inner theater's shadow-maker *stagehands* and chained *audience*, with shadows also projected outside the cave.

What I am calling the inner *character* network, as presentation of self to others in everyday life[24], has been mapped by Lieberman with hubs in the lateral prefrontal cortex (LPFC) on the sides of the forehead, by asking subjects to look at themselves in a mirror. (This may involve more scripted functions on the left and mimetic on the right, regarding various left-cortical *scriptwriter/critic* and right-cortical *improviser/designer* networks.) The Theory of Mind network, or inner *director* (as I call it), with subjects' ideas of how others view them, is centered in the dorsomedial prefrontal cortex (DMPFC), just above the MPFC, between the eyes. The inner *stage manager*, monitoring one's own behavior, with subcortical *stagehand* emotions and temporal-lobe *audience* memories, has its hub in the ventromedial prefrontal cortex (VMPFC), below the MPFC. (It also includes the anterior cingulate cortex, mentioned above regarding alien hand syndrome.) These various aspects of self and Otherness in the inner theater might be considered as further permutations of Plato's enchained prisoner shadow-play, freed prisoner fire-puppetry, and sunlit seeing with episodic stream-monitoring *stage manager*, mimetic *actor*, and mythic *character* vis-à-vis *director* networks. But how do such inner theater functions relate to the theoretic, Trojan Horse devices of mass and social media, producing collective, shadow-play "likes," as fetishes and addictions, with periodic copycat violence?

Trojan Horses or Tragic Catharsis

According to Baars, a conscious event can alter the scene-setter frames and "shape future conscious events without itself being conscious" again (2019, 343). Hence, the "more we are exposed to an extreme belief, the less extreme it seems, while the perceived norm will shift toward the extreme" (359). Psychological experiments show that people can be motivated by unconscious processors to perform a specific action, such as picking a consumer item, and they will give a different reason, rationalizing the choice afterward "with an air of conviction" (491). More specifically, Lieberman's brain mapping experiments with young adults found a "Trojan horse self" in the MPFC *actor* network. If that circuitry was activated by a message to quit smoking or use sunscreen, it predicted subjects' later performances better than their own reported "beliefs and intentions" (2013, 198–200). This showed that the Other's influence altered the private sense of self, like the Greek soldiers sneaking inside the walls of Troy. Thus, there is increasing evidence of the Trojan Horse effect that Donald theorized, as current theoretic media "play" our cognitive instrument, directing our minds.

Research on "mortality salience" in Terror Management Theory has shown that reminding people of death increases "worldview defense" and pursuit of self-esteem, with stronger attitudes of punishing criminals (in judges deciding bail amounts), rewarding heroes, and valuing symbols such as the crucifix and American flag (Schimel et al. 2019, 4–5). Such group and ego defensiveness correlates with activity between the temporal lobe (amygdala) and neocortex (anterior cingulate), including the left and right ventrolateral prefrontal cortex, for worldview maintenance and emotion regulation, plus VMPFC self-concepts (Quirin et al. 2019, 350–353), as inner *audience, character,* and *stage manager*. Various experiments found that death reminders increase ingroup liking and outgroup animosity, regarding religion, nationality, and race, even to the point of "actual aggression against worldview violators" or verbal support for "pro-martyrdom" causes and "extreme military actions" (Schimel et al. 2019, 6–7), such as using nuclear weapons and pre-emptive strikes against threatening nations. Another experiment found that subjects with low "trait empathy" became less forgiving toward outgroup members than ingroup, when given mortality reminders, yet those with high trait empathy were forgiving toward both (8). Thus, people with prosocial values tied to their self-esteem, or primed to remember them, showed increased environmental concern and intention to help others—when reminded of death (9). However, mortality salience may encourage self-esteem attitudes that increase the risk of death, including "suicidal martyrdom" to gain "symbolic immortality" (9–10).

Personal and intergroup conflicts can be creative through cooperative competition, as with sports or drama onstage and onscreen. But peers or political leaders may push a person's cognitive frames, as consciousness scene-setters, toward mortality fears and specific threats. This can have rippling inner- and inter-theatrical effects, especially through current mass and social media, with the paranoid style of conspiracy theories. Playfulness as the hinge between basic (survival, reproduction, territoriality, care, hierarchy) and more distinctly human drives (grooming-gossip and meaning-purpose) may then develop toward melodramatic conflicts of victims, villains, and warped heroes.

For example, the 1999 Columbine High School shooters in Colorado, two heavily armed male teens who became famous in the news media for killing twelve classmates and one teacher (plus themselves), made several videos prior to that event, with the help of another student who later said: "They always wanted to be the intimidators, the guys out to get the bad guys" (Alvarez 1999). They were well known in school for admiring Hitler and they picked his birthday for the shooting (Duggan et al. 1999). One of them, the son of an Air Force pilot, yet rejected by the Marine Corps, created new levels of a first-person-shooter videogame, *Doom*, and shared them online, with numerous monsters to fight, for virtual survival and reproduction, territoriality and hierarchy, in anxious/avoidant attachment fantasies. (The U.S. Marines used a modified version of *Doom* to train troops in the late 1990s.) Together, the teens insulted Jewish, Hispanic, and African Americans, but especially hated evangelical Christians and popular athletes at school.[25] They made a video wearing black trench coats, as "Hitmen for Hire," with guns as transitional object props and friends acting as bad-guy "jocks" (athletes) shot by them, falling and bleeding fake blood. It was a rehearsal for committing such violence in real life, when they wore the same costumes and yelled at jocks to stand up and be killed, showing their mimetic rivalry as perverse melodramatic heroism, in paranoid-schizoid terror-ecstasy. This mass shooting inspired other young men toward copycat violence, including a 23-year-old Asian-American who killed thirty-two people at Virginia Tech University in 2007, after making a video that referred to the Columbine shooters as "martyrs."[26] Their sacrifice of others also inspired several fiction films and a 2005 videogame, *Super Columbine Massacre RPG!*, with players as the shooters and flashbacks shown to earlier motivations, such as being bullied.[27]

Reportedly, the teenager who killed 19 children and two teachers at Robb Elementary School in Uvalde, Texas, in May 2022, in the classroom where he had been a student, got angry while playing an online videogame, shortly before the shooting, and suggested he would "shoot up a school" (Propper 2022). He was also called "school shooter" by coworkers, prior to the act (Bogel-Burroughs 2022). The mass shooter in Highland Park, near Chicago, in July 2022, who killed seven people at an Independence Day parade, previously made videos that he posted in forums, "glorifying and fantasizing about violence," according to Jared Holt, a researcher on domestic extremism (Sullivan 2022). Cooperating and competing playfully, he was seeking "perverted clout among other people in the same online spaces," through like-minded performers who "pride themselves on this fetishization of violence, of being as offensive as humanly possible" (ibid.).

Mass shooters, nearly always male, show a consistent pattern: early childhood trauma, such as home violence, sexual assault, parental suicide, or extreme bullying, with suicidal self-hatred turned *outward*, against a rival group, through a quest for fame (Peterson and Densley 2021). Inner-theater shame is projected as melodramatic blame upon "jocks" or others. Thus, a severely alienated Devil's Advocate *improviser/designer* re-identifies as a predatory *scriptwriter/critic*, with twisted scene-setter frames, in the staging of self as perverse hero, objectifying others, through melodramatic mimesis, subcultural myth, and Trojan Horse media. According to the Gun Violence Archive online, there were 656 mass shooting incidents (at least four victims killed or injured) in the United States in 2023, an average of 1.8 per day, after 646 in 2022, 689 in 2021, and 610 in 2020.

Such terrible examples of creative destruction, turning survival-reproductive play into video-real violence, relate to the danger that Plato saw in art and artists, rejecting them from his ideal republic, especially their mythic mimetic "pathos" onstage, as falsifying truth and misleading others, like the "shadow-play" and its puppeteers in the cave (Lawtoo 2023b, 89–115). Apparently, making videos that acted out violence and sharing them with schoolmates in the 1990s, or playing violent videogames and sharing videos with a vast online audience in the twenty-first century, did not purge the melodramatic impulses of existential terror management for male teens who became mass shooters, though it might have been a plea for help. In some cases, it was a way to rehearse, gather audience support, and perform vengeful violence, as worldview defensiveness and self-esteem building. In each teen, it involved left-cortical predatory *scriptwriter/critic* and right-cortical anxious *improviser/designer*, along with subcortical trickster *stagehand* and temporal-lobe memorial *audience* networks, objectifying perceived bad guys or random people as villainous outgroup threats. This perversion of rational idealism not only projects melodramatic cave shadows in current media, but also onto real-life scapegoats. However, the melodramatic impulse to save victims from a villain can also stage positive heroes, as with Riley Howell (a 21-year-old *Star Wars* fan) sacrificing his life to stop a classroom shooter by running toward that fellow student, who shot him in the body and head, but then stopped shooting, in April 2019 at the University of North Carolina at Charlotte, the campus where I teach.

Plato's student, Aristotle, argued for the value of ancient tragedy (onstage or in reading) to evoke admiration, sympathy, and fear for complex heroes, yet also awareness of their errors, which cause suffering for many. This is unlike simplistic identifications evoked by melodramatic heroes on numerous screens today, through righteous vengeance objectifying villains as deserving violence. Ancient Greek theater was stylized with choral odes between episodes and males performing all roles while wearing masks. According to most extant scripts, violent acts were *not shown onstage*. They were heard offstage or described by a messenger, sometimes with a bloody mask or dead body revealed afterward (such as Oedipus's gouged eyes, Pentheus's decapitated head, or Medea's murdered children), emphasizing the tragic effects on various characters. And yet, even with direct spectacles of pleasurable violence in today's screen entertainments, tragicomic twists may challenge melodramatic identifications, rebalancing competition and cooperation, through hierarchy and territoriality, yet also care and play, in the viewer. Catharsis as clarifying such emotional drives (from *kathairô*, to wash) occurs through complex perspective changes,[28] in the left and right cortical "reappraisal" of ego and group phantoms, with VMPFC *stage manager* and amygdala *audience* "compassion" (Engen and Singer 2018, 176; Pizzato 2016). This depends on the artwork's plot/character twists with recognition moments (as Aristotle put it), along with verbal, scenic, and acoustic ironies, altering identifications. But it also depends on how we watch and later perform, and for whom, in our patho(-)logical pathways of hypermimetic, contagious attachments (Lawtoo 2023b), with sunlight, fire, and shadow-puppetry projections.

Notes

1   On the importance of Plato's cave allegory for mimetic studies from an evolutionary (Nietzschean) perspective, see Lawtoo 2022, 69–91; on the cave and media violence, see Lawtoo 2023b, 75–122.
2   Not all neuroscientists are materialists. See McGilchrist 2021.
3   See Lawtoo 2023b, 181–196.
4   See Baars 2019, 102–103, 140, 164, 394–395, 576.
5   See Ramachandran and Blakeslee 1998, 103–104.
6   See Damasio 2010, 140–141, 152, 189–190.

7   See Ramachandran 2011, 64, 287.
8   On Girard's debt to Lacan and Kojève's Hegelian dialectics of the "desire of the other," see Lawtoo 2013, 286.
9   See Redekop and Ryba 2014.
10   See Girard 1977, 52–55, 143.
11   See Corballis 2014, 62, and Iacoboni 2008, 6–7, 14.
12   See Pizzato 2024.
13   See Panksepp and Biven 2012, 100, 295–98.
14   See Graeber and Wengrow 2021, 510.
15   See de Waal 2006, 48.
16   See Goettner-Abendroth 2012.
17   See Hrdy 2009. See also Lawtoo 2022, 63–64, 72–73.
18   See Dunbar 2004.
19   See Pizzato 2019, 7–9.
20   See McGilchrist 2009, 25–28.
21   See McGilchrist 2009, for details in this paragraph on right and left hemisphere characteristics. See Ramachandran and Blakeslee 1998, 135-47, about the right as Devil's Advocate scout to the left as war-room general.
22   Baars 2019, 580, 625.
23   See Holtmann et al. 2020 and Siep et al. 2019.
24   On this, see Goffman 1959.
25   See Larkin 2007; "Trenchcoat" 1999.
26   See "Shooter" 2007.
27   On the relation between media violence, videogames, and mass-shootings, see also Lawtoo 2023b.
28   Cf. Lawtoo 2023a, especially 103–110, on catharsis as affective medical embodiment and purging through sacred music, according to Aristotle's *Politics*, yet involving "distance" with theater or reading in his *Poetics*. Using Nietzsche, Lawtoo critiques the idea of catharsis as "purging" the psyche or community, through emotional (unconscious memory) expression or violent (ritual scapegoat) expulsion—in Freud, Girard, and popular views of current screen media.

Bibliography

Alvarez, Maria (1999). "Violent Video Was Just a Dress Rehearsal." *New York Post*, 23 April.
Baars, Bernard J. (2019). *On Consciousness*. New York: Nautilus.
Becker, Ernest (1973). *The Denial of Death*. New York: Free Press.
Bogel-Burroughs, Nicholas (2022). "The Gunman in Uvalde Left Multiple Hints Before His Attack Began." *The New York Times*, 27 May.
Calvo-Merino, Beatriz, Daniel E. Glaser, Julie Grèzes, Richard E Passingham and Patrick Haggard (2005). "Action Observation and Acquired Motor Skills." *Cerebral Cortex* 15.8, 1243–1249.
Cavarero, Adriana (2016). *Inclinations*. Stanford: Stanford University Press.
Corballis, Michael C. (2014). *The Recursive Mind*. Princeton: Princeton University Press.
Damasio, Antonio (2010). *Self Comes to Mind*. New York: Pantheon.
de Waal, Frans (2006). *Primates and Philosophers*. Princeton: Princeton University Press.
Donald, Merlin (2001). *A Mind So Rare*. New York: Norton.

Duggan, Paul, Michael D. Shear, Michael and Marc Fisher (1999). "Shooter Pair Mixed Fantasy, Reality." *Washington Post*, 22 April.

Dunbar, Robin (2004). "Gossip in Evolutionary Perspective." *Review of General Psychology* 8.2, 100–110.

Engen, Haakon G., and Tania Singer (2018). "Fighting Fire with Fire," in *The Nature of Emotion*, ed. Andrew S. Fox, Regina C. Lapate, Alexander J. Shackman, Richard J. Davidson. Oxford: Oxford University Press, 173–177.

Freedberg, David, and Vittorio Gallese (2007). "Motion, Emotion and Empathy in Esthetic Experience." *Trends in Cognitive Sciences* 11.5, 197–203.

Fuentes, Augustín (2019). *Why We Believe*. New Haven: Yale University Press.

Girard, René (1977). *Violence and the Sacred*. Baltimore: Johns Hopkins University Press.

Goettner-Abendroth, Heide (2012). *Matriarchal Societies*. Bern: Peter Lang.

Goffman, Erving (1959). *The Presentation of Self in Everyday Life*. New York: Anchor.

Graeber, David, and David Wengrow (2021). *The Dawn of Everything*. New York: Farrar.

Harris, Lasana T. (2018). "Movement and Manipulation," in *The Nature of Emotion. Fundamental Questions*, eds. Andrew S. Fox, Regina C. Lapate, Alexander J. Shackman, Richard J. Davidson. Oxford: Oxford University Press, 257–261.

Holtmann, Olga, Maximilian Bruchmann, Constanze Mönig, Wolfram Schwindt, Nico Melzer, Wolfgang H. R. Miltner and Thomas Straube (2020). "Lateralized Deficits of Disgust Processing After Insula-Basal Ganglia Damage." *Frontiers in Psychology* 11.1429, 1–13.

Hrdy, Sarah Blaffer (2009). *Mothers and Others*. Cambridge, MA: Harvard University Press.

Iacoboni, Marco (2008). *Mirroring People*. New York: Farrar.

Larkin, Ralph W. (2007). *Comprehending Columbine*. Philadelphia: Temple University Press.

Lawtoo, Nidesh (2013). *The Phantom of the Ego: Modernism and the Mimetic Unconscious*. East Lansing: Michigan State University Press.

—— (2022). *Homo Mimeticus: A New Theory of Imitation*. Leuven: Leuven University Press.

—— (2023a). *Violence and the Oedipal Unconscious: vol. 1 The Catharsis Hypothesis*. East Lansing: Michigan State University Press.

—— (2023b). *Violence and the Mimetic Unconscious: vol. 2 The Affective Hypothesis*. East Lansing: Michigan State University Press.

Lewis-Williams, David (2002). *The Mind in the Cave*. London: Thames and Hudson.

Lieberman, Matthew D. (2013). *Social*. New York: Crown.

McGilchrist, Iain. (2009). *The Master and His Emissary*. New Haven: Yale University Press.

—— (2021). *The Matter with Things*, 2 vols. London: Perspectiva Press.

Melley, Timothy (2021). "The Melodramatic Mode in American Politics, and Other Varieties of Narrative Suspicion." *symplokē* 29.1–2, 57–74.

Panksepp, Jaak (1998). *Affective Neuroscience: The Foundations of Human and Animal Emotions*. Oxford: Oxford University Press.

Panksepp, Jaak, and Lucy Biven (2012). *The Archaeology of Mind*. New York: Norton.

Peterson, Jillian, and James Densley (2021). *The Violence Project*. New York: Abrams.

Pizzato, Mark (2016). *Beast-People Onscreen and in Your Brain*. Santa Barbara: Praeger.

—— (2019). *Mapping Global Theatre Histories*. London: Palgrave.

—— (2024). *European Churches and Chinese Temples as Neuro-Theatrical Sites*. London: Bloomsbury.

Propper, David (2022). "Texas Shooter May Have Revealed Sick Massacre Plan in Video Game Rant." *New York Post*, 26 May.

Quirin, Markus, Johannes Klackl and Eva Jonas (2019). "Existential Neuroscience," in *Handbook of Terror Management Theory*, ed. Clay Routledge and Matthew Vess. Cambridge: Academic Press, 347–367.

Ramachandran, Vilayanur S. (2011). *The Tell-Tale Brain*. New York: Norton.

Ramachandran, Vilayanur S., and Sandra Blakeslee (1998). *Phantoms in the Brain: Probing the Mysteries of the Human Mind*. New York: William Morrow.

Redekop, Vern Neufeld, and Thomas Ryba (eds.) (2014). *René Girard and Creative Mimesis*. Lanham, MD: Lexington Books.

Schimel, Jeff, Joseph Hayes and Michael Sharp (2019). "A Consideration of Three Critical Hypotheses," in *Handbook of Terror Management Theory*, eds. Clay Routledge and Matthew Vess. Cambridge: Academic Press, 1–30.

"Shooter" (2007). *CNN*, 18 April.

Siep, Nicolette, Franca Tonnaer, Vincent van de Ven, Arnoud Arntz, Adrian Raine and Maaike Cima (2019). "Anger Provocation Increases Limbic and Decreases Medial Prefrontal Cortex Connectivity with the Left Amygdala in Reactive Aggressive Violent Offenders." *Brain Imaging and Behavior* 13, 1311–1323.

Solms, Mark (2021). *The Hidden Spring*. New York: Norton.

Sullivan, Becky (2022). "Highland Park Suspect's Online History Reveals a Fascination with Violence." *National Public Radio*, 5 July.

"'Trenchcoat Mafia' was Well-Known at Columbine." (1999). *Pocono Record*, 22 April. https://www.poconorecord.com/story/news/1999/04/22/trenchcoat-mafia-was-well/51097379007/.

PART 2

THEORETICAL RE-TURNS TO HOMO MIMETICUS

CHAPTER 6

NIETZSCHE'S NIHILISM
AND MIMETIC STUDIES

Marina Garcia-Granero

It is uncontroversial to present Friedrich Nietzsche's diagnosis of nihilism as one of his most important legacies for contemporary thought. Among his ideas, the thought of the death of God has significantly impacted European culture; it also provokes vivid discussions within mimetic theory and is now under the lens of mimetic studies as well. Although Nietzsche was not the first thinker to speak of nihilism, and there is an important "prehistory" of nihilism crucial to understanding where his originality and contribution lie, he is responsible for formulating nihilism as a vital question in philosophy.

My goal is to provide an alternative, mimetic account of nihilism, starting from Nietzsche's texts, complementing them via the theoretical filter of mimesis and drawing on his reception within mimetic theory and legacy within mimetic studies. Indeed, Nietzsche is central to Girard's thinking, even if as antagonistic rivalry, as attested by Lawtoo's work (2024). He is also one of the most influential philosophical references to promote a mimetic re-turn internal to *homo mimeticus* and the emerging field of mimetic studies.[1]

The general goal of mimetic studies is to develop a new transdisciplinary theory of imitation that includes not only Girard but also other genealogical foundations, such as Nietzsche, among many other philosophical and literary sources, as attested by the diverse contributions to this volume. Methodologically speaking, mimetic studies has a problem-solving approach and pays attention to different disciplines (philosophy, aesthetics, anthropology, psychology, medical sciences, media studies, and so forth) relevant to the problem at hand, in this instance, the emergence of nihilism out of mimetic relations. As a result, new mimetic studies redraws the boundaries of subjectivity, aesthetics, and politics for contemporary times by adopting perspectival, immanent, and affective approaches.

The chapter furthers mimetic studies from the still underdeveloped problematic of nihilism. It aims to display the differences between, on the one hand, Girard's pathological reading of Nietzsche and, on the other, mimetic studies' focus on patho-logies. Mimetic studies, in fact, reads Nietzsche without unilaterally pathologizing his thoughts. Moreover, contrary to mimetic theory's *nihilistic* anxiety after the death of God, it comprehends nihilism as both a challenge and an opportunity to overturn transhistorical, totalizing hypotheses—which include not only the Christian-moral hypothesis but also Girard's transhistorical theory of mimesis.

The chapter will underline how this perspectival approach is a positive product of the phenomenon of nihilism, resulting in a primacy of immanence over transcendence, which appears as heavily eroded after the death of God. Mimetic behaviors are not imposed from the outside, as by gods, for example. Our human faculty to imitate is actually rooted in our human nature *tout court*, whose intrinsic mimetic logic justifies its designation as *homo mimeticus*, and, as we now know, has received empirical confirmation via the discoveries of mirror neurons in the 1990s and brain plasticity.[2] Contrary to mimetic theory's longing for transcendence, mimetic studies, then, remains rooted in material reality in connection to human and non-human beings, nature, and Earth. These material foundations are necessary to understand mimesis as "*conditio humana*" and to move beyond the traditional metaphysical conception of mimesis as a copy, representation, or adequation.[3] Lastly, this chapter addresses myth as the fundamental hermeneutic resource to respond to nihilism. In line with mimetic studies that have already stressed the centrality of mythic identification in the context of fascism (old and new),[4] I will analyze myth as an affective mechanism that ties humans to a shared belief for good and ill. As a result, the chapter will reveal the mimetic implications of Nietzsche's thoughts on nihilism for us nowadays and will outline nihilism as a Janus-faced mimetic problem manifesting both as a salvation and a threat.

The Different Levels and Meanings of Nihilism

Nietzsche's most extensive and systematic treatment of nihilism is a posthumous fragment from 1886 famously known as "Lenzer Heide" because of the location in Switzerland where it was written. Drawing on this crucial fragment, prominent Nietzsche scholar Paul van Tongeren (2018) argues that Nietzsche conceptualizes nihilism in at least three stages, each of which represents a particular meaning of nihilism. Temporally speaking, the absurdity and meaninglessness of life represents the first, initial stage whereas the protective structure—Christian ideals—is a second stage aiming to hide the tragic insight of life. Finally, the corrosion of those Christian ideals—the event also known as "the death of God"—represents the third stage. Therefore, to have a full understanding of nihilism, one must consider all the stages. Paul van Tongeren's interpretation provides a documented and ambitious account that rigorously ensembles the different meanings and layers of Nietzsche's vision of nihilism. Hence, his scholarship represents a solid, reliable foundation for us to build upon and further the dialogue between Nietzsche studies and mimetic studies.

We will start from the initial layer of nihilism and move from the bottom-up. First, nihilism-1 is the absolute lack of logic in the order of the world, and its paradigmatic form or manifestation is Greek pessimism—the original pessimism beyond good and evil, that is, before any consolatory, philosophical, or religious ideal is projected onto it. Nihilism-1 is the tragic experience of life, the sense of our insignificance in the context of radical becoming and passing away. The archaic (or pre-Platonic) Greeks are Nietzsche's paradigmatic model and example. Their strength lies in the fact that they not only endured the tragic experience but also desired it strongly "as a worthy foe against which it can test its strength and from which it intends to learn the meaning of fear" (Nietzsche 1999, 4) instead of fleeing from fear.

Second, nihilism-2 is the construction of "God," "Truth," "Being," and so on, as part of humanity's self-defense against nihilism-1. It is the history of European culture from Plato up to the nineteenth century, including Christian religion, democracy, scientific positivism, and romanticism. Paradigmatically, Christian religion succeeded in part because "it served the advocates of God to the extent that, despite suffering and evil, it let the world have the character of *perfection*—including "freedom"—and evil appeared full of sense" (Nietzsche 2010, 385).[5] Christianity provided meaning to suffering, to death, and to the tragic insight of life. Following van Tongeren's account, any ideal attempting to conceal that original nihilism will be considered nihilistic in this sense because all ideals, by definition, contain a negation of what they are opposed to: namely, a negation of the meaninglessness of the world or nihilism-1 (van Tongeren 2018, 76). Nietzsche's alternative is to embrace the innocence of becoming and a radically immanent standpoint that does not aim to impose an external, ideal perspective on life to life itself.

Such a quest for meaning is a parallel strategy, symptomatic of the same inability to endure or love life as it is. In the "Attempt at Self-Critique"—the prologue Nietzsche added to the second edition of *The Birth of Tragedy*, thirteen years after its original publication—he realizes that the very quest for meaning is intrinsically nihilistic; it is at the center of the problem and threatens to fulfill the same consoling and redemptive functions as Socratism, Christianity, Romanticism, or scientism. In that new prologue, he argues instead for "pessimism of strength" (Nietzsche 1999, 4), capable of affirming the absurd character of life and its inherent lack of meaning without resorting to the traditional, metaphysical-moral consolations. Nietzsche himself was guilty of pursuing a nihilistic ideal of life when he argued, in the first edition of the book, for a regeneration of German culture via Schopenhauer's philosophy and Wagner's music. Hence, in the "Attempt at a Self-Critique," he criticizes his past romantic quest to find meaning in life through art because he, in his youth, was not strong enough to endure the original meaninglessness of life.

Third, Nietzsche argues that Socratic philosophy and Christian morality inculcated truthfulness, and the longing for truth led to its corrosion and self-undermining manifesting in the event of the death of God (nihilism-3). The death of God is the corrosion and undermining of the meaning previously provided by different walls of protection against pessimism and absurdity.

Nihilism-2 had its condemnation inscribed for at least two reasons. The first reason is that Socratic philosophy and Christian morality inculcated truthfulness and the will-to-truth, which materialized, for instance, in the progressive development of modern science. The advances of evolutionism in the nineteenth century also led to the loss of authority of religion and morality, and therefore, to their corrosion and self-destruction. The very will-to-truth of nihilism-2 discovers the illusory nature of Good, Truth, and Beauty, which acted as walls of protection and prophylactic ideals against the insight of the original nihilism. The will-to-truth is what causes the corrosion of nihilism-2 toward nihilism-3.

The second reason is that nihilism-2 is a "physiological contradiction" in which life ideals deny life itself, and Europeans have been raised and educated with the predisposition to despise and devalue their existence.[6] This aporetic situation opens an abyss between life, action, and values. When ascetic values become the absolute judges over life, even life has to sacrifice itself, and these values are resented as unattainable and obsolete. For these two reasons, God is dead, "and we have killed him" (Nietzsche 2001, 120), which is what Nietzsche truly adds to the phrase "*Gott ist tot*" already pronounced by Hegel in *The Phenomenology of Spirit*.

An interesting detail contradicts superficial understandings of nihilism reduced to the idea that everything would be in vain. The generalized feeling that "everything is in vain" is nothing more than a pathological response to the death of God. In the Lenzer Heide fragment, Nietzsche writes that "*one* interpretation has collapsed, but because it was considered *the* interpretation," now the world in its entirety seems worthless. He lamented that extreme positions—by which he explicitly referred to "God"—are succeeded not by "moderate" positions but rather by "equally extreme but *opposite* ones" (Nietzsche 2010, 386). The interpretation opposite to the extreme idea that everything has meaning in the context of a Christian worldview and eschatology is the also extreme idea that nothing in the world has sense. When one interpretation falls, people become suspicious of every kind of meaning and perceive all their moral needs to be dissatisfied. But, Nietzsche contends, the loss of credibility of one interpretation is not reason enough to devalue the entire world. Therefore, the persistent prejudice according to which nihilism would mean that "everything is in vain" and "nothing in life matters" is incorrect in Nietzsche's account.

Instead of such an "extreme" conclusion, Nietzsche argues for a more "moderate" position. He argues that human power has grown to such an extent that people should no longer need consolatory processes to soothe despair. Thus, people could endure nihilism-1. Nowadays, given our position of power over nature, we should be able to live with a somewhat diminished sense of the value of human existence. While "weak people" long for a replacement of "the dead God" to provide said sense of value, powerful and strong people, Nietzsche writes in the Lenzer Heide note, can live with a certain degree of randomness and nonsense (Nietzsche 2005, 386–389). By strong and powerful, Nietzsche does not mean people with power over others but people strong enough to live without dogmas and to endure and affirm the inherent meaninglessness of the world as a positive aspect of life. It is positive, for instance, in the sense that before the death of God there was no space for pluralism. Even more so, our capacity to transcend ourselves and such an absurdity is what makes us human (Roodt 2018). The original lack of meaning in life will come out forever; what defines our essentially human experience is to try to make sense of it.

As we can see, in Nietzsche's account, nihilism designates simultaneously (1) a human condition, namely, the fundamental meaninglessness and absurdity of life, which cannot be overcome; (2) the nihilistic ideals created to protect humanity against that tragic insight of life; and (3) the event of the death of God, manifesting in a feeling of aimlessness after the values articulating a given culture—for example, Christian values—lose their authority. As a result, one can go backwards in time and conclude that nihilism is "(3) the decline of (2) the protective structure that was built to hide (1) the absurdity of life and world" (van Tongeren 2018, 100). As we will later see, René Girard's misinterpretation of nihilism and pathological reading of Nietzsche are largely due to reducing nihilism to the event of the death of God, thus oversimplifying Nietzsche's true insight into our human, mimetic, and nihilistic condition.

The Shadows of God, or the Aftermath of the Event

God is dead, but the shadows still survive. Even after God's death, there is still faith in the idea that truth will save us, and we need someone to provide that truth. The shadows of God designate the axiological structure of some values given to us because we want it that way. Even if the emancipation from authority represents one of the main motifs in nihilism, Nietzsche warned that the more frequent response to the event of the death of God is to look for another authority that speaks unconditionally and can order goals and tasks.[7] Thus, other instances come to occupy the position of the dead God. The shadows of God constitute a new danger of religions "without God," of worship without divinity. They provide an ideal, unique truth, points of reference, and moral appreciation, which replace the "dead God" and deliver the same security and comfort once provided by the metaphysical-moral hypothesis of God as the absolute and ultimate foundation of the world.

It is not a question of eliminating a belief in God but of becoming aware of this heteronomous habit of mimicry and that other instances occupy the position of the dead God and are in charge of answering the questions of where to and what for. Such powerful intrusion in the ego deprives the person of their autonomy and individuality. This constant anxiety of losing the "purpose" of "being" is symptomatic of a mimetic dispossession.[8] Therefore, nihilism will remain until we assume the burden of creating values, purpose, and meaning for our lives, previously delegated to (particular types of) theology.

Nihilism destroys the differences within a herd, a herd of obedient beings who incorporate a totalizing myth (such as Girard's anthropology) for the security promised to them, mimetically replacing individual differences with collective sameness. In Nietzsche's account, this dynamic happens because the experience of nihilism has an affective basis.[9] Nihilism will not disappear through simple awareness because living conditions that have been inculcated and incorporated as needs by a long educational tradition for centuries do not disappear with the sole force of theoretical arguments. It requires a long-term reworking and reconfiguration of our affects.

Therefore, nihilism is an affective and relational problem, manifesting as the inability to create meaning when the purpose is missing, an incapacity to create or posit productively a goal for oneself. Thus, like mimesis, nihilism is a human condition manifesting in affective, bodily, and relational behaviors. One of the main goals of mimetic studies is to sketch a diagnostic of good and ill forms of mimesis. And one can do the same with good and ill forms of nihilism. Hence, the parallels continue to grow.

It should be noted that even before famously announcing the death of God in aphorism § 125—via the mask of the madman—Nietzsche had already proclaimed its death in § 108, immediately followed by a warning concerning new struggles with his remaining "shadows":

> *New battles.*—After Buddha was dead, they still showed his shadow in a cave for centuries—a tremendous, gruesome shadow. God is dead; but given the way people are, there may still for millennia be caves in which they show his shadow.—And we—we must still defeat his shadow as well! (Nietzsche 2001, 109)

This mimetic trope of a "shadow" suggests a projection of human needs and a desire for unconditional authority. This is a mimetic trope that echoes Plato and is different from it. These shadows are not merely illusions or appearances in Plato's sense; they are akin to a phantom as far as they take possession of weak bodies and egos.[10] But they also have the characteristics of a bodily/affective mimesis because Nietzsche is critiquing the affective emergence of nihilism out of mimetic relations. Humans may lament the loss of a god who could communicate clear commands or draw us closer to the fundamental design of things and substitute God with surrogates that claim to provide meaning and protect against the world's fundamental nihility. These shadows can emerge, for instance, in modern science and technology and politics.[11]

The death of God can be experienced as a liberation because the bankruptcy of transcendence and traditional norms and values represents an opportunity for self-legislation, experimentation, and individuality. It raises the awareness that there is no inherent meaning in the world because meaning is a human creation that we introduce into the world—and, in this sense, it is fictional, as it has no correspondence in the world. However, the death of God is also dangerous since it not only impacts Christian morality. Institutions and political ideals such as democracy, traditionally legitimized by Christian values—for instance, altruism and love for thy neighbor—are also affected by the loss of orientation. This is why nihilism represents a threat not only at a personal level but also has significant consequences for any form of community now that these ideals have been revealed as constructs and have lost their divine guarantee. The loss of a "given" reference point is so unbearable that people cannot help but search for God/*arché*, to whom they remain attached even though they can no longer believe in them.[12]

Now that our definition of nihilism is clear and aligned with mimetic studies' Nietzschean inspiration, we will see that understanding mimesis as a human condition allows us to understand better how nihilism works, how to promote its patho-*logical* side, and how to avoid its pathological manifestations.

Nihilism as Patho(-)logy

In what follows I will analyze the specific dynamic of this pathological contagion and the logos Nietzsche uses to diagnose this nihilistic *pathos*, parallel to his critique of mimetic *pathos*.[13] I will argue that Nietzsche's nihilism follows the same paradoxical diagnostic movement coined by Lawtoo through the term "patho(-)logies" (Lawtoo 2013, 6–8). As I see it, this interwoven dynamic between *pathos* and *logos* applies to nihilism, first, in the form of affective contagion or "pathology"—nihilism is a mimetic pathology because it has the contagious characteristics of a sickness—and second, "patho-*logy*": a critical, liberating discourse or *logos* on mimetic *pathos* that is central to the experience of nihilism and, specially, the event of the death of God.

Indeed, Nietzsche uses pharmacological vocabulary in Lenzer Heide supporting our reading of nihilism as a pathology. He writes that the Christian moral hypothesis "prevented man from despising himself as man, from taking against life, from despairing of knowing [*Erkennen*]: it was a *means of preservation*—in sum: morality was the great antidote against practical and theoretical nihilism" (Nietzsche 2010, 385). The death of God can aggravate the symptoms of such despair, but it also can lead to recovery and emancipation from nihilistic ideals. Therefore, nihilism is a malady and remedy in one. It is a mimetic patho(-)logy in the sense that it goes beyond good and evil, generating both contagious pathologies, such as despair, suffering, dependency, and critical discourses on mimetic *pathos*. People can discuss values and consider alternative values when these appear contingent instead of dogmatic. Therefore, nihilism represents a dawn, a new light, because it opens new horizons. Old ideals fade, and new opportunities emerge to transform humanity, society, and culture, as Nietzsche hoped with his idea of "transvaluation of values."

In his reading of Nietzsche, René Girard senses the mimesis–nihilism connection but restricts it within his schema whereby identification with a model determines the object of desire, leading to rivalries that, in his view, trigger envy and resentment (1965 [1961]). This identification prompts people, especially when assembled in a crowd, public or virtual, to involuntarily mimic, feel, and reproduce the effects of the leader qua model. The imitative structure of desire produces a "mimetic crisis" and "loss of difference" in Girard's terms, or, in Nietzsche's terms, a gregarious society, easy to manipulate. Moreover, this transformation of differences into sameness is a defining characteristic of (negative) mimesis and nihilism.

Instead of only mimetic desire, the theory of homo mimeticus provides a broader, alternative frame of mimetic *pathos*, including all affects and not just desire. All affects, sympathy, pain, jealousy, resentment, disgust, fear, panic, trust, and happiness, tend to generate mimetic affects, both positive and negative, sadness or joy, as theorized by Spinoza and Nietzsche, among many other modernist philosophers. A pathos possesses us; it unfailingly hits us like madness, anger, fear, rejection, or love—a drive that is so primal and deep-rooted that it acts as instinct and produces an internal tension toward something.[14] The power of pathos overflows intentional consciousness and generates unconscious pathologies. As a precursor of mimetic studies, Nietzsche engages a conception of affect that is not simply intra-corporeal but flows *across* bodies like anger, revenge, or inspiration. Likewise, the new theory of imitation internal to *homo mimeticus* is a theory about the transmission of affect via mimesis between human (and non-human) beings who are part of a "social network" (Lawtoo 2022a, 48).

Not surprisingly, Girard and other Girardian mimetic theorists, such as Giuseppe Fornari, seem to only consider or understand nihilism as the event of the death of God because they do not agree with the other levels or dimensions of nihilism. Indeed, informed by their theological beliefs, they do not characterize Christian ideals as nihilistic (nihilism-2) or agree with Nietzsche's anthropology and anti-realist depiction of the world as fundamentally meaningless and absurd (nihilism-1). On the contrary, Girardians start from a very particular anthropological structure that acts a total explanatory theory, so much so that Jesuit philosopher Paul Valadier (1982), also a prominent Nietzsche scholar who specialized on the topic of religion, famously criticized Girard for reducing Christianity to an all-encompassing sociological theory.

Interestingly, some aspects of Nietzsche's critique of religion can be used to critique Girard, and we will see that there are mimetic theoretical stakes at play. At the end of *Ecce Homo*, Nietzsche signaled the direction of his transvaluation or inversion of values (*Umwertung*): "Dionysus versus the Crucified One," insisting that the "disciples of the philosopher Dionysus" have the task to propagate new values, as opposed to those designated by the symbol of "the Crucified One." There are two antagonisms at play. The first is the prominent and well-known antagonism between Dionysus (or Nietzsche) and the Crucified. The second, less known antagonism, but equally important for our account of mimetic nihilism *contra* Girard, lies on the very designation of "the Crucified," specifically, the fact that Nietzsche creates a second antagonism between Jesus and Christ.

Karl Jaspers (1961) and Jörg Salaquarda (1985) convincingly argued that Nietzsche's criticism of Christian religion does not target the historical figure of Jesus, and pointed toward the disparity between Paul's theology and Jesus's teaching. Paul the Apostle turned Jesus into Christ, substituting his love with guilt (the cross). The historical Jesus did not know ressentiment, he accepted his helplessness, he was strong in his weakness, he welcomed life and death equally, and he learned to endure life's afflictions, meaning, he was closer to Nietzsche's values (Vitiello 2006). Although one could still debate Nietzsche's depiction of the historical Jesus, there is no doubt that he mostly worried about the use of Christ as a cognitive and moral weapon, and that he preferred the life of Jesus over the miscreation of Christianity, as attested by § 39 of *The Anti-Christ*.

> Even the word "Christianity" is a misunderstanding—there was really only one Christian, and he died on the cross. The "evangel" *died* on the cross. What was called "evangel" after that was the opposite of what *he* had lived: a "*bad* tidings," a dysangel. It is false to the point of absurdity to think that Christians are characterized by their 'beliefs,' like a belief in salvation through Christ: only the *practice* of Christianity is really Christian, living like the man who died on the cross... A life like this is still possible today, for *certain* people it is even necessary: true, original Christianity will always be possible... Not a believing but a doing, above all a *not*-doing-much, a different *being*. (Nietzsche 2005, 35)

Evidently, Nietzsche is critical of ecclesiastical institutions and attacks Christian morality, but, as attested by the paragraph above, he still suggests an immanent and personal form of religiosity, anchored in responsibility.[15] Thus, Nietzsche's critique of Christianity can serve as a basis for reconstructing the religious experience after the death of God. What has fructified for two thousand years is a misinterpretation that denies Jesus's true Christianity. In the face of the growing psycho-sociologization of religion in contemporary life, Nietzsche points out the dangers of using the cross as a verdict and an argument, that is, of reducing religion to a nihilistic, anesthetic instance of salvation. In *The Anti-Christ*, he suggests other ways of living religion, for instance, through the example of Jesus of Nazareth's way of life as an authentic tragic Christian.

On the other hand, Girard, from his particular theologically informed standpoint, argued for "the central relevance of Christianity, the truth of Christ crucified as against the falsehood of Dionysus" (Fornari 2021, 490). Girard's account centered on Christ, and not Jesus, because Christ's sacrifice as a scapegoat will cease vengeance and violence. The worship of his sacrifice is supposed to bring peace, whereas Nietzsche's message was to forget about salvation, and, in line with his immanent thinking, he suggested that "true original Christianity" should consist in "a doing," that is, a patho-*logical* way of life characterized by love in Earth. This question lies at the heart of nihilism, specifically the transition from nihilism-2 to nihilism-3, because as we have already seen, Nietzsche hints multiple times at the idea that European culture murdered God by pathologically associating Jesus, or Christian religion in general, with ascetic values, which are not necessarily the values that the historical Jesus practiced in life. This is to say, Christian religion could have experienced a different fate had it been more faithful to the life of the man who died on the cross.

The Perspectival and Hermeneutic Shift in Mimesis and Nihilism

In what follows, I will show how mimetic studies has benefited from a perspectival shift inaugurated after the event of the death of God and its liberatory outcomes in the form of patho-*logies*. The hermeneutic school is intrinsically characterized by recognizing that there is no way back to the old certainties, and many of its key representatives, such as Heidegger, Gadamer, Figal, Ricoeur, and Vattimo, found inspiration in Nietzsche.

Most authors in the hermeneutical tradition, such as Gianni Vattimo, focus on the liberating outcomes of nihilism and the absence of fixed orientation points. They value the death of God as the moment of Modernity when hermeneutics came into its own, or better, the event marking the human challenge to think of reality from a multitude of perspectives. The death of God is a hermeneutic event because it goes hand in hand with a human awareness of the role of worldviews and interpretations of reality, and it entails the lesson that worldviews do not claim to represent, mirror, or duplicate reality as it is in itself since there is no impulse of truthfulness inside them. Worldviews are mere "pragmatic interpretations embraced by our language-world" (van der Heiden 2018, 156).

As a result, authors in the hermeneutic tradition stress that the conditions in which we find ourselves now should prove fertile: modern manifestations of morality are "more pluralistic, religion less dogmatic, philosophy more critical" (van Tongeren 2018, 88). Humans have power over how they interpret and live in the world. They have the power to make sense of nonsense and create meaning out of the absurd. In these conditions, western culture—traditionally articulated by Christian religions—could learn to live *within* nihilism, as Nietzsche suggested calling for a "pessimism of strength." The key takeaway for mimetic studies is to argue for a new way to respond to what one is faced with, that is, how we respond to the tragic insight of life so that it increases our relational capacity and prevents its instrumentalization via an alleged leader or model. It is not a question of avoiding pain, denying the harmful elements of life, its absurdity, and meaninglessness via a new, totalizing, redeeming anthropology. It is instead a question of being strong enough to live without such redemption and finding a new way of experiencing the tragic insight.

It is fascinating that Gebauer and Wulf, even if without mentioning the death of God, also stress the importance of the nineteenth century as the period in which "*perspectival mimesis*" emerges and "individuals begin to have a relatively free hand in interpreting the world within the frame of their own social experience" (Gebauer and Wulf 1995 [1992], 238), that is, the period where individuals are faced with the opportunity to form an interpretation of their own. However, they stress that the novelty resides in "the fact that this can occur at all" because, sadly, the reality is that, more often, "the subject misses its chance by subjecting itself to an already existing interpretation, which is present in an inner medium" (238).

Based on this realization, Gebauer and Wulf further critique Girard, and, specifically, the triangular structure of his theory of mimesis, by stating that the key issue is not the identification with a model. Radically, the interpretation determines that said model is worth imitating and, therefore, the object is desirable. The interpretation is the internal medium and "has the power to guide wishes, fantasies, desires, and dreams, which is to say, extensive areas of the imagination" (1995 [1992], 238), and they conclude their argument by alluding to the power of interpretation in Nietzsche's account. Whoever has control over the interpretation will have power and control as an individual, social group, or institution, such as the Church, over the individual who internalizes it as a compulsion. The key factor in perspectival mimesis is the interpretation itself, not the model—and there are always multiple interpretations at play, meaning, *there are alternatives.* Such awareness provides a route to solve mimetic pathologies without the promises of a fundamental anthropological structure such as Girard's, which is nothing more than a perspective, hence the need to struggle against his pathological interpretation.

One of the hermeneutic powers or resources to navigate the event of the death of God is the mimetic resource of myths. Notwithstanding the mainstream bad reputation of myths as a false narrative standing in contrast to logos, myth means "formulated speech," belongs to the domain of *legein*, and does not originally stand in contrast to logoi (Vernant 1980). On the contrary, myth makes the development of logos possible, which is why, despite Girard's faith in the Gospels to discredit mythologies and bring an end to the mechanisms of prosecution,[16] mythology can never be brought to an end because it is part of our human ability to think and fantasize about the world.

Myths are also *logos*; they are narrations that play a role in education and provide general references and orientation of socially accepted behaviors. Myths have a formative character: they give form and inform and ultimately result in impressing a particular shape or type into a form. Mythic figures have the power to impress, form, and in-form impressionable and plastic subjects—a process that Lacoue-Labarthe (1989) called "typography."[17]

Fiction, especially in the form of narration, is also one of the primary moral sources of the hermeneutic tradition because, in fiction, meaning is not indexed to reality or truth. The same fictional principle existing in novels—as Girard himself diagnosed in *Deceit, Desire, and the Novel*—exists in society—despite Girard's fundamental anthropology in *Violence and the Sacred*, which does not recognize its necessary fictional character in the hermeneutic sense.

Even if there is no truth claim but simply an interpretation (conscious of itself as an interpretation) that is valued as *superior* to others, it is still possible to functionally find, create, and evaluate meaning, for example, "in terms of power relations, tactics, and strategies" (Becker 2018, 69). There is no truth-claim behind hermeneutics, but there is still, at the very least, a criterion for value discernment. One could elaborate an infinity of interpretations of a text—or points of view about an event—but not all those interpretations will be valid or of the same worth.

In fact, despite prejudices that still associate Nietzsche with relativism, he foregrounded the pluralization of perspectives—enabled by the death of God—as a major opportunity to compare and choose.

> [T]o see differently, and to want to see differently to that degree, is no small discipline and preparation of the intellect for its future "objectivity"—the latter understood not as "contemplation without interest' (which is, as such, a non-concept and an absurdity), but as *having in our power* the ability to engage and disengage our "pros" and "cons": we can use the *difference* in perspectives and affective interpretations for knowledge. (2006, 87)[18]

Any interpretation, narration, or myth is open to being contested by alternative perspectives that prove themselves as more valuable and as having a more positive impact on life, which Nietzsche recognizes as the key criterion in *Beyond Good and Evil* § 4. Nietzsche's perspectivist philosophy (and hermeneutics after him) recognizes all reality as interpretative, and such hermeneutic awareness helps find new ways to live *within nihilism* and avoid its pathological manifestations.

Nihilism, Mimesis and Mythic Identification

As we have seen, authors in the hermeneutic tradition tend to focus on the liberating side of nihilism as patho-*logical*. This perspective should be supplemented with important lessons on the politics of mimesis by key figures of mimetic studies who have also stressed the catastrophic, pathological, and dangerous side of nihilism. Continuing with our argument, we will see that the search for myths is a patho(-)logical strategy to respond to the insight of nihilism.

As already pointed out, Nietzsche warned that the State, nationalism, the market, or science often act as shadows of God because they provide consolation as omnipotent myths and exempt people from autonomous decision-making. This nihilistic logic and relationship manifests in a search for candidates to replace the dead God, and such a nihilist diagnosis or subtext is implicit in multiple texts by precursors of mimetic studies that have dealt with "the politics of mimesis."

Already Philippe Lacoue-Labarthe and Jean-Luc Nancy explicitly allude to the paradoxical situation of a "double bind" in German culture from which the "malady of National Socialism" emerged (Lacoue-Labarthe and Nancy 1990, 300). The unstable state of German culture at the end of the nineteenth century between, on the one hand, "the collapse of religious transcendence and its corresponding social and political structures" and "popular romanticism [which] founded itself on a nostalgia for medieval Christianity" (300), on the other, gradually created a breeding ground for the allegedly saving mission of Nazism and its restoration of the sacred, particularly, sacred identities: a people unified by a chief, a community a fatherland, race, blood, soil, and nature. Sociologically speaking, Nazi symbolism could partially emerge out of a pathological experience of weakness and nihilistic impotence.

Let us recall that Nietzsche diagnosed this double bind and became particularly wary of Romanticism after breaking ties with Wagner in 1876. In writings such as *The Case of Wagner*, *Ecce Homo*, and *Nietzsche contra Wagner* (Nietzsche 2005), he denounced that romantic art, like Wagner's spell-binding spectacles, did not stay true to the tragic insight of Greek tragedy but instead performed a magnetizing, political function analogous to the solemn mass. Wagner profited from his audiences' "need to *anaesthetize* feelings of hunger and monotony using a narcotic art" in such a way that his art became instrumental in fostering obedience to the political interests of Bismarck's regime and promoting the Germanic type itself (Nietzsche 2005, 118). Since Christian religion no longer created intense, communal bonds of solidarity, art received a new political mission: erecting mythical figures in which humanity could recognize itself and create a new, or not-so-new, identity. Lacoue-Labarthe and Nancy point to this "aesthetic solution" as actually not merely aesthetic, since it also "beckons to the political" (Lacoue-Labarthe and Nancy 1990, 303).

Furthering Philippe Lacoue-Labarthe, Lawtoo (2013, 76–83) developed Nietzsche's critique of Wagner's magnetism on the masses. Continuing this genealogy, I will foreground the problematic of nihilism, showing how myth represents a patho(-)logical strategy to respond to the death of God. At the basis of the strategy is the awareness that myth is not merely a representation, but instead a performative power put into moral and political practice. In the words of Lacoue-Labarthe and Nancy:

> Myth is a power more than it is a thing, an object, or a representation. Myth is the power to bring together the fundamental forces and directions of an individual or a people, the power of a subterranean, invisible, nonempirical identity. (Lacoue-Labarthe and Nancy 1990, 306)

In line with our understanding of mimesis as mimetic *pathos*—embodied, affective, and relational—myth should not be understood in representational terms. Nietzsche's recourse to pathos represents a mimetic critique of European metaphysics since Plato's founding defense of *logos* against *pathos* and *mythos*.[19] Indeed, Nietzsche's lesson is that the dichotomy is mistaken. Paying attention to the pathological side is not equivalent to renouncing rationality but rather represents an opportunity to enrich and amplify our understanding of reason so that social phenomena, such as nihilism and mimetic heteronomies, can be better comprehended.

Myths become central to the question of patho(-)logically responding to nihilism. They are plastic fictions that do not remain in the sphere of realistic representations, as a myth is a primary medium for mass communication. As a narration, it provides meaning to life, the exact meaning that is missing after the death of God. A myth provides models, types, and forms of imitation through which a person, a city, or a people manages to understand and identify itself. The power of myth is bodily, mimetic, and contagious: it rests on a desire to be somebody via an affective identification, the desire to acquire an identity, even if it is not an original identity. Myths act as an identificatory mechanism. In fact, according to Lacoue-Labarthe and Nancy, they are "*the* mimetic instrument par excellence" (1990, 298). The ancient Greeks resorted to myths as part of their mimetic *paideia*. With their myths (namely, Homer's epic and Greek tragedy), they learned to perceive beauty in life and the world, despite their pessimistic awareness about the meaninglessness and absurdity of the World (nihilism-1, following van Tongeren's terminology), captured by the wisdom of Silenus.

Later, in the twentieth century, the "Nazi Myth" is, of course, only one of many possible myths. The loss of transcendence after the death of God teaches us that interpretations and myths are performative in the sense that they depend on their reiteration and reenactment to persist in time. Citizens have the power to reflect and decide which myths they give credibility to and choose to reenact and project onto the world. Therefore, like mimesis, myths act beyond good and evil: they are fictional narrations that affect and infect our psychic lives and can shape either ethical citizens or uncritical masses.

Therefore, mimetic studies furthers a critique of fascist leaders that finds in Nietzsche a genealogical starting point still relevant today. The more someone wishes to have a "master," the more power the master achieves because the latter is aware of such dependence and need. On the basis of such awareness, tyrannical leaders exploit rhetorical tactics that spread affectively—not triangularly—as well as strategies of demonization of minorities and specific demographic groups.[20] Tyrannical leaders appear charismatic and tempting to mimetic subjects because they present themselves as powerful enough to solve the moral disorder and social disintegration that arises after the death of God, which suggests a connection between nihilism, fascism, and the politics of mimesis worth pursuing in forthcoming mimetic studies.

Conclusion

This chapter has shown that accounts that reduce nihilism solely to the event of the death of God are inadequate. In particular, they fail to comprehend and target the pathological heteronomies spreading out of mimetic relations, already present before the death of God in the form of ascetic ideals and continuing after the event in the form of shadows of God. Moreover, nihilism, at least in its fundamental sense of nihilism-1—namely, the meaninglessness and absurdity of life—shares with mimesis its definitory characteristics as *conditio humana*, as they both materialize and manifest in affective, embodied, and relational behaviors. Understanding nihilism as a mimetic human condition and its Janus-faced character as both salvation and threat allows us to understand better how nihilism works and how to avoid its pathological manifestations via patho-*logical* discourses that emerge precisely after the exposure to nihilism, or better, thanks to the loss of transcendence intrinsic to nihilism.

As a result, it becomes clear that it is not a question of rejecting or condemning nihilism and mimesis or disavowing morality, mythology, poetry, and imitations but reorienting them. Liberation from mimesis and nihilism are impossible as they are both part of our human condition. It is instead a question of liberating ourselves from their ill, pathological forms and their limitations, and such liberation will work within mimesis and mythology. Likewise, freeing ourselves from nihilistic ideals—originally intended to protect ourselves from the abysmal insight of the meaninglessness and absurdity of life—will necessarily entail coming to terms with our nihilistic condition. Girard's pathological response to nihilism reveals itself as intrinsically nihilistic, as it is a strategy to conceal the fundamental meaninglessness of life and protect from it. Instead, as we have seen in the chapter, genealogical precursors and representatives of new mimetic studies have proven themselves as being more capable than mimetic theory of providing a nuanced, multi-layered assessment of nihilism and its implications for both good and ill.

Nihilistic ideals can be overcome (nihilism-2); what is more, they are condemned to be overcome because our will-to-truth will ultimately reveal them as contingent and undermine their legitimacy, prompting a critical discourse on its pathos, patho-*logical*. Dependent, mimetic relationships with deceiving idols acting as 'shadows of God' can be overcome. But the pessimistic nature of existence (nihilism-1) and its tragic antagonism can never be overcome. As shown in the chapter, attempting to overcome this tragic insight and experience of fundamental nihilism gives rise to heteronomous and potentially dangerous mimetic relations, in which the mimetic subject becomes instrumental, for instance, for a pre-determined socio-political project.

Notes

1   See Lawtoo 2013, 3–83; 2022a, ch.1; and Garcia-Granero 2024.

2   See Lawtoo 2022a and the Coda with Vittorio Gallese in this volume.

3   On mimesis as "*conditio humana*," see Gebauer and Wulf 1995 [1992]; Lawtoo 2022b.

4   The concept of "(new) fascism" intends to stress both the genealogical continuities and discontinuities, the repetition with differences happening in the re-emergence of new fascist phantoms and their specific forms of mimetic communication (Lawtoo 2019, xli).

5   Emphases and italicizations in Nietzsche's texts are always those from his original manuscript, here and in all subsequent citations.

6   See the posthumous fragment 14[91] from 1888. As a complete, English edition of Nietzsche's posthumous fragments is still underway with Stanford University Press, I will refer to *Nietzsche Source*, the electronic, open-access edition of Nietzsche's texts in German (Nietzsche 2009).

7   See the posthumous fragment 9[43] from 1887 (Nietzsche 2009).

8   On Nietzsche's critique of "mimetic dispossessions" as an alternative to Girard's challenge, see Lawtoo 2013, 47–52.

9   For a recent, affective account of nihilism, see Creasy 2020.

10   On Nietzsche's use of "phantom" as part of a genealogy that goes back to the Platonic critique of mimesis, see Lawtoo 2013, 55–56.

11   On nihilism and technology, see Gertz 2018. On nihilism and politics, see Eden 1984.

12   Paul van Tongeren designates the paradoxical awareness of this antagonism as nihilism-4, a nihilism to which there is no beyond (van Tongeren 2018, 100–102).

13   Lawtoo proposes the concept of mimetic *pathos* "to account for the relational power of human bodies to be unconsciously affected by human and nonhuman others via a shared sympathy, or *sym-pathos*" (2022a, 37). For more on mimetic pathos and Nietzsche as its key genealogical source, see 53–58.

14   In fact, as already underscored by Lawtoo (2013), Nietzsche defines the hypothesis of the will to power as a *pathos*: "the will to power is not a being, it is not a becoming, but a *pathos*, it is the most elementary fact, only from which a becoming results, a producing effects..." (Nietzsche 2009, posthumous fragment 14[79] from 1888).

15   See Conill 2021.

16   See Girard 1986.

17   On the power of myth today in relation to (new) fascism, see Lawtoo 2019, ch. 3, where the author engages with Lacoue-Labarthe and Nancy as key genealogical sources for mimetic studies, now revisited from the angle of nihilism.

18   See also the posthumous fragment 23[85] from 1876: "The virtue of our culture is *comparison*. We bring together the most diverse products of older cultures and appraise them; it is our job to do this well. Our strength shall be shown as we *choose*; we shall be judges" (Nietzsche 2009, my trans.).

19   See Müller 2005.

20   See Connolly 2017.

Bibliography

Becker, Marcel (2018). "Nietzsche, Virtue Ethics and Hermeneutics," in *Beyond Nihilism?*, eds. Chris Bremmers, Andrew Smith, and Jean-Pierre Wils. Nordhausen: Verlag Traugott Bautz, 47–70.

Conill, Jesús (2021). *Nietzsche frente a Habermas. Genealogías de la razón*. Madrid: Tecnos.

Connolly, William E. (2017). *Aspirational Fascism: The Struggle for Multifaceted Democracy under Trumpism*. Minneapolis: University of Minnesota Press.

Creasy, Kaitlyn (2020). *The Problem of Affective Nihilism in Nietzsche. Thinking Differently, Feeling Differently*. Cham: Springer.

Eden, Robert (1984). *Political Leadership and Nihilism: A Study of Weber and Nietzsche*. Gainesville: University Presses of Florida.

Fornari, Giuseppe (2021). *Dionysus, Christ, and the Death of God*. East Lansing: Michigan State University Press.

Jaspers, Karl (1961). *Nietzsche and Christianity*. Chicago: Henry Regnery Co.

Garcia-Granero, Marina (2024). "Nietzsche's Legacy for Posthuman Mimesis: Metamorphoses, Embodiment, Immanence," in *Mimetic Posthumanism: Homo Mimeticus 2.0 in Art, Philosophy, and Technics*, ed. Nidesh Lawtoo. Leiden: Brill, 178–199.

Gebauer, Gunter, and Christoph Wulf (1995 [1992]). *Mimesis: Culture, Art, Society*, trans. Don Reneau. Berkeley: University of California Press.

Gertz, Nolen (2018). *Nihilism and Technology*. London: Rowman & Littlefield International.

Girard, René (1965 [1961]). *Deceit, Desire and the Novel: Self and Other in Literary Structure*, trans. Yvonne Freccero. Baltimore: The Johns Hopkins University Press.

—— (1984). "Dionysus versus the Crucified." *MLN* 99.4, 816–835.

——— (1986). *The Scapegoat*, trans. Yvonne Freccero. Baltimore: Johns Hopkins University Press.

Lacoue-Labarthe, Philippe (1989). *Typography: Mimesis, Philosophy, Politics*, ed. Christopher Fynsk. Cambridge, MA: Harvard University Press.

Lacoue-Labarthe, Philippe, and Jean-Luc Nancy (1990). "The Nazi Myth," trans. Brian Holmes. *Critical Inquiry* 16.2, 291–312.

Lawtoo, Nidesh (2013). *The Phantom of the Ego: Modernism and the Mimetic Unconscious*. East Lansing: Michigan State University Press.

——— (2019). *(New) Fascism: Contagion, Community, Myth*. East Lansing: Michigan State University Press.

——— (2022a). *Homo Mimeticus: A New Theory of Imitation*. Leuven: Leuven University Press.

——— (ed.) (2022b). "The Mimetic Condition," *CounterText* 8.1.

——— (2023). *Violence and the Oedipal Unconscious: vol. 1 The Catharsis Hypothesis*. East Lansing: Michigan State University Press.

——— (2024). "Nietzsche contra Girard: Agonistic Steps for Mimetic Studies." *Contagion* 31, 145–176.

Müller, Enrico (2005). *Die Griechen im Denken Nietzsches*. Berlin: de Gruyter.

Nietzsche, Friedrich (1999). *The Birth of Tragedy and Other Writings*, eds. Raymond Geuss and Ronald Speirs, trans. Ronald Speirs. Cambridge: Cambridge University Press.

——— (2001). *The Gay Science: With a Prelude in German Rhymes and an Appendix of Songs*, ed. Bernard Williams, trans. Josefine Nauckhoff, poems trans. Adrian del Caro. Cambridge: Cambridge University Press.

——— (2005). *The Anti-Christ, Ecce Homo, Twilight of the Idols, and Other Writings*, eds. Aaron Ridley and Judith Norman, trans. Judith Norman. Cambridge: Cambridge University Press.

——— (2006). *On the Genealogy of Morality*, ed. Keith Ansell-Pearson, trans. Carol Diethe. Cambridge: Cambridge University Press.

——— (2009). *Digitale Kritische Gesamtausgabe, Werke und Briefe [eKGWB]*, ed. Paolo D'Iorio, Paris, Nietzsche Source. Available open-access in www.nietzschesource.org

——— (2010). *The Nietzsche Reader*, eds. Keith Ansell Pearson and Duncan Large. Oxford: Blackwell Publishing.

Roodt, Vasti (2018). "Living with Nihilism," in *Beyond Nihilism?*, eds. Chris Bremmers, Andrew Smith, and Jean-Pierre Wils. Nordhausen: Verlag Traugott Bautz, 71–84.

Salaquarda, Jörg (1985). "Dionysus versus the Crucified One: Nietzsche's Understanding of the Apostle Paul," in *Studies in Nietzsche and the Judaeo-Christian Tradition*, eds. James C. O'Flaherty, Timothy F. Sellner, and Robert M. Helm. Chapel Hill: University of North Carolina Press, 100–129.

Tongeren, Paul van (2018). *Friedrich Nietzsche and European Nihilism*. Newcastle upon Tyne: Cambridge Scholars Publishing.

Valadier, Paul (1982). "Bouc émissaire et Révélation chrétienne selon René Girard." *Études* 357.2/3, 251–260.

van der Heiden, Gert-Jan (2018). "A Hermeneutics of Attestation," in *Beyond Nihilism?*, ed. Chris Bremmers, Andrew Smith, and Jean-Pierre Wils. Nordhausen: Verlag Traugott Bautz, 155–168.

Vernant, Jean-Pierre (1980). *Myth and Society in Ancient Greece*, trans. Janet Lloyd. Sussex: Haverster Press.

Vitiello, Vincenzo (2006). "Nietzsche contra Pablo." *Estudios Nietzsche* 6, 83–100.

CHAPTER 7

ESSENTIAL VIOLENCE AND RENÉ GIRARD'S MIMETIC THEORY

William A. Johnsen

In *La Rovina di Kasch,* Roberto Calasso tagged René Girard as a hedgehog (1983, 205–10) using Archilochus's distinction between knowing many things and one thing.[1] For Calasso, Girard's one thing was the scapegoat mechanism. Girardians have inevitably increased this number to at least two, to include Girard's mimetic theory as well as his Christian conversion as an epistemology (Kirwan in Girard, 2008, xii–xiii). In my title I have called attention to a less-recognized feature of violence as discussed within Girard's "mimetic theory" to feature what Girard called in *La violence et le sacré* "la violence essentielle" (1972, 332). But such additions to our customary reading of Girard need to be at least mapped in a preliminary way *within* the incorporative, consolidating method of at least *this* hedgehog's iteration of his theory of human imitation, intraspecies violence, and the origin of culture (hominization). My subject is the oscillating relation between Girard's own mimetic theory, which includes the scapegoat mechanism and interdividual mimetic rivalry and entanglement, all part of *his* role in the "mimetic turn" (see Lawtoo 2022, 2023a), and "essential violence" that Girard depicts in *La violence* implicitly as a self-organizing, self-regulating mechanism. This relation might suggest that other versions of the mimetic turn might well recognize an interpenetration of the radical dependence of mimesis on others for guidance and the seemingly contrary hypothesis of self-organization.

To sketch this large project out I will need to hold *essential* violence somewhat apart from the commonly accepted ideas by mimetic theorists of all kinds about violence's "contagion," polarization," and "catharsis," before relocating essential violence to these key concepts.

From Romantic Rivals to Twins in Anthropology and Mythology

Girard explained that after completing *Mensonge romantique* in 1961, his friend and colleague at Hopkins Eugenio Donato suggested that Girard's special literary subject (the circumstance in novels of friends who become rivals, even more like each other as they compete more aggressively until they become violent antagonists), was in fact the primary subject of myth currently being studied by structural anthropologists and classicists. This suggested line of investigation encourages the standard view of Girard's hypothesis, a straightforward development from violent modern rivals in fiction, to the enemy twins so recurrent in myth, then to the primitive prohibitions that prevent rivalry, and ultimately to the scapegoat mechanism embedded in ritual that incites but then redirects and finally purges rivalry in archaic culture. For Girard, ritual founded on scapegoating reveals the traces of the foundation of culture itself that enabled the passage from proto-human to human by curtailing reciprocal, intraspecies violence. In other words, this path would describe a straight line from Girard's work on fiction, *Mensonge romantique* and his short book on Dostoievski (1963), to *La violence* in 1972.

Yet Eric Gans, one of Girard's earliest students asked, according to Girard: "why didn't you start with mimetic theory at the beginning of *La violence*, rather than introducing it half-way through?" Girard's provisional answer was that he wanted this book recognized as having a new subject (2008, 38). Perhaps Girard worried that the collection of essays he edited on Proust in 1962, and the short monograph on Dostoievski in 1963 that followed *Mensonge romantique*, would lock him in as a *literary* scholar, and he would not attract the attention of his next target audience of anthropologists and social scientists to his new area of research.

Mechanisms and Self-Ordering Systems

Gans asked a very good question that begs a more complex answer than readership. One might think that the curious personalization of violence as a being with autonomy, intentions, and even desires that begins *La violence* was to give *first* the mythical version of (collective human) violence misunderstood, misrepresented as a divinity. This "deity" is shown to have desires to be placated or diverted by ritual practices that are in effect, on Girard's full understanding, only placebos, only capable of producing catharsis as long as violence is *not* recognized as initiated and perpetuated solely by humans themselves.

The clue to a deeper understanding of "la violence essentielle" is to note Girard's frequent description of it in *La violence* as a *"mécanisme"* (he uses the term 124 times), but *once* especially as a "self-regulating *system* [*un mécanisme autoregulateur*] (1972, 377).

First, let us map the emergence of a theoretical context for "mécanisme" in *Mensonge romantique et vérité romanesque* (1961). For the English translation of *Mensonge romantique* that was published in 1966, Girard inserted several paragraphs in the first three pages that identified "intersubjectivity," "structural models" and "systems" as vital concepts for his analysis (1966, 2–3). It is likely that Girard was formally reorienting his mimetic theory and in particular his observation of its status as a mécanisme (the word occurs twenty-five times in *Mensonge romantique* alone) in advance of the Languages of Criticism and the Sciences of Man conference (which would be called the "Structuralist Controversy" when published) that he would co-host the following year at Hopkins. Girard's lifelong and largely one-sided public dialogue with Levi-Strauss in particular, and structuralism/poststructuralism, especially in his insistent credit of Derrida,[2] is forecast by this intervention into the English translation of *Mensonge romantique*.

But to map a contemporaneous relation to the research in self-regulating systems suggested by Girard's use of the term "un mécanisme *autoregulateur*" is more difficult. It is unclear who Girard was reading on self-regulating systems in the late 1960s. Although I will be placing this facet of Girard's hypothesis within the cadre of self-organization theorists, it is probably impossible to know where Girard came upon "autoregulateur" before 1971, when he had finished the manuscript of *La violence*. Edgar Morin, a masterful creator and long-time instigator of breakthrough ideas, published *Le paradigme perdu: La nature humaine* in 1973, which shows *his* attention to self-organizing systems in Heinz von Foerster and Henri Atlan. Girard spent his academic career in or near French departments, his summers in France, so it wouldn't be difficult to place him in proximity to the thinkers of the re-emerging paradigm Morin discusses; but genealogies of the mimetic turn such as Lawtoo's, a godsend to us, a veritable *paideuma*, often are resisted by their subjects not through dishonesty but because that is how they keep faith with, how they remember these ideas, how they "came to them," especially how to start them up again from their beginning. Later on in the 1980s, Jean-Pierre Dupuy together with Paul Dumouchel personally and formally integrated Girard's mimetic theory with theories of self-organizing systems in an influential series of conferences and books.[3]

Thus, Girard's idea of an autoregulating mechanism that seems to express intention maps out more easily ten years later, after the remarkable Disorder/Order conference at Stanford in 1981 that gathered a whole generation of what Dupuy classed as the "second-order cybernauts" who were researching self-regulating natural machines: Edgar Morin himself, Heinz von Foerster, Henri Atlan, Francisco Varela, Michel Serres, Ilya Prigogine and Isabel Stengers among many others. There were several important subsequent meetings throughout the decade. In an interview with Nadine Dormoy later in the 1980s, Girard reported appreciatively that Ilya Prigogine approved of Girard's scapegoat hypothesis as "non déterministe" (2018, 189) for the order of a human community emerging from the disorder of mob violence of all against all. This group saw clearly and enthusiastically the kinship of Girard's ideas to their own work.

Girard then has three methods of describing violence: (1) as a being with intentions and desires to be placated and displaced, as a mechanism that is self-regulating, as in myth; (2) as a human collective behavior that can only work toward "catharsis" if humans disown their own violence; (3) to disown "myth" in the skeptical sense, demythologizing it by acknowledging it as our own. These methods sometimes overlap, sometimes interfere with one another in *La violence et le sacré*. Girard sometimes describes ritual purgation as a real social process, a therapy, but also otherwise recognizes it as a placebo, which works only as long as misunderstanding of sacrifice survives. So, we must be especially careful about suggesting that violence is "contagious" but can be "purged," two terms that, applied indiscriminately, can deform Girard's thought and hijack our own thinking about human violence, doing it for us.

Girard's final context for mimetic theory and essential violence that began with *Violence and the Sacred* is his reading of Clausewitz and total war theory in *Achever Clausewitz* (2007): religion and the judicial system are the successive institutions humans have put their faith in to prevent as much violence as possible by using as small a dose of violence as possible, but decisive enough to keep the peace. When belief in these institutions fails in the modern world, we have nothing left but essential violence that can now produce nothing but itself, the world of "neverending wars" as Ann Hironaka terms it (2005).

Modelling Essential Violence as an Emerging Self-Organizing System

To develop my suggestion for what essential violence represents in Girard, I will slow-walk through a hypothetical episode of originary breakaway violence that *could be* generative of the social order that regulates it by repeating it in ritual. I will hold off for as long as possible from using terms like "contagion," "polarization," and "purgation" to describe its emergence, development, and conclusion; I will be following Girard's model as carefully as I can, just going slow, real slow to invite scholars of the mimetic turn to recognize where their paths intersect with Girard and "Girardians."

If spontaneous scapegoating is a *nondeterministic* mechanism, then when all-against-one fails to emerge, fails to end violence (and it must have failed often, in fact almost always), when something else happens, we might get a look at the threshold state, the point of bifurcation (Prigogine's term) just before the scapegoat mechanism locks in (or doesn't), a state where we might imagine ourselves inside the individual participants about to merge in a frenzy, but moved at first by some simple motive of just defending themselves against violence, a motive that we might minimally recognize as theirs but ours also. We might also see what else might occur after bifurcation, perhaps the emergence of sacrificial mechanisms for reconciliation *other* than scapegoating, such as the well-attested dual systems analyzed by Simon Simonse in *Kings of Disaster* (Simonse, 1992, 2007) that keep the peace relatively constant internally for both moieties, managing a low state of external strife short of total war between both moieties or even single champions fighting for each side that formed in opposition.

And we should have confidence. Consciousness is a problem, of course, as neuroscientists usually confess to us, yet we are better positioned than those researching 'natural' self-organizing systems that, unlike human, living organisms, cannot confess, testify, answer questions, and whose orderly and seemingly determined behavior must therefore be cautiously described using limiting terms like "dispositions," "emergence," and "attractors" to avoid the accusation of introducing divine causation, or especially some consciousness determining their behavior.[4]

To describe this human motive to violence simply: we move emotionally against violence or its possibility because we fear it, never daring to recognize our own responses as violent, as aggressive. It is important to emphasize (which Girard doesn't always do) that human violence is not solely the result of mimetic

desire, of needs or appetites altered by human imitation.[5] But preemptive violence anticipating the violence of the other, which as a behavior it would be
somewhat misleading to classify primarily as imitative behavior, *is* frequently
discussed by Girard, especially when discussing Clausewitz, but also in referring
to simple exchanges in advanced societies such as the exchange of greetings and
gifts, or even facial gestures to manage violence. 'Self-defense' looks like imitation to an outside viewer because both antagonists become more like each other
the longer they fight, but antagonists are warding off, matching, countering the
attacks of the other, not 'imitating' in the way we use this word.

Andrew Meltzoff, Vittorio Gallese and many others were part of the
Mimesis and Science project funded by The Templeton Foundation and directed by Scott Garrels (2011). We all owe them for their work, for concepts central to my own thinking, like Gallese's "shared manifold" and Meltzoff's role in
reintroducing imitation as a subject for research (*The Imitative Mind*), and his
demonstration that very young children are not mere mimes, they recognize,
understand the intentions of an action they imitate. Yet I wonder about one of
the most famous images of Meltzoff's engagement with a newborn, sticking out
his tongue and the child reciprocating. Does the child's expression look like the
beginning of the haka dance to you? As if the child says, 'I know my mother, we
go way back, but who the hell are you?' Perhaps Meltzoff's face did not indicate
carefully enough his benign intentions when he sticks out his tongue (admittedly, difficult then to smile at the same time) but the baby's face is anything but
welcoming. Is this imitation or necessary defensive matching? Might we consider, as a conjectural exercise, mirror neurons as part of some neural defensive
system, prudently matching the potentially hostile gestures of another?[6]

Girard credits Konrad Lorenz (1966) for suggesting that anger is an anthropological invariant across cultures, that nothing more resembles an angry
person than another angry person (especially when, as they usually are, they are
angry with another angry person). But in fact, if you understand what Girard
assumes that you understand at the beginning of *La violence* when he reminds us
of "Kick the dog" as an example of displacing violence on another (simply, someone who can't strike back at his boss takes it out on the dog when he gets home),
you have acknowledged as common knowledge nearly everything in Girard's
scapegoat hypothesis. This bit of folk wisdom recognizes that (1) anger as an
emotion persists beyond the scene of its incitement because it is reciprocal, it
must be answered in kind; (2) when direct reciprocity is impossible, humans will
try to violently offload their payback anger on a safer substitute, even an animal
substitute[7] who is paradoxically almost a sure bet for an affectionate greeting,

a "welcome home." Sir James Frazer is Girard's perfect example of méconnaissance, Girard's preferred term for misunderstanding "violence and the sacred," which he uses in order to avoid the misleading notions of "the" unconscious, an internal psychic organ, Freud's black box; Frazer dismisses archaic religion as nonsense because it believes such displacement, believing that you can load your sins on another like handing your luggage over to a porter. Thus, Frazer misrecognizes his own expulsion of archaic religion and its modern progeny as also religious—in Girard's sense.

Anticipating our turn to Girard's late turn from discussing archaic violence to modern warfare as understood by Clausewitz, we might ask 'what are the earliest signs of intra-specific human violence, especially armed conflict?' Forensic archaeologists like Chris Knüsel (Knüsel and Smith 2014) read forearm damage on skeletal remains as the result of warding off the blow of an antagonist's weapon in his alternate arm. (Is there any primitive "tool" we can think of that could not have served also as a weapon?) Human violence can produce adversarial 'matches' for the historical record, which it would be misleading to class as pre-programmed mimetic mirror-effects. Violence 'itself' as a threatening condition (not contagion, not catharsis) erases differences between opponents. It is their attempt to extinguish the other's violence that makes "opponents" increasingly resemble each other, which is the furthest thing from what they want, or what they "desire."

As Aristotle puts it in a famous passage of the *Poetics* central to mimetic studies,[8] Girard argues that humans are natural creatures, but more mimetic than other creatures; they copy each other with greater effect. Going further, Girard insists that when they copy each other's desires, they will become conflictual whenever the objects desired cannot be shared. Beyond a certain threshold, simply beyond a certain size population perhaps susceptible to a Dunbar calculation, hominid groups cannot restore peace through the dominance patterns that pacify animal and proto-human groups. One individual's brute power and intimidation over others can only carry so far.

But however, violence begins, perhaps over water, foraging, scavenging or later[9] hunting, from need, from self-defense, or basic needs mediated by desire, it can spread throughout, entangling whoever is nearby. This is Girard's special subject: breakaway human violence and attempts to end it. How does this engulfment in violence happen, and how can order emerge from it? We must try to reason out this sequence that recurs everywhere in the world, in the same few patterns where violence ends violence, that it recurs as a nondeterministic mechanism. Moreover, we should not short-circuit our own thinking by "ritually" depending on mythical conceptual shortcuts or agencies such as "contagion," "polarisation," or "purgation" that depict, copy the steps or algorithms of behavior that emerge as a community urgently increases the speed of these practices to get to the violent resolutions to violence that it remembers as successful. Like the theorists of crowd behavior such as Gabriel Tarde, Gustave Le Bon, and Elias Canetti that came before him, Girard (and Girardians) see sameness in 'mobilizing' crowds from an outside point of view, then in a somewhat circular manner hypothesize this behavior as motivated by imitation on the inside. I am trying to isolate the initial less-than-hysterical steps of preventing violence on the inside taken one by one which leads to the group frenzy of a self-organizing system of accusation against a single culpable victim.[10]

Then we must ask: why is violence copied, how is violence "contagious"? Why does it "snowball," why does it spread so far, so fast, like wildfire? We must not give the quick (non-)answer, 'because that is the way people are—violent, and that is the manner of violence, to be contagious.' As violence spreads, it creates a compelling center of attention. Bystanders or "outliers" *must* address this event emerging among them that was not at first "their" fight; they must match, counter, equalize this expanding violence at the center that violence creates, or surely be engulfed themselves as violence's (next) victim.

Girard begins with the universal claim of humans that they want peace from violence. It is as true now as it ever was: we all want peace, but we never admit to being aggressive. It is all these others who seem to be aggressive, who threaten our security, who want what we need, who want "our" things, and violence is the only way to retrieve the peace that they violently interrupted.

In the ensuing mêlée, everyone returns the violence against them. With interest, as Girard says, for we all love peace and hate violence, violently. As they contest with one another, combatants become more like one another. If violence makes all the same, then, as Girard reasons, it becomes easier for one (violently angry) person, ultimately, to be the same single enemy, to stand for everyone's enemy. Easier, yes, but how could that happen? One against one everywhere, then what? Two against one? Almost inevitably. What happens next after two against one? Three against one? Why does *that* happen?

This is the world of *essential* violence, entered perhaps initially through a conflict over needs (food, water, a habitat), not necessarily mediated desires. In fact, any contested object is superseded by violence itself, the need to survive rivalry, to dominate the other's violence. In other words, it becomes a contest over who has the greatest violence, the violence that cannot be answered.

It is useful here to invoke more fully Ilya Prigogine's influential model[11] for the emergence of limited self-regulating systems, beginning in a "bifurcation point" emerging out of a state "far from equilibrium," which would be for our model a place where a third person joins one of the two rivals to stop the violent "other" one, but perhaps also to hide oneself from becoming the potential next victim to the violence of the victors, as the attention of the victors expands to see if there is any more violence to be put down. This third or additional person increases their group's size when joining their collective violence on yet another person, or by inviting the group to join its own violence against another (which is perhaps itself a "copy" of the group's violence) and, perhaps consciously, but perhaps not, deflecting the group's violence away from itself.

One might even argue that a kind of mediating triangle recurs here when a third joins one side of the two inaugural antagonists to attack the same person, two able to share an anger, an antagonism that is more successfully integrative than two sharing a desire. If the human dynamic of the violence mechanism is not understood, the staging itself is well recognized. To build an accusatory movement toward unanimity-minus-one, Deuteronomy 19:15 advises: "You must not convict anyone of a crime on the testimony of only one witness. The facts of the case must be established by the testimony of two or three witnesses." Simply put, to get the ball rolling down the hill, you must begin with an "attractive" two-against-one.

How then does peace return from everyone matching one another's violence, from blow and counter-blow, when reciprocal violence engulfs everyone? Eventually a *mêlée* will exhaust the group's limited human resources, will wear down into a few left, into finishing off one last. Thus, peace would return when the last antagonist or antagonists are vanquished by all who are left. Violence pushes all the way through to the most successful but least likely of all things "not impossible the most difficult" (1918, 85). The more lop-sided the final result is, the better it is for group survival, now and in the future; the best score for any future iteration is all against one. Violence that spreads as if "contagiously," engulfing all against all, in appearance and effect "polarizes," "purges" finally, exhaustively, into all against (the last) one.

Ritual Models Regulate Violence

Ritual sacrifice commemorates, formalizes (and we can surely say here, at this point, imitates) this spontaneous outbreak and resolution of runaway violence, economizing it, but still (mis-) attributing ritual's efficacy and order to some causative force external to itself. Where does the increasingly formalized ritual come from, as opposed to a runaway mechanism? It is as if the group asked itself, "what were we doing the last time peace arrived, or the last time the transcendent powers or forces that control everything, indicated to us the proper direction towards peace in the midst of everyone fighting?" They remember the spectacle of peace's first emergence: all were united in opposition to the last antagonist. Again, for the survival of the group, the best, final score is all against one, the sooner the better. So: ritual copies spontaneous violence, essential violence, which is interdividual but nondeterministic for achieving a self-regulating system. Ritual, however, *has* designs on a particular and successful outcome: to *determine* the sturdiest peace process possible, the best placation of the gods or forces who must be the controllers of what they believe that humans cannot themselves control. Three likely scenarios for a nondeterministic mechanism emerging from the chaos of all-against-all, yield after some point of bifurcation the three most attested sacrificial models: all against one, the dual systems (fifty–fifty), and the ritual contest of champions who represent their opposing moieties.

Modern Violence

Girard's entry into his research and reflection on the archaic, on the passage from hominid to the human, was to ask the question: how did early humans deal with their worst threat, the problem of reciprocal violence without a judicial system like ours that has the last violent word?

But this *determining* sacrificial system that mimics a nondeterministic mechanism depends on misunderstanding the genuine source of the chaos and its random result. As Yeats's wonderful poem "Meru" says, "Man's life is thought" and modern thinking culminates in deconstructing "méconnaissance" without any further "religious" solutions.

Civilisation is hooped together, brought
Under a rule, under the semblance of peace
By manifold illusion; but man's life is thought,
And he, despite his terror, cannot cease
Ravening through century after century,
Ravening, raging, and uprooting that he may come
Into the desolation of reality. (Yeats 1989, 289)

The mind is like a tongue, which behaves with independent curiosity. The dental hygienist tells the patient to keep his tongue away from a certain place in his mouth, but the struggle to investigate is powerful. For Girard as well, our life is thought, finding the truth. If you come to "acknowledge" (a useful term to oppose to the untranslateable *méconnaissance*) that you are scapegoating, that the victim is not uniquely guilty, then it will not work, the placebo is revealed, the rule of the "manifold illusion" delivering what Yeats terms above as the "semblance of peace" is broken.

Girard suggests in several places that the judicial system inherits the role (and retains some of the accoutrements) of religious sacrifice, and his idea remains compelling that the primary role of the judicial system is to take revenge in its own impartial hands, out of the hands of the aggrieved, to respond so powerfully that no further response is possible.

Because of Girard's exemplary commitment to making these ideas that came to him as clear as possible, he did not always leave time to remind us[12] that most cultures did not survive the loss of their sacrificial protection, and it was by no means determined that the judicial mechanism would automatically emerge from sacrificial systems. In the same way, just as the sacrificial world cannot survive without misunderstanding, the suspicion that the judicial system is not impartial dangerously weakens its 'religious' authority as the last word.

Girard reports in *Achever Clausewitz* that we are now experiencing an acute loss of belief in the judicial system. At the global level we have never had one, at best we have only the dual system analyzed by Simon Simonse in a more complex form, or "neverending wars" in Ann Hironaka's phrase (2005).

Achever Clausewitz

Girard's reading of Clausewitz and essential violence, of radical violence, in the modern world takes center stage in his last book. For Girard, Clausewitz burrows down to disclose the generative radical of war, which is still the two antagonists[13] in the *Wechselwirkung* of hand-to-hand strife. War can get out of hand, out of our hands, into its own hands, we might say, striving to complete itself despite us ("Das Streben nach dem Aussersten" in Clausewitz, "la montée aux extrêmes" for Girard and Benoît Chantre, who follow Pierre Naville's French translation). "In our end is our beginning;" we are now back to our origins, where, as Girard says, violence cannot produce anything but itself.

Girard voices two alarms in particular in *Achever Clausewitz*. He says that his friends who are legal scholars tell him that law is finished, no one believes in it anymore. We might find this weakening of the judicial system in each of our own countries, which have avoided the escalation of rivalry and revenge by the suppositious social contract of turning over retribution to the State. Of course for global relations there is no such arrangement. As an American I note that in my country that our "social contract" ostentatiously allowed us to keep our guns.

The other warning concerns viral contagion in a world where humans affect everything:

> Terrorist wars and looming pandemics recall the plague in Thebes. The devastating nature of bird flu virus H5N1, which is a mutant that can kill hundreds of turkeys in a few hours, spreads through bird migrations, but especially thanks to air traffic. It is a pandemic that could cause hundreds of thousands of deaths in a few days, and it is a phenomenon typical of the undifferentiation now coursing across the planet. We can counter it with vaccines, so long as we *share them*, and do not limit them to rich nations, seeing how porous borders have become between countries, and between all differences in general. (Girard 2009, 23–24)

We can no longer blame the gods or the system, we cannot blame Nature, the weather, dubious instincts or even the somatic for contagion, polarization, catharsis, or interdividual echopraxia for the violence that threatens us. It belongs to us.

Battling to the End

The special preface that Girard wrote to *De la violence à la divinité* (the Grasset collection of four of his books preceding *Achever Clausewitz* but published concurrently in 2007) constitutes part of Girard's final consideration of his set of hypotheses that, he declares, are even more pressing now than when they first came to him, concerning the question of violence in its relation to religion.

Religion, he came to feel, was always about peace, even in its most virulent form. In *Achever Clausewitz* he says, implacably, that Christianity has left us with a terrible choice: "ou croire à la violence, ou ne plus y croire. Le christianisme, c'est l'incroyance" [To believe in violence, or no longer believe in it. Christianity is disbelief] (Girard 2007, 58).

Further, Girard calls for research into a mimetic history that is partially a history of the perfecting of violent warfare, paradoxically alongside a history of bettering our concern for other humans, rejecting persecution, developing hospitals and other forms of care. But as Girard says warningly: "history has meaning, and its meaning is terrifying"(2009, xvii).

In 2009, Girard and Chantre[14] chose the English title, *Battling to the End* (2009), to emphasize a side very different from the French original title, *Achever Clausewitz*, to their conversations, thus recasting a more positive prompt for every time one picks up the book to read it, and its tone weighs counter to observations and insights in the book that are by themselves quite frightening, even despairing. But I take my cue from that English title, and from Girard's lifelong reading of Hölderlin:[15]

> Nah ist
> und schwer zu fassen der Gott
> Wo aber Gefahr ist wächst
> das Rettende auch.

Notes

1 "πόλλ' οἶδ' ἀλώπηξ, ἀλλ' ἐχῖνος ἓν μέγα" in Zenob. 5.68 (Paroem. Gr. i. 147.7 L.-S.). Archilochus, *Fragments*, Loeb Classical Library, fragment 201, p. 216.

2 And the use by both Girard and Derrida of the work of Jean-Pierre Vernant, who was present at the conference. See Lawtoo 2022, ch. 3. For Derrida's unacknowledged use of Girard see Chantre, *René Girard: biographie*, 437–996, passim.

3 A few titles will have to serve as a holding-place in lieu of a proper historical/analytical narrative. See Dumouchel and Dupuy 1983, from a conference held on 10–17 June 1981 at Cerisy-la-Salle that prepared for the forthcoming Stanford conference in the fall of 1981; Livingston 1984, from the conference at Stanford University, 10–17 September 1981; Deguy and Dupuy 1982; Dumouchel 1985, from a conference at Cerisy-la-Salle 11–18 June 1983; a selection of these texts was published in English in Dumouchel 1988. Varela and Dupuy, 1992 contains papers from a conference at Stanford University 13–16 September 1987. This period of collocation with Girard needs its own intellectual history as the third wave of cybernauts to follow after Dupuy's history of the cybernetic second wave in *The Origins of Cognitive Science* (2009). Dupuy himself would be one of the central figures of this history as participant and convener.

4 These difficulties have not prevented some neuroscientists such as Antonio Damasio (2010, 2021) and more recently Kevin J. Mitchell (2023) from running the board with a model of the development of human consciousness from the single cell to the present.

5 Also see *Evolution and Conversion*: "Mimetic theory is the only theory that assumes a violent component both in primitive and modern culture, considering man as ethologically violent, but with the cultural capacity (given by religion), to control this violence, promoting ethical behavior. Mimetic theory, in this sense, has a strong ethical component, for it acknowledges that we are all orientated towards a violence that is mimetically engendered" (172). It is important to note here also that violence can be instigated to meet, to match up with another's violence.

6 Nidesh Lawtoo has drawn my attention to *Morgenröthe*, 142 passim, where Nietzsche locates the origin of sympathy (*Mitempfindung*) achieved by means of bodily imitation of the other, in a primitive human early warning system for sensing the other's aggression. This fear of the other's violence is „die *Lehrmeisterin jener Mitempfindung ....[und] des Verstehens.*" [See Lawtoo 2013, 38–41, editors' note.]

7 We might even remember here Girard's proposal that animal domestication is an accidental benefit coming from keeping sacrificial animals ready to hand.

8 "Imitation is a part of men's nature from childhood, and he differs from the other animals in the fact that he is especially mimetic and learns his first lessons through imitation as is the fact they all get pleasure from imitation" (*Poetics*, 1448b6–10). See Else 1957, 124.

9 As Roberto Calasso often noted, the term "hunter-gatherer" is too slack. If hominids only came to flesh-eating later, according to dental remains, then they foraged before they scavenged, gathered before they hunted, learning from their gatherer-hunter competitors in the animal kingdom.

10 The frenzy itself that group violence comes to, perhaps answerable to some approximate Dunbar threshold number of group disintegration, or to the results of those experiments that put too many Norwegian rats in a cage, requires a separate treatment not possible here.

11 For a full mapping of how this essential formulation changes the contours of modern science, see Ilya Prigogine and Isabelle Stengers 1984.

12   But see *Evolution and Conversion:* "I have never said that the mimetic mechanism is deterministic. We can hypothetically assume that several prehistoric groups that did not survive precisely because they didn't find a way to cope with the mimetic crisis; their mimetic rivalries didn't find a victim who polarized their rage, saving them from self-destruction. We could even conceive of groups that solved one or two crises through the founding murder but failed to re-enact it ritually, developing a durable religious system, and therefore succumbing to the next crisis" (Girard 2008, 67). See also Dormoy: «En fait, le mécanisme ne fonctionne à peu près jamais de manière absolue, mais nous devons le penser comme tel pour pouvoir penser tous les cas possibles» (2018, 100).

13   It is remarkable that Clausewitz's resolves modern warfare down into two wrestling for dominance, "die zwei Ringende" (Clausewitz 1952, 191), and Goya's two antagonists in "Fight with Cudgels" occur at the same historical moment, both with their eyes on the world that Napoleon's new warfare of total conscription has created. Wilfred Owen's unfinished Great War poem "Strange Meeting" ends (left incomplete in manuscript) on the Clausewitzian *Wechselwirkung* of the *zwei Ringende* when two opposing soldiers meet in Hell. The German victim says to his British killer: "I parried/But my hands were loathe and cold./Let us sleep now." This is Leibnitz/Kant's perpetual peace of the graveyard. See Johnsen 2017.

14   Personal communication.

15   Nidesh Lawtoo has told me of Lacoue-Labarthe's lifelong devotion to this poem. Such comparisons, Erich Auerbach taught us, are a *wechselseitige Befruchtung, eine guter Weg.*

Bibliography

Calasso, Roberto (1983). *La rovina di Kasch.* Milano: Adelphi

Chantre, Benoît (2023). *René Girard: biographie.* Paris: Grasset.

Clausewitz, Carl (1952). *Vom Kriege.* Bonn: Ferdinand Dümmlers.

Damasio, Antonio (2010). *Self Comes to Mind: Constructing the Conscious Brain.* New York: Pantheon.

—— (2021). *Feeling and Knowing: Making Minds Conscious.* New York: Pantheon.

Deguy, Michel and Jean-Pierre Dupuy (eds.) (1982). *René Girard et le problème du mal.* Paris: Grasset.

Dormoy, Nadine (2018). *L'univers de René Girard.* Paris: Orizons.

Dumouchel, Paul (ed.) (1985). *Violence et vérité.* Paris: Grasset.

Dumouchel, Paul and Jean-Pierre Dupuy (eds.) (1983). *L'auto-organisation: De la physique au politique.* Paris: Seuil.

Dumouchel, Paul (ed.) (1988). *Violence and Truth: On the Work of René Girard.* Stanford: Stanford University Press.

Dunbar, R.I.M. (1993). "Coevolution of Neocortical Size, Group Size and Language in Humans." *Behavioral and Brain Sciences* 16.4, 681 735.

Dupuy, Jean-Pierre (2009). *On the Origins of Cognitive Science. The Mechanization of the Mind,* trans. M.B. DeBevoise. Cambridge, MA: MIT Press.

Else, Gerald F. (1957). *Aristotle's Poetics. The Argument.* Cambridge, MA: Harvard University Press.

Gallese, Vittorio (2011). "The Two Sides of Mimesis: Mimetic Theory, Embodied Simulation, and Social Identification," in *Mimesis and Science: Empirical Research on Imitation and the*

Mimetic Theory of Culture and Religion, ed. Scott R. Garrels. East Lansing: Michigan State University Press, 87–108.

Garrels, Scott (2011). *Mimesis and Science: Empirical Research on Imitation and the Mimetic Theory of Culture and Religion*. East Lansing: Michigan State University Press.

Girard, René (1961). *Mensonge romantique et vérité romanesque*. Paris: Grasset.

—— (1962). *Proust: A Collection of Critical Essays*. Englewood Cliffs: Prentice Hall.

—— (1963). *Dostoïevski, du double à l'unité*. Paris: Plon.

—— (1966). *Deceit, Desire and the Novel*. Baltimore: The Johns Hopkins University Press.

—— (1972). *La violence et le sacré*. Paris: Grasset.

—— (1978). *Des choses cachées depuis la fondation du monde*. Paris: Grasset.

—— (2007). *Achever Clausewitz*. Paris: Carnets Nord.

—— (2008). *Evolution and Conversion: Dialogues on the Origin of Culture,* with Pierpaolo Antonello and João Cezar de Castro Rocha. London: Bloomsbury.

—— (2009). *Battling to the End: Conversations with Benoît Chantre*. East Lansing: Michigan State University Press.

Hironaka, Ann (2005). *Neverending Wars: the International Community, Weak States, and the Perpetuation of Civil War*. Cambridge, MA: Harvard University Press.

Johnsen, William A. (2017). "Wilfred Owen's 'Strange Meeting' and René Girard's Clausewitzian Apocalypse." *Cosmopolis* 16.1–2. http://www.cosmopolisonline.it/articolo.php?numero=XIV122017&id=11

Knüsel, Christopher, and Martin Smith (eds.) (2014). *The Routledge Handbook of the Bioarchaeology of Human Conflict*. London: Routledge.

Lawtoo, Nidesh (2013). *The Phantom of the Ego: Modernism and the Mimetic Unconscious*. East Lansing: Michigan State University Press.

—— (2022). *Homo Mimeticus: A New Theory of Imitation*. Leuven: Leuven University Press.

—— (2023a). *Violence and the Oedipal Unconscious: vol. 1 The Catharsis Hypothesis*. East Lansing: Michigan State University Press.

—— (2023b). *Violence and the Mimetic Unconscious: vol. 2 The Affective Hypothesis*. East Lansing: Michigan State University Press.

Livingston, Paisley (ed.) (1984). *Disorder and Order*. Saratoga, CA: Anma Libri.

Lorenz, Konrad (1966). *On Aggression*. New York: Harcourt, Brace and World.

Meltzoff, Andrew N. (2011). "Out of the Mouths of Babes: Imitation, Gaze, and Intentions in Infant Research—the 'Like Me' Framework," in *Mimesis and Science: Empirical Research on Imitation and the Mimetic Theory of Culture and Religion*, ed. Scott R. Garrels. East Lansing: Michigan State University Press, 55–74.

Meltzoff, Andrew N., and Wolfgang Prinz (2002). *The Imitative Mind*. Cambridge: Cambridge University Press.

Mitchell, Kevin J. (2023). *Free Agents*. Princeton. Princeton University Press.

Nietzsche, Friedrich (1887). *Morgenröthe*. Leipzig: E.W. Fritzsch.

Prigogine, Ilya, and Isabelle Stengers (1984). *Order Out of Chaos*. London: Heineman.

Simonse, Simon (2007). *Kings of Disaster*. Kampala, Uganda: Fountain Publishers. Revision of (1992). *Kings of Disaster*. Leiden: E.J. Brill.

Varela, Francisco J., and Jean-Pierre Dupuy (eds.) (1992). *Understanding Origins*. Dordrecht, The Netherlands: Kluwer Academic Publishers.

Yeats, William B. (1918). *Per Amica Silentia Lunae*. London: MacMillan.

—— (1989). *The Collected Poems of W. B. Yeats*, ed. Richard J. Finneran. New York: MacMillan.

CHAPTER 8

BATAILLE ON MIMETIC HETEROLOGY[1]

Nidesh Lawtoo

Virtually unknown during his life, Georges Bataille started to cast a shadow after his death. This long shadow now reaches, via mimetic studies, into the present opening up of new perspectives on homo mimeticus for the future as well. Recuperated from oblivion in the 1970s and 1980s by different thinkers we now conveniently group under the heterogeneous category of "poststructuralism,"[2] Bataille soon became synonymous of an untimely writer whose voluntarily disordered thought slipped through stable linguistic oppositions, transgressed the boundaries dividing the margins and the center, the sane and the insane, life and death, the imaginary and the symbolic, and went as far as anticipating groundbreaking theoretical innovations such as the death of the author, sexual transgressions, the *mise en jeu* of language, the death of the subject, the gestation of inoperative communities, and, we may now add, the birth of homo mimeticus as well.[3]

   After Nietzsche, it is in fact Bataille who arguably went furthest in developing a protean thought that investigates the centrality of mimesis in intersubjective forms of non-verbal communication mediated by affective contagion: from laughter to collective effervescence, festivity to expenditure, drunkenness to ecstasy, erotism to sacrifice, trance to death, all these manifestations of sovereign communication rest on a "mimetic communication" (Lawtoo 2013, 209–280) that traverses his entire corpus. Moreover, Bataille's focus on what Nietzsche called "inner experience" (1990, § 45) also led him to transgress the boundaries of individuation via Dionysian dramatizations that, as a genealogy that goes from Nietzsche all the way back to Plato made clear, are at the roots of mimetic studies more generally. Strangely, Bataille's career-long focus on the relation between eroticism, violence and the sacred remained at the margins of mimetic theories of the past century.[4] It is thus now important to keep foregrounding the centrality of Bataille for mimetic studies in the present century.

For this genealogical operation, the possible starting points in Bataille's corpus are multiple: from "The Psychological Structure of Fascism" to *Inner Experience*, *Guilty* to *Theory of Religion*, *Eroticism* to the trilogy on *The Accursed Share*, among other heterogeneous texts, Bataille insistently returns to what he calls the "gay contagion [*heureuse contagion*]" flowing, like a river, from self to other(s) generating an "intense current of communication" (1954, 112–113; my transl.) that finds in mimetic pathos, rather than rational logos, its primary medium of transmission. Having traced Bataille's general contribution to mimetic studies elsewhere, I now take a genealogical step back to the dawn of Bataille's intellectual career. In particular, I re-turn to the transgressive subject matters out of which his mimetic thought is born. Early on, in fact, Bataille practiced an interdisciplinary thought *avant la lettre*, which, along with Roger Caillois' "diagonal science" already discussed in volume one of *Homo Mimeticus*, inspired mimetic studies. Bataille's simultaneous engagement with the human sciences of his time allowed him to develop, via the productive logic of mimetic agonism, an alternative "science" of heterogeneous subjects that are "totally other," cannot be reduced to rational discourse; yet, in his view, could be studied nonetheless, from the interdisciplinary angle of what he called, oxymoronically, the science of "heterology" or, alternatively, the "science of the *heterogeneous*, that is to say, the science of the *excluded part*" (Bataille 2018, 31)—an accursed mimetic part that now returns to haunt, phantom-like, the contemporary human sciences.

Bataille not only as a thinker who anticipates post-structuralist concerns with difference, language, and mediation, then. Rather, Bataille as a pre-structuralist thinker of sameness, affect, and contagion, a mimetic contagion that is intimately felt in *ek-static* instants of communication that reveal the palpitating homology of heterology vital to furthering the mimetic turn or *re*-turn. This is, in a nutshell, the hypothesis that leads me to reopen the "Dossier Heterology" from the angle of mimetic studies.

"Definition of Heterology:" Reopening the Dossier

The recently translated "Definition of heterology," which is not included in the 12 Volumes of the *Oeuvres complètes*, appeared in English for the first time in 2018 (Bataille 2018), opening up new perspectives to further the patho-*logies* of homo mimeticus. Originally conceived as part of a project titled, "Dossier Heterology" collected in volume II of the *Oeuvres complètes,* this short, previously unpublished, and impressively dense theoretical "Definition" illuminates sacred, mimetic experiences Bataille never stopped interrogating, in their throbbing movement of emergence. This previously unpublished piece shines like a precious pearl in the formless magma of his unpublished papers. Furthering orthodox disciplines in the human sciences, Bataille accounts for the ambivalent feelings of "attraction and repulsion" at the heart of transgressive experiences whose syncopated movement generates "ecstatic horror."

This double movement is, indeed, characteristic of the pathos of distance that distinguishes *homo mimeticus*; it is also the beating heart of Bataille's heterogeneous thought and animates his major theoretical preoccupations, including preoccupations with fascist leaders endowed with the will power to horrify and hypnotize individual bodies, as well as the entire body politic. True for fascism and Nazism a century ago, this lesson remains valid for "aspirational" (Connolly 2017) or "(new) fascism" (Lawtoo 2019) in the present century that still benefits from a Bataillean lens.[5] As William Connolly puts it in diagnostic terms Bataille would have appreciated and that are now central to mimetic studies, "there is never a vacuum on the visceral register of cultural life"—hence the urgency to pay attention to "bodily stresses" and mimetic modes of "affective communication" (Connolly 2022, 689, 891) that continue, via new media, to galvanize the body politic.

At the same time, the implications of "Definition of Heterology" cannot be restricted to Bataille's well-known political preoccupations with monocephalic leader figures in 1930s still relevant a century later. Rather, they immediately transgress the boundaries between politics and religion, anthropology and psychology, and open up heterogeneous questions that inform the general economy of what he calls "heterology" and continue to inform what we call mimetic patho(-)logies. For instance: how can what is "totally other" and, thus, "heterogeneous," become the object of a discursive "*logos*" that, by definition, belongs to the sphere of the "homogenous"? How can we know, or feel, the *pathos* of an "other" whose distance, Bataille says, is "absolute," yet is intimately experienced nonetheless? Above all, why do heterogeneous matters that are "holy and unclean" (Bataille 2018, 30) both hypnotically attract us and physically repel us, in a double movement that animates what Bataille calls "ecstatic horror" (34)? These questions cut through the heart of Bataille's heterogeneous thought. They directly inform his conception of the sovereign subject "whose *exterior objective* aspect is always inseparable from the *interior*" (VIII 284),[6] as he puts it in *Sovereignty*. In particular, the early Bataille helps us understand the complex interplay between the *inside* and the *outside* of the subject essential to follow the transgressive dynamic of mimetic communications that have been neglected during the linguistic turn but are central to both the affective and mimetic turn.

"Definition" reveals more clearly and succinctly than any other writings the theoretical foundations of Bataille's thought by making visible the continuities and discontinuities between heterology and emerging human sciences now internal to mimetic studies. Bataille, in fact, relies on the insights of pioneering figures such as Émile Durkheim and Sigmund Freud in order to cast new light on the fundamental "ambivalence" sacred experiences generate. Hetero-logy is thus as much an anthropo-logy (*logos* on man) as a psycho-logy (*logos* on the soul). But it is not only that. For Bataille, in fact, these scientific disciplines are, *volens nolens*, complicit with a long-standing idealizing trend in western philosophy that can be traced back to Plato and whose tendency is to exclude the obscure subject matter they attempt to illuminate, freezing the movement of heterology in unitary, ideal, and transcendental forms. Furthering a mimetic line of inquiry in Bataille studies[7] now informing mimetic studies, I argue that the laws of attraction and repulsion that animate heterology find their polarized foundations in the patho-*logies* of imitation (*mimesis*) understood in its heterogeneous—anthropological, ontological, and psychological—manifestations. Mimesis, for Bataille, was never restricted to a visual and stabilizing economy of ideal representation. Instead, it entails a destabilizing form of bodily communication he will later call "sovereign" for it introduces a general movement of affective participation with privileged others introducing a troubling sameness at the heart of difference. In his "Dossier on Heterology," Bataille, following the French psychologist and philosopher Pierre Janet—a key and so far, largely unacknowledged precursor of mimetic studies—will call this heterogeneous other who is indistinguishable from the self, a "socius" (II, 287).

Paradoxically, then, heterology, while being the "science" (*logos*) of the "totally other" (*hetero*) may actually point toward an abyssal mimetic experience of homology, an ecstatic, transgressive, yet sacred homology that escapes homogeneous definitions, but has nonetheless the mimetic power to transform pure spirits into impure matters, abject horrors into loving angels, thereby bringing Bataille's mimetic heterology into being.

Polarized Anthropology: Recharging the Sacred

In "Definition," Bataille immediately places the movement of his emerging thought in an impossible position, generating a double movement that will animate the entirety of his career. In the opening paragraph, in fact, Bataille defines heterology as "the science of *the excluded part*" (2018, 31), by which he means an "accursed" (*maudite*) part that includes "sacred elements," "objects of disgust" and "erotic life" (30). This is, indeed, an oxymoronic definition; if only because "excluded" matters (that is, the heterogeneous) are, by their very essence, inaccessible to the sphere of objectifying "science" (that is, the homogeneous). Just as light cannot illuminate a shadow, so science cannot cast light on the heterogeneous. The material *objects* of Bataille's project and his scientific *objective* are thus radically at odds, generating a methodological oscillation toward/away from heterogeneous matters that will continue to animate Bataille's account of sacred experiences. Whether his focus is on abject objects in the 1930s, on mystical subjects in the 1940s, or on the experience of sovereign communication in the 1950s, Bataille's thought follows as much what he calls "the path of work" as "the path of transgression" (1986: 261). Hence, this double-path sets up a tension between intellectual distance (*logos*) and affective proximity (*pathos*); it also generates a polarized oscillation that reproduces, shadow-like, the double movement sacred matters themselves produce. This paradoxical methodological position informs influential human sciences concerned with the ambivalence of sacred emotions, such as anthropology of religion and psychoanalysis. Bataille is thus not naïvely in search of originality. Rather, his thought emerges from a mimetic, sometimes agonistic, but always productive relation with these neighboring discourses (*logoi*) whose conceptual limits Bataille will test first and, eventually, transgress.

Bataille's general debt to anthropology of religion is well known. Heterology in particular has often been approached from a Durkheimian Perspective (Richman 2002) that is attentive to the "contagious" (ffrench, 2007, 38) and in our sense "mimetic" experiences the sacred generates. And yet, Bataille also relies on mimetic agonism to mark his distance from his anthropological predecessor. Thus, he specifies that Durkheim did not go far enough in his exploration of the polarization of the sacred: "Although Durkheim did not neglect the polarized nature of the elements of the sacred, he did not feel able to assign them an important role in his theory" (Bataille 2018, 33). Consequently, he claims that Durkheim is partially responsible for "a classic confusion between *impure* and *profane*" (33), a confusion later accentuated by members of Durkheim's school. As Bataille makes clear, anthropology is a scientific *logos* in line with a "purifying development" (34) that excludes impure, magical elements from the sacred, relegating them to the profane. In an emancipatory, agonistic move, then, Bataille outlines a fundamental *différend* between heterology and anthropology. And he does so to reintroduce a base, material impurity into an idealizing, anthropological tendency that freezes the movement of the sacred in pure, ideal forms.

In a way, Bataille's heterogeneous thought comes into being precisely in his attempt to regenerate a polarity, which, for him, is missing in the science of anthropology but functions as the beating heart of the sacred itself. He argues for the return of unclean, heterogeneous matters on the theoretical scene, emerging from the shadow of a purifying, homogenous tradition that sought to exclude them as he writes:

> The confusion between the impure and the profane, writes Bataille, is one of the fundamental principles of any purifying development, seeking to remove religion of the original cesspool [*cloaque*], in which the sludge [*boue*] itself was sacred. It gradually becomes necessary to devalue the mud and that is why we call it profane. (2018, 34)

The language here is already characteristically Bataillean, and so is the movement of his thought. Bataille, in fact, counters an idealizing confusion that purges the idea of the sacred from impure, abject matters. As this passage indicates, these excluded, "accursed" (*maudite*) parts, comprise "mud," and "sewers," but he also adds: "'the leftovers, the litter, nail clippings and cut hair, faeces, foetuses, garbage'" (34)—the latter being "ingredients used by witches" (35) in their magical participations.

The reason Bataille wants to include these abject matters and the magic that animates them within the sphere of the heterogeneous is clear. For him, the double movement of attraction and repulsion at the heart of the heterogeneous depends precisely on the systolic and diastolic interplay between right and left sacred, pure and impure matters. Without the experience of rejection heterogeneity generates, there is no polarity within the sacred; and without polarity, there is no possible "transmutation" between high sacred and low sacred, or, as he also says, between what is "pure and impure, angelic and obscene" (2018, 36). Bataille's theoretical operation that will drive his entire thought is already present in embryo here. It consists in repolarizing the sacred so as to render it *sacer* again, that is, both holy and accursed. And by doing so, he sets in motion a palpitating double movement between high and low sacred, generating a circulation of affective energy whereby impure matters turn into pure spirits, loving angels into obscene bodies.

But Bataille's operation touches deeper. In fact, his recuperation of the impure within the sphere of the sacred entails an immanent move that brings human beings back in touch with the muddy origins from which they stem, introducing a sacred continuity at the heart of profane discontinuities. Paradigmatic examples of heterogeneity such as "nail clippings and cut hair, faeces, foetus" (2018, 34) and so forth are, indeed, *excluded* in disgust, and subjected to different forms of social taboos in profane periods of homogenous stability. And yet, at sacred times, these abject elements are nonetheless materially *included* in heterogeneous, destabilizing ritual practices that recognize them as constitutive of the human subject itself. Notice in fact that these abject products are not only originating from accursed, bodily parts; they also include the original material out of which the subject, as foetus, grows. What is excluded, then, is actually already included within the very subject that operates the exclusion. If we peel off the first layer of straightforward formal discontinuity we find a material base of continuity that traces "nail clippings" back to fingers, "cut hair" to heads, "faeces" to bowels, the "foetus" to *ipse*. It is thus no accident that these taboo elements are also the ingredients witches use in their practices, magical practices whose goal is to generate transgressive forms of mimetic participation that break down the boundaries of individuation. As Bataille learned as an "apprentice sorcerer" (I, 523) from Henry Hubert's and Marcel Mauss's theory of magic (as well as from James Frazer and Lucien Lévy-Bruhl), "magic takes place in a sacred world" in which figures loaded with the "force of *mana*" trigger "a spiritual action at a distance that is produced between sympathetic beings" (Mauss and Hubert 1995, 105). Heterogeneous matters, then, introduce not only unclean (physical) continuities, but also sympathetic (spiritual) continuities at the heart of "absolute" discontinuities, generating a sense of what Bataille, following Lucien Lévy-Bruhl, also calls "mystical" participation with the world (I, 347). Similarly, as Bataille will later say in *Erotism*, at sacred or erotic times, taboos are indeed transgressed; and out of this transgression a "discontinuity" of beings turns into what he calls a "miraculous continuity between two beings" (1986: 19)—or, more generally, "continuity of being" (16).

As the language of "being" suggests, and the scope of heterology confirms, this double-movement of attraction and repulsion is not without destabilizing ontological effects: if it explicitly reintroduces mystical transformations that, for better and worse, recharge the sacred, it also implicitly throws mud on an entire classic tradition that conceives of being in terms of pure, ideal forms. Mimetic studies re-turns to this muddy ontology.

Muddy Ontology: Un-forming Idealism

At stake in Bataille's quarrel with an idealizing tendency in anthropology that excludes the impure is not only a redefinition of what the sacred is, or should be; it is also, and more fundamentally, a philosophical interrogation of the onto-logical foundations of being itself. Bataille's general anti-idealism is well-known given his genealogical alignment with figures like Nietzsche, but we still need to further his materialist ontology to further mimetic studies. If we have seen from an anthropological perspective that heterogeneity (the sacred) introduces mimetic continuities between human beings, we now turn to see from a phil-osophical perspective that it also introduces a mimetic continuity at the very heart of being.

Bataille's paradigmatic examples of mimetic heterology indicate an un-derlying dialogue with a much more ancient tradition, a classical, metaphysical tradition whose ideal forms Bataille sets out to deform or, better, un-form. In a much-discussed passage on the "formless," in fact, Bataille counters "academic men [*hommes académiques*]" for whom "to be happy, the universe would have to take shape [*prenne forme*]" by stating that the "formless [*informe*]" "universe is something like a spider or spit [*crachat*]" (1929, 382; 1985, 31). Less known is that, as the anti-academic tone of this paragraph suggests, the origins of this philosophical tradition can be traced back to that *homo academicus* par excel-lence who is, of course, Plato. After a confrontation with the father of anthropol-ogy of religion, a brief dialogue with the father of philosophy will allow us to see how deep the anti-idealist foundations of Bataille's mimetic studies go.

The base, materialist spirit of Bataille's definition of heterology is clearly an-ti-Platonic in conceptual orientation, but when it comes to the movement of his thought, matters are far from being clear-cut: underlying mimetic continuities emerge between Bataille's materialist heterology and Plato's idealist ontology. In *Parmenides* (1961a), for instance, a notoriously difficult yet founding dialogue in western metaphysics, the ancestral father of ontological thought, Parmenides, sets out to interrogate the foundations of Socrates' (Platonic) theory of forms. Let us simply recall that in Plato's transcendental metaphysics, immanent, plural phenomena (*phainomena*) are modeled on a corresponding, singular form in the transcendental sphere of ideas (*eidos*), an intelligible sphere in which sensible phenomena are said to "participate" via the medium of imitation (*mimesis*)— that is, by "being made in their image" (1961a, 927).[8] From the outset, however, Parmenides is not at all convinced that "forms themselves" can be neatly peeled away from the material phenomena that mimetically "participate" in them. Thus, he asks Socrates a series of materialist questions that resonate strikingly with Bataille's heterogeneous concerns with formless matters. Let us partake in a part of this dialogue:

> **Parmenides**: "[Is there] a form of man, apart from ourselves and all other men like us—a form of man as something by itself? Or a form of fire or water?"
> **Socrates**: "I have often been puzzled about those things, Parmenides…"
> **Parmenides**: "Are you also puzzled, Socrates, about cases that might be thought absurd, *such as hair or mud or dirt or any other trivial and undignified objects*? Are you doubtful whether or not to assert that each of these has a separate form distinct from things like those we handle?"
> **Socrates**: "Not at all, said Socrates. In these cases, the things are just the things we see; it would surely be absurd to suppose that they have a form. *All the same, I have sometimes been troubled by a doubt whether what is true in one case may not be true in all.*" (Plato, 1961a, 130c–d; emphasis added)

Parmenides contra Socrates, Plato contra Plato: this is, indeed, an ancient mimetic quarrel. Dramatically put, Parmenides's materialist questions unbalance Socrates' idealism and force him into an impossible double bind, throwing a wrench in the very origin of Plato's metaphysics and, by extension, western philosophy as a whole. Either Socrates admits that not all material phenomena have a corresponding intelligible idea. *Ergo* the world of forms is incomplete, deficient and perhaps even illusory—that is, the ideal world turns out to be a fable! Or he admits that impure, formless elements such as "hair, or mud, or dirt" do have a corresponding form in which they participate. *Ergo* pure forms turn out to be as formless as impure mud—that is, the ideal origin is stained by a muddy reality! There is no easy way out from this mimetic stranglehold, and the dialogue does not offer a dialectical resolution. Instead, old Parmenides benevolently admonishes young Socrates for dismissing these formless, heterogeneous matters. In his view, Socrates has not been fully possessed by philosophy as yet, and cares too much for the world's opinions (*doxa*), a tendency Parmenides hopes Socrates—and with him perhaps also Plato, and the idealist philosophy he engendered—will perhaps overcome "someday:" "You will not despise any of these objects then," Parmenides quips, "but at present your youth makes you still pay attention to what the world will think" (1961a, 130e).

To be sure, more than two millennia later, as Bataille explores the muddy waters of heterogeneous matters, he is certainly not concerned with what the world thinks. On the contrary, he turns precisely to such "undignified objects" in order to subvert a longstanding metaphysical tradition that considers base phenomenal matters as a debased imitation of ideal forms. That Bataille, in "Definition," is implicitly engaging with the same "academic" tradition he denounces in "Dictionary" is confirmed by the shadow of mimetic language that frames his recuperation of impure matters within the sphere of the sacred. For instance, he writes:

> [T]he role of heterology consists precisely in taking out from the shadows [*ombre*] what they had made horrible, and to do that it first had to remove as explicitly as possible a confusion that had resulted from protection from all investigation for the very thing [*chose même*] that had for humankind immeasurable importance. (Bataille 2018, 34)

The "origin" of our being, which, for Bataille, is the "very thing" (*chose même*)—he does not say the "thing itself" (*chose en soi*) to avoid the idealizing tendency he seeks to overturn, preferring to speak of the "original cesspool" (*cloaque initial*) (34) instead—has indeed been relegated to the world of mimetic "shadows" by an ontological tradition that privileges dignified, unitary forms over and against undignified, formless phenomena. Bataille, on the other hand, like other figures of Nietzschean inspiration, continues to be haunted by illusory "shadows" or "phantoms," whose originary nature has progressively been rendered "unintelligible" by a western "need to idealize" (2018, 30). Thus, he specifies:

> By moving away from these unpleasant phantoms [*phantasmes*], a new purpose was realized: the unspeakable sense of ecstatic horror, which is at the root of religion as well as erotic activity, was rendered unintelligible, as were polarization phenomena as their heterogeneity increased... (34; trans. modified)

Bataille's concept of "phantom" should not be confused with a psychological phantasm here. As it was already the case with his references to "shadows," it stems from the same philosophical tradition that excludes unformed matters into a cavern of darkness. As is well-known, in Book 10 of the *Republic*, as the question of what mimesis is in general returns to haunt the philosophical scene, Socrates describes the world of phenomena as mere "phantoms" (*phantasma*) and the world of art as "an imitation of a phantasm" (1961b, 598b) three times removed from reality. In sum, Bataille's playful relegation of the *homo academicus'* "need to idealize" to the illusory world of "unintelligible" "shadows," or "phantoms," far removed from the "original sewer" out of which we are born, is wrapped up in deep layers of (Socratic) irony. In a deft metaphysical move, Bataille turns mimetic "shadows" into "original" realities, the "sewer" into something "originary," while at the same time relegating the "need to idealize" to what he significantly calls a place of "darkness."

And yet, Bataille does not paint the world in black and white. Despite the violent, idealist exclusion of the low (formless) sacred from the high (formed) sacred, the movement of Bataille's heterology indicates that there is no simple opposition between light and darkness, pure ideal forms and impure material phenomena, but a mimetic continuity instead. Just as a shadow cannot easily be detached from the form that casts it, so the formless side of the sacred cannot easily be detached from the formal side that rejects it. In fact, it is precisely through this "classic," "purifying" exclusion, Bataille suggests, that the origins of our being are "made horrible." And, conversely, he says that "the role of heterology consists precisely in bringing out from the shadows [*ombre*] what they [the idealists] had managed to make horrible" (34; emphasis added). For Bataille, then, the purifying movement of exclusion of heterogeneous matters into a cavern of "shadows" is far from remaining unstained. On the contrary, this idealist move is directly responsible for generating the muddy "horror" it seeks to keep at bay, unwittingly contributing to the movement of attraction and repulsion it attempts to freeze. Paradoxically, then, Bataille finds in Plato's idealist ontology an inversed, mirroring counterpart of the movement of heterology. That is, a *transformative* movement in which an originary experience turns into a formless shadow, a pure intention into an impure effect, ideal forms into muddy sewers, angelic spirits into abject bodies. Perhaps, then, at stake in Bataille's move is not only a metaphysical inversion that posits formless matters over and against ideal forms; nor solely a psychological diagnostic that shows the impure, material consequences of pure, rational reflections (though it is both). It is also a heterological realization that despite their absolute otherness, formless, abject matters are nonetheless intimately connected to the origins of our being—if only because, for Bataille, it is from a formless "universe" in general, and from bleeding "wounds" in particular, that human beings both originate and continue to participate.

We are now in a position to confirm the destabilizing effects of Bataille's mimetic heterology whereby we started and its general importance for a re-turn of homo mimeticus that transgresses idealist forms. If the rigor of orthodox science Bataille inherits from Durkheim's religious anthropology forces him to set up a radical *conceptual* difference between the sacred and the profane, the ontological undercurrent that animates the *movement* of Bataille's heterogeneous thought transgresses the neat positivistic distinctions on which he relies. Bataille, in fact, not only cuts through homogenous disciplinary traditions, spilling over to contaminate the ontological foundations of western idealism; it also melts the formal boundaries of heterogeneity itself, generating inclusion and continuity at the heart of exclusion and discontinuity. This also means that, for Bataille, the "study of human polarity as an autonomous science" (2018, 33) is predicated on the realization that oppositions, no matter how "absolute," are never static and unmovable, but entail a transformative polarization that turns polar opposites into mimetic polarities. And if this was true for anthropological and ontological polarizations, we now turn to see that it is equally true for psychological communications.

Transgressive Psychology: Communicating with the *Socius*

Eroticism, phantasms, and the ambivalence generated by sexually oriented bodily matters. Indeed, as Bataille unfolds his definition of heterology, sailing away from the idealism of anthropology, while deftly avoiding the whirlpool of Platonic ontology, he is nearing yet another disciplinary shore that turns sexual taboos into a privileged object of inquiry that is, psychoanalysis. Heterology's proximity to psychoanalysis was already latent in Bataille's suggestion that rationalist exclusions are responsible for turning heterogeneous matters into something abject and horrible—what psychoanalytic critics will theorize under the rubric of "the powers of horrors" (Kristeva 1982). But Bataille makes this connection manifest as he says that psychoanalysis "reaches directly to eroticism, genitalia and *excreta*" (2018, 35), which is the sphere of heterology as well. Like heterology, psychoanalysis focuses on the impure, excluded matters at the "root of religion as well as erotic activity" (34). And, again like heterology, psycho-analysis is concerned with the contradictory double movements generated by irrational, emotional currents. Thus, Bataille acknowledges that in chapter 2 of *Totem and Taboo* (1940), titled "Taboo and the Ambivalence of Emotions," "Freud speaks of the conjugation of attraction and repulsion," giving the exam-ple of the "neurotic fear of touching and the desire to touch at the same time" as an indication of a type of psychic ambivalence "causing nausea and erection, disgust and love at the same time" (2018, 34–35; see Freud 1940, 48–54).

At first sight, the psychoanalytical concept of "ambivalence" seems to of-fer a privileged door to account for the movements of repulsion and attraction taboo subjects generate. As Freud makes clear such an "ambivalent attitude to-ward...taboo prohibitions," characteristic of so called "obsessional neurotics" and "primitive people" (1940, 54) has ultimately its origin in an unresolved Oedipal conflict. Sexual desire for the parent of the opposite sex, the story goes, generates a rivalrous hostility toward the parent of the same sex who is perceived as an obstacle, and as this conflict between the pleasure principle and the reality principle is internalized into a psychic conflict between the "id" and the "su-perego," we have what Freud calls "the prototype of the ambivalence of human emotions" (1940, 91–92)—*alias* the Oedipus complex.[9] From this "prototype," then, Freud extrapolates an anthropological theory that, in *illo tempore*, the same desire led young "savages" to the actual murder of the ancestral father figure in a sacrificial transgression responsible for the emergence of taboo prohibitions and, by extension, religion and culture as a whole. As Bataille faithfully reports, for Freud, what is at stake in this original transgression is a "'projection of un-conscious hostility' that the children had nourished against the dead parent dur-ing his lifetime" (2018, 34; see Freud, 1940, 77). With psychoanalysis, then, het-erology seems to have reached the bottom of the affair. Bataille, in fact, touches a discipline that not only makes the sphere of the impure its privileged object of scientific investigation, but also individuates the very origins of the ambivalent oscillation responsible for the polarization of erotic experiences.

And yet, having traveled so far, Bataille is extremely careful not to frame the movement of heterology within neat, prototypical (that is, triangular) forms, lest he reproduce the idealist movement he has been deftly averting all along. Bataille's suspicion of psychoanalysis—what he also calls in *Sovereignty* "*la pensée abstraite*" (VIII, 18)—is expressed at different points in his work, but "Definition" shows how deep his anti-Oedipal critique of Freud actually goes, clarifying the fundamental *différend* that divides the Oedipal unconscious from the mimetic unconscious. Bataille, in fact, specifies that psychoanalysis is based on a "defective method (which, besides, did not belong to it, since it was borrowed from general scientific method) (2018, 34)," and compares Freud's homogeneous approach to the one of "the chemist or the physiologist working in their laboratories" (35). That is, scientific figures that do not follow the flow of blood that animates living organisms, but dissect dead bodies instead. For Bataille, this methodological distance is the reason "Freud did not manage to think of impure objects as a specific reality" (34) and, consequently, missed the very origins of the ambivalence he set out to illuminate. It is thus no accident that Bataille sardonically speaks of "psychoanalysis's impotence" (*impuissance*) (34), deriding the castrating methodological effect of applying a homogeneous scientific method to heterogeneous sacred matters. Finally, for Bataille, the perverse effect of framing "primitive" people's sacred emotions in an Oedipal account of "obsessional neurotics" confined to familial, pathological dramas renders Freud seemingly "unaware that [in the 1930s] human life in its totality has become a function of demented reactions" (35). We can now understand why in "Dossier Heterology" Bataille insists that heterological investigations "are to be opposed to the theme of Oedipus" (II, 171). This is a firm and decisive claim. It clarifies, once and for all, that no matter how close to psychoanalysis Bataille might sound at first sight heterology, and the conception of the unconscious it presupposes, is radically "opposed" to the founding Oedipal theme on which psychoanalysis, in its Freudian, Lacanian, or other derivations, ultimately rests—if only because Bataille, like Nietzsche before him, is an advocate of the mimetic unconscious instead.

As we have now come to expect, Bataille's references to the father of psychoanalysis are not simply antagonistic; they rest on a mimetic agonism that serves a double diagnostic operation: symptomatic of a psychoanalytical impotence to account for the ambivalence of heterogeneous objects, the case of Freud also provides a springboard for immanent and material operations into heterogeneous subjects. Here is a Freudian diagnostic that gestures toward a heterological backdoor Freud himself did not actually open, but gives us access to the unconscious sources of the emotional currents we have been following all along:

> "The corpse, the newborn," he [Freud] said, "women in their state of suffering [*die Frau in ihren Leidenszustanden*], attract *by their inability to defend themselves*, the individual who has reached maturity and sees this as a source of new pleasures. That is why these people and these states are taboo." (Bataille 2018, 34)

The corpse, the newborn, and the suffering woman: what could these heterogeneous subjects possibly have in common? Freud's explanation is typical: it is their shared vulnerability, their "peculiar helplessness" (1940, 55), their openness to being violated, that generates an ambivalent feeling of attraction and repulsion, opening up transgressive "new pleasures" to be later repressed by social taboos. This is, indeed, a classical psychoanalytical explanation that frames the movement of heterogeneous affects within the Oedipal "prototype" Bataille warns us against. What, then, we may wonder, is the Bataillean alternative to access the labyrinth of the unconscious?

Bataille does not open this door completely, but he offers us a key. To capture the unconscious sources of heterological polarization it is necessary to situate these Freudian examples within the mimetic currents and undercurrents that inform the general economy of Bataille's thought, while at the same time supplementing a definition Bataille left partially incomplete from the angle of mimetic studies. We have seen so far that what is totally other and *discontinuous* at the level of science (work) might intimately be the same and *continuous* at the deeper level of communication (transgression). We have equally seen that the ingredients witches and sorcerers use in their magical rituals (nails, hair, etc.) are not only in a direct *physical* continuity with the body, but also in a *spiritual* participation with the soul, going as far as touching the *ontological* origins of being itself. What we must add now is that this mimetic continuity at the heart of human beings is even more intimately experienced with the three taboo cases mentioned above (corpses, newborns, suffering women). The repulsion and attraction they generate should in fact not simply be defined in terms of a "peculiar helplessness" that opens the door to Oedipal pleasures (Freud 1940, 55). Nor should our emphasis on mimesis lead us to automatically think in terms of a mimetic "identification" with an image (Lacan 1966, 94); or, alternatively, of a "mimetic desire" in which "mimesis" determines the object of desire (Girard 1977, 146). Rather, these examples are defined by an intrinsic feeling of *mimetic participation* generated by the fact that this heterogeneous "other" is not simply "totally other," but is also experienced as being intimately the same—what Bataille, following the French psychologist and philosopher Pierre Janet, also calls a "socius."

The importance of Janet's "psychological analysis" in the discovery of the unconscious has been traced by Henri Ellenberger's monumental study, *The Discovery of the Unconscious*, but largely due to the shadow psychoanalysis's romantic agonism cast on competing figures it is still largely unknown in the humanities.[10] This is the moment to retrieve Janet from the shadows. In fact, he developed an "intersubjective psychology" that gives birth to phantom egos open to mimetic influences that are now under the lens of mimetic studies.[11] Bataille, for one, was well-red in Janet's analytical psychology: he even collaborated with Janet by serving as the vice-president of the Society of Collective Psychology, presided by Janet.

In a lecture for this short-lived Society in 1937, for instance, Bataille relies on Janet's "psychology of the socius" in order to go to the origins of the ambivalent feelings of attraction and repulsion generated by heterogeneous others that trouble the boundaries of individuation. He writes: "Janet insisted on the fact that the individual subject," as he is caught in the movement of sacred communications, "is not easily distinguished from the fellow creature with whom he is in rapport, from the socius" (Bataille II, 287; Janet 1938, 145). The socius, then, as a distinct figure who is "not easily distinguished" from the "individual subject" opens up a mimetic continuity at the heart of discontinuity. And specifying this opening, Bataille adds a heterogeneous touch to Janet's definition as he adds: "the dead is a socius, which means that he is very difficult to distinguish from oneself" (II, 287). This is indeed a strange claim to understand, especially in technologized, homogeneous societies where corpses tend to be excluded and confined to profane institutions used to keep the feeling of sacred horror at a distance. Yet, as anyone who has experienced the loss of someone dear intimately knows, the death of the other is very difficult to keep outside—for her pathos is felt inside. Thinking of death, Bataille will also later speak of a "gulf which separates us" (1986, 12), yet he immediately adds, "death is hypnotizing" (13), suggesting the possibility of a mimetic union. The corpse might thus be excluded in its physical manifestation as corpse, but as socius she is immediately included in a "rapport," a hypnotic rapport generating what Bataille will also call a "passage, communication, but not from one the other insofar as the *one* and the *other* have lost their distinct existence" (1954, 74). This also means that the dead qua socius might indeed be "totally other" from the exterior point of view of homogeneity (science), but from the interior perspective of a transgressive communication (heterology) this other is actually difficult to disentangle from the self.

The socius, then, is a mimetic other who is formative of *ipse*, but not in the homogeneous sense that she reflects a unitary image in a mirror, or directs desire in yet another structure of rivalry. Rather, she is mimetic in the heterogeneous sense that her hypnotizing effect transgresses neat distinctions between self and other, inside and outside, introducing an affective continuity whereby "human unity" is unformed—or as Bataille figuratively says, is "shattering" it "like glass" (2018, 36). In sum, the socius is not the origin of an ideal, representational form, but of a formless bodily communication; she does not freeze the ego in a unitary *imago* but opens up the boundaries of individuation allowing the communication of mimetic affects to flow.

I have shown elsewhere that Janet's "psychology of the socius" informs not only the entirety of Bataille's heterogeneous thought but also opens up an alternative, mimetic backdoor to the unconscious.[12] Following up on this dossier, we should notice that Bataille moves from the figure of the "dead" to the one of the "newborn" as paradigmatic case of communication with a socius. Bataille was in fact quick to recognize that from the very first weeks of life, newborns are open to non-linguistic forms mimetic communication that turn exterior affects originating in the other into interior experiences that animate the self. For instance, speaking of that contagious affect par excellence that is laughter, Bataille says: "A child, who is a few weeks old, respond[s] to an adult's laughter" (in Hollier 1995, 107). Along similar lines, but thinking about the origins of feelings of disgust, he writes: "During the formation of behavioral attitudes in childhood, the act of exclusion is not directly assumed. It is communicated from the mother to the child through the medium of funny faces [*grimaces*] and expressive exclamations" (II, 220). And in *Erotism*, still thinking of children, he specifies that we "have to teach them [disgust] by pantomime" (1986, 58), suggesting that even such visceral affects such as disgust do not originate in the subject herself, but emerge from a mimetic reproduction of the facial expressions of the other/socius. An unconscious reflex triggered by an external expression of attraction (laughter) or repulsion (disgust) is thus at the source of a polarized emotional experience within the subject; the affect of the other/*socius* is not only reproduced but also felt, experienced, as the affect of the self/*ipse*.

This heterogeneous view of pre-verbal, unconscious communication flies in the face of the homogeneous doxa that dominated the twentieth century and considered that imitation was a belated, Oedipal phenomenon; yet it anticipates by nearly a century cognitive, mimetic discoveries that are now informing educated readers in the twenty-first century. Experiments in developmental psychology have in fact confirmed the presence of mimetic responses in newborns that allow them to reproduce facial expressions right after being born, records ranging about 42 minutes old (Meltzoff and Moore 1999), leading to the evolutionary hypothesis of the "imitative mind" (Meltzoff and Prinz 2002) in line with mimetic studies. More recently, as we noted in the Prelude, the discovery of "mirror neurons" in the 1990s (initially found in monkeys and later confirmed in humans as well) entailed the discovery of motor neurons that fire not only when we enact a movement but also when we observe someone else's movements or expressions. Still under discussion, mirror neurons are responsible for unconscious forms of imitation that can communicate basic emotions along embodied, affective and communicative lines postulated by precursors like Bataille. The most philosophically inclined among neuroscientists go as far as claiming that mirror neurons "may provide a key neural mechanism for understanding the mental states of others" (Iacoboni 2008: 33). Above all, contemporary neuroscience confirms a genealogical hypothesis on the birth of homo mimeticus: namely that the presence of an "unconscious intersubjective mimesis" (Gallese and Ammaniti 2014, 13) entails that "we should abandon the Cartesian view of the primacy of the ego and adapt a perspective emphasizing that the other is co-originally given as the self" (24), which is exactly that a genealogy of the phantom ego suggested. Familiar with a long tradition in mimetic theory—from Plato to Nietzsche, Tarde to Janet—and attentive to the formative power of mimesis in the birth of the ego Bataille modestly couched his groundbreaking heterological observations in the language of mimesis by saying: "I have thus only stated in other terms the well-known principle of contagion, or if you still want to call it that, fellow feeling, sympathie" (in Hollier 1997, 109).

After this detour via the laws of imitation responsible for affective communications with a socius, we should be in a better position to address the third, and last case of heterology: the suffering woman. When Freud speaks of "*die Frau in ihren Leidenszustanden*" (1920, 44) he might actually be alluding to the pain of menstruation, a bodily production that is traditionally included among taboo, heterogenoues objects. And yet, since the focus is on the suffering subject herself, we should be careful not to objectify our interlocutor and essentialize our mimetic diagnostic, if only because suffering [*Leiden*] transgresses gender barries in order to open up the self to a suffering that takes place with the other [*Mitleid*]. That this case can be diagnosed from the perspective of the psychology of the socius is clear. In both its physical and psychic manifestation, suffering is a contagious affect that communicates itself mimetically, from self to other, introducing an affective continuity at the heart of discontinuity that is experienced from the inside. Thus, in the experience of *Mitleid* or sympathy (*sym-pathos*, feeling with not feeling for) for a suffering woman or man—why be biased?—the self is caught in a relation of communication so profound that the distinction between self and other, inside and outside, my pathos and sym-pathos, no longer holds. As Bataille will specify later in his career, such an other allows me to "participate in his emotion from inside myself. This sensation felt inside me communicates itself to me" (1986, 153). The subject who speaks from "inside myself" is thus not myself, and yet an experience in which the heterogeneity of what is supposedly "totally other" turns into an intimately felt homology of what is experienced as radically the same.

We should now better understand why in the midst of writing what is arguably his most influential work, *Inner Experience*, Bataille stated: "Then I started reading Janet, imagining it necessary to use his subtlety in order to go further" (V, 430). Indeed, in Janet's much-neglected (some would say excluded) psychology of a socius who is oneself, while being someone other, he finds a subtle tool to diagnose the laws of imitation that underlie his persistent fascination for sacred forms of sovereign communication. Whether he speaks of the self in terms of a "space of communication, of fusion between subject and object" (1954, 21) in *Inner Experience*, of an "interpenetration (contagion)" that opens up "the passage, the fall of one's being into another [*la chute d'un être de l'un dans l'autre*]" (V, 392) in *Guilty,* or of "our obsession with a primal continuity linking us with everything that is" (1986, 15) in *Erotism*, he is consistently referring to the experience of mimetic homology generated by heterogenous and, thus, sovereign communications with the other/socius. This is why, he, Bataille, in a confessional mode, goes as far as saying: "I cannot distinguish between myself and those others with whom I desire to communicate" (1954, 55).

In sum, the corpse, the newborn, and the suffering (wo)man are paradigmatic examples of heterogeneous subjects and should be considered as "totally other" from the mediated perspective of "discursive knowledge" (Bataille 1954, 11). Yet, as anyone who a lost a loved one, loves a newborn, or has made a lover suffer, intimately knows from the experience of what Bataille calls "emotional knowledge" (11), these others, far from being "totally other," engender what Bataille calls a "fusion, precarious yet profound" (1986, 20). This precarious fusion, Bataille specifies, provisionally melts the unity of the ego, dragging it back to a type of muddy and originary, yet *ek-static* homology in which the ego can no longer be contained in neat, ideal forms and is rendered formless and precarious instead. Hence, the experience of communication with the socius introduces a polarized attraction, a *passage*, in which self and other are no longer on the boat of individuation but slide (*glisse*) in the currents and undercurrents of the ocean itself, "two waves losing themselves in the neighboring waves" (1954, 64). Be it at political meetings, at a funeral, in childbirth, or in a lover's bed, the subject is magnetically, or as Bataille likes to say, "hypnotically" attracted toward an experience with the socius that merges the ego in a "primal continuity linking us with everything that is" (1986, 15). Until the very end, Bataille will continue to insist that we are irresistibly attracted by heterogeneous communications because "we yearn for our lost continuity" (15).

And yet, precisely because of the socius's fatal attraction toward the ecstatic sphere of communication, *ipse* also shivers with an originary terror that violently swings her in the opposite direction, lest she loses her identity in a formless experience of self-dissolution. Hence this communicating subject is not only radically pulled *toward* originary experiences with others qua socii who have the power to open up the channels of the ego to its unbounded outside; it is also pulled *away* from it, horrified by the possibility of a permanent loss of identity in a muddy pond without form. We can thus better understand why Bataille, at the beginning of his career, as he is about to open his "Dossier Heterology" jots down a reminder for himself that reads: "say also the heterogeneous is what we *love* and what horrifies us" (II, 171). And, many years later, as the end is nearing, he echoes the following reminder for others: "We ought never to forget that in spite of the bliss love promises its first effect is one of turmoil and distress" (1986, 19). If heterology generates ambivalent feelings of attraction and repulsion, then, the origins of this double movement do not stem from the vulnerability of the object alone; nor from the openness of the subject alone; but from the irresistible currents and undercurrents of sovereign communication that open up the ego to the sacred ecstasy of eroticism, while making her shiver in front of the terror of death. That this deeply subjective experience touches the heart of the matter is confirmed, one last time, as Bataille specifies: "this ambivalence inherent in the sacred things has not only the effect of tearing apart the feeling of which it is the object, *it rips apart as well the sacred itself*" (2018, 35; emphasis added). In this final heterological incision, the sacred is indeed ripped apart—so that its palpitating heart can keep beating.

***

We were wondering: what are the laws that govern the movement of "attraction and repulsion" whose pathos of distance constitutes the palpitating heart of mimetic studies? We are now in a position to see and feel that Bataille's heterology may appear impossible from a purely homogenous, scientific perspective that considers the sacred from without. Yet it is rendered possible by a heterogeneous perspective that adopts *anthropological*, *ontological*, and *psychological* lenses to consider the homology of heterology from within. What appears other and excluded from an exterior, scientific perspective actually turns out to be intimate and included from an interior, affective perspective; what is discontinuous in the path of work is continuous in the path of transgression. This is also what Bataille himself suggested, in a truncated footnote whose formless logic we are now perhaps in a position to recompose:

[I] expressed the impossibility of a science of the excluded or heterogeneous part, but in practice? It is not necessary to take into account the
fundamental difference from the point of view of knowledge, between
the excluded part and the mode of exclusion; and it is easier to speak of
the science of the heterogeneous: this fiction can only cause inconvenience if one has not indicated it from the outset [The sentence stops
here]...(Bataille 2018, 38; trans. modified)

Indeed, the "fiction" of a science heterology can only "cause inconvenience" if
one does not take into consideration what Bataille indicated at the outset: namely, that heterology "refers" to what he describes as "*lived states* [états vécus]," and
its method of investigation rests on "lived, *affective* experience" (I, 339, 348).
And as he will continue to emphasize, heterology is not only a science based on
discursive "knowledge" of a rational *logos*; it is also, and above all, a science based
on the "practice" of a felt *pathos*. From this "practical" angle, the absolute otherness of the heterogeneous might actually be less other than "the point of view of
knowledge" (or work) thought it to be; if only because from the point of view of
"lived experience" (or transgression) this other qua "socius" is in a homologous
continuity with the self qua "ipse."

"I" have argued that the laws of heterology are tightly intertwined with
the laws of imitation, in the sense that *mimesis*—conceived not as homogenous
representation, but in its heterogeneous anthropological, ontological and psychological manifestations—reveals the underlying homology of being that, at
sovereign instants of communication, opens up *ipse*, for better and worse, to the
experience of what is totally other, yet is intimately the same. For Bataille, it
is because our muddy origins are in a relation of mimetic continuity with our
universal destiny that we remain intimately fearful, yet radically open to the ecstatic and squandering horror these heterogeneous forces generate. This is the
beating heart that keeps Bataille's sacred thought in motion, a communicative,
oscillating, and above all palpitating thought that realizes, time and again, that
what is most distant and totally other (heterology) may actually be closest and
intimately the same (homology). From the systolic and diastolic interplay between sameness and difference, logos and pathos, work and transgression, the
homology of mimetic heterology must thus be constantly renewed. For Bataille,
this is, indeed, a life-affirming operation that transformed impure bodies into
pure angels, the horror of death into the ecstasy of love—whether we could turn
this *ek-stasis* into a labor of love out of which mimetic studies was born, is not up
to any ego to say, but for future phantoms to evaluate.

Notes

1   This is a revised version of an article titled "Bataille and the Homology of Heterology" first published in a 2018 special issue of *Theory, Culture & Society* devoted to "Bataille & Heterology."

2   For a critical reader of canonical poststructuralist essays on Bataille from Maurice Blanchot to Michel Foucault, Jacques Derrida to Jean-Baudrillard, Denis Hollier to Mikkel Borch-Jacobsen among others, see Botting and Wilson 1997.

3   On Bataille and mimetic studies see Lawtoo 2013, 209–305; on Bataille and community, see Nancy 1991, Lawtoo 2019, 53–128, Nancy and Lawtoo 2022, 35–38.

4   As Philippe Lacoue-Labarthe was quick to note: "Bataille, though invoked just once, unless I am mistaken, in *Violence and the Sacred*, continuously underlied the Girardian problematic" (1989, 106, n103). This neglect is revelatory of the logic of "romantic agonism" (Lawtoo 2023a, 54–57) that led Girard to consistently erase or downplay influences of theorists of mimesis of the past, which mimetic studies now aims to re-turn to.

5   On Bataille and (new) fascism see Lawtoo 2019, 53–128.

6   References to Bataille's *Oeuvres complètes* (1970–1988) are indicated by volume number instead of date.

7   See Borch-Jacobsen 1997, ffrench 2007, Lawtoo 2011, 2019.

8   For a more detailed discussion on the role mimesis plays in Plato's metaphysics, see Staten, ch. 2 in this volume, and Lawtoo 2022, ch.2

9   For a more detailed genealogy of the Oedipal unconscious and the way it intersects with mimetic theory, see Lawtoo 2023a.

10 As Mikkel Borch-Jacobsen and Sonu Shamdasani put it in their informed account of the history of psychoanalysis sensitive to mimetic strategies at play in "Freud's theory," which "was one of the many possible philosophies of the unconscious": "What was good in psychoanalysis was not new, and stemmed from Janet's work. What was new was not good, and could safely be left to Freud" (2012, 94, 75).

11 See Lawtoo 2013, 247–281.

12 See Lawtoo 2013, 254–281.

Bibliography

Bataille, Georges (1929). "Informe. " *Documents* 7, 382.
—— (1930). "L'esprit moderne et le jeu des transpositions." *Documents* 8, 49–52.
—— (1954). *L'expérience intérieure*. Paris: Gallimard.
—— (1970–1988). *Oeuvres complètes*. 12 vols. Paris: Gallimard.
—— (1985). *Vision of Excess: Selected Writings, 1927-1939*, ed. Allan Stoekl. Minneapolis: University of Minnesota Press.
—— (1986). *Erotism, Death and Sensuality*. San Francisco: City Lights Books.
—— (2011). "Définition de l'hétérologie," ed. Marina Galletti. *Cahiers Bataille 1*, 229–236.
—— (2018). "Definition of Heterology." *Theory, Culture & Society* 35.4/5, 29–40.
Bois, Yve-Alain, and Rosalind E. Krauss (1987). *Formless: A User's Guide*. Cambridge, MA: MIT Press.
Borch-Jacobsen, Mikkel (1997). "The Laughter of Being," in *Bataille: A Critical Reader*, eds. Fred Botting and Scott Wilson. Oxford: Blackwell, 146–166.

Borch-Jacobsen, Mikkel, and Sonu Shamdasani (2012). *The Freud Files: An Inquiry into the History of Psychoanalysis*. Cambridge: Cambridge University Press.

Botting Fred, and Scott Wilson (eds.) (1997). *Bataille: A Critical Reader*. Oxford: Blackwell.

Connolly, William E. (2017). *Aspirational Fascism: The Struggle for Multifaceted Democracy under Trumpism*. Minneapolis: University of Minnesota Press.

—— (2022). "Bodily Stresses, Cultural Drives, Fascist Contagions." *Theory & Event* 25.3, 689–709.

Didi-Huberman, Georges (2003). *La Ressemblance informe: ou le gai savoir visuel selon Georges Bataille*. Paris: Vues.

Durkheim, Émile (2001). *The Elementary Forms of Religious Life*. Oxford: Oxford University Press.

Ffrench, Patrick (2007). *After Bataille: Sacrifice, Exposure, Community*. London: Legenda.

Freud, Sigmund (1920). *Totem und Taboo: Eine Uebereinstimmungen im Seelenslenben der Wilden und der Neurotiker*. Wien: Internationaler Psychoanalytischer Verlag.

—— (1940). *Totem and Taboo: Resemblances between the Psychic Lives of Savages and Neurotics*. Harmondsworth: Penguin.

Gallese, Vittorio, and Massimo Ammaniti (2014). *The Birth of Intersubjectivity: Psychodynamics, Neurobiology, and the Self*. New York: W.W. Norton & Company.

Girard, René (1977). *Violence and the Sacred*. Baltimore: Johns Hopkins University Press.

Hollier, Denis (ed.) (1995). *Le Collège de sociologie 1937-1939*. Paris: Gallimard.

Iacoboni, Marco (2008). *Mirroring People: The New Science of How We Connect to Others*. New York: Ferrar, Straus and Giroux.

Janet, Pierre (1938). "Les conduites sociales," in *Onzième Congrès International de Psychologie*, eds. H. Piéron and I. Meyerson. Paris: Alcan, 138-149.

Kristeva, Julia (1982). *The Powers of Horror*. New York: Columbia University Press.

Lacan, Jacques (1966). "Le stade du miroir comme formateur de la function du Je," in *Écrits*. Paris: Seuil, 93-100.

Lacoue-Labarthe, Philippe (1989). *Typography: Mimesis, Philosophy, Politics*, ed. Christopher Fynsk. Stanford: Stanford University Press.

Lawtoo, Nidesh (2011). "Bataille and the Birth of the Subject: Out of the Laughter of the *Socius*." *Angelaki* 16.2, 73–88.

—— (2013). *The Phantom of the Ego: Modernism and the Mimetic Unconscious*. East Lansing: Michigan State University Press.

—— (2019). *(New) Fascism: Community, Contagion, Myth*. East Lansing: Michigan State University Press.

—— (2022). *Homo Mimeticus: A New Theory of Imitation*. Leuven: Leuven University Press.

—— (2023a). *Violence and the Oedipal Unconscious: vol. 1, The Catharsis Hypothesis*. East Lansing: Michigan State University Press.

—— (2023b). *Violence and the Mimetic Unconscious: vol. 2, The Affective Hypothesis*. East Lansing: Michigan State University Press.

Mauss, Marcel, and Henry Hubert (1995). "Esquisse d'une théorie générale de la magie," in *Sociologie et anthropologie*. Paris: Presses Universitaires de France, 1-141.

Meltzoff, Andrew N., and Keith Moore (1999). "Persons and Representation: Why Infant Imitation Is Important for Theories of Human Development," in *Imitation in Infancy*, eds. Jacqueline Nadel and George Butterworth. Cambridge: Cambridge University Press, 9–35.

Meltzoff, Andrew N., and Wolfgang Prinz (eds.) (2002). *The Imitative Mind: Development, Evolution, and Brain Biases*. Cambridge: Cambridge University Press.

Nancy, Jean-Luc (1991). *The Inoperative Community,* ed. and trans. Peter Connor. Minneapolis: University of Minnesota Press.

Nancy, Jean-Luc, and Nidesh Lawtoo (2022). "Mimesis: A Singular Plural Concept." *CounterText* 8.1, 23–45.

Nietzsche, Friedrich (1990). *Beyond Good and Evil*, trans. R. J. Hollingdale. New York: Penguin Books.

Plato (1961a) "Parmenides," trans. M. F. Cornford, in *The Collected Dialogues of Plato,* eds. Edith Hamilton and Huntington Cairns. New York: Pantheon Books, 920–955.

—— (1961b) "Republic," trans. Paul Shorey, in *The Collected Dialogues of Plato,* eds. Edith Hamilton and Huntington Cairns. New York: Pantheon Books, 575–843.

Richman, Michelle (2002). *Sacred Revolutions: Durkheim and the Collège de Sociologie*. Minneapolis: University of Minnesota Press.

CHAPTER 9

A NEW LOGIC OF PATHOS

The Anti-Oedipal Unconscious in
Hysterical Mimesis

María del Carmen Molina Barea

> What do imitation, suggestion, and contagion have in common?
> A historical oblivion, one might initially say.
>
> —Nidesh Lawtoo, "The Mimetic Unconscious"

Introduction

The purpose of this chapter is to expand on Gilles Deleuze and Félix Guattari's critique of the Oedipal unconscious in the *Anti-Oedipus* (1972) from the perspective of the mimetic unconscious central to mimetic studies. Both the anti-Oedipal and the mimetic unconscious provide a sound alternative to the psychoanalytical unconscious rooted in phantasmatic structures of representation. Such a model framed unconscious mimesis within repetitive, fixed roles derived from familial relations only. However, Deleuze and Guattari stress that unconscious desire breaks with prescribed mimicry and develops free flows of affective identifications. More specifically, I will argue that the unconscious can fully rearticulate the mimetic relation with normative pathos. Under these circumstances, following Nidesh Lawtoo, if humans defined as *homo mimeticus* are *pathologically* inclined to the contagion of mimetic affections, I maintain that the unconscious understood as "desiring-production" (Deleuze and Guattari 2000, 1) fosters pathological affection against the representational mimetic model. Deleuze and Guattari's anti-Oedipal critique provides, thus, a starting point to broaden the genealogy of the mimetic unconscious. In this context, the anti-Oedipal hypothesis constitutes a stimulating field for mimetic studies insofar as it promotes a new logic of pathos that expands the analysis of mimetic subjectivation.[1]

In this chapter I focus on mimesis in hysterical subjects to demonstrate an anti-Oedipal approach to the mimetic unconscious. The ultimate objective is to develop a specific model to further the potential of the mimetic unconscious, so as to counteract representational affective domination. I will focus on hysterical mimicry to highlight the power of anti-Oedipal desiring mimesis central to autohypnosis, autosuggestion and automatism.[2] Hence, hysterical performances generate suggestive simulations that spread anti-Oedipal characteristics like anti-representation, anti-essentialist subjectivity, and non-idealistic and immanent embodiment, among other phenomena. As we shall see, the hysterical mimetic unconscious introduces procedural techniques that question what Deleuze and Guattari call the "theater of representation" (2000, 86, 271). In this context, Antonin Artaud's "Theater of Cruelty" (1973, 157–161) —that Deleuze and Guattari take as a fundamental reference—provides concrete strategies to unleash the desiring force of the mimetic unconscious, which has the ability to disrupt affective identification.

To give my analysis aesthetic specificity, I will take as a case study the play *Mary Said What She Said* (2019) by Robert Wilson, starring Isabelle Huppert, with a script by Darryl Pinckney and music by Ludovico Einaudi. I will pay special attention to gestures and mechanical movements in order to explore the scope of disrupting mimetic pathologies in this work. I argue that *Mary*'s protagonist constitutes an extension of the mimicry of hysterics. Above all, this chapter addresses the double bind mirroring process at the core of mimetic pathos: on the one hand, the mimetic unconscious in hysterical subjects imitates almost everyone, thanks to the intensity and plasticity of its flows of affect or pathos; on the other, this phenomenon is able to resist normative manifestations of Oedipal desire.

Deleuze and Guattari Rethink the Mimetic Unconscious

The mimetic unconscious differs from the Oedipal model that the psychoanalytic tradition created. Since it is not based on the interpretation of dreams and clinical symptoms, representational processes do not subdue the mimetic unconscious. Instead, the unconscious is better understood as a mimetic realm that embodies mirroring flows running through a relational plane of immanence. In this sense, the unconscious is mimetic rather than repressive. Deleuze and Guattari's anti-Oedipal unconscious aligns with the genealogical reach of the mimetic unconscious, which can be traced back to pre-Freudian mimetic devices found in the nineteenth century hypnotic tradition. Thus reframed, the unconscious has a long history of misinterpretation, for which psychoanalysis, in particular, is largely responsible. It is true that Sigmund Freud established that the unconscious is closely related to mimetic processes, such as "identification," which as Mikkel Borch-Jacobsen and Lawtoo have shown remains central to mimetic studies.[3] However, as they have also shown, the way Freud saw such a connection was strongly determined by a theatrical model restricted to several techniques of representation. This is based on the figure of Oedipus in Sophocles' play—that formulates the homonymous complex—as well as on the Shakespearean tragedy *Hamlet*. Freud states that these two plays have a great impact on the audience because they illustrate the functioning of the unconscious mind: the young child is driven by his desire for his mother, and directs his aggressive instincts toward his father, who threatens the boy with castration.[4] Hence, Freud established a parallelism between the unconscious mimetic drive and a male-centered theater of representation. The Oedipal unconscious's motto is "daddy, mommy and me" (Deleuze and Guattari 2000, 101), each one performing a prescribed role.

The psychoanalyst directs the mimetic unconscious and transforms it into a theater: in his confrontation with his father the little boy surrenders to the powerful adversary, thus abandoning the previous libidinal subversion and taking his place in society like a good child. However, if the boy persists in his attitude and does not pass through the Oedipus complex, then he becomes a disturbed individual who will need psychoanalytic healing. This is, of course, the Freudian stance on the issue. In such a scenario, "Oedipus" constitutes an effective controlling tool that forces the unconscious to repress its desiring potential and repeat the enactment of the same tragedy over and over again. However, Deleuze and Guattari's critique of representation supports a subversive turn with regards to affective and embodied mimesis. Oedipus is not the truth about the unconscious, but rather just a violent imposition. As Brian Massumi puts it, following Deleuze and Guattari: "Oedipus has no truth value. It is a matter of force: it is a categorical overlay, an overpowering imposition of regularized affects" (1992, 94). The resulting unconscious typifies a specific *pathos of representation*: the mimetic unconscious colonized by Oedipus. Mimetic studies understand pathos as an affective force that takes possession of the ego. It also distinguishes between mimetic pathos and mimetic desire while separating the Oedipal unconscious from the mimetic unconscious. Considering that mimetic pathos is the relational power of humans to be unconsciously affected by others via a "shared sympathy, or *sym-pathos* (feeling with)" (Lawtoo 2022, 37), the Oedipal unconscious establishes a mimetic pathos forcing the mimetic unconscious to adopt patterns of representation, thereby putting desiring mimesis under control.

Such a psychic scene, thus, requires a critical analysis in relation to the "phantom of the ego" (Lawtoo 2013). According to Lawtoo, this Nietzschean concept refers to contagious affects that have the power to turn the ego into a phantom; that is, to render the self open to the influence of others and impede the process of individuation. In other words, the "phantom of the ego" is the phenomenon through which human vulnerability to mimetic pathos opens the subject up to influences that blur the boundaries of individuation, generating a porous, relational, and permeable ego.

Let us consider the phenomenology of the mimetic unconscious via its relationship to pathos. The unconscious proceeds mimetically, inasmuch as it replicates identification processes spread by social, cultural, and political actors. Thus, it operates at the level of passions —the perfect terrain for unconscious dynamics—by means of affective contagion. Therefore, *mimetic pathos* —and *patho-logy* as its inner logic—refer to the actor's power to disseminate such a contagion. For example, in the political realm, this logic has been defined as a fascist technique that leads people to "reproduce the affects of the leader qua model" (Lawtoo 2019a, xxxii). In the words of Lawtoo: "Crowd behavior, violence, propaganda, (new) fascist insurrections, conspiracy theories, and war are manifestations of what I call *mimetic pathologies*" (2022, 38). Unconscious mimetic drives may generate negative manifestations of pathos based on Oedipal pathos. Deleuze and Guattari's philosophy implies a powerful anti-Oedipal alternative in line with mimetic studies, pursuing a new understanding of the unconscious against Oedipus and vindicating affirmative desiring mimesis. They take a clear stand on this:

> Oedipus is a factitious product of psychic repression. It is only the re-
> presented, insofar as it is induced by repression [...]. Oedipus is not a
> state of desire and the drives, it is an *idea*, nothing but an idea that re-
> pression inspires in us concerning desire; not even a compromise, but
> an idea in the service of repression, its propaganda, or its propagation.
> (Deleuze and Guattari 2000, 119)

As Deleuze and Guattari put it, unconscious desire operates without submission to the affective demands of representation. As mimetic pathos builds upon *sym-pathos*, the mimetic unconscious entails a certain degree of identification. In this respect the Oedipal unconscious is an expert: Oedipus constitutes a *phantom*, a distorted image, the illusion of an inverted mirror that forces unconscious identification with the "daddy-mommy-me" (Deleuze and Guattari 2000, 23) schema. Therefore, the theater of representation is never the unconscious's truth; rather, it entails a mimetically reproduced repressive enactment, a pathologically imposed negative embodiment. This is why Deleuze and Guattari argue that psychoanalysis is unable to fully grasp the unconscious's potential, because it relies on pure representation. The analyst looks for Oedipus in every manifestation of mimetic pathos so as to represent a recurring unconscious desire: the child *must* love his mother and *must* hate his father. Thus, patients will never heal unless they identify with—and consequently mimic—the representational unconscious model.

At this point, Deleuze and Guattari claim that the unconscious is not about representation, but rather *production*: the unconscious generates productive mimesis under the auspices of an anti-Oedipal pathos. Deleuze and Guattari insist that the unconscious is a matter of desiring-production, and complain that it becomes a form of theater instead of a *factory*:

> The unconscious ceases to be what it is—a factory, a workshop—to become a theater, a scene and its staging. And not even an avant-garde theater, such as existed in Freud's day (Wedekind), but the classical theater, the classical order of representation. The psychoanalyst becomes a director for a private theater, rather than the engineer or mechanic [...] (2000, 55)

Whereas Freud considered desire to be produced by the Oedipal triangle, Deleuze and Guattari argue that desire must be understood as the unleashed articulation of machinic assemblages. This explains the label "desiring machines" that the authors use to describe the unconscious. "For desiring-machines are precisely that: the microphysics of the unconscious, the elements of the microunconscious" (2000, 183). Therefore, from the anti-Oedipal perspective, desire takes the form of a process of production marked by moments of anti-production (flow and cuts). There can thus be no organizing structure to fix the unconscious, but just desiring connections and disruptions. The consequence of such a machinic device is a combination of affective ups and downs. The main contribution of these anti-Oedipal insights is that desire is not a representation of lack (produced by the forbidden object of desire), but desiring-production itself.[5] "From the moment lack is reintroduced into desire, all of desiring-production is crushed, reduced to being no more than the production of fantasy" (2000, 111). Consequently, there is no reason for symptomatic—Oedipal—interpretations of the unconscious, inasmuch as it does not *represent*. There is no prior role to be embodied; subjectivity is produced along with the desiring process, which is free from phantasmatic capture. Deleuze and Guattari's approach, thus, restores the unconscious with the productive capabilities that had been subtracted by the Oedipal sign.

The Inverted Mirror of Hysterical Mimesis

The anti-Oedipal unconscious reverses normative mimetic pathos by producing desiring mimesis, which questions representation and identification. This illustrates a new logic of pathos that critically invests affective contagion. Given that the mimetic unconscious draws on a pre-Freudian tradition that had "hypnosis as a via regia" (Lawtoo 2023b, 169–196), one of the most powerful examples of such a mimetic unconscious can be found in hysterical mimesis, thanks to the development of autohypnosis and automatism.

To meet our protagonists, it is necessary to attend the "theater" of Jean-Martin Charcot, specifically "the spectacle of pain" (Didi-Huberman 2003, 3), which took place at the Salpêtrière on a weekly basis. Charcot used to give a lecture to a full hall of students every Tuesday, and for those occasions he chose a hysterical patient. The woman selected was the star actress, as it were, in a private theater or circus show, whose stage director, Charcot, seemed to possess hypnotic powers. He induced poses and gestures by means of his commands exercised through affective suggestion. This mechanism set the stage for a Panoptic-like system aimed at the interpretative dissection of the unconscious. It should come as no surprise, then, that the young Freud studied under Charcot. Nevertheless, it is my belief that the infamous Salpêtrière theater can be interpreted as a subversive scenario. The reason is that the hysterical unconscious does not simply reproduce mimetic patterns. Rather, it puts into practice a radically different mimetic impulse. In short, the hysterical unconscious does not only replicate external models, but also exaggerates them, rendering them meaningless and distorting identification, thereby placing an inverted mirror in front of the already inverted representational mirror.

Hysterics' mimetic pathos fosters new trajectories within unconscious production through intense desire in such a way that it reverses normative patho-logy. One way to do this is through hyperbolic mimicry: it is known that hysterics' most characteristic feature is that they imitate everybody. Women at the Salpêtrière played the role of the analyst, and the audience, and eventually imitated themselves. "They imitate, then, imitation itself" (Didi-Huberman in Charcot and Richer 1984, 146; my trans.). Hysterics' mimetic practice can be related to what Lawtoo calls "the human chameleon," responding to mirror neurons (2022, 191–223). The extent to which these women enact mimesis makes them the perfect example of pathological subjects, as they are sym-pathetic and relational, by definition; so much so that the hysterical holistic mimesis makes it virtually impossible to distinguish between what is the original and what is a performance.[6] However, as hysterics identify with everybody, they simultaneously identify with nobody, and thus representational, fixed roles vanish. The unconscious plasticity in hysterical mimesis becomes a twofold phenomenon that redefines contagion. On this point, it is important to revisit Lawtoo's study on plasticity in order to clarify this dual articulation. He goes back to Philippe Lacoue-Labarthe's account of mimesis so as to shield us from a persistent risk:

> On the one hand, Lacoue-Labarthe stresses that mimesis is a plastic concept in search of an identity that assumes different dramatic forms. Thus, he defines it as a concept whose essence is to "lack a stable essence," whose proper being is, paradoxically, a "lack of being-proper" —in short, an unstable, malleable, and thus plastic concept that, like the protean *mimos* it designates, constantly changes form, fashioning, modeling, fictioning different conceptual protagonists on the theatrical/theoretical scene. [...] On the other hand, the fact that mimesis cannot be stabilized in a theoretical form does mean that typical psychic formations are not already at play in theatrical practice. (Lawtoo 2022, 139)

Plastic virtuosity, then, is the property of a subject *without property*, whose defining characteristics are to *receive form* but also *give form*. Put differently, the plastic subject is both the subject of a *passive reception of form* (like wax) and also the subject, who *gives form* (the subject that assumes different roles), including formless, protean roles that challenge Oedipal representational forms.[7]

Furthering this line of inquiry in mimetic studies we could specify that the hysterical subject is a subject of *active reception* of pathological forms, a pathos that gives form to a phantom of ego in destabilizing ways. Due to their extreme malleability, driven by desiring mimesis, hysterics interact excessively, giving form to an anti-form that subverts the enactment of their roles. This is because the hysterical unconscious's affective qualities are stronger and exceed contagious pathos. Hence, we prefer to say that the hysterical subject receives form and *destroys form*. In short, what the unconscious *factory* produces is, ultimately, the destruction of mimetic representation. It is a question of deconstructive and disarticulating performances.

There are several ways to do this. Firstly, the hysterical unconscious does not merely react according to hypnotic pathos but undergoes a sort of mimetic "autohypnosis" as well; that is, an autonomous reenactment of external patterns filtered through desiring mimesis. This goes hand in hand with hysterics' "autosuggestion:" dealing with desiring-production, the hysterical subject manufactures pathological affection by challenging negative investments. This phenomenon is not an endogenous notion of mimesis but a two-way mirroring simulacrum that turns affective suggestion upside down, bearing in mind that hysterics imitate what, at the same time, they reject:

> *Mimesis* is the hysterical symptom par excellence. Hysteria is considered to be "a whole art," the art and manner of "theatricalism," as is always said in psychiatry, and which no theatricality is strong enough to equal in its swaggers. Hysteria reveals itself in histrionics and a tragic mask turned flesh; and at the same time there is a veil, dissimulation; and at the same time a naive, sincere gift of multiple identifications. A hysteric will repeat anything she hears around her; a hysteric wants to be everyone, or rather she wants to have the being of anyone and everyone. But she only seems to want this, in a perpetual distraction, smashing all roles into pieces. (Didi-Huberman 2003, 164)

The way in which hysterics manufacture pathological affection is primarily unconscious and intuitive; "automatic," we might say. Hysterics' mimesis reinforces unconscious automatism, but not as a manifestation of *echopraxia*; that is, the involuntary imitation of another person's action without explicit awareness under hypnosis.[8] It is more like Bernheim's idea, according to which automatic activity is at the foundation of the "mirroring" principle as an "instinctive" phenomenon (Lawtoo 2022, 212). Labeling this instinctive drive desiring mimesis, automatic mimesis gains subversive resonances against representation. Desiring mimesis can rearticulate our natural tendency to mimetic pathos by producing a distorted embodiment of normative affects. On this line, hysterics display an incredibly powerful machinery for unconscious desire; the Salpêtrière patients' performances were not mimetic representations, but rather a questioning of representation by means of unconscious mimesis. Metaphorically, they were actresses, but they did not perform *theater*. Consequently, the hysterical unconscious cannot simply be thought of as a puppet theater of hypnotic imitation. Thus, we should not confuse it, for instance, with Richard Foreman's Ontological-Hysteric Theater or Edward Gordon Craig's Uber-Marionette Theater, both created to transform actors into marionettes at the director's disposal. It is more like Antonin Artaud's Theater of Cruelty, which radically reshaped representational theater, having a great impact on the audience, in the sense that this theater really succeeded in shocking affection, eliminating identification and unleashing the unconscious potential.[9] Highly admired by Gilles Deleuze and Félix Guattari as desiring unconscious model, "Artaud was one too. In 1924 he wrote: 'I am a walking automaton'" (in Baudrillard 2005, 236).

The mimetic plasticity of the hysterical unconscious adopts the form of mechanical automatism. Josef Breuer, considered the "father" of hysteria, along with Charcot, situated the source of movement and the transmission of driving forces in electrical fluids (Breuer 1976, 94). Hence, it is not surprising that mental treatments at the Salpêtrière included experiments with electrical discharges. The general idea was that the hysterical body expresses unconscious desire by means of automatic symptoms caused by disrupted electrical fluxes. Apart from electricity, the unconscious was also understood as a result of magnetic forces. This idea came from Franz Anton Mesmer and his theory of "animal magnetism."[10] Thus, the pathos of the hysterical unconscious was read in terms of magnetic suggestion (Thornton 1976, 6).[11] Mesmer himself was a great master of suggestion, another theater director, like Charcot.[12] Nevertheless, the mimetic unconscious continuously eludes being colonized by representation. The hysterical unconscious manages to do so by developing mechanical mimicry as if gestures were prompted by electrical shocks, but these do not actually come from mesmerizing affects. As seen before, hysterical automatism redefines unconscious desiring fluxes as a pathological production that counteracts normative mimesis, which exemplifies the double bind process's function at the core of the hysterical unconscious.

A New Logic of Pathos

Now the objective is to study the production of the desiring unconscious through the mimetic devices put into play in the experimental theatrical piece *Mary Said What She Said* (hereafter *Mary*).[13] The performance consists of a single actress on stage—Isabelle Huppert—declaiming a monologue in three parts. She plays Mary, Queen of Scots, who recalls memories and disseminated fragments of her letters and biographical events, along with her desires, ambitions, and personal struggles. She waits for her execution as if she were Lucky or Pozzo waiting for Godot, constantly coming and going in an incessant repetition. Huppert's alienating movements and gestures put spectators into a disturbed, although raptured, state of mind, producing a non-cathartic but very moving theater. In *Mary* the human figure appears as the solitary silhouette of a woman against a neutral background standing in front of the audience. Her bodily presence becomes mysterious and almost ethereal, although somehow disturbingly physical and dehumanized. The pale makeup transforms Mary, Queen of Scots, into a grotesque mannequin, and her slender figure inspires a pronounced sense of anxiety. The stylized, non-conventional gestures that she makes with her hands, arms and entire body constitute a disruptive choreography that contributes to a growing effect of alienation, thus echoing Artaud's Theater of Cruelty. In *Mary*, the main distinguishing features, among her wide range of postures, are basically discontinuity, rupture, and strangeness. These gestures bear no direct relationship with representational devices. Inversely, they manifest a mimetic activity that embodies the production of a different model of affective replication. This specific gesticulation invites us to consider its potential as an alternative pathos.

It is striking that *Mary*'s gestural panoply closely resembles the *Iconographie Photographique de la Salpêtrière*, a catalogue of hysterical poses illustrated by Bourneville and Régnard, which had a strong impact on the cultural imaginary and made its mark in theater and the visual arts. Charcot wrote *Les démoniaques dans l'art*, which included similar illustrations by Paul Richer and some photographic materials that constituted a novelty in clinical literature. Charcot listed four stages to analyze what he called a hysterical attack: epileptoid crisis, contortions, and acrobatic poses (clownism), emotional and religious gestures (*attitudes passionnelles*), and finally, delirium. He compiled numerous drawings in a collection illustrating these eccentric postures: hysterical arch, cataleptic convulsions, ecstasy, catatonic rigidity caused by hypnosis, etc. In particular, *Mary* presents many similarities with poses resulting from cataleptic suggestion, a kind

Figure 1: Female patient with catalepsy. Photograph by Albert Londe. *Nouvelle iconographie de la Salpêtrière*, 1890. Wellcome Collection. Source: Wellcome Collection (Creative Commons Attribution 4.0 International)

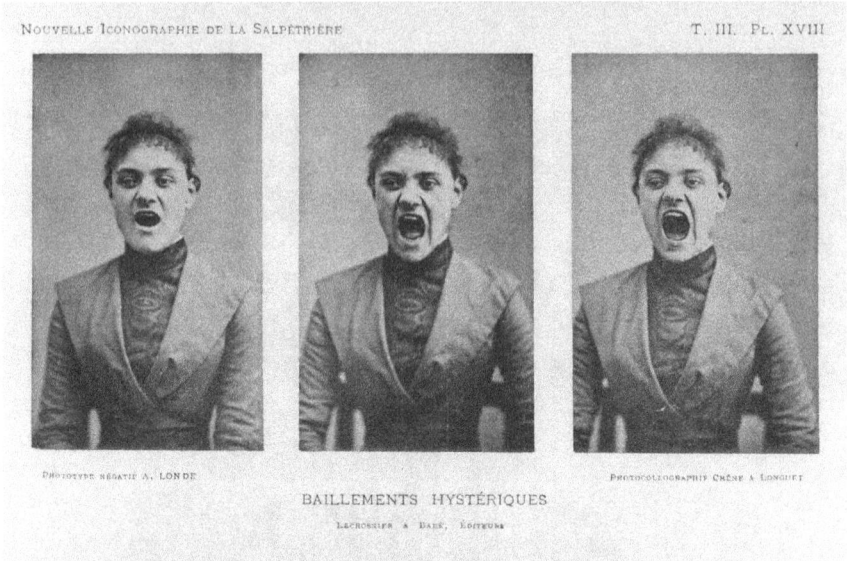

Figure 2: Three photos in a series showing a hysterical woman yawning. Photograph by Albert Londe. *Nouvelle iconographie de la Salpêtrière*, 1890. Wellcome Collection. Source: Wellcome Collection (Creative Commons Attribution 4.0 International)

of automatism that operates in the form of somnambulist spontaneous hypnotism (fig. 1). Such a procedure figuratively expands the extent of hysterical autohypnosis. *Mary* closely approaches this sort of autosuggestion by means of her automatic, even mechanical, repetitive movements, which seem utterly instinctive, as if she were guided by unconscious desire. This idea differs, for example, from Mesmer's pupil, Puységur, who coined "magnetic somnambulism," a sort of induced somnambulism. However, as we already know, mimetic pathos does not always copy, as such, insofar as desiring mimesis spurs the unconscious to recreate contagious affects by disrupting referential models. In this sense, *Mary* impersonates a kind of cataleptic automaton whose mimetic unconscious turns pathological representation around.

Mary also rejects representational discourse. Artaud himself also attacked language because he believed that words were oedipally dominated: "The theater, as well as the word, has the necessity to be released" (Artaud 1997, 114; my trans.). This explains why, in the Theater of Cruelty, the actors shout, grunt, and gasp, and thus transgress language with irritating guttural sounds and aphasic onomatopoeias whose phonetic automatism disarticulates consistent language.

Figure 3: Filippo Lippi, *The Feast of Herod: Salome's Dance*, detail. ca. 1464. Public Domain.

Artaud defined this phenomenon as a physical language named "affective athleticism," and Deleuze and Guattari see it as language reshaped by unconscious desire. Therefore, affective athleticism performs a distorted mimesis of language, as it conveys affective pathos in language in a completely different way, so much so that it evacuates normative pathos installed within language. In this way, the automatic mimetic language would not be limited to *echolalia*, in other words, the involuntary repetition of another person's speech. *Mary*'s short-circuited voice also breaks with representational speech. The vibrating movement of her mandible, caused by diction and increasing speed, stops abruptly when Huppert stands with her mouth completely open in a strong green light, like a Kabuki *mime*. On this point, physiognomic photographs taken at the Salpêtrière constitute a powerful visual twinning that links *Mary* and the hysterics (fig. 2).

As an example of subjugating mimetic pathos, it is worth mentioning that, following his colleague Charcot, G.-B. Duchenne electrically stimulated the facial muscles of hysterical women and actresses of the Comédie Française with the intention of inducing artificial mimicry. Transcending theatrical colonization, the hysterical unconscious was taken up by dancers and vaudeville actresses, fascinated by the eccentric gesticulation of hysteria, who enthusiastically embraced the iconography of the Salpêtrière.[14] These included, just to mention a few, Sara Bernhardt, Isadora Duncan, Loïe Fuller, and Tórtola Valencia.[15] Hysteric poses helped them build subversive affective personas in the public domain, questioning the pathology behind women's "mimetic condition" (Clúa Ginés 2007, 161). They developed a concept of pathos reminiscent of art historian Aby Warburg, whose central interest in gesture was guided by *pathosformel* (Didi-Huberman 2016), the surviving affects' formula (*Nachleben*) inspired by the figure of the *nympha* in Quattrocento's frescos (fig. 3). She embodies an unconscious *phantom* that randomly traverses the history of affection with no subjection to representation.[16] *Mary* dances as if she were possessed by desiring pathos, in a sequence of discontinuous motion, going back and forth as if following an invisible point on the horizon and increasing the speed of her walking while rhythmically raising her arms. She embodies a desiring machine with its connected and disconnected fluxes. *Mary*'s dancing is an autohypnotic choreography—*Mary*, the last *nympha*.

Conclusion

Mimesis, as we have seen, has often been confined within a stabilizing theatrical genealogy restricted to the visual logic of representation. Psychoanalytic readings of the unconscious helped forge this image of mimesis, in line with an affective theater where imitation was restricted to a theater of fixed familial representations. The resulting schema is named "Oedipus." Gilles Deleuze and Félix

Guattari heavily criticized its perverse phantasmatic mirror, especially because it traps mimetic pathos in an extremely narrow direction. Equally narrow will be the mimetic subject under the influence of such an Oedipal unconscious model.

In this chapter, I have gone back to Deleuze and Guattari looking for a picture of the unconscious, shaping a subject whose desiring mimesis is free from constraining repetitions and prescribed affective embodiment. I have found a perfect example of this in hysterics, by means of processes like self-hypnosis, autosuggestion, and automatism. In brief, the unconscious potential of hysterical "puppets" boils down to their power to produce mimetic affection through reiterative gestural processes so excessive that they deconstruct referential patterns. This being the case, hysterics show that the unconscious is a matter of production rather than mere reproduction, as Deleuze and Guattari observed.

Consequently, the hysterical unconscious demonstrates that it would never *give stabilizing form* to Oedipal pathologies. In other words, to say that the hysterical mimetic unconscious corresponds to the anti-Oedipal unconscious is the same as saying that it entails an anti-representational mimetic unconscious. Hysterics become a fascinating typology of the mimetic subject: on the one hand, they are quintessentially mimetic individuals; on the other, they articulate a programmatic device in order to deconstruct certain pathologies of the mimetic unconscious that have "hypnosis, suggestion, contagion, and mirroring reflexes as a *via regia*" (Lawtoo 2023b, 164).

Finally, I have proposed desiring mimesis as the key to articulating such a double mirroring effect, through which the unconscious paves the way for a new logic of mimetic pathos: "*homo mimeticus* is, thus, not only passively subjected to the affective experience of imitation; it can also actively resist the powers of imitation and keep them at a distance" (Lawtoo 2022, 37). In this regard, hysterics demonstrate a high degree of skill. They imitate almost everything, but in so doing, they struggle against structuring mimetic pathos. Hysterical mimesis can do this because of a markedly creative production capacity based on desiring unconscious's affective flows. The subsequent mimetic excess functions as an inverted mirror for an inverted phantom.

Ultimately, *Mary Said What She Said* shows that the mimetic unconscious easily frustrates Oedipal schemas and impacts the audience in a way that sweeps away representation. Indeed, *Mary*'s rupture with identification is especially noteworthy. Mary's gestural plasticity continues the genealogy of hysterical women, the "queens" of Charcot's theater. In this sense, Mary fights the same battle as the hysterics. Hysterical performance is never simplistically at the disposal of an influential reference, a "stage director," the actor of affective contagion – in short, Oedipus. On the contrary, it turns the mimetic situation around. Hence, the anti-Oedipal unconscious of hysterical mimesis delineates a new definition of pathos.

Notes

1. For an initial connection between the anti-Oedipal and the mimetic unconscious, see Lawtoo 2013, 195–197; and Lawtoo 2023b, 19–34.

2. Although "mimetic desire" is traditionally linked to René Girard, my reframing of this concept as "desiring mimesis" emerges from the connection between Deleuze and Guattari's anti-Oedipal focus on productive desire and mimetic studies' focus on mimetic pathos. This link opens up the problematics of mimesis to all affects. It also yields a conception of desiring mimesis with a double advantage: first it critiques the Oedipal unconscious that, for Lawtoo, still informs Girard's model; and second it is in line with theories of hypnosis internal to the mimetic unconscious. See Lawtoo 2023a, 2023b.

3. For two foundational texts on Freud's theory of identification that remains paradoxically indebted to theories of hypnosis and affective mimesis he seeks to move beyond, see Borch-Jacobsen 1982, 1993. On identification, hypnosis, and mimetic studies see Lawtoo 2013, 234–247 and 2023b, 91–99.

4. The reason for such affective—*empathic*—power over the spectators' unconscious can be traced back to Aristotelian catharsis, which plays a role in the "birth of psychoanalysis."

5. This claim is in line with Nietzsche's definition of will to power as pathos, which inspires the theory of mimetic pathos in mimetic studies.

6. See Agamben 2013.

7. The formless/excessive Bataillean foundations of mimetic studies contribute to challenging Platonic/Oedipal ideals of representational form. See Lawtoo 2013, 209–279 and ch. 7 in this volume [editors' note]

8. "The symptom of echopraxia also occurred frequently in the hypnotic state. Voluntary movements being abolished, the subject imitated like an automaton all movements made before him when these were made purposely to attract his attention. A hypnotized person for example, would follow when someone walked in front of him with loud steps or clench his fist when that gesture was made in front of him" (Thornton 1976, 163).

9. See Artaud 1997. Jean Baudrillard states that Artaud destroyed any possibility of identification: "Everywhere Artaud challenged the process of identification. He said that people should identify with actors materiality through gestures and signs—pure signs and events. It was totally opposed to the modern psychology of the actor. Actors create affects, but they don't belong to them" (Baudrillard 2005, 222).

10. "I observed that magnetic material is almost the same thing as electric fluid, and that it is propagated by intermediary bodies in the same way as is electrical fluid" (Mesmer 1980, 27). On the genealogical link between Mesmer's magnetism and mimetic pathos see Lawtoo 2013, 79–80.

11. This can be appreciated, for example, in literature. In 1813, E.T.A. Hoffman, well-known for his stories about automata, wrote *The Magnetizer*, and in 1882, Guy de Maupassant, who attended Charcot's course at the Salpêtrière, wrote *Magnetism* in defense of women accused of committing crimes under hypnotic induction.

12 "He [Mesmer] effected 'rapport' by various means, for example by pressing his knees against those of the patient or rubbing the latter's thumbs against his own, while in magnetic passes his fingers lightly stroked part of the subject's body with a view to inducing a 'crisis'. Imbued with his theory, Mesmer saw the magnetic fluid as the sole agent in the relationship between therapist and patient. [...] In his own words, animal magnetism 'must in the first place be transmitted through feeling'" (Chertok and de Saussure 1979, 5).

13 See Theatre de la Ville Paris: https://www.youtube.com/watch?v=Iw2PeSO6Uto.

14 Some of them, like Lucia Joyce, daughter of *Ulysses*'s author, and Jeanne Bernhardt, Sara's sister, suffered imprisonment in mental hospitals (Jeanne was, interestingly enough, interned at the Salpêtrière). For further insight, see Antliff 1997, and Garelick 2007.

15 "Through his theatrical lecture-demonstrations (Sarah Bernhardt, acting in cross-dressed parts at the same time, was often compared to the hysterical Queens of Charcot's amphitheater), and even more through the photographic atelier that captured images of the hysterical women for the volumes of iconographies, Charcot emphasized the visual manifestations of hysteria and the hysterical body as an art object" (Gilman et. al. 1993, 310).

16 Research into the *nympha* can be found in Warburg's *Bilderatlas Mnemosyne*, in which he addresses pathos by means of juxtaposed images. In contrast, when Charcot investigated Art History looking for hysterical symptoms to include in *Les démoniaques dans l'art*, what he found was a codified collection of postures. Warburg's phantom is quite different: it swarms around like Dionysian maenads whose dancing movements evoke hysterical gesticulation. In the book *Nymphs* (2005), Giorgio Agamben linked Warburg's *pathosformel* to the Renaissance book *De la arte di ballare et danzare* by Domenichino, in which the term *phantom* refers to a sudden stop between two movements that rearranges bodily memory and makes the limbs move (2013).

Bibliography

Agamben, Giorgio (2013). *Nymphs*, trans. Kevin McLaughlin and Amanda Minervini. London: Seagull Books/University of Chicago Press.

Antliff, Mark (1997). *Inventing Bergson. Cultural Politics and the Parisian Avant Garde*. Princeton: Princeton University Press.

Artaud, Antonin (1997). *Le Théâtre et son double*. Paris: Gallimard.

Baudrillard, Jean (2005). *The Conspiracy of Art. Manifestos, Interviews, Essays*. New York, Los Angeles: Semiotext(e).

Borch-Jacobsen, Mikkel (1982). *The Freudian Subject*, trans. Catherine Porter. Stanford: Stanford University Press.

——— (1993). *The Emotional Tie. Psychoanalysis, Mimesis, and Affect*, trans. Dougals Brick et al. Stanford: Stanford University Press.

Breuer, Josef (1976). *Contribuciones a los "Estudios sobre la histeria."* Mexico: Siglo XXI.

Charcot, Jean-Marie, and Paul Richer (1984). *Les démoniaques dans l'art*. Postface by Georges Didi-Huberman. Paris: Macula.

Chertok, Leon, and Raymond de Saussure (1979). *The Therapeutic Revolution. From Mesmer to Freud*. New York: Brunner/Mazel.

Clúa Ginés, Isabel (2007). "El cuerpo como escenario: actrices e histéricas en el fin de siècle." *Dossiers Feministes* 10, 157–172.

Deleuze, Gilles, and Félix Guattari (2000). *Anti-Oedipus*. Preface by Michel Foucault. Minneapolis: University of Minnesota Press.

Didi-Huberman, Georges (2003). *Invention of Hysteria. Charcot and the Photographic Iconography of the Salpêtrière*. Massachusetts: MIT Press.

—— (2016). *The Surviving Image. Phantoms of Time and Time of Phantoms: Aby Warburg's History of Art*. Pennsylvania: Penn State University Press.

Garelick, Rhonda (2007). *Electric Salome: Loie Fuller's Performance of Modernism*. Princeton, Oxford: Princeton University Press.

Gilman, Sander L., Helen King, Roy Porter, George S. Rousseau, and Elaine Showalter (1993). *Hysteria Beyond Freud*. Berkeley, Los Angeles, Oxford: University of California Press.

Lawtoo, Nidesh (2013). *The Phantom of the Ego. Modernism and the Mimetic Unconscious*. East Lansing: Michigan State University Press.

—— (2019a). *(New) Fascism. Contagion, Community, Myth*. East Lansing: Michigan State University Press.

—— (2019b). "The Mimetic Unconscious. A Mirror for Genealogical Reflections," in *Imitation, Contagion, Suggestion. On Mimesis and Society*, ed. Christian Borch. London, New York: Routledge, 37-53.

—— (2022). *Homo Mimeticus. A New Theory of Imitation*. Leuven: Leuven University Press.

—— (2023a). *Violence and the Oedipal Unconscious: vol. 1, The Catharsis Hypothesis*. East Lansing: Michigan State University Press.

—— (2023b). *Violence and the Mimetic Unconscious: vol. 2, The Affective Hypothesis*. East Lansing: Michigan State University Press.

Massumi, Brian (1992). *A User's Guide to Capitalism and Schizophrenia. Deviations from Deleuze and Guattari*. Cambridge, MA: MIT Press.

Mesmer, Franz Anton (1980). *Mesmerism. A Translation of the Original Medical and Scientific Writings of F. A. Mesmer, M. D.*, trans. George J. Bloch. London: William Kaufmann.

Thornton, E. M. (1976). *Hypnotism, Hysteria and Epilepsy. An Historical Synthesis*. London: William Heinemann Medical Books.

CHAPTER 10

EXHIBITION/EXPOSITION

Irigaray and Lacoue-Labarthe on
the Theaters of Mimesis

Niki Hadikoesoemo

This chapter is an investigation into the relationship between theater and mimesis based on the work of two contemporary French thinkers who have rarely been discussed together but who are at the forefront of the *re*-turn to mimesis – namely, Luce Irigaray and Philippe Lacoue-Labarthe. Following the mimetic turn in its "shift from a still dominant translation of mimesis as a representation of reality [to a] performative, embodied, affective, relational, and deeply troubling manifestation of mimesis" (Lawtoo 2022, 31–33), my aim in this chapter is to put the notion of theater at the forefront of materialized processes of imitation. In an age in which the theater is no longer culturally dominant, it is worth highlighting the theoretical importance of *Homo Mimeticus*' recuperation of the theatrical origins of *mîmos*—"whose meaning is already double, as it signifies both the actor or mime and a type of dramatic performance" (Lawtoo 2022, 13)—that go back to pre-Platonic times, with the help of Irigaray and Lacoue-Labarthe. Both will help to shift the attention from visual representation to the materialized processes of theatrical mimesis. More specifically, I would like to confront their accounts of the mimetic (sexuate) subject qua *mime* with an elemental feature of the theater, which is the ability to *display, exhibit* or *expose*.[1]

Rather than reserving the act of display and exhibition for the theater stage that represents this or that reality (a model reminiscent of a Platonic mimesis), I am interested in how all living human beings, individually and collectively, can expose, on theatrical grounds, the mimetic processes to which they are subject.

When does mimetism become the display of not just pre-existing qualities but also the exposition of how those qualities become mimetic and potentially the subject of a different kind of theatrical matter? Accounting for display or exposition as paradigmatic for mimetic processes of subjectivity is important for the *re*-turn to *homo mimeticus* this volume proposes as it shifts the focus from the visual representation of a (fictional) character to a more process-driven and transformative account of subjectivation *before* and *informing*—"giving form and receiving form" (Lawtoo 2022, 155)—the world as a stage. The idea of the world stage is not explicitly used by Irigaray and Lacoue-Labarthe. Nevertheless, considering the central role that the eighteenth-century thinker Denis Diderot plays in Lacoue-Labarthe's foundational works, key sources for mimetic studies, such as *Typographie* (1975), and *Le sujet de la philosophie: Typographies I* (1979) and *L'Imitation des modernes: Typographies II* (1981), which start with an essay on Diderot's *Paradox of the Actor* (1773–1777), I believe it can help us in our consideration of theatricality as mimetic exposition. More specifically, building on these sources, the re-turns to *homo mimeticus* allow us to think the exhibiting qualities of transformation both inside and outside the theater—the world stage as *activity* rather than as *entity*. This also ties into possible future conceptualizations of mimetic metamorphoses in the Anthropocene, a promising new pillar of mimetic studies.

Irigaray and Lacoue-Labarthe are two contemporary "philosophers of difference" who have pushed non-representational mimesis in areas as broad as philosophy, psychoanalysis, linguistics, feminism, politics, literature and poetry. Both authors are known for their work on and with mimesis. They play a key role as precursors of mimetic studies, as featured in recent work on the plasticity (Lawtoo 2022, 129–156), (sexuate) fluidity (Hadikoesoemo 2021), and musical affectivity (Villegas Vélez 2022) of mimesis. They share a deconstructive approach to (especially) Plato and Aristotle's theories of mimesis; and they are confronted with the problem that (women) philosophers in the West are inevitably embedded in the history of mimesis, albeit differently. The concept of mimesis cannot be a mere object of philosophical reflection because, as history has shown, it has often served as the very instrument of that reflection.

Mimesis' nature is such that it partakes in and configures "regimes" of language, thought and meaning. This is an insight that Irigaray and Lacoue-Labarthe, among other philosophies of difference developed by the likes of Derrida, Deleuze, and Levinas, took particularly seriously. Theoretically and practically, one has to face one's embeddedness in mimetic processes and make it the central problem of philosophizing and living more generally. In this light, and fascinatingly, Irigaray and Lacoue-Labarthe in their own way turn to *theatricality* as their concept of choice to explore the practical and ethical layers provoked in more affective modifications of mimesis. They make explicit the relation between behavioral imitation (mimetism) and the communal aspect of theater in pre-Platonic times, focusing on the affective bond constituted by the interplay between actor and audience. This is expressed in the idea of *theater-as-mimetic-event*, a structure of subjectivation and community that also allows Irigaray en Lacoue-Labarthe to expose the materialized dimension of their own practice as philosophers. In their view, philosophizing is necessarily relational; it presupposes a (mimetic) conversation with the past and the future. It does not stand outside but arises from and dramatizes theatrical mimesis as displayed in western philosophies, making them exceptionally apt thinkers for this chapter's examination.

First, I will start with a brief deconstruction to mimesis as representation, as this is central in the philosophies of Irigaray and Lacoue-Labarthe; this will allow me to reconsider the act of staging beyond the limits of theater generally understood. I will then expand on Lacoue-Labarthe's notion of exhibition/exposition/display, based on André Hirt's definition of the term (2009), followed by a poststructuralist account of mime. Second, I will continue with a crucial conceptual link between poststructuralist thought and feminism on mime: the distinction between "two mimeses" in Plato (in Irigaray's *This Sex*) or a "restrictive" and "general" form of mimesis (in Lacoue-Labarthe's *Typography*). This will allow me to come finally to an account of theatrical display as an embodied, affective encounter that calls for a new ethics and poetics of human life in the twenty-first century.

Lacoue-Labarthe and Theater's Display

"What is on display in the theater is what is on display, not what is displayed." (Hirt 2009, 43; my trans.) With these words André Hirt dramatizes Lacoue-Labarthe's "déconstruction mimétique," foregrounding the theater as a place "improper" (Nancy et al. 2007; Hirt 2009, 23–24). In Lacoue-Labarthe's notion of impropriety, which comes from Plato, lies the idea of a false coincidence between two designated terms: the subtle but significant difference between what is on display and what is displayed. Moving away from theater as visual representation, Lacoue-Labarthe wants to highlight the theater's presentation of characters, voice, movement, text, as not so much adhering to an objective reality preceding or outside the theater (the re-presentation of a figure) but instead, in the most literal sense, as them *being on display*. Theater is always about the display itself.

Impropriety also means without property, or without a proper origin. For Lacoue-Labarthe, the notion of origin, although important, cannot be contained in one definite term or sentence. It cannot provide a unified meaning production, following a premeditated path in shared histories, emotional lives and thought; "there" is always something in its iterations that escapes us and that cannot be recuperated or reintegrated—through Hegelian dialectics resulting in a synthesis of opposites or through a teleologically motivated matter reaching for its final form. It is precisely this "there" of origin that is put on display in the theater. Not as a proper, fixed, stable, identifiable subject but as a plastic, constantly changing, *poetical* one instead.

Theater always has to do with what Lacoue-Labarthe called with Diderot a "disquieting *plasticity*" generating an unnerving and unsettling quality at the heart of the theatrical encounter (1989, 115).[2] For Lacoue-Labarthe this has to do with the fact that literally anything and any character can be assumed, appropriated and presented on the stage, which is no small thing, it is an insight that designates the protean actors predating Plato. The protean actor is a recurring figure that runs all the way through western culture and finds new conceptualizations in recent work on *homo mimeticus*.[3] Hence, with Lacoue-Labarthe, if one were ever to designate the "origin" of theater it would entail that it keeps differing from itself, like a protean character, its qualities keep differentiating and presenting as other. He often called this unnerving sense of the lack of origin experienced in the theater encounter, with Blanchot, "*caesura*" (Lacoue-Labarthe 1989, 208–235). By no accident, it is a literary term.

How, for Lacoue-Labarthe, is this deconstructive moment—where origin is sensed as a lack or loss of origin—of theater related to mimesis? We find a useful clue in one of Lacoue-Labarthe's key phrases, a conceptual matrix (following Irigaray) in the poststructuralist turn to homo mimeticus: the *mime de rien*, or mime without a model.[4] With this notion, Lacoue-Labarthe not only wants to shift the concept of mimesis from simple imitation to *mime*, a rather obscure and unknown term in philosophy, but he goes one step further by positing mime as the engendering, activating mechanism of imitation. In the act of miming [*mimer*] some "thing" is mimed, but this thing is—echoing Derrida's "Double Session" (1981)—"nothing" for it has no substance, no reason, no goal, and no objective. What is left is the act of the displaying or the event of theatricality *as such*. What interests Lacoue-Labarthe in short is the operation that enables mimetic relations to occur; it enables stories, discourses, rhythms, ideas, desires, melodies and emotions to be transferred not just from one subject to another, but among communities and intergenerationally. The idea of the *mime de rien* foregrounds mimesis as the working principle or stage that displays subjects in relation to each other and, simultaneously, as the production mechanism of the societies that are articulated through those operative mimeticisms.

Mime is not the prescriptive determination of imitative behavior, but the unpredictable description "of" and "after" the fact of a relational structure, that which binds subjects together without fixing them in their sameness as they remain open. Put differently, what connects us is our irresolvable need to mime— or "will to mime" (Lawtoo 2022, 51) indicating the immanent Nietzschean foundations of mimetic studies that animate Lacoue-Labarthe as well—to participate in an operation that by nature defies subjective boundaries. Mime is not a choice for Lacoue-Labarthe but a necessity. This also means that the question of theater as the event of mime should not be articulated in terms of a "why" (why (not) theater? why do we (not) need theater? why do we (not) make theater?)—these questions are beside the point because they are based on an already-established definition of theater. Instead, Lacoue-Labarthe wants to direct our attention toward the moment where theater "happens" before any definition could find its proper place in thought. The question of theater is better articulated in terms of a "when" and "how" (when does theater become the operational principle? when does theater (not) acknowledge its theatricality? and how (deep) are we enveloped in its dramaturgy or scenography?).[5]

Narrowing down the question of theater to that of the *actor*, a surprising and paradigmatic move in understanding Lacoue-Labarthe's shift from imitation to mime crucial for *homo mimeticus*, Lacoue-Labarthe writes in a short essay: "the actor is a mime in this sense: he is a spokesperson. To put it more accurately: he (we) represents that we are all such spokesmen, mimes. Theater is not mimesis, but the revelation of mimesis" (Lacoue-Labarthe 1983, 196). Although we are all mimetic creatures, as Aristotle and Plato stated, imitation is not an activity that originates in and can be appropriated by a subject or group of subjects. Rather, imitation as mime underlines that we are the ungrounded ground of mimesis, less imitating than emoting, emersed in and at the same time theatrically (re)phrasing our mimetic relations as we display them. There is a close correspondence between how subjects are configured in and through mimetic relations—for Lacoue-Labarthe, this is related to the question of language and its long western history in both the appeal to a universalizing logos and poetry or literature—and the theater's operation of *display*: both are marked by impropriety, both "are" not mimesis but "reveal" mimesis, and both transmit meaning that short-circuits rather than opposes the representational laws of imitation. Reformulating Hirt's definition, then, mime "designates less what we see and what we contemplate, thus what is represented in representative objectivity," but rather denotes "a meaning [that] passes through us that we cannot close in a figure" (Hirt 2009, 42).

From Ancient *Mimos* to Poststructuralist *Mimeuse*

It is important to reflect for a moment on the historical context and etymological roots of ancient mimesis, as this is one of the driving forces behind the contemporary *re*-turn to mimesis and features in particular in the works of our two central authors. It is no coincidence that Lacoue-Labarthe revivifies the idea of mime. Mimesis comes from the Greek verb *mimesthai* meaning to imitate, to portray, derived from *mimos*, referring simultaneously to performer and performance (Halliwell 2009, 17). However, regarding the type of performance, "[*mimos*] is not confined to a technical use but has a wider use, namely to exhibit something vividly and concretely by means of typical characterizing qualities" (Sörbom 1966, 38). There is an interesting conceptual link here with the origins of mimesis in mime that volume 1 of *Homo Mimeticus* traces (Lawtoo 2022, 13, 117, 138). Indeed, this genealogy does not stop in the 1960s with the work of classicists but is picked up, via Lacoue-Labarthe in the 2010s and 2020s, as part of the mimetic turn.

There is a conceptual and cultural distinction underlying the definition of the ancient mime present in this genealogy that deserves attention. Compared to other ancient performing styles such as tragedy, mime is closest to life in subject matter but in execution far removed from what we call, since the nineteenth century, *realism*. Where tragedy complies to models of the hero, monster, deity, god, and goddess, mime "is confined to the way we, ordinary human beings, behave" (Sörbom 1966, 24). At the same time, while mime exhibits life "as it is" (1966, 24), the *performative style* of mime does not comply with realism. Mime had as its primary task the deployment of performative means to make a phenomenon that is recognizable by people of all walks of life *vivid*, *active*, and *dynamic*, regardless of its aesthetic outcome. It is about finding the most effective way to (re-)activate an everyday situation or phenomenon without using reality as such as an aesthetic model.[6] This paves the way for a new material understanding of performance as mime in philosophical terms: mime designates the most basic human capacity to present life. That is, to display or exhibit what is *alive*, which is fundamentally distinct from what is "present" and "re-presentable," as poststructuralists show.

The historical insight that the ancient mime bypasses the aim for representation and is not first and foremost concerned about sustaining a similarity relation between aesthetic representation and life will be radically rethought by poststructuralist thinkers such as Lacoue-Labarthe, Derrida, Nancy, Agacinski, Kofman, and the feminist philosopher Irigaray who, as I hope to make clear, functions as a key pre-cursor of the mimetic turn proposed in this volume. An important reference to mention here is *Mimesis des articulations* (Agacinski et al. 1975), an edited volume featuring the above-mentioned French thinkers, among others, in which the philosophical concept of mimesis is deconstructed alongside the logocentrism of the western tradition—Derrida's "metaphysics of presence"—that in their view underlies representional conceptions of mimesis. Their focus is specifically on the mime [*la mimeuse*].[7] Derrida writes about "mime's articulations" [*des articulations des mimeuse*]:

> *Mimesis* could be played out, could be sketched out, elsewhere, a gesture, a mime, music from a stage already older, younger than these speeches, figures of actors striking a pose, movements of dissatisfied spectators roaming the stage, noises, street rumours, animal cries, rustling plants. (Agacinski et al. 1975, 14; my trans.)

In *Mimesis*, Derrida announces the deconstructed stage, or "page," as he calls it in his "Double Session," that the philosophical concept of mimesis necessarily "is" in the western tradition. Rather than referring to the heroic figures in western history, theatrical mimesis always also evokes an echo or "phantom," a "minor" figure like a mime (Lawtoo 2013; Hadikoesoemo 2020b). The mime "is" in light of a dominant tradition "elsewhere" or, in Lacoue-Labarthe's words, following Aristotle's definition of mimesis, designates "another presentation—or the presentation of something other, which was not there yet, given, or present" (Lacoue-Labarthe 1989, 247). How should we evaluate this poststructuralist view today in light of the genealogy mimetic studies trace? The question I pose myself that Derrida did not answer is the following: could it be that his theatrical description of "figures of actors striking a pose, movements...noises, street rumors, animal cries, rustling plants" leads us to unknown, ancient, embodied, musical, vibrant forms of theatricality exhibiting constantly differing forms of individuation, through and beyond subjectivation?

Lacoue-Labarthe might take Derrida's deconstruction toward that direction through Nietzsche.[8] In the context of theater, Nietzsche plays in the background of Lacoue-Labarthe's engagement with "the well-known thesis concerning enthusiasm" (1989, 253), central to Diderot's *Paradox of the Actor*, a key text for the turn to *homo mimeticus* that moves beyond deconstruction toward a more materialist philosophy (although calling Lacoue-Labarthe a materialist would go too far).[9] What Lacoue-Labarthe adds to Derrida's mime through his discussion of Diderot is an emotional or, rather, emotive layer to the mime as a theatrical figure. With Lacoue-Labarthe, we are talking more concretely about the actor as a human being of flesh and blood. He elevates the mime from the page, out of the purely textual realm, into the theater.[10]

Diderot's Paradox of the Actor

In his essay "Diderot: Paradox and Mimesis," featured in *Typography* (1989), Lacoue-Labarthe revivifies Diderot's "art of the actor," which entails a performer on the stage materializing a "phantom" [*fantôme*]. This phantom is, according to Diderot, paradoxically tied to the physiological—modern but fundamentally ancient—phenomenon of enthusiasm [*sensibilité*]" (Diderot and Archer 1957, 40; Lacoue-Labarthe 1989, 248). Enthusiasm refers to the excesses of human passions in mind and body, troubling the actor's judgment. In light of the performer's practical quest for continuity and consistency of action, Diderot argues against enthusiasm in favor of the theory of alienation—long before Brecht—celebrating "self-command" over emotional identification and praising the actor's lack of self, also known as the actor as "nothing"—we will come back to this point.[11]

However, in a much less extreme formulation, Diderot admits that affective engagement [*inspiration*] in and through an imaginary phantom is essential for a great performance.[12] Without analyzing the *Paradox* in full, what is important for our analysis is Lacoue-Labarthe's emphasis on what he calls the "hyperbological" structure of Diderot's dialogue (1989, 252). Lacoue-Labarthe argues that the *Paradox* resists the modern tendency to let the mind "win" over the body or vice versa. Instead, the dialogue shows that affects can paradoxically co-exist with reflection, that feeling does not exclude intellect but that they in-form (receive and give form to) each other, generating a "dynamic and spiraling interplay" between logos and pathos for which Lawtoo coined the term "patho(-)logy"

(2022, 21). The hyperbological aspect of the *Paradox* lies in the fact that Diderot does not *demonstrate* his argument of the productive interplay between pathos and logos as a "philosopher" per se—in Diderot's own words, that would make him a mediocre man—but instead *displays* or *exhibits* it in dialogical, nonlinear, a-logical, ironical, theatrical fashion, just as actors are using theatrical tools to emote an audience. What Diderot highlights in Lacoue-Labarthe is the inclination to hold together thought and drama, "adjusting theater to theory and theory to theater," as his long-time collaborator in the theater, Michel Deutsch, phrased it, which Lacoue-Labarthe seemed to have had all his professional life.[13]

Sober Theater as Patho(-)*logy*

In *Au théâtre*, currently edited by Aristide Bianchi and Leonid Kharlamov, as well as *Scène* (2013), Lacoue-Labarthe develops the idea of the exhibiting qualities of the theater through the principle of sobriety, a term borrowed from the eighteenth-century German poet Friedrich Hölderlin:

> It's the principle of sobriety, which is the opposite, therefore, of all forms of hysterization [...] This is what I expect from theater, from art in general. To offer as little as possible to any phenomenon of identification, which does not mean, once again, to forbid emotion. That's the confusion we generally make. (Lacoue-Labarthe n.d., 168)

Contrary to the idea of sobriety as a total lack of emotion (an "anti-mimetic" solution of distance from pathos), Lacoue-Labarthe argues for a mimetic principle of non-identification that at the same time involves emotion that includes *distance* as well as *pathos* and where the interplay between the two opens a stage, a theater of affective exchange. This touches on an idea that Lacoue-Labarthe has coined elsewhere; namely, the theater's power to generate an emotion of thought. The idea that thought *itself* carries emotion, rather than the actor, character or even spectator, is fascinating. In this understanding, emotion is not a subjective property but a mimetic property—not opposed to thought but precisely carried through it. In a sober theater one is being provoked to think, and this thinking *has emotion*. If we connect this to homo mimeticus' "patho(-)*logy*," we could say that the theater reaches a point of productive sobriety when the interplay between pathos and distance is masterfully balanced, where one is emotionally and intellectually involved in equal measure because and in spite of a mimetic principle that defies subjective boundaries.

Where does this Lacoue-Labarthean plea for a sober theater—against a theater of hysterization—come from? In his essay *Typography*, Lacoue-Labarthe historically links hysterization to passivity and feminization, a convergence mimetically intertwined with the western obsession with appropriation: "Whence the obsession with appropriation that dominates through and through every analysis of mimesis, of mimetism, and works to create its full economic (and consequently political) bearing" (1989, 126–129)—a thought well-developed in mimetic studies already.[14] The "political" aspect of hystericized mimetism builds, of course, on Nietzsche (and is carried over to Heidegger). But it also has a specifically feminist stamp due to Lacoue-Labarthe's intensive reading of Irigaray, which becomes clear in a footnote:

> As regards the 'question of woman,' we are passing very close here (as has been indicated throughout this essay by the motif of the specularization of mimesis) to the trail followed by Luce Irigaray, in *Speculum, de l'autre femme*. (Lacoue-Labarthe 1989, 129)

It is the feminist undertones of Lacoue-Labarthe's consideration of the sober theater that has remained understudied in mimesis research so far that I aim to develop further in what follows. In *Speculum* as well as *This Sex Which is Not One*, Irigaray deconstructs, like Derrida, Plato's mimesis and displays mimetically—patho(-)*logically* (with affect and distance)—the gendered nature of the western tradition. She does so by distinguishing between "two mimeses" in Plato, which in turn informed Lacoue-Labarthe's distinction between a restrictive and general form of mimesis, pivotal for mimetic studies.

Two Mimeses

Although Irigaray is well-known for her "strategic" use of mimicry in her early work, her reading of Plato's "mimeses" also announces the possibility of a positive ontology of/in the feminine, generally attributed by commentators to her later work. This reveals not only the richness and scope of Irigaray's philosophy

of sexuate difference, but it also indicates the many layers of the concept of theatrical mimesis yet to be developed from this point of view. In *This Sex*, Irigaray
argues that

> in Plato, there are two *mimeses*. To simplify: there is mimesis as pro-
> duction, which would lie more in the realm of music, and there is the
> mimesis that would be already caught up in a process of *imitation, spe-
> cularization, adequation,* and *reproduction.* It is the second form that
> is privileged throughout the history of philosophy and whose effects/
> symptoms, such as latency, suffering, paralysis of desire, are encoun-
> tered in hysteria. The first form seems always to have been repressed,
> if only because it was constituted as an enclave within a "dominant"
> discourse. Yet it is doubtless in the direction of, and on the basis of,
> that first *mimesis* that the possibility of a woman's writing may come
> about. (1985, 131)

There are two elements I want to highlight in this passage. The first is Irigaray's
equation of productive mimesis with the realm of *music*; the second is Irigaray's
terminology of mimesis in terms of a *place*. Let me start with the second. Irigaray
is clearly repeating Plato's language when she calls mimesis' productive forces an
"enclave," which is a small part of a country completely surrounded by another
country. This imagery is reminiscent of Plato's *chora*, the birthing place of "woman's writing," "suppressed" by the surrounded dominance of a masculine logic
that works according to "specularization" (in *Speculum*, most clearly, Irigaray
mimes the "flat" mirrors in Plato and Freud). She *disappropriates* the *chora* from
Plato's sphere of philosophical demonstration and allows it to be the driving
force behind a different place of writing, *her* woman's writing, instead, where
multiple repetitions are at work at once and through which meaning can seep
due to her modifications of its sexuate matter. She puts on display the improper
origin of her own language next to the dominant masculine one not to create a
confusing web of references but to make more vivid and characteristic the concrete forms of imitation that women are victim of in language and can as well
inflict upon themselves and other women through becoming that mirror object
of man's self-image. How does this work?

Irigaray's mimetic display is that place of impropriety in the same way as
theater has been doomed improper by Plato. At the same time, and this is an important complication, by inhabiting and playing on that improper stage, Irigaray is
not miraculously freed of its dominant historical traces. She is leaving it up to the

spectator or reader of her mime to experience and contribute to what theater of mimesis *exactly* she is activating in her repetitions and how far we see ourselves immersed in it. This presupposes a mastery of patho(-)*logy*, where affect and thought, pathos and distance, are held together, passing through and over a hysterical undercurrent. In my view, Lacoue-Labarthe's insistence on the theatricality of mimesis carries an Irigarayan insight: the importance of understanding the anxiety-driven and violating "why" question ("why is she converting to mime?" and "why am/can I (not) be included in that mime"?) emerges as a phallogocentric quest for identification/appropriation. On the other hand, questions of the "how" and "when" display a thinking in the feminine that always already understands itself as mimetic. In Lacoue-Labarthe's vocabulary, the first theater of mimesis is "restrictive," the second theater of mimesis is "general," productive; the first has "forgotten" its "own" theatricality, the latter acknowledges it as its very principle (1989, 225).

In Irigaray, crucially, this insight cannot be blind to the reality of sexuate difference. The question of mime or mimetic exposition takes on a particular weight when it comes to the concrete lives of women. In Irigaray's view, the western world is generally configured around a logic of sexual indifference, which means that women's relation to imitation, including its presupposed theatricality, gains a particular societal and political meaning and impact. I will not enter the feminist debates that surround this issue because it would lead us too far from the topic at hand.[15] It suffices to say that imitation in western cultures implies a sexual imbalance, historically, as women tended to be put on the side of passive, receptive matter (copy) and men on the side of active form (original).[16] Against this background, mime is a pertinent question for women because they have to move through the site of logical sameness that constitutes and organizes a phallogocentric thought production and has occupied representations of Woman. In any case, for Irigaray, the feminine is neither the brute force of pure biology nor a lofty model to aspire to in our dreams, and that remains in obscure and unknowable spheres. Instead, we should see the mime as/in the feminine as a productive theater of thought that is always already material. An *écriture féminine* (a term Irigaray never used for herself) may be writing, but its texture is of flesh, three-dimensional, and not flat and two-dimensional as a piece of paper. Irigaray's mime-in-the-flesh activates all the significant differences that make up our sexuate subjectivities and is understood by us, readers or spectators, as a kind of collaboration with life's forces in which we, sexuate-specific beings, always already partake and that asks of us a noble response.

Let me return to Irigaray's mention of music. Perhaps it is here that we see most clearly Irigaray's resonance in Lacoue-Labarthe: they both tap into an ancient account of productive mimesis that recalls the act of mime within the boundaries of the musicopoetic arts also known as *mousikè*.[17] By calling upon "mimesis as production," lying "within the realm of music," Irigaray highlights that mimesis is not restricted to visual representation, which she associates with the act of specularization (to make specular, reflective or visible). Instead, she accounts for performative forms of expression like dance and music, which has an explicit exposing (rather than demonstrating) function. This is the main paradigm shift mimetic studies aims to foreground. The mime's exposition in sound and movement *in the feminine* principally and performatively does not comply with a logic of verisimilitude and visual resemblance. Rather it focuses on finding the performative means to explore vividly a phenomenon of life, which also involves forces coming from animals, the elements, and instruments.[18] When Irigaray speaks of a productive mimesis she is hence speaking of a very distinct practice that should be differentiated from more established ancient theater forms like tragedy.

A Theater of Activating, Musical Bodies

Let me give an example where music and movement play a role in Irigaray's work. In *Elemental Passions* (1992), Irigaray speaks in the first-person, describing herself as "your mime" [*ton mime*] that transforms into the forces of nature: "I had become all kinds of things at play [*en jeux*], all kinds of sound" (1982, 74–75; 1992, 60–62, my trans.). She describes herself as being "at play" and in terms of an instrument or natural element producing different "kinds of sound." In so far as she is "at play" as woman, she is to be considered as becoming not just an imitator of sound but the kinds of sound *themselves*. There is no separation between her as an autonomous being, a pre-existing *subiectum*, and the sounds that are produced. She is the ungrounded yet engendering force of sound where the act of producing and her as what is "at play" *mean the same thing* (remember the ancient mimos that designates performer and performance simultaneously). Now there is always a double dynamic—"two mimeses"—going on in Irigaray where, on one side, the miming of woman is passive, subsuming to a phallogocentric logic of the Same where coincidence (of "woman" and "sound") presumes a metaphysics of presence and identity. On the other side, however, Irigaray subverts the logic of mimesis by simultaneously accounting for the creative, always-in-movement, and excessive process of subjectivation or becoming in the feminine. This time, the "I" is mimetic on the grounds that she (the "I" who speaks here is Irigaray and thus sexuated [*sexué*] as a woman) understands the natural, musical, and rhythmic qualities as being "at play" on quite another plane, creating an affective and corporeal encounter with the (sexuate) other or others.

By example, in *Elemental Passions*, Irigaray displays a productive relational mimesis, already present in Plato and probably well before him, prefiguring the *re*-turn to mimesis, through a poetical, musical language:

> Where the wind's song fills [*emplit*] the air with a harmony that has no cries or silent agonies. The whole murmurs [*tout bruit*] so softly that the melody makes way [*laisse place*] for the highest and the lowest note, the sharpest and the deepest. Should a bird sing, the whole joins in an accompanying choir [*le chœur du tout l'accompagne*]. But the appearance or disappearance of this song is not heart-breaking. If nothing happens, nothing is missing. If no sound is detached, the atmosphere remains full of music [*l'atmosphère demeure musique*]. (1982, 85; 1992, 70)

Attuned to the productive forces of mimesis, an "atmosphere" where "nothing happens" is a place still full of music. According to an affective account of mimesis, and within Irigaray's philosophy, music without demarcations is neither with nor without property; rather, it is like a theater with no "roof, no frame, no fence," (1992, 24–25) and yet with the power to potentially present or display everything. Indeed, it is crucial not to think of this "becoming everything" of women in a skeptical, passive manner, as a figure dispersed. Irigaray precisely attests to the fact that it is a *task* (of patho(-)logy?) to keep dismantling that logic while pointing to the creative sides that always already produce another plane of relationality.

It is not farfetched to link the delineations that women face in a predominantly masculine discourse with the delineations of the theatrical stage in the way we have been conceptualizing it with Lacoue-Labarthe as a restrictive form of mimesis. In my view, Irigaray's feminine mime refers to an embodied stage beyond writing because she engages in qualities that have precisely historically been linked to theater, such as fluidity and plasticity—think of Diderot's plastic actor transforming into everything or, indeed, Plato's Ion, a similar chameleon figure.[19] Like Lacoue-Labarthe's Diderot, Irigaray is following the path of creatively inhabiting, or *giving birth to*, several roles at once without producing her "self" as a stable core or "representative" of such roles. She exposes the feminine voice as exceeding subjective boundaries and in a fluid manner. More concretely, she gives a body and a voice—in essence a *sexuated nature*—to Lacoue-Labarthe's suggested figure of the "feminization" of mimesis in *Typography*.

By Way of Conclusion: The Gift of Nothing

Was it Irigaray who taught Lacoue-Labarthe about the productive forces of mime?[20] In her latest book, *Sharing the Fire* (2019), Irigaray writes: "if we have not opened in ourselves the void space that the respect for the difference of the other involves, we do not perceive all that their touch tells to us" (2019, 14). Again, traditionally, a void space means *lack*, lack of property, an ontological nothingness that does not "seize," "become" or "exist." Irigaray speaks of a fruitful and rich void, a void that allows us to hear the other's voice and to feel the other's touch as different from ours. Without this void space, one would be absorbed in a circular dynamic where the other becomes the instrument of self-affection; a "neutrality [that] does not enable us to distinguish an 'it is me' from an 'it is you'" (Irigaray 2019, 15). In *Typography*, Lacoue-Labarthe writes that nothingness is a gift that the actor gives themselves. He is echoing Diderot's *Paradox*: that actor who is "neither a pianoforte nor a harp, nor a spinnet, nor a violin, nor a violoncello [...] and he can take up any," that actor has that specific "gift of nature" that is "the gift of being nothing," in short, "the gift of nothing" (of course the void/nothing for Lacoue-Labarthe is also of Heideggerian inspiration and Sartre was still in the air (Diderot and Archer 1957, 46; Lacoue-Labarthe 1989, 259). In Irigaray, this gift is irrevocably intersubjective: it is *because of you* that I can give myself the gift of nothing and potentially become everything. It is, as such, the basis of *another* theater or *another* stage of mimetic togetherness. Following this chapter's analysis, Irigaray's fruitful void requires the notion of mimetic display. As we saw, the act of miming [*mimer*] not only produces repetition but it displays it in light of its potential nothingness. Even more importantly, because emerging from theatrical and, hence, communal structures, it can be transmitted on those grounds (Irigaray 1992, 25).

In this chapter's investigation, I have aimed to make the case for an Irigarayan undercurrent in one of the most prominent sources for mimetic studies—namely Lacoue-Labarthe's *Typography*—inscribing her corporeal phi-losophy of/in the feminine in the theatricality of mimesis, central to the *re*-turn to mimesis that this volume proposes. Inspired by Hirt's definition of theater as display/exhibition/exposition, and moving away from visual representation, I analyzed Lacoue-Labarthe's interest in theatrical (restrictive and productive) forms of mimesis through his reading of Diderot. This allowed me to offer an account of a so-called sober theater based on a paradoxical interplay between "pathos" and "logos" (Lawtoo 2022, 37). This double sidedness of mimesis in Lacoue-Labarthe, finally, bears the traces of Irigaray's deconstruction of "two mimeses" in Plato. This distinction has not only (partly) provided Lacoue-Labarthe with the conceptual means to link the notion of the feminine to mi-mesis. It has also, and together with Lacoue-Labarthe's *Typography*, allowed us, today, to help shift the binary logic of both theater (re-presentation of reality) and the feminine (re-creation of a masculine imaginary) toward a more sensu-ous, relational, process-oriented display of mimeses.

Notes

1   On exhibition as an elemental feature of theater, see Guénoun 1998.

2   See Kirkkopelto 2009, 2010.

3   See Hadikoesoemo 2020a and Lawtoo 2018, 2021, 2022.

4   In one of his notes, published after Lacoue-Labarthe's death, Nancy qualified the *mime de rien* as Lacoue-Labarthe's "main philosophical exercise" (Nancy and Girard 2015, 40–41). For the role of this notion in Lacoue-Labarthe, see also Murena 2022.

5   Together with Nancy, Lacoue-Labarthe investigated the political implications of this *mimétisme* – for example, as regards the emotional and artistic undercurrent of the Nazi regime in Germany in "The Nazi Myth" (1990). The communal aspect of the politics of mi-mesis is an important dimension of Lacoue-Labarthe's work, especially in his collaborations with Nancy and has been central to the mimetic turn (see Lawtoo 2019, ch. 3). As Nancy was the first to acknowledge, it cannot be underestimated how much of this work is embed-ded in and directly informed by Lacoue-Labarthe's (first hand) insights on theater (Nancy and Lawtoo 2022, 28–35).

6   Interesting to point out is the recent focus on an "alternative history of mimesis" (in contrast to the dominant tradition of tragedy as a form of theatrical mimesis) through the lens of comedy, which has strong links with ancient mime, expanding mimetic studies in the field of performance. On this, see Ortega Máñez 2023.

7   Derrida, Nancy, Lacoue-Labarthe, and other contributors of *Mimesis* invented a variety of different words designating "mime" to make the diversification and plurality of mimesis' production processes in thought and action visible, in particular in light of the history of thought in the West; see also their "débat à propos de la mimesis" in *La Quinzaine* (Agacin-ski et al. 1975).

8   I do not have the space to do justice to Lacoue-Labarthe's engagement with Nietzsche here. It suffices to say that he is an important precursor for the ritual origins of theatrical mimesis both for Lacoue-Labarthe and mimetic studies. See Lawtoo 2008; 2022, 44–47.

9   See Lawtoo 2022, 132, 147.

10 See also Lacoue-Labarthe n.d; Bianchi and Kharlamov 2017.

11 See Diderot and Archer 1957, 17, 46; Lacoue-Labarthe 1989, 259; Von Held 2010; Hadikoesoemo 2020b.

12 See Diderot and Archer 1957, 17.

13 "An academic was going to work in the theater with actors and actors would go to the University to take philosophy courses" (Deutsch 2018, 108; my trans.).

14 See Borch-Jacobsen 2009; Lawtoo 2022, 29, 207, 319. For Lacoue-Labarthe's use of "economy" I refer to Derrida's important contribution to *Mimesis: des articulations*, titled "Economimesis" (1975). Lacoue-Labarthe's reference of Derrida's "The Double Session" in *Typography* (Lacoue-Labarthe 1989, 101) is also worth mentioning.

15 It is worth highlighting the work of Butler, Cavarero, Malabou, and other allies of the *Gendered Mimesis Project* here, which shows that mimetic studies are foregrounding feminist mimesis as well. See https://genderedmimesis.com/

16 See also an important footnote in "Typography," where Lacoue-Labarthe re-articulates "passivity" and "activity" as complying to "a certain sexual—so to speak—modelization of ontideo-typo-logy" (Lacoue-Labarthe 1989, 126).

17 See Villegas Vélez 2019. For a classical account of the notion of *mousikè*, in line with mimetic studies, see Halliwell 2009, 19.

18 For an in-depth analysis of Irigaray's thought as a feminist philosophy of life, see Seely 2016.

19 See Lawtoo 2022, ch. 2; Cavarero 2005.

20 To support the idea of Irigaray as a precursor of mimetic studies, see also Lawtoo 2006.

Bibliography

Agacinski, Sylviane, Jacques Derrida, Sarah Kofman, Philippe Lacoue-Labarthe, Jean-Luc Nancy, and Bernard Pautrat (1976). "Philosophes occupés à déplacer le philosophique à propos de la 'mimesis.'" *La Quinzaine Littéraire* 231, 19–22.

Agacinski, Sylviane, Jacques Derrida, Sarah Kofman, Jean-Luc Nancy, Philippe Lacoue-Labarthe, and Bernard Pautrat (1975). *Mimesis des articulations: La philosophie en effet*. Paris: Aubier-Flammarion.

Bianchi, Aristide, and Leonid Kharlamov (2017). "Passer au théâtre." *L'Esprit Créateur* 57.4, 10–21.

Borch-Jacobsen, Mikkel (2009). *Making Madness: From Hysteria to Depression*. Cambridge: Cambridge University Press.

Cavarero, Adriana (2005). *For More Than One Voice: Toward a Philosophy of Vocal Expression*. Stanford: Stanford University Press.

Derrida, Jacques (1975). "Economimesis," in *Mimesis des articulations. La philosophie en effet*. Paris: Aubier-Flammarion, 57–93.

—— (1981). *Dissemination*, trans. Barbara Johnson. London: Athlone.

Deutsch, Michel (2018). *Souvenirs épars: Philippe Lacoue-Labarthe, les années théâtre*. Paris: Christian Bourgois.

Diderot, Denis, and William Archer (1957). *The Paradox of Acting: Masks or Faces?* New York: Hill and Wang.

Guénoun, Denis (1998). *L'exhibition des mots et autres idées du théâtre et de la philosophie.* Belfort: Circé.

Hadikoesoemo, Niki (2020a). "Altering Bodies: Thinking of Intervention through Impersonation." *Performance Philosophy* 5.2, 316–331. https://doi.org/10.21476/PP.2020.52281.

—— (2020b). "Phantoming the Subject: Diderot, Lacoue-Labarthe and the Actor's Paradox." *Brazilian Journal on Presence Studies* 10.3, 1–25. https://doi.org/10.1590/2237-266092334.

—— (2021). "In Favour of an Ontology of Sexual Difference. Luce Irigaray on Mimesis and Fluidity." *P.O.I. – Points of Interest. Rivista di indagine filosofica e di nuove pratiche della conoscenza (Italian Journal of Philosophical Investigation and New Practices of Knowledge)* 8.1, 106–29. https://doi.org/10.5281/zenodo.5714520.

Halliwell, Stephen (2009). *The Aesthetics of Mimesis: Ancient Texts and Modern Problems.* Princeton: Princeton University Press.

Hirt, André (2009). *Un homme littéral: Philippe Lacoue-Labarthe.* Paris: Kimé.

Irigaray, Luce (1982). *Passions élémentaires.* Paris: Les Éditions de Minuit.

—— (1985). *This Sex Which Is Not One*, trans. Catherine Porter and Carolyn Burke. Ithaca, NY: Cornell University Press.

—— (1992). *Elemental Passions*, trans. Joanne Collie and Judith Still. London: Routledge.

—— (2019). *Sharing the Fire: Outline of a Dialectics of Sensitivity.* Cham: Springer.

Kirkkopelto, Esa (2009). "The Question of the Scene: On the Philosophical Foundations of Theatrical Anthropocentrism." *Theatre Research International* 34.3, 230–242.

—— (2010). "On the Structure of the Scenic Encounter," in *The Event of Encounter in Art and Philosophy: Continental Perspectives*, eds. Kuisma Korhonen and Pajari Räsänen. Helsinki: Gaudeamus, 69–96.

Lacoue-Labarthe, Philippe (n.d.). *Au Théâtre* [unpublished manuscript], eds. Bianchi Aristide and Leonid Kharlamov.

—— (1989). *Typography: Mimesis, Philosophy, Politics.* Cambridge, MA: Harvard University Press.

—— (2008). "Bye Bye Farewell (1983)." *L'animal* 19–20, 191–198.

Lacoue-Labarthe, Philippe, and Jean-Luc Nancy (1990). "The Nazi Myth." *Critical Inquiry* 16.2, 291–312. https://doi.org/10.1086/448535.

—— (2013). *Scène: suivi de Dialogue sur le dialogue.* Paris: Christian Bourgois.

Lawtoo, Nidesh (2006). "Dissonant Voices in Richard Rodriguez's *Hunger of Memory* and Luce Irigaray's *This Sex Which Is Not One.*" *Texas Studies in Literature and Language* 48.3: 220–249. https://doi.org/10.1353/tsl.2006.0011.

—— (2008). "Nietzsche and the Psychology of Mimesis: From Plato to the Führer," in *Nietzsche, Power and Politics: Rethinking Nietzsche's Legacy for Political Thought*, eds. Herman Siemens and Vasti Roodt. Berlin: de Gruyter, 667–696.

—— (2013). *The Phantom of the Ego: Modernism and the Mimetic Unconscious.* East Lansing: Michigan State University Press.

—— (2018). "The Critic as Mime: Wilde's Theoretical Performance." *Symploke; Lincoln* 26.1–2: 307–328.

—— (2019). *(New) Fascism: Contagion, Community, Myth.* Michigan: Michigan State University Press.

——— (2021). "The Human Chameleon: Zelig, Nietzsche and the Banality of Evil." *Film-Philosophy* 25.3, 272–295.

——— (2022). *Homo Mimeticus: A New Theory of Imitation*. Leuven: Leuven University Press.

——— (2023). "Shared Voices: Lacoue-Nancy's Mimetic Methexis," in *Thinking With—Jean-Luc Nancy*, ed. Susanna Lindberg, Artemy Magun and Marita Tatari, Zurich/Berlin: Diaphanes, 289–307.

Murena, Nicolas. (2022). *Le 'Mime de Rien' de Philippe Lacoue-Labarthe*. Paris: Hermann.

Nancy, Jean-Luc (2007). "Lettre à Philippe Lacoue-Labarthe." *Lignes* 1.22: 178–181.

Nancy, Jean-Luc, and Mathilde Girard (2015). *Proprement Dit: Entretien Sur Le Mythe*. Paris: Lignes.

Nancy, Jean-Luc, and Nidesh Lawtoo (2022). "The CounterText Interview: Jean-Luc Nancy Mimesis: A Singular-Plural Concept." *CounterText* 8.1, 23–45.

Ortega Máñez, María J. (2023). "Comedy: Towards an Alternative History of Mimesis," in *Second Nature: Comic Performance and Philosophy*, eds. Josephine Gray and Lisa Trahair. Lanham: Rowman & Littlefield, 1-15.

Seely, Stephen D. (2016). "Does Life Have a Sex? Thinking Ontology and Sexual Difference with Irigaray and Simondon," in *Feminist Philosophies of Life*, eds. Hasana Sharp and Chloë Taylor. Montréal: McGill-Queen's University Press, 108–125.

Sörbom, Göran (1966). *Mimesis and Art: Studies in the Origin and Early Development of an Aesthetic Vocabulary*. Stockholm: Svenska Bokförlaget.

Villegas Vélez, Daniel (2019). "Interruption—Intervention: On the Interval between Literature and Music in Jean-Luc Nancy's 'Myth Interrupted.'" *Performance Philosophy* 5.2, 183–202.

——— (2022) "Musical Affects: Genealogies and Diagnoses," in *The Routledge Companion to Gender and Affect*, ed. Todd Reeser. London: Routledge, 299–310.

Von Held, Phoebe (2010). *Alienation and Theatricality: Diderot after Brecht*. London: Legenda.

PART 3

NEW MIMETIC STUDIES FROM AESTHETICS TO BIOMIMICRY

CHAPTER 11

NEGATIVE EMPATHY IN FICTION

Mimesis, Contagion, Catharsis

Carmen Bonasera

> But another man's soul is murky, and the Russian soul is murky; it is
> so for many. Here he had long been getting together with Rogozhin,
> close together, together in a "brotherly" way—but did he know
> Rogozhin? And anyhow, what chaos, what turmoil, what ugliness
> there sometimes is in all that!
>
> —Fyodor Dostoevsky, *The Idiot*

Establishing a connection with the mind and feelings of another person is a complex endeavor, as the above passage, taken from Fyodor Dostoevsky's *The Idiot* (1869), suggests. Here, the novel's protagonist, Prince Myshkin, is reflecting on his ambiguous relationship with his dear friend Rogozhin—who will later attack Myshkin with a knife in a fit of jealousy—and on the unintelligible nature of human souls, evocatively described as "murky."[1] What this quote also indicates, however, is that humans are naturally going to attempt entering into that murky cave. Dostoevsky is thus depicting the all-too-human inclination to embrace that darkness and turmoil. This contradictory tendency of being caught on the threshold of another's soul, oscillating between stepping into the dark and recoiling, is at the heart of a specific aesthetic and literary experience that is bound to express the patho(-)logical[2] side of the mimetic engagement with other people: namely, negative empathy.

While post-critical studies on readerly empathy have highlighted its beneficial effects, a re-turn to mimetic approaches in the study of empathy actually seems more suitable to encompass its multifaceted nature.[3] The latter was particularly clear to one of the precursors of the modern research on empathy: the early twentieth-century German psychologist and aesthetician Theodor Lipps. Albeit a neglected figure in the genealogy of the study of empathy, Lipps had a key role in developing a systematic understanding of *Einfühlung* in aesthetics, which literally translates as "feeling-into" a work of art or another person.[4] Not only did he envision empathy as the "objectification of myself in an object that is different from me" (Lipps 1909, 222); he was also the first to consider empathy as either positive or negative. Empathy thus entails experiencing a connection with a person or an object based on either a feeling of accord and pleasure (positive empathy), or a feeling of conflict and unpleasure (negative empathy).[5]

This chapter is conceived as an assessment of Lipps's concept of negative empathy via the recent reappraisal in literary studies. My main aim is to add a tile to the interdisciplinary mosaic of the mimetic turn, so as to show its relevance for literary and reception studies. The chapter is organized into three sections, each revolving around one fundamental concept in the theory of *homo mimeticus*: namely, mimesis, contagion, and catharsis. In the first section, I discuss the mimetic turn in the humanities that has prompted a renewed interest in empathy. The second section delves into the literary approach to narrative (and negative) empathy seen as a form of emotional contagion that spreads among authors, works of art and readers, while also describing some fictional strategies capable of eliciting character identification and negative empathy. Finally, the third section focuses on the effect that negative empathy allegedly exerts—catharsis—and it establishes a tangible conjunction with the theory of homo mimeticus via the notion of the *pathos of distance*, a Nietzschean concept re-evaluated by mimetic studies to express the double-bind between "mimetic and anti-mimetic tendencies" (Lawtoo 2022a, 37). Throughout the chapter, literary analyses of excerpts from two novels by Fyodor Dostoevsky contribute to showing how emotional contagion, negative empathy, and the pathos of distance are theoretically interrelated and also dramatized in fiction for cathartic and transformative purposes.

Mimesis: A Change in Perspective

The opening move of the mimetic turn, in its recent proposal by Nidesh Lawtoo, is to highlight how a transdisciplinary gamut of theorists is now revisiting and challenging the traditional interpretation of mimesis understood as mere representation of reality. There has been a progressively shared awareness of the multifaceted nature of mimesis in the humanities; in fact, its intertwining with complex notions such as identification, embodied simulation, and affective contagion makes it barely plausible to narrow its meaning down to aesthetic and literary realism, Auerbach notwithstanding.[6]

Lawtoo's work furthers a return to mimesis in order to reveal the ways in which this concept encompasses "the anthropological, psychological, sociological, biological, neurological and ontological foundations of an eminently relational species that perhaps prematurely designated itself as *Homo sapiens sapiens*" (2022a, 2). In this sense, following Gunter Gebauer and Christoph Wulf's anthropological take on mimesis as a *conditio humana* (1995, 1), Lawtoo proposed a 'relational' interpretation of mimesis as:

> rooted in an immanent, embodied, and shared human condition on planet Earth that is constitutive of our [...] lives, a mimetic condition which, in different ways and with widening degrees of inequality, infects and affects the embodied materiality of an eminently relational, communal, and plastic species we call [...] *homo mimeticus*. (2022a, 5)

While the far-reaching consequences of this rethinking can be witnessed across the humanities, I argue that this challenge may be mostly felt in aesthetics and literary studies, since the long history of mimesis in literary theory makes it the arena where it may display the highest potential for inquiry. For instance, the widespread enthusiasm about the discovery of mirror neurons as a possible biological basis for mimetic behavior—including mental simulation and emotion-sharing skills—rekindled interest in human mimetic abilities, leading to claim that "if we needed an empirical confirmation that we are mimetic creatures, now we have one" (12).[7] Literary studies have been particularly receptive to the view of mirror neurons as the fundamental mechanism for human mimesis, especially with regards to affective and empathic processes encouraged by fiction, which may have positive transformative effects on human behavior.[8] In fact, our acknowledgement of the feelings, emotions and troubles of others, including fictional others, makes us easily understand their motives and value systems; it also "enable[s] us to recognize a similar complex of feelings and motives in ourselves, thus illuminating or even helping shape an aspect of our own identity" (Miall 2011, 285).[9]

By incorporating social psychology and (neuro)cognitive studies, literary theorists recently translated this interest in mimetic responses into a surge of new theoretical and empirical research on the beneficial effects of reading on interpersonal skills, associating the experience of readerly empathy with altruism and improved relational abilities.[10] Conversely, several investigations in developmental and social psychology and neuroscience have shown that empathy can indeed have positive as well as negative articulations, just as Lipps had foreseen, each one activating different regions of the brain and triggering different behaviors.[11] Nevertheless, these studies merely defined positive empathy as a mirroring of positive emotions of other people, and negative empathy as engaging with negative emotions of others. When it comes to the aesthetic realm, however, these working definitions fail to sufficiently depict the sophisticated and contradictory forms of mimetic engagement that readers experience. While reading fiction, the most challenging case is in fact represented by negative empathy, which may be aroused by stories that foreground unreliable, deviant or immoral characters. These narratives are shaped in a way that makes them capable of eliciting ambivalent affects, which may spread contagiously from the work of art to readers.[12] The next paragraph will account for a description of this empathic form by relating it to the broader context of the study of empathy in literary theory.

Contagion: Narrative and Negative Empathy in Literature

The issue of the readers' empathetic engagement with fiction has been widely discussed in literary studies, specifically while considering imaginary characters not as mere textual signifiers, but as real entities[13] with whom readers can experience "a projective fusing" (Keen 2007, 28). Post-critical interpretations have progressively equated fictional characters with real persons on the grounds of shared qualities and idiosyncrasies. As a consequence, the primal disposition to be curious about the thoughts, feelings and motives of others, that is, the draw "to make sense of other people" (Felski 2019, 83), is symmetrically translated into fiction, in the relationship that is established with characters through narrative empathy.[14]

Although readers' experiences and empathic abilities are clearly subjective and differ in degree from one individual to another, narrative empathy has been generally described as "the sharing of feeling and perspective-taking induced by reading, viewing, hearing, or imagining narratives of another's situation and condition" (Keen 2014, 521). Most importantly, it is an experience that encompasses both affect and cognition, since it is not limited to a mimetic sharing of emotions and sensations; on the contrary, it extends to complex cognitive acts that are involved in reading, such as imagination, projection, and absorption. This process, entailing an interaction between affect and cognition, relates to Lawtoo's understanding of mimesis as a "patho-logy," a term he uses "to indicate the dynamic and spiraling interplay between affect and reason, body and mind, *pathos* and *logos*, animating the two sides [...] of homo mimeticus" (2022a, 21).

But is it possible to experience empathy for negative and morally flawed characters? This issue has been at the center of a heightened debate in literary studies and aesthetics. Felski, for instance, states that since empathy is linked to altruism and fellow feeling, it would be "exceptionally ill-suited to the demented, destructive, antinomian, and asocial heroes of much modern and postmodern fiction" (2019, 111–112), despite the fascination that these characters may exercise. On the contrary, I argue that morally challenging characters are often crafted with a view to arousing ambiguous affects. Following Lipps's early intuition regarding works of art, this affective and aesthetic experience has been termed "negative empathy" (Ercolino 2018). We can certainly be captivated by works that depict tragic emotions, suffering human beings, as well as repulsive or immoral characters, but we could also be capable of *resonating with* them.[15] In theory, negative empathy evolves from the general frame of narrative empathy in more elaborate and unpredictable ways, resulting in a "*cathartic identification* with characters [...] that are *disturbingly* portrayed as markedly *negative* and *seductive* at the same time" (Ercolino and Fusillo 2022, 70; my transl.). The peculiar ways in which these individuals are characterized make them capable of prompting a complex affective experience that oscillates between closeness, identification, and empathy, on the one hand, and distress, angst and, eventually, detachment, on the other. As I will discuss in section 3, the aftermath of this experience is a form of catharsis that does not occur for its own sake; rather, it leads the recipient to engage in a moral evaluation of the characters and their stories and, finally, to assume an ethical position for self-transformative purposes.

This profound patho(-)logical experience consisting of both affective closeness and critical detachment might ultimately "involve a darker aspect of emotional contagion" (Keen 2007, 135), by "transferring" the author's own affection for a negative character to the reader in order to exorcise an involuntary empathy felt for such figure. This pathological emotional contagion ties inextricably the issue of narrative (and negative) empathy to the theory of *homo mimeticus*, since, as Lawtoo suggests

> all affects are mimetic and thus contagious [...] all affects—from sympathy to grief, jealousy to resentment, disgust to fear, panic to trust,

happiness to joy—tend to generate mimetic effects, for both good and ill, triggering both sad and joyful affects. (2022, 10)

Nevertheless, negative empathy still remains an *aesthetic* experience. While it is rather difficult to feel a mimetic and empathic connection for ordinary people whose actions violate our moral boundaries, the extra-ordinary prerogatives of fiction and some specific narrative strategies may allow people to temporarily disregard their moral sense and engage with characters that commit abominable crimes or that are portrayed as twisted and immoral.

Fictional Strategies to Elicit Negative Empathy

Consider, for example, the unfortunate vicissitudes of murderer Raskolnikov in Dostoevsky's *Crime and Punishment*, the tragic downfall of pedophile and rapist Humbert Humbert in Nabokov's *Lolita*, or the evolution of *Breaking Bad*'s Walter White from passive chemistry high-school teacher into ruthless drug lord. Although we are aware of these characters' journey toward immorality, something in their portrayal lures us into *feeling with* them, despite our ethical restraints.

Identifying the narrative strategies that elicit negative empathy is, at this point, a paramount question. Among the variety of textual techniques associated with empathy in literary reading, specific aspects in the characterization of immoral fictional people may fuel the readers' potential for identification and empathy, beyond moral limitations. For instance, the roundness of a character and the representation of their thoughts, feelings and consciousness may well lead the reader to experience a higher degree of closeness toward them, despite the unsettling nature of such thoughts. A poignant example is the following passage, taken from Dostoevsky's *Crime and Punishment* (1866), where Raskolnikov is gradually realizing the misery of his financial situation and his unbearable reliance on an old evil pawnbroker, which would lead him to commit the titular murder:

[Raskolnikov's] trouble kept increasing more and more. On his way down the stairs he even stopped several times, as if suddenly struck by something. [...] "Oh, God, how loathsome this all is! And can it be, can it be that I... no, it's nonsense, it's absurd!" he added resolutely. "Could such horror really come into my head? But then, what filth my heart is capable of!... Above all, filthy, nasty, vile, vile!" [...] But

neither words nor exclamations could express his agitation. The feeling of boundless loathing that had begun to oppress and sicken his
heart while he was still only on his way to the old woman now reached
such proportions and became so clearly manifest that he did not know
where to flee from his anguish. (1993, 9–10)

Here, the mimetic representation of the character's distressing thoughts and
feelings while they are forming in his mind compels us to feel closer to him,
to experience some sort of pity or compassion, even though we sense that his
thoughts are, in fact, fantasies about committing a horrific crime. Moreover, the
shaping of the narrative situation is equally at play when it comes to activating
readers' empathy, especially with regards to the perspective from which the story
is told and individuals are characterized. Quite intuitively, an internal perspective—achieved with either first-person narration or third-person narration with
a focus on the representation of the character's consciousness via direct or free
indirect speech, as in the above quote—encourages the reader to adopt the character's point of view,[16] even when they display unreliable or unethical behaviors.

Furthermore, the representation of conflicting emotions can contribute to
the reader's oscillating movement between identification and detachment that is
key to negative empathy.[17] The following quote explicitly describes Raskolnikov's
feelings while carrying out the murder of the pawnbroker and of her sister, by
highlighting not only his fear of the consequences of his actions, but also the
distressing conflict between pathos and logos, affect and reason:

Fear was taking hold of him more and more, especially after this second, quite unexpected murder. He wanted to run away from there
as quickly as possible. And if he had been able at that moment to see
and reason more properly, if he had only been able to realize all the
difficulties of his situation, all the despair, all the hideousness, all the
absurdity of it, and to understand, besides, how many more difficulties
and perhaps evildoings he still had to overcome or commit in order
to get out of there and reach home, he might very well have dropped
everything and gone at once to denounce himself, and not even out of
fear for himself, but solely out of horror and loathing for what he had
done. (Dostoevsky 1993, 79–80)

These narrative strategies may play a part in the arousal of negative empathy.
However, the chief aspect that allows for this experience to fully occur is the

text's fictionality itself. Several theoretical and empirical studies agree on the role of the perception of fictionality in facilitating engagement with characters and thus in the activation of empathy,[18] through the act of "sneaking into the minds of strangers" (Felski 2019, 84) and aligning to their perspective during the immersive readerly experience. Our ability to empathize with negatively portrayed characters is thus allowed by the "protective fictionality" (Keen 2007, xiv) of the narrative's world-making, which establishes a safe space for us to be affected by these people, a space "within which to see through the eyes of the psychopath" (131), without experiencing demanding repercussions on our reality. The next paragraph will delve into the deeper workings and cathartic effects of negative empathy as prompted by the safe space of fiction.

Catharsis and the Pathos of Distance: Unraveling Negative Empathy

Protective fictionality not only allows for identification with negative characters; it also paves the way for a potentially cathartic experience, which is the element that allegedly distinguishes negative from narrative empathy *tout court* (Ercolino 2018, 248–252). While tracing a genealogy of the cathartic hypothesis in mimetic studies through Aristotle, Freud, and Girard, Lawtoo explains that Aristotle's classical notion of catharsis as purgation of emotions was famously put forth as a reply to Plato, who argued that tragedy generates socially threatening forms of mimetic contagion (Lawtoo 2023a, 101–126). In the *Poetics*, Aristotle instead envisioned tragedy as imitating actions that excite certain emotions (pity and fear) only to exorcise them. Whilst attending a tragic play, which is a mimesis of a real action, spectators are bound to identify with the suffering hero on stage, to feel both pity and fear for his fate, and through this identification they are able to exorcise these emotions from their real-life experience.

In reception studies, the Aristotelian notion of catharsis thus helps to understand the purposes of identifying with characters; for instance, as Ercolino (2018, 248–252) shows, Hans Robert Jauss proposed the idea of cathartic identification to define "the aesthetic attitude that frees the spectator from the [...] affective engagements of his world and puts him into the position of the suffering and beset hero so that his mind and heart may find liberation through tragic emotion" (1982 [1977], 177). Prior to Jauss, Sigmund Freud had argued that the aesthetic and cathartic pleasure of identifying with fictional heroes is fostered by the spectators' realization of the fictionality of the story they are witnessing. A reader or a spectator can successfully experience a cathartic release of repressed emotions, while also profoundly enjoying the work of art and possibly empathizing with a suffering character, because their distress is "mitigated by the certainty that, firstly, it is someone other than [themselves] who is acting and suffering on the stage, and, secondly, that after all it is only a game, which can threaten no damage to [their] personal security" (1953, 306). Protective fictionality thus acts as a prerogative of character identification and, in turn, of catharsis.

In all likelihood, Freud's account of catharsis was influenced by a medically oriented interpretation of the concept by classical philologist Jacob Bernays, who, as Lawtoo reminds us, happened to be Freud's uncle-in-law (Lawtoo 2023a, 85–87).[19] In Bernays's account, the catharsis generated by Greek musical rituals heightens states of physical and affective frenzy so as to purify men of burdening affects, such as pity and fear. Freud and Josef Breuer then expanded on this diagnostic view of catharsis as a psychoanalytic treatment capable of exciting emotional states, in order to relieve the individual from their oppressive effects. They then turned it into the cathartic method of "abreaction" (1953, 8), that is, the experience of reliving emotions associated with a trauma to discharge its emotional excesses by talking about it in a sort of psychoanalytic confession, or, "a first-person dramatic and thus mimetic re-presentation and reenactment that makes present the very affects that had not been allowed outlet in the first place, were strangulated and stuck, and are now introduced into 'normal consciousness'" (Lawtoo 2023a, 94).

An effective literary strategy for arousing negative empathy could then entail the choice of first-person perspective and the adoption of a confessional register, which paves the way for the characters' (re-)enactment of their inner torment, similarly to what happens during a psychoanalytic session. Both Dostoevsky's *Crime and Punishment* and *Demons* (1873) display several instances in which the confessional register takes over in order to highlight the characters' anguish. For example, in the following quote from *Crime and Punishment*, Raskolnikov is attempting to confess to Sonya, his lover, that he had murdered the pawnbroker; he does so by referring to himself in the third person and, later, without actually saying a word, thus highlighting the unspeakable nature of the crime:

> "This Lizaveta... he didn't want to kill her... He killed her... accidentally [...] So you can't guess?" he suddenly asked, feeling as if he were

throwing himself from a bell-tower. "N-no," Sonya whispered, barely audibly. "Take a good look." Again, as soon as he said this, a former, familiar sensation suddenly turned his soul to ice: he looked at her, and suddenly in her face he seemed to see the face of Lizaveta. He vividly recalled the expression of Lizaveta's face as he was approaching her with the axe and she was backing away from him towards the wall, her hand held out, with a completely childlike fright on her face [...] (Dostoevsky 1993, 410).

While Sonya is gradually realizing that Raskolnikov himself is the culprit behind the murder, he is described as somehow *reliving* the traumatic experience of the crime he committed, when he painfully recognizes the frightened expression of his victim in Sonya's face. The readers' ethical position, which would ordinarily condemn Raskolnikov's crime, may well vacillate here because of the suffering and anguish that the character pathetically conveys.

In *Demons*, the confessional register finds narrative actualization in the chapter popularized as "Stavrogin's confession," which was censored in early editions. It includes a written confession given by the protagonist, Nikolai Stavrogin, where he admits raping a vulnerable ten-year-old girl, Matryosha, and doing absolutely nothing to avoid her suicide. In the following quote, he displays his torment and self-loathing after committing the rape, especially at the sight of the little girl's despair; at the same time, however, he is described as belittling her reproachful gestures as "funny," and this may prompt readers to suddenly estrange and detach from their compassionate feelings:

But this time I was frightened and really felt fear, I do not know why, for the first time in my life—a very tormenting sensation. [...]. Contempt together with boundless revulsion would spring up in me for the way she had rushed into the corner after it all and covered herself with her hands; [...] she suddenly began shaking her head rapidly at me, as people do when they reproach very much, and suddenly she raised her little fist at me and began threatening me with it from where she stood. For the first moment this gesture seemed funny to me, but I could not stand it for long; I got up and moved nearer to her. There was despair in her face, such as was impossible to see on the face of a child. (Dostoevsky 1995, 697–698)

The tension between mimetic (that is, empathic) and anti-mimetic (that is, estranging) readerly tendencies that is exemplified by the above passage is not peculiar only to negative empathy; it is also associated to the Nietzschean concept of *"pathos of distance,"*[20] which informs the mimetic turn. As Lawtoo puts it, it entails a movement that "renders subjects both open and vulnerable to the inner experience of pathos and—simultaneously and without any contradiction or aporia—puts us in a position to set up a critical distance from such pathos" (2022a, 11). This movement therefore exemplifies the oscillation in which *homo mimeticus* is caught, shifting back and forth between affective and mimetic impulses on the one side, and rational anti-mimetic dispositions on the other.

As a defense mechanism against overwhelming emotions, distance is the core aspect of protective fictionality and cathartic identification, both of which are prerogatives of negative empathy. To explain the crucial role of distance in negative empathy and to come full circle, it is necessary to journey back again to Theodor Lipps and his early theory. In fact, Lipps's aesthetic view of negative empathy sees the subject as experiencing a resistance against the projection of something unpleasant inside of themselves, which in turn generates "interior detachment [*inneren Abkehr*]") (1909, 229). Detachment is clearly essential to the experience of aesthetic and narrative empathy *tout court*, in order to avoid overwhelming sensations that would prevent any aesthetic enjoyment. However, keeping a safe distance is even more crucial when it comes to negative empathy, because no matter how enticing the evil character may appear, the disturbing aspects of their actions must estrange us to activate our ethical sense. Being an aesthetic experience that forces readers to *oscillate* between identification and detachment, negative empathy bears striking resemblance to the inner structure of the pathos of distance, which revolves around the same mimetic patho(-)logy, that is, a "fundamental oscillation towards/away from mimetic reactions" (Lawtoo 2013, 3).

Interestingly, catharsis may complete the triangulation with negative empathy and the pathos of distance. In fact, several interpretations of the aesthetic reception of Greek tragedies see it as an interplay between a state of mimetic entrancement and a return to reason, for which painful emotions are eventually converted into pleasurable ones. Catharsis, especially the one triggered by negative empathy, is not merely characterized as a discharge of oppressive affects, it is "not just the end-result of watching a tragedy" (Halliwell 2011, 31), but the "product of a mimetic patho(-)logy" (Lawtoo 2018, 179) that leads to transformative ethical experiences, thanks to the interplay between mimetic affect and critical discourse. These transformative cathartic effects are especially conveyed at the end of "Stavrogin's confession" in Dostoevsky's *Demons*, when the protagonist confesses that, after Matryosha's tragic suicide, he has been tormented by her haunting presence, repeatedly seeing her threatening him just as she did the last time he saw her alive:

> I saw before me (oh, not in reality! and if only, if only it had been a real vision!), I saw Matryosha, wasted and with feverish eyes, exactly the same as when she had stood on my threshold and, shaking her head, had raised her tiny little fist at me. And nothing had ever seemed so tormenting to me! The pitiful despair of a helpless ten-year-old being with a still unformed mind, who was threatening me [...]. Is this what is called remorse of conscience or repentance? I do not know, and I cannot tell to this day. Perhaps even to this moment I do not loathe the memory of the act itself. Perhaps this remembrance even now contains something pleasurable for my passions. No—what is unbearable to me is only this image alone, and precisely on the threshold, with its raised and threatening little fist, only that look alone, only that minute alone, only her shaking head. (Dostoevsky 1995, 703–704)

The unbearable remorse that Stavrogin confesses and, at the same time, the sadistic pleasure felt for the memory of the crime are aimed at pressuring readers into a disturbingly ambivalent affective relationship toward the character. This fluctuation between pathos and distance is explicit when Stavrogin is able to perceive the devastating effects of his abjection on the little girl; simultaneously, the narrative strives to persuade and entice readers into a sort of "emotional understanding" (Halliwell 2011, 30), which is certainly not directed toward the protagonist's crime, but at least toward his anguish and remorse. His pathetic regret cannot justify his atrocious actions; nevertheless, it succeeds in increasing the emotional intensity of the narration, allowing for Stavrogin to appear both abhorrent and vulnerable, therefore estranging readers and simultaneously prompting a patho-logical empathic connection.

In conclusion, negative empathy can be considered as an aesthetic experience that ultimately questions the moral boundaries of human agency. Through the pathos of distance, it drags us into the dark cave of the character's mind and, through catharsis, it leads to a transformative reading experience while also leaving us bewildered by the force of our empathic response to a monster. As readers, we cannot help but remain caught in the pendulum-like oscillation between identification and estrangement, empathy and detachment, pathos and distance – an oscillation that characterizes the murky soul of the individual called *homo mimeticus*.

Notes

1   Other versions translate the original Russian term used by Dostoevsky, потёмки (*potjómki*), as 'darkness.'

2   A key concept for mimetic studies, patho(-)logy combines emotional involvement (*pathos*) and critical discourse (*logos*). See Lawtoo 2013, 6–9.

3   For works that address the definition of empathy, see Batson 2009, Coplan 2011, Maibom 2020.

4   For an in-depth exploration of Lipps's aesthetic theory of empathy, see Burns 2021.

5   Interestingly, Lipps's idea of *Einfühlung* is also grounded in a reflection on mimicry and motor imitation, showing his awareness of mirroring reflexes long before they could be proved by neuroscientists. See Lawtoo 2013, 257, and the Coda to this volume.

6   In fact, in literary studies, mimesis has been generally circumscribed to the study of the Western literary tradition and it has long coincided with the identification of the forms of representation and reproduction of reality, as Erich Auerbach's foundational essay demonstrated. See Auerbach 2003.

7   For a systematic overview on mirror neurons, see Rizzolatti and Sinigaglia 2008. On the relation between mirror neurons and empathy, see the pioneering studies by Vittorio Gallese 2001, 2003, and the Coda to this volume.

8   On transformative reading, intended as a cognitive and affective process with which readers may gain fresh insights into themselves and others through reading literature, see Fialho 2019, 2024.

9   Miall's view of readerly empathy suggests that this ability clearly evokes abstract concepts and imagery in our minds, but it may also ignite bodily responses, such as motor and kinesthetic reactions. This embodied perspective of literary reading may reasonably be influenced by the notion of embodied simulation, which is core to both mimetic studies and neuroscientific investigations on the mirror neuron system; see Miall 2011, 291–292.

10   On empathy in literary studies, see Keen 2007 and Hammond and Kim 2014; for a survey of empirical approaches to literature and empathy, see Burke et al. 2016.

11   On the separability of positive and negative empathy, see Andreychik and Migliaccio 2015; Morelli, Rameson, and Lieberman 2014; Morelli, Lieberman, and Zaki 2015.

12   See Ercolino 2018 and Ercolino and Fusillo 2022 for a thorough reevaluation of Lipps's idea of negative empathy in aesthetics, literature, art, and media.

13   On the nature of fictional characters, see Anderson, Felski, and Moi 2019.

14   Postcritical and affect studies have extensively focused on this aspect of tuning in and being attached to works of art and fictional characters; in particular, see Felski 2020.

15   This view may be influenced by the Platonic hypothesis of mimetic contagion as a trigger of violent and irrational pathologies, which underpins the mimetic turn and shows its overlap with related theories of narrative empathy and affect studies; see Lawtoo 2023b, 19-35, and part I of this volume.

16   Felski defines this as "alignment," an aspect of character identification for which a text "shape[s] a reader's or viewer's access to character" so that it indicates "whose perspective we are invited to adopt" (Felski 2019, 93–94), without necessarily siding with the character's immoral behavior.

17   See Bonasera 2023 for an account of the effects of emotional shifts and fluctuations in the semantic representation of feelings.

18   For empirical evidence supporting this, see Altmann et al. 2014; with specific regards to negative empathy, see de Jonge et al. 2022.

19   As Lawtoo emphasizes, while Bernays's medical and diagnostical interpretation of catharsis was appreciated in critical theory, it sparked controversy regarding its effects for therapeutic practice, leading Freud to eventually abandon it, and it also promoted "a medical translation of catharsis that, while doing hermeneutical violence to its original aesthetic meaning, continues to inform the critical, theoretical and popular imagination" (Lawtoo 2023a, 147).

20   In Nietzsche's *oeuvre*, the concept refers to a distinction between anti-mimetic masters and mimetic masses, who are subject to "different forms of psychic dispossession" (Lawtoo 2013, 3–6, 27–83), that is, mimetic pathos.

Bibliography

Altmann, Ulrike, Isabel C. Bohrn, Oliver Lubrich, Winfried Menninghaus, and Arthur M. Jacobs (2014). "Fact vs Fiction—How Paratextual Information Shapes our Reading Processes." *Social, Cognitive and Affective Neuroscience* 9.1, 22–29.

Anderson, Amanda, Rita Felski, and Toril Moi (eds.) (2019). *Character: Three Inquiries in Literary Studies*. Chicago: University of Chicago Press.

Andreychik, Michael R., and Nicole Migliaccio (2015). "Empathizing with Others' Pain versus Empathizing with Others' Joy: Examining the Separability of Positive and Negative Empathy and their Relation to Different Types of Social Behaviors and Social Emotions." *Basic and Applied Social Psychology* 37.5, 274–291.

Auerbach, Erich (2003). *Mimesis: The Representation of Reality in Western Literature*, trans. Willard R. Trask. Princeton: Princeton University Press.

Batson, Charles Daniel (2009). "These Things called Empathy: Eight Related but Distinct Phenomena," in *The Social Neuroscience of Empathy*, eds. Jean Decety and William Ickes. Cambridge, MA: MIT Press, 3–15.

Bonasera, Carmen (2023). "Exploring the Potential of Sentiment Analysis for the Study of Negative Empathy." *Journal of Literary Semantics* 52.2, 163–189.

Burke, Michael, Anežka Kuzmičová, Anne Mangen, and Theresa Schilhab (2016). "Empathy at the Confluence of Neuroscience and Empirical Literary Studies." *Scientific Study of Literature* 6.1, 6–41.

Burns, Timothy (2021). "Theodor Lipps on the Concept of Einfühlung (Empathy)," in *Theodor Lipps (1851-1914): psychologie, philosophie, esthétique, langage*, eds. David Romand and Serge Tchoughounnikov. Genève: sdvig press.

Coplan, Amy (2011). "Understanding Empathy: Its Features and Effects," in *Empathy: Philosophical and Psychological Perspectives*, eds. Amy Coplan and Peter Goldie. Oxford: Oxford University Press, 3–18.

de Jonge, Julia, Serena Demichelis, Simone Rebora, and Massimo Salgaro (2022). "Operationalizing Perpetrator Studies. Focusing Readers' Reactions to *The Kindly Ones* by Jonathan Littell." *Journal of Literary Semantics* 51.2, 147–161.

Dostoevsky, Fyodor (1993). *Crime and Punishment*, trans. Richard Pevear and Larissa Volokhonsky. New York: Vintage Classics.

——— (1995). *Demons: A Novel in Three Parts*, trans. Richard Pevear and Larissa Volokhonsky. New York: Vintage Classics.

—— (2003). *The Idiot*, trans. Richard Pevear and Larissa Volokhonsky. New York: Vintage Classics.

Ercolino, Stefano (2018). "Negative Empathy. History, Theory, Criticism." *Orbis litterarum* 73:3, 243–262.

Ercolino, Stefano, and Massimo Fusillo (2022). *Empatia negativa. Il punto di vista del male*. Milano: Bompiani.

Felski, Rita (2019). "Identifying with Characters," in *Character: Three Inquiries in Literary Studies*, eds. Amanda Anderson, Rita Felski, and Toril Moi. Chicago: University of Chicago Press, 77–126.

—— (2020). *Hooked: Art and Attachment*. Chicago: University of Chicago Press.

Fialho, Olivia (2019). "What is Literature For? The Role of Transformative Reading." *Cogent Arts & Humanities* 6.1, 1692532.

—— (2024). *Transformative Reading*. Amsterdam: John Benjamins.

Freud, Sigmund (1953). "Psychopathic Characters on the Stage (1905)," in *The Standard Edition of the Complete Psychological Works of Sigmund Freud*, vol. 7, trans. and ed. James Strachey, in collaboration with Anna Freud. London: The Hogarth Press and the Institute of Psychoanalysis, 305–310.

Freud, Sigmund, and Josef Breuer (1953). "On the Physical Mechanism of Hysterical Phenomena: Preliminary Communication (1893)," in *The Standard Edition of the Complete Psychological Works of Sigmund Freud*, vol. 2, trans. and ed. James Strachey, in collaboration with Anna Freud. London: The Hogarth Press and the Institute of Psychoanalysis, 3–17.

Gallese, Vittorio (2001). "The 'Shared Manifold' Hypothesis: From Mirror Neurons to Empathy." *Journal of Consciousness Studies* 8.5–7, 33–50.

—— (2003). "The Roots of Empathy: The Shared Manifold Hypothesis and the Neural Basis of Intersubjectivity." *Psychopathology* 36:4, 171–180.

Gebauer, Gunter, and Christoph Wulf (1995). *Mimesis: Culture, Art, Society*, trans. Don Reneau. Berkeley: University of California Press.

Halliwell, Stephen (2011). *Between Ecstasy and Truth: Interpretations of Greek Poetics from Homer to Longinus*. Oxford: Oxford University Press.

Hammond, Meghan Marie, and Sue J. Kim (eds.) (2014). *Rethinking Empathy through Literature*. New York: Routledge.

Jauss, Hans Robert (1982 [1977]). *Aesthetic Experience and Literary Hermeneutics*, trans. Michael Shaw. Minneapolis: University of Minnesota Press.

Keen, Suzanne (2007). *Empathy and the Novel*. Oxford: Oxford University Press.

—— (2014). "Narrative Empathy," in *Handbook of Narratology*, vol. 2, eds. Peter Hühn, Jan Christoph Meister, John Pier, and Wolf Schmid. Berlin: de Gruyter, 521–530.

Lawtoo, Nidesh (2013). *The Phantom of the Ego. Modernism and the Mimetic Unconscious*. East Lansing: Michigan State University Press.

—— (2018) "Violence and the Mimetic Unconscious (Part One): The Carhartic Hypothesis: Aristotle, Freud, Girard." *Contagion: Journal of Violence, Mimesis, and Culture* 25, 159–192.

—— (2022a). *Homo Mimeticus: A New Theory of Imitation*. Leuven: Leuven University Press.

—— (2022b). "Guest Editor's Introduction. The Mimetic Condition: Theory and Concepts." *CounterText* 8.1, 1–22.

—— (2023a). *Violence and the Oedipal Unconscious: vol. 1, The Oedipal Hypothesis*. East Lansing: Michigan State University Press.

—— (2023b). *Violence and the Mimetic Unconscious: vol. e, The Affective Hypothesis*. East Lansing: Michigan State University Press.

Lipps, Theodor (1909). *Leitfaden der Psychologie*. Leipzig: Verlag von Wilhelm Engelmann.

Maibom, Heidi L. (2020). *Empathy*. London and New York: Routledge.

Miall, David S. (2011). "Enacting the Other: Towards an Aesthetics of Feeling in Literary Reading," in *The Aesthetic Mind. Philosophy and Psychology*, eds. Elisabeth Schellekens and Peter Goldie. Oxford: Oxford University Press, 285–298.

Morelli, Sylvia A., Matthew D. Lieberman, and Jamil Zaki (2015). "The Emerging Study of Positive Empathy." *Social and Personality Psychology Compass* 9.2, 57–68.

Morelli, Sylvia A., Lian T. Rameson, and Matthew D. Lieberman (2014). "The Neural Components of Empathy: Predicting Daily Prosocial Behavior." *Social Cognitive and Affective Neuroscience* 9.1, 39–47.

Rizzolatti, Giacomo, and Corrado Sinigaglia (2008). *Mirrors in the Brain: How Our Minds Share Actions and Emotions*, trans. Frances Anderson. Oxford: Oxford University Press.

CHAPTER 12

FERNANDO PESSOA AND THE ([P]RE)BIRTH OF HOMO MIMETICUS

Kieran Keohane and Carmen Kuhling

Man is an invention of recent date. And one perhaps nearing its end.
If those arrangements were to disappear as they appeared, if some event
of which at the moment we can do no more than sense the possibility—
without knowing either what its form may be or what it promises—
were to cause them to crumble, as the ground of Classical thought did
at the end of the 18th century then one can certainly wager that man
would be erased, like a face drawn in sand at the edge of the sea.

—Foucault, *The Order of Things*.

I see boats moving on the sea.
Their sails, like wings of what I see,
Bring me a vague inner desire to be
Who I was without knowing what it was.
So all recalls my home self, and, because
It recalls that, what I am aches in me.

—Pessoa, "I See Boats Moving"

History, Liminality, Mimesis

In historical situations of liminality, when the previously taken for granted order of things becomes confused and formerly credible models are scrambled, imitative processes come to the fore—along with calls for restoration of authority by a strong leader. And so, we see the historical recurrence of contagious populist authoritarianism. Whether in the "old" forms as *Führer* and *volk,* Party and proletariat, or in the varieties of (new) fascism White Christian Nation and its native-born citizens, and "Market fundamentalism" and its "rational choice sovereign individuals" all authoritarian orders, old and new, are replete with their scapegoats: Socrates and Jesus in Classical and Biblical eras; "Jews" and "counter revolutionaries" in Hitler's and Stalin's regimes; and among current scapegoats are "illegal migrants" and "LGBTQ." Scapegoats are sacrificed so that all the diversities and internal divisions that characterize any and every human community are cathected and discharged onto an "Other," so that the social and body politic is purged of "contaminations" and "impurities," and everyone else, through their unanimous condemnation of the scapegoat, is assimilated into a unified whole (Girard 1979). But "Nature is parts without a whole" (1998, 65) Fernando Pessoa[1] says, and he embraces the incompleteness of identity and the "mimetic" rather than the "sovereign" subject. Mimesis "casts the very idea, or ideal, of originality into crisis" (Lawtoo 2022, 33) and Pessoa's mimetic identit(ies) playfully subverts the potentially totalitarian desire to make whole what had never been whole to begin with. Fernando Pessoa's life(s) and work(s) straddle the agonal conjuncture of mimetic desire-violence (Girard) and mimetic patho(-)logies (Lawtoo), with all of the overdetermined complexities, ambivalences, paradoxes and possibilities that mimesis entails. And in so far as Pessoa suggests a form of life other than spiraling toward violent sacrificial crisis it is helpful for the project of new mimetic studies to fold Fernando Pessoa into its kin.

History and Biography, Methods and Models

Our method[2] as a way into understanding the world of Fernando Pessoa and his heteronyms, his [their] life(s) and time(s) as an intervention in mimetic studies—is by interpolating Pessoa's biography and the history of modern Portugal particularly, and of Modernity generally—for "neither the life of an individual nor the history of a society can be understood without understanding both" (Mills 1959, 3). To interpolate biography and history in the case of Fernando Pessoa we have *The Book of Disquiet*, "a factless autobiography," by Pessoa's semi-heteronym Bernardo Soares; we have Pessoa's fragmentary accounts of "himself" in poems such as "*Autopsicografia*," and we have Richard Zenith's (2022) comprehensive biography, *Pessoa: An Experimental Life*. Our method also includes browsing Pessoa's books, for one can tell a great deal about a person by the books they have on their bookshelf, Walter Benjamin says; in Pessoa's room, recreated in Lisbon's *Museu Casa Pessoa*, many of his books are arranged as they were and can be viewed online.

Two of the most densely annotated books on Pessoa's bookshelf are Freud's *Leonardo da Vinci and a Memory from his Childhood*, and Shakespeare's *The Tempest*, of which Pessoa had three copies. Refracted through the model of Leonardo da Vinci Fernando Pessoa came to see his lifelong celibacy in terms of repressed (homo)sexuality sublimated into his frequent inability to finish his work. And mediated through Shakespeare as a model and the question of Shakespeare's identity Pessoa learned to desire to dissimulate himself through the heteronyms. (Younger) Fernando Pessoa identified with Hamlet—Pessoa's mother's new relationship immediately upon the death of Fernando's father parallels the 'wicked haste' of Gertrude and Claudius' marriage; and the parallel between Hamlet's Ophelia and Pessoa's girlfriend, also named Ofélia / Ophelia: just as Hamlet tells Ophelia "get thee to a convent" Pessoa spurned his Ofélia, telling her that he had important literary work to do. (Older) Fernando Pessoa identified with *The Tempest's* Prospero, wherein Prospero is Shakespeare, coming to terms with divided parts of himself represented by the spirits of Caliban and Ariel;[3] with his bi-sexuality; and having come through the tempests of his own private life and tumultuous historical times, now seeking reconciliation and harmony in what was Shakespeare's last (or penultimate) play before retiring.

Nidesh Lawtoo's literary and cultural-anthropological genealogy of the subject as "homo mimeticus" (2022) and "patho-logies" (2023a, 19) as a method of theorizing gives us a key for understanding Fernando Pessoa. We read Fernando Pessoa's troubled and ebullient 'identity' as arising from the spiraling interplay of affect and reason, *pathos* and *logos* under historical and political conditions of liminality—*pathos* in Pessoa's grief for the 'death' of Portugal, and *logos* in Pessoa's words creating form and beauty out of liminality. In Pessoa's lifetime (1888–1935) liminality and mimetic contagions were associated with Portugal's transition from monarchy to republic to dictatorship and the conditions of the inter War period in

Europe generally. In so far as the conditions associated with Pessoa's life and times resemble our own troubled times he is our uncanny doppelganger, harbinger of the person suffering under conditions of the neoliberal and digital revolutions: a vulnerable, malleable, flexibilized subject; a person with multiple parallel existences "online" and "IRL"; a purportedly autonomous, individual sovereign 'self' but that in actuality is "a phantom ego who is easily possessed by others, affected by crowds, manipulated by leaders, and now dispossessed by a plurality of social media that catch homo mimeticus in spirals of becoming other" (Lawtoo 2022, 15). In Pessoa's time, and again presently, as Foucault anticipated, "those arrangements of words and things"—*les mots et les choses,* the symbolic order and imaginative structures within which "man" has been invented are "crumbling and disappearing." Fernando Pessoa lived and experienced 'himself' as a phantom ego being erased—or as already having been erased; or even never to have been drawn at all—a "self" as precarious as "a face drawn in sand at the edge of the sea." Here is Bernardo Soares (one of Pessoa's heteronyms) in a typical passage from *The Book of Disquiet*:[4]

> I'm always thinking, always feeling, but my thoughts lack all reason, my feelings all emotion. I'm falling though a trapdoor, through infinite, infinituous space, in a directionless, empty fall. My soul is a black maelstrom, a great madness spinning around a vacuum, the swirling of a vast ocean around a hole in the void, and in the waters, more like whirlwinds than waters, float images of all I ever saw or heard in the world: houses, faces, books, boxes, snatches of music and fragments of voices, all caught up in a sinister, bottomless whirlpool.
>
> And I, I myself, am the centre that exists only because every circle has one, I, I myself, am the well in which the walls have fallen away to leave only viscous slime. I am the centre of everything surrounded by the great nothing. (Pessoa 2010, 28)

Portugal's Interregnum and the Birth of Pessoa (and the Heteronyms)

Interregnum (from *inter,* between and *regis,* king)—means the liminal period between the end of one sovereign and the enthronement of another; a period during which—"the old is dying and the new cannot be born; in this interregnum a great variety of morbid symptoms appear" (Gramsci 1971, 276). In anthropology an interregnum corresponds with the "liminal stage" in a "rite of passage" (van Gennep 1960), a period characterized by confusion, ambiguity, and ambivalence; not an either/or dis-junction, but rather a conjunction of complexity and possibility, for better and for worse. At such moments in history, Nietzsche says:

> [W]e behold, mutually involved and entangled with one another, a splendid, manifold, jungle like upward growth and striving, a kind of *tropical* tempo in rivalry to grow and a tremendous ruin and self-ruination, as the savage egoisms that have turned, almost exploded against one another wrestle each other "for sun and light" and can no longer find any limit, restraint, or consideration from their previous morality... a dangerous and uncanny point has been reached where a more manifold, more comprehensive life *lives beyond* the old morality... (1989, 262)

Just as Shakespeare was born out of the conditions of the English Renaissance with Hamlet, Macbeth, and others too dramatizing explicitly the liminality of interregnum, Fernando Pessoa (and the heteronyms) were born out of the liminal conditions of Portugal's interregnum, between "death" and the protracted labor and "birth" of new forms of life, an ongoing crisis with a profusion of morbid symptoms and social pathologies, forms of life that are both *patho*-logical and patho-*logical*—emotion and reason "mutually involved and entangled with one another." These overdetermined and ambiguous movements, "wrestling" and "exploding against one another" included republicanism, monarchism, nationalism, anarchic radical libertarianism, pluralist democracy and fascist military bureaucratic authoritarianism, and Fernando Pessoa (and the heteronyms) were, variously and simultaneously assimilated and swept along in their *pathos* while expressing and giving form to their *logos*. Pessoa includes a "more manifold life" reaching "beyond the old morality." Lisbon's travails were mirrored throughout the Portuguese world, especially in Brazil, where recursive mutual influences circulated between fatherland / mother tongue and the former colony, which was now, ambiguously, an independent power and a post-colonial dependency.

The complex recursive mimetic relationship between Lisbon and Rio de Janeiro is exemplified by Joaquim Maria Merchado de Assis; grandson of freed African slaves, married to a white Portuguese, who eked out his livelihood as a scrivener and middling bureaucrat in sundry newspapers and government departments to support his literary life. Merchado's double life in Rio de Janeiro paralleled the double life(s) of Fernando Pessoa / Bernardo Soares in Lisbon. Among Merchado's books was *The Posthumous Memoirs of Brás Cubas,* a paradoxical title that reverberates in Pessoa's / Soares "factless autobiography," and Pessoa wanted to publish Merchado's book in his Ibis Press (one of Pessoa's many dreams and schemes that died in infancy). In the mimetic recirculation of influences between Lisbon and Rio antitheses of "original" and "copy" are not so much synthesized and sublimated into a higher unity, but, rather, they are dissolved and dissimulated, dispersed and disseminated.[5] Out of the liminality and complexity of Portugal's interregnum Pessoa brought to life his "heteronyms," all fictions, phantom egos, all mimeses, with fully elaborated biographies and personalities, aesthetic styles and tastes and political views; even their handwriting and signatures were different. For many years Pessoa and the heteronyms wrote poetry, published letters in newspapers and journals, critically reviewed one another's work, argued with one another about culture, politics, and current affairs, met with people in cafes and bars, and played active roles in Lisbon's and Portugal's cultural and political public sphere.

Pessoa: Persona, Mimos, Mimesis

Among the many remarkable things about Fernando Pessoa is his name, for *pessoa* means both "person" and "persona." As the etymology of "persona" means a "theatrical mask" and as the etymology of mimesis is *mimos* (performance) there is already an elective affinity between Fernando Pessoa and mimetic studies. "Fernando Pessoa" is understandable to us as a person—a "self" an elusive, fugitive self, that even as he asserts himself ("I, I myself")—swirls away and vanishes in the void. "My home self" as Pessoa wistfully recalls it in "I See Boats Moving" is a person who, as Erving Goffman says, only "is" in terms of their dramaturgically realized "presentations of self in everyday life" (1959). Goffman takes his cue from Shakespeare: "All the world's a stage, And all the men and women merely players; They have their exits and their entrances; And one man in his time plays many parts..." (*As You Like It,* II. Vii). There is no "real" "self" outside of these many parts; the entire human drama is predicated on mimesis; and so, as Pessoa [heteronym Álvaro de Campos] says, "to pretend is to know ourselves" (Zenith 2022, 332).

For Goffman, as for Shakespeare and Pessoa, a person is first and foremost a homo mimeticus, involved in the performance of roles, personas, enacted on social stages, for audiences, in contexts, discursive and normative frames that may be more or less stable, always troubled and troubling. As Judith Butler has shown, even "gender," heretofore purported to be identical with "sex," fixed as a natural biological state, is actually no more, and no less, than an ongoing performative mimetic accomplishment (Butler 1990). For a genealogy that goes from Shakespeare to Pessoa, Butler to Lawtoo, the dramaturgical-performative-mimetic paradigm confronts the person with the challenge of "defining the situation." To take up Foucault's question of "the order of things" in dramaturgical-mimetic terms means that however prescribed and rigid the taxonomies, scripts and stage-settings may appear to be, there is always room for improvisation and variation in the human drama. We can always draw new faces of man, whether in the theaters of everyday life and on the stages of History.

The Lisbon Earthquake and the Genealogy of *Saudade* and *Fado*

More than a geological event, the Lisbon Earthquake of 1755 was a seismic historical-social-cultural, even civilizational event; it entailed a rupture in cosmology, a fracturing of the order of things, a quickening in thinking and a powerful impetus of social acceleration. Great debates in Religion and Science flared and flourished not only in Portugal but throughout Europe: "What caused the Lisbon earthquake?" Was the earthquake divine retribution for Lisbon's sins? Lisbon was the epicenter of a Catholic globe-spanning empire from Macau and Goa, to Brazil and the Caribbean, to Angola and Mozambique. Henry the Navigator, Bartolomeo Diaz and Vasco de Gama's circumnavigations of the Earth in Portugal's Golden Age of exploration had made Lisbon fabulously rich through the spice trade, that quickly developed into the nefarious sugar and slave trades.[6] Lisbon was devout, but it was also wicked and decadent. Or was the earthquake an entirely Natural event, the cause of which could be revealed not by Religion but by Science? For Voltaire the Lisbon earthquake refuted pious platitudes about a benevolent God overseeing the best of all possible worlds; and a young Immanuel Kant published three papers explaining the Lisbon earthquake in terms of Natural Philosophy, establishing his name as a father of Reason and Enlightenment.

The Lisbon Earthquake is the genealogical collective historical "stamping experience" that left its characteristic mark on Portuguese culture. It did so specifically in *Fado* ["fate"] as the disconsolate musical expression of the terrible fate that has befallen the Portuguese; also in *Saudade*, sadness, loneliness and constant longing for an (impossible) return in the wake of a loss,[7] the melancholy and complex grief for a lost loved object of an ideal Portugal as "Fatherland" that has "died" in the Earthquake. *Saudade* and *Fado* are cathexis and catharsis of individual and collective Portuguese *pathos*, and one hundred and fifty years after the Lisbon Earthquake Fernando Pessoa as victim-survivor of that historical trauma bears its characteristic melancholic stamp.

Saudade as *pathos* may seem to be uniquely Portuguese but *saudade* belongs to Modernity generally, because the Lisbon earthquake was not a Portuguese historical event, but one of the formative traumas in the genealogy of Modernity. As Ganeri puts it: "Only the Portuguese have a single term for an emotion that is, nevertheless, arguably universal. More than merely loneliness or nostalgia or homesickness, *saudade* instead evokes a melancholic yearning for something absent, something that perhaps never was and never will be, but still haunts one's psychological life in one's memory and desire. A sense of loss for that which one never had; the anticipation of a future that will never be" (Ganeri 2023). In response to that civilization-level trauma *saudade* is Modern *pathos*: grief and suffering in the wake of the "death of God" and also longing and desire for there to be "something" rather than Nothing. And even deeper than the *pathos* of *saudade* in the genealogy of Modernity, beyond modernocentric historicism *saudade* is even more universal and anthropologically deep-seated: the *pathos* of *saudade* belongs to the ontology and phenomenology of the human being. Edmund Husserl's "embodied phenomenology" (2002) and Martin Heidegger's "phenomenology as the way back into the ground of metaphysics" (1975) tell us that the particularity of human beings—*Dasein,* "being-with-others," who, like ourselves, "stand open to the openness of being in which we stand" (1975, 271). That is, it is because human beings stand in need of one another, that to constitute ourselves we imitate one another.

In Hartmut Rosa's (2019) sociology of resonance, which has a strong affinity with mimetic studies, human beings, at the most fundamental, deep anthropological, constitutional level of our being need to have relations of resonance with one another and with the world. *Homo mimeticus* and *homo resonans* go hand in hand because we reciprocally and recursively stand in need of one another and constitute one another by our embodied trans-subjective inter-relationality with other human beings in a generative and recursive "physio-bio-anthropo-social ecosystem of complexity" (Edgar Morin 2008). The phenomenology of mimesis and resonance is our ontology and metaphysics. *Saudade,* and Fernando Pessoa's *patho-logos*, in so far as he and the heteronyms imitate and emulate many and various models, proliferating and resonating with one another joyfully and playfully and without doing violence to any of them rather than escalating in envious rivalry into sacrificial crisis and scapegoating, suggest ways to think beyond Girard's theological theory toward a-theological foundations of mimetic studies in embodied phenomenological anthropology, ontology and metaphysics.

Pessoa's Face, Erased and Re-Drawn

Fernando Pessoa was born into, grew up, and lived through the most intense period of modern Portuguese history, a time of liminal collapse and transition from monarchy to republic to dictatorship: the assassination of the king and his son and heir to the throne in 1908 was preceded and followed by prolonged and intense rivalry among several republican factions, with frequent paroxysms of scapegoating violence and sacrificial re-foundings of leader, state, government, constitution, and society; wave upon wave of economic crises; the dissolution of the church, confiscation of its properties and the expulsion of clergy (later re-instated); teeming plots and conspiracies; coups d'états; anarchism, socialism, monarchist restorationism and fascism.[8] The Portugal of Fernando Pessoa's life was a time in which "everything that man pronounces or expresses is a marginal note in a text that has been totally erased..." (Pessoa 2011, 144). As he puts it:

> [I]n this twilight age of all the disciplines, in which beliefs are dying and religions are gradually gathering dust.... I belong to a generation— or part of a generation—that has lost all respect for the past and all belief or hope for the future. This is why we live in the present with the desperate hunger of someone who has no other home. ...the world into which we were born had no security to offer us as regards religion, no anchor as regards morality, no stability as regards politics. We were born into a state of anguish, both metaphysical and moral, and of political disquiet. Drunk on external formulae, on the mere processes of reason and science, the preceding generation destroyed the foundations... (Pessoa 2011, 41)

Conditions of accelerating liminal collapse cause destabilized "situational identities" and "situational politics" (Rosa 2013, 20) that are radically contingent and open to the prevailing influences of "the situation." In Pessoa's Portugal this has especial resonance, where the *situação* of liminal collapse and interminable transition, the anguished *situação* of "permanent liminality" (Szakolczai 2001) was always the topic of conversation among Pessoa and his coterie—a conversation involving real ["actually existing"] people as well as Pessoa's heteronyms; a *situação* wherein everyone—"real" or "fictive" (like today's fake online personas, trolls, influencers and "coordinated inauthentic identities") are all seeking resonance and mimesis, for better and for worse.

In the wake of the earthquake, in the context of crumbling and disappearance, even when rebuilding out of the ruins Lisbon borrowed its plans and designs from European Enlightenment's architecture—the gird of streets and boulevards and grand squares, the mansions and townhouses and apartments, the interior décor, the fashions in the streets—everything, all copies and imitations of the current styles in Paris, Vienna and London. Having suffered the loss of its own soul, Lisbon (and Portugal) had become a mimetic city, a city with no style or character of its own, Pessoa said, and its people too, its economic and cultural elites, its writers and artists and intelligentsia having less and less native Portuguese genius became more and more mimics. Fernando Pessoa himself was not immune from mimetic contagions, and he immersed himself in the fashionable ideas in philosophy and literature and social and political thought circulating in Europe, imitating others' ideas and styles. For while the public face of Lisbon was being erased and re-drawn by earthquakes, aftershocks, and tempests; Fernando Pessoa's private, personal face was similarly liminal and indeterminate.

Ironically, even though he experienced the disappearance of those "arrangements of words and things," of social institutions all crumbling to ruins, and with them the face of man being erased, Pessoa's face is drawn everywhere in Lisbon today: on museums and bookstores, on statues and monuments, on busses and streetcars, on cafes and laundromats, on T-shirts and souvenirs. Pessoa has become "the face of Lisbon," which would cause him some disquiet, for on the one hand he suffered from lack of recognition and he wanted to be well known, and at the same time he wanted to be an anonymous, faceless "man of the crowd." A pathos of distance, of presence and absence is always in play with Pessoa. Slight, softly spoken, seeming shy and self-effacing, he was enigmatic and ethereal. Always neatly dressed in a well-tailored, plain, dark three-piece suit, hiding under the shadow of a broad homburg, he wore the standard camouflage of a modern city man. One of Pessoa's literary acquaintances who met with him frequently at the Café Martinho da Arcadia, reported the uncanny sensation that after their conversations, while walking in the city with him, if Pessoa disappeared around a corner in a downtown street he had really disappeared, and would be nowhere to be found were he to run after him.[9]

While Pessoa "himself" was ethereal, the heteronyms are more than *noms de plume* or literary avatars but fully realized individual persons. "They are utterly human realities to me... I hear, I see, I feel them. I receive greetings from them" (Pessoa 1998, 9). The heteronyms were personae that Pessoa completely inhabited; or perhaps it is truer to say that the heteronyms inhabited him. He was taken over by his heteronyms, as if through powers of mimesis and metempsychosis their spirits "possessed" him. Another acquaintance tells of paying a visit to Pessoa's apartment, knocking on the door, which was duly answered, but to his visitor's consternation, Pessoa, with the voice and demeanor of a different person, said, politely, "Fernando Pessoa is not here today" and closed the door.

Ofélia Queiroz, Pessoa's girlfriend, a very intelligent, beautiful, and playful woman who loved him, unrequitedly, for many years, describes going on a date with him. Their meetings were often in the streets, at streetcar stops and in similar liminal transitional city spaces. But rather than "Fernando Pessoa" the person she met with was heteronym Álvaro de Campos, and throughout their entire evening together he remained so, without once ever losing what Goffman calls "expressive coherence" or "breaking character" (1959, 56). Still, this would be a somewhat inaccurate usage, for to break character would suggest "method acting," which would mean that "Álvaro de Campos" was just a *dramatis persona* of Fernando Pessoa, whereas Álvaro de Campos is much more "real" than that. In fact, to Pessoa the heteronym Álvero de Campos is "really real," a person, just as "real" as—maybe even more "real" than Fernando Pessoa "himself." Álvaro de Campos often accompanied Fernando and Ofélia on their dates, and in these elaborate dramaturgies Ofélia actively played along, entering into the mimetic spirit of the situation seriously and in all earnest.

Pessoa had as many as seventy-two heteronyms, though four major ones (five including "semi-heteronym" Bernardo Soares, and six if we count Fernando Pessoa 'himself') and even though many of the heteronyms had relatively brief lives and personalities and biographies, they all 'have their exits and their entrances'; all of them are simultaneously "phantom egos" as well as "real" "selfs," persons, as "real" as Fernando Pessoa "himself."

> Since childhood I had the tendency to create around me a fictitious world, surrounding myself with friends and acquaintances that never

existed (I don't know, of course, if they didn't exist or if it was I who didn't exist...) Since knowing myself to be the one I call myself, I remember fixing mentally by countenance, movement, character and history, various unreal figures that were to me as visible as those we perhaps abusively call real-life. (Pessoa 1988, 8)

The conditions of erasing and liminality that characterized Lisbon's history and public life mirrored Pessoa's biography, which was marked by private troubles and liminality in his family life. He suffered the loss of the father, literally as well as figuratively. His father, a middle-grade civil servant and a theater reviewer for a daily newspaper, suffered from tuberculosis (TB), "consumption" as it was called then, and in his early childhood Fernando saw his father being consumed, "erased," and eventually dying when Fernando was just five years old; and within the same year Fernando's baby brother, Jorge, also died. Very soon after the double death of his father and his baby brother Fernando Pessoa's mother fell in love with a new man, a redoubtable Portuguese Navy Captain, Rosa, who was soon promoted to the position of Port Captain in Durban, South Africa. Fernando Pessoa's mother's plan at that time was to leave Fernando to be raised by his grandmother, and to go to South Africa with her new lover soon-to-be husband, Captain Rosa. It was in fact this terrible Oedipal drama / trauma that was the birth of Pessoa's first poem, which he read to his mother:

To My Dear Mother
Here I am in Portugal,
In the lands where I was born.
However much I love them,
I love you even more.

Pessoa's mother had hardened her heart to leave her son behind and move to South Africa, but this poem so moved his mother that her heart melted, and she changed her mind about taking Fernando with her. This is the precise genealogical moment when Fernando Pessoa became a poet, when he discovered the power of words, *logos,* to bring about *metanoia,* generating a pathos with the power to change reality.[10] When he recited "To My Dear Mother" (on 26 July 1895) Fernando was barely seven years old. Still in the throes of the intensely liminal formative drama of the Oedipal stage, Pessoa discovered the incantatory and phallic power of *logos.* By the metanoiac patho-logical power of his first poem Fernando changed his mother's heart and mind, and thereby he changed the whole world; the world that had been crumbling into antistructure and chaos af-ter the deaths of his father and his baby brother was re-formed into a structured cosmos. All be it an imperfect cosmos, for his brother and father were really dead, and his fatherland was to be left behind; his mother loved another man, and Fernando Pessoa would have to leave Lisbon and his fatherland and go with his mother and stepfather to a strange new world in South Africa.

That his incantatory power to bring about metanoia, transforming *pathos* by *logos* was only partly successful helps us to account for Pessoa's lifelong enthusiasm for rituals of initiation into secret societies and cults, whether of Rosicrucianism, millenarianism or astrological spiritualism, always acting as though there was an order to the cosmos rather than chaos, and he was always in search of a cosmology. Close to Pessoa in terms of artistic sensibility was William Butler Yeats, whose poetry was often "automatic writing" by "spirit guides" "channeled" through his wife Georgiana, including the famous verse in "The Second Coming," "Things fall apart / the centre cannot hold / mere anarchy is loosed upon the world..." (Yeats 1920, 19) the quintessential image of the liminal interwar period; and Yeats too was under the spell of Mussolini's fascism for a while, just as Pessoa was with Salazar.

Part of the vexed complex of mimetic selves that is "Fernando Pessoa" is his conflicted sexuality, which caused him anguish throughout his life. He (or the heteronyms) wrote homoerotic poetry, dissimulated and ambiguous, as per Shakespeare's sonnets on the "Fair Youth" and "Mr W. H." Pessoa's friends were almost exclusively male, among whom were several "out" gay men, whose literary work Pessoa and the heteronyms defended and promoted in letters and reviews. Walt Whitman was another important model, and Pessoa had a keen interest in Oscar Wilde, particularly in the fate that befell Wilde when his homosexuality, tacitly acknowledged but discretely masked as a persona affected by an aesthete, was exposed during the libel trial as having been physically consummated, and the scandal and persecution that followed. Pessoa came to understand himself—or some part of his multiple selves—as homosexual,[11] though this "self" was re-pressed in favor of a "straight acting" presentation of self in everyday life. Pessoa's (once only) girlfriend, Ofélia, decades later gave Pessoa's biographers intimate details of their relationship, which included occasional passionate kissing and petting, but never anything beyond that. And, of course, one must ask, was this kissing and petting with "Fernando Pessoa," or was it with the more worldly het-eronym Álvaro de Campos?!. Fernando Pessoa was a life-long celibate; but, later in life at least, he was not necessarily frustrated and unhappy, like a contempo-rary "incel." Rather, Pessoa had come to think of his involuntary celibacy as per

Freud's analysis of Leonardo da Vinci's, that Pessoa's own genius was due to his repressed conflicted sexuality sublimated into art and imagination; and like his model Leonardo, who left countless unfinished canvases, sketches, and inventions but only twenty finished paintings, Pessoa had great difficulty completing anything. His literary legacy was a trunk of some 27,000 unfinished pieces of writing, in many different hands and voices and languages, for Fernando Pessoa had many models; but above all he imitated Shakespeare.

'Shakespeare'(?): Pessoa's Model(s)

Fernando Pessoa was seventeen years of age when he returned from Durban to Lisbon. No longer a child, not yet an adult, he was a teenager, literally "between ages," a quintessentially liminal condition wherein a young person is vulnerable and open to influences: just as Hamlet is "young Hamlet" when he returns from university to Denmark and Elsinore, an in-between, half-formed person, entering into a liminal social, cultural, and political situation—a dead Father-King, usurped by a pretender. "The time is out of joint" Hamlet says (2008, I.V.211-2); "something is rotten in the state of Denmark" (I. IV. 67), which is a historical pre-*corso* of the state of Portugal when Pessoa returned from South Africa.

Back "home" in liminal Lisbon, young Fernando Pessoa was gripped by the debates surrounding the identity of Shakespeare: namely, that "Shakespeare" was in fact someone else, writing under the name William Shakespeare, perhaps Francis Bacon, or Edward deVere, or perhaps there were multiple authors, several "William Shakespeares." This serious debate in the history of literature was raging at the time, and Pessoa was not only gripped by that debate (he planned to write a book on it and drafted the first thirty pages) he was *in the grip* of it, in the sense of being caught up in a mimetic relationship with Shakespeare, an agonal and playful mixture of envy, admiration, and emulation. With Shakespeare as his model Pessoa learned to desire what Shakespeare desired, to create characters as "real" and "alive" as Shakespeare's. Imitating Shakespeare, Pessoa's heteronyms were as real, even more real than Hamlet, whose existence is realized "on stage," in a fictitious historical Denmark, whereas Pessoa's heteronyms enjoyed an existence "in real life" in contemporary Portugal: they argued with one another; they wrote letters to newspapers; they supported this or that political cause; they even met with people in Lisbon's streets and had conversations with them in cafes.

Suffering and surviving the storms of his life and times, the storms at the intersections of history and biography, the younger Fernando Pessoa who identified with Hamlet becomes an older and wiser Fernando Pessoa who identifies with Prospero. In *The Tempest* "Shakespeare was thinking about himself and his own theatre" Girard says:

> ...a dynamic history of Shakespeare's *oeuvre*, which is divided in two periods, one signified by Caliban and the other by Arial. ... Caliban symbolizes uneducated poetic feeling, poetry before language, formless, amoral, even immoral, dangerous therefore ... in Arial conversely, there is something serene, noble and orderly that recalls Nietzsche's idea of the Apollonian. (Girard 1991, 344, 348)

Whether read in terms of *ego* forming between *id* and *superego* central to psychoanalysis or as the agonal drama of Dionysus and Apollo central to mimetic studies, in this mimesis Pessoa becomes "Prospero-Shakespeare." *The Tempest* is Shakespeare's last (or second to last) play, and Prospero "is" Shakespeare in what's known as Shakespeare's fourth period, when Shakespeare has been made wise by life's often bitter experiences and is transcending his desire for revenge on his betrayers and rivals.[12] Just as Prospero had been usurped and overthrown by his brother Antonio, and just as young Fernando Pessoa's dead father's place in the cosmos of his mother's love had been taken by his stepfather, Captain Rosa, Shakespeare-Prospero-Pessoa is a wizard who has dreamed up and brought many "people" to life, and by doing so he has come to know a deep truth, that "We are such stuff as dreams are made on, and our little life is rounded with a sleep" (*The Tempest* IV.I. 55–56). This radical insight—the knowledge that what we call "reality" is always and ever no more than discursive-dramaturgical-performative mimetic realizations of dreams, fantasies, myths; imaginary structures, woven within the symbolic orders of history, society, culture, and language, all arrangements of words and things that are drawn in sand at the edge of the sea; all only ever radically contingent social constructions of "reality" to discretely mask the Void. This knowledge that wizards and artists come to know, the phantasmagorical nature of what we call "reality," is power. Knowledge of homo mimeticus and the transformative power of mimesis can be a power wielded by tyrants to manipulate and control what people take to be "reality," but equally mimesis can be a beautiful, playful, subversive, and emancipatory power to re-create new realities.

Pessoa's fascination with psychic phenomena, astrological "influences" and "powers," the "spiritualism" that he had in common with W. B. Yeats and many

others[13] of the generation of artists and poets of the liminal-transitional era
of inter-war Europe, can be redeemed in a much better light if we see them in
light of concepts central to mimetic studies: they were reaching for a language
to account for the form of life that is homo mimeticus, the *vita mimetica,* and
the mimetic unconscious.[14] From the perspective of the Oedipal unconscious
Freud would rather speak of an un-discovered "dark continent" of an anthropologically deep-seated all-too-human mimetic drive that Enlightenment and
Modernity repudiates and represses in favor of an impoverished and constricted
idea of Reason and the sovereign individual. Wherever I go I find the poets have
been there before me! Freud exclaims, and Fernando Pessoa is one of those poets who is an early explorer of the dark continent of the unconscious, both the
mimetic one via his dramatic personae and Oedipal due to his familial drama.
Like Prospero's Island, this psychic continent is animated by unseen powers of
Caliban and Arial, *patho-logos,* ambiguously sinister and benevolent, ambiva-
lently dark and light.

"To Pass beyond Bojador One Must Pass through Pain:" Odysseus as Model

In *The Odyssey* "ever resourceful" Odysseus, with the help of "bright eyed"
Athene and Hermes the "giant slayer," assumes fake names and puts on many dis-
guises, personas, and masks that afford him all of his feints and ruses. Athene's
epithet in *The Odyssey* is "bright eyed," signifying the intelligence that the goddess bestows on Odysseus; and Hermes' epithet is "giant slayer," for having killed
Argos Panoptes the all-seeing giant with one hundred eyes; so Hermes as we
meet him in *The Odyssey* is the model through whom intelligent "quick-witted"
Odysseus becomes the "subtle man of twists and turns" who is able to get by in a
world of pervasive panoptic powers.[15]

   Fernando Pessoa gives us hope that a beautiful life—many lives—can be
lived during our own weird and paradoxical times. We can have a *ricorso* of "the
ruin of all space, shattered glass and toppling masonry" (Joyce 1998 [1922]) and
at the same moment, even as things fall apart, we are assimilated in swarming
digital surveillance and social media. "Whoever wants to pass beyond Bojador
/ Has to pass through pain" Pessoa says.[16] Bojador is a cape on the desert coast
of northwest Africa, known to the Portuguese explorers and since then to all

navigators as "The Point of No Return," because beyond Bojador the prevailing winds are so strong that it was impossible to turn back. Fernando Pessoa knows that there can be no going back; but like the Portuguese navigators if we pass beyond Bojador, pass through the pain, we may round the Cape of Good Hope and find our way, if not to a new world, then perhaps to better ways of living in the old world. "On the old sea always the Homeric, O Ulysses!" heteronym Alvaro de Campos declares in "Maritime Ode." The name Odysseus (Ulysses) means "no name," no one. This affords Odysseus the clever trick that he plays on Polyphemus the Cyclops, so that when Polyphemus cries out for help and the other Cyclopes asks, "who is hurting you?" Polyphemus says "Odysseus ('no one') is hurting me," so they ignore him, and Odysseus escapes. Having "no name" being "no one" gives Odysseus wriggle room to escape. Free of the in-terpellating nets of signification and the order of words and things that would entrap him Odysseus is a prototypical homo mimeticus: he is a "man in search of identity that is no(t) one," who, "precisely because of his ability to evade the question of personal identity, this founding scene and the journey that follows dramatizes a plurality of exemplary experiences that go from the affective to the psychological, the mythical to the religious, the political to the ethical, the ped-agogical to the educative" (Lawtoo 2022, 18). Mimetic studies also makes clear that as a homo mimeticus Ulysses is both a trickster whose logos develops cun-ning patho-logies and vulnerable to violent pathologies.

For instance, even as he is making his escape, Odysseus cannot resist the urge to taunt the Cyclops, boasting that no-name Odysseus is in fact his proper name, and having given himself away by his fault of pride and desire for recog-nition the Cyclops invokes his father Poseidon to punish Odysseus for blinding him, and consequently Odysseus brings a world of trouble and pain, or pathos, upon himself. Odysseus "identifies himself as a man of pain" (Shay 2002, 13); and "long suffering" Odysseus is a warrior who has caused pain to his enemies during the Trojan war and to the suitors who he slaughters for pestering his wife and ransacking his household. But Odysseus has also been a 'man of pain' to his own crew, who have all perished along the way, to his wife Penelope, to his son Telemachus, to his father Laertes, to all his family and household whom he abandoned and neglected. Odysseus is his own worst enemy, and a vital source of the trouble is that the 'man of pain' was scarred as a child. Odysseus / Ulysses *Oulixes* (L) is from *oules*, scar was gored by a boar's tusk while under the dubious care of his maternal grandfather Autolycus, a wolfish man—*auto lycus* means literally "the wolf himself," "the most accomplished thief and manipulator of oaths of his day" (Homer 1991, 19:395). It was Autolycus who gave Odysseus his tricky, subtle, polyvalent name: "I will give you a name for him. I have been at odds with people up and down this bounteous earth, so let his name Odysseus signify this" (19:406). It is by his childhood scar that his nurse, his wife and his father recognize that "the stranger" is in fact really "our own Odysseus"; and, like ourselves, all of us are somehow or other scarred, damaged, by, among so many other things the thrownness of our being in the world.

Tricky Odysseus is a bit of an animal; one who cannot keep from stirring up trouble and putting people at odds with one another. No sooner has he settled himself with Penelope then civil war erupts again, with Odysseus, Telemachus, and their household facing off against the suitors' clans:

> Uttering a terrifying war cry [Odysseus] gathered himself together and pounced on them like a swooping eagle. ...But at this very moment... Zeus flung a flaming thunderbolt which fell in front of the bright eyed Athene who called to Odysseus: "Odysseus, favorite of Zeus, resourceful son of Laertes, hold your hand! Stop fighting your countrymen, in case you incur the wrath of Zeus the Thunderer." Odysseus obeyed her, and his heart rejoiced. Then, Pallas Athene, Daughter of aegis-bearing Zeus, still using Mentor's form and voice for her disguise, established peace between the two sides. (24: 535, 545).

At the end of *The Odyssey* bright eyed Athene in the form of Mentor is the good model for Odysseus's son Telemachus to imitate, lest he repeat the sins of his father; as Leopold Bloom is a model and mentor for Stephen Dedalus, as Italo Svevo was Joyce's model for Bloom whose father John Stanislaus Joyce was rolling chaos; and as Fernando Pessoa can be a model and mentor for us.

Fernando Pessoa is a metempsychosis of a spirit from Portugal's Golden Age, a person who has "sailed beyond Bojador" into uncharted waters. "Here be monsters," certainly, but there is also a Cape of Good Hope. Pessoa helps us to understand and embrace the pains and possibilities of a strange new world and its native peoples—*homines mimeticus*; people whom, with Pessoa as our model, we may come to recognize the strangers among us—and the strangers within us, as having been "ourselves" all along.

Notes

1   Heteronym Alberto Caeiro. As the name Fernando Pessoa is mentioned his heteronyms will always be implied [editors' note].

2   "Method" is *hodos* (Gr) a "path," a "way."

3   See Girard 1991, 343.

4   Here, we make use of two (of the many) editions of *The Book of Disquiet*. See Pessoa 2010, 2002.

5   As well as being an influential model for Pessoa, Merchado also became the model and inspiration for Jorge Luis Borges and for Gabriel Garcia-Marques. Beckett says that "the task of the artist now is to find a form that accommodates the mess," and magic realism is a form that accommodates the mess of baroque, often morbid, and always extravagantly fecund mimetic complexities characteristic of the convulsions and transitions, liminality and stasis in late modern civilization whether in Latin America, Eastern Europe (Milan Kundera), India (Salman Rushdie), or China (Mo Yan).

6   Portugal alone was responsible for 6 million of the 12 million people captured, bought, and sold in the transatlantic slave trade.

7   *Saudade* is a "Portuguese way of life": a constant feeling of absence, the sadness of something that's missing, wistful longing for completeness or wholeness, and the yearning for the return of what is now gone. Saudade…is a vague and constant desire for something that does not and probably cannot exist (Bell 1912). The etymology of "saudade" is *solitudo* (L), meaning solitude, being alone, being on one's own, and feelings of loneliness; and *salutare* (L) meaning "to say goodbye," with "*salut*," carrying the rich semantic cluster of associations in good-byes and fare-wells; of parting gifts and good wishes for health and hopes for future happiness.

8   A precipitating event occurred during the so called "scramble for Africa" in which Portugal suffered a mortifying humiliation. While trying to hold onto and expand its old interests in Africa, which spanned east to west, Mozambique and Angola but with Congo in-between, brought Portugal directly into confrontation with England, culminating in a "British ultimatum" of 1890, escalating towards a war that Portugal would certainly lose, and so Portugal backed down… a terrible blow to Portuguese collective self-esteem, underlining yet again the shameful fact that Portugal was a spent power, diminished and lacking.

9   See Zenith 2022.

10 *Metanoiein* (Gr) means "to change one's mind" (from *meta-* after, beyond, and *noein* to think, from *nous* mind). Metanoia means "a change in the trend and action of the whole inner nature, intellectual, affectional and moral"; a "transmutation of consciousness" (Merriam Webster; OED). Metanoia means "conversion," that is, being "turned," "turned around," "turned towards" sources of illumination, ideals that lead us in a higher direction. Metanoia, a complete change of heart and mind, accords with Plato's famous definition in *Republic* of education as the "turning of the soul."

11 "[T]he nature of the phenomenon [his 'self'] is a repressed sexual inversion" (Pessoa 1988, 5). "Sexual inversion" was the diagnostic term for "homosexuality" current at the time in psychiatry and psychoanalysis, literature that Pessoa read avidly, so Pessoa's self-analysis is quite straightforwardly that he was a repressed homosexual. However, in Pessoa's case, he says, "It stops in the mind. … I am not saying that I would then practice the sexuality that corresponds to the impulse, but the desire to do so would be enough to humiliate me. Many

of us of this type occur throughout history, especially through the history of art. Shakespeare and Rousseau are amongst the most famous examples or exemplars. An obsession with their cases being deeply rooted in me" (ibid.).

12   According to Stephen Dedalus [Joyce] Shakespeare's brother Edmund had an affair with Ann Hathaway; see *Ulysses* episode 9 "Scylla and Charybdis."

13   Pessoa's involvement in spiritualism and astrology while extensive wasn't systematic, but he envied Yeats and others who were more committed and who had undergone initiation rituals into "mystical" "orders." Pessoa may have suspected that it was all bogus, but he feigned his belief and played along with it, for to play along with feigned belief is at least as "authentic" as "truly believing," and in the end to believe in "something" was perhaps better than to face the Nothing. In this Pessoa was anticipating Samuel Beckett at least thirty years before *The Unnamable* and *Endgame*, wherein Beckett shows that outside of the human drama playing out on whatever stage there is only the Void of silence, madness and death.

14   On the differences between the "mimetic unconscious" and the "Oedipal unconscious," see Lawtoo 2023a,b.

15   See also the Prelude to this volume pp. [editors' note].

16   From "Portuguese Sea" in *Mensagen* [*Message*], the only book published in his lifetime, in Portuguese, the product of a convoluted plot where Pessoa was inveigled into being a sort of poet laurate for Salazar's New State, set up by an old acquaintance who had become the Minister for Culture [propaganda]; a situation that Pessoa was deeply ambivalent about, for while he was, as usual, desperate for the money and the recognition, this was the wrong kind of recognition!

Bibliography

Bell, Aubrey F. (1912). *In Portugal.* London, New York: John Lane.

Brown, Susan M. (1991). "The Whitman-Pessoa Connection." *Walt Whitman Quarterly Review* 9.1, 1–14.

Butler, Judith (1990). *Gender Trouble: Feminism and the Subversion of Identity.* London: Routledge.

Foucault, Michel (1970). *The Order of Things: An Archaeology of the Human Sciences.* New York: Pantheon.

Freud, Sigmund (1959 [1917]). "Mourning and Melancholy," in *Sigmund Freud Collected Papers,* ed. James Strachey. New York: Basic Books, 152–170.

Freud, Sigmund (2001 [1910]). *Leonardo da Vinci and a Memory from his Childhood.* London: Routledge.

Ganeri, Jonardon (2023) "Solace and Saudade: How to Find a Strange Solace in the Indifference of the Universe," *AEON,* 17 July 2023, accessed 20 July 2023, https://aeon.co/essays/how-to-find-a-strange-solace-in-the-indifference-of-the-universe

Girard, René (1979). *Violence and the Sacred.* Baltimore: The Johns Hopkins University Press.

——— (1991). A *Theatre of Envy.* Oxford: Oxford University Press.

Goffman, Erving (1959). *The Presentation of Self in Everyday Life.* New York: Random House.

Gramsci, Antonio (1971). *Selections from the Prison Notebooks.* New York: International Publishers.

Homer (1991). *The Odyssey,* trans. E. V. Rieu. London: Penguin Classics.

Heidegger, Martin (1975). "The Way Back into the Ground of Metaphysics," *Existentialism from Dostoevsky to Sartre*, selected and introduced by Walter Kaufmann. New York: New American Library, 206–221.

Husserl, Edmund. (2002). *Ideas: General Introduction to Pure Phenomenology*. London: Routledge.

Joyce, James (1998 [1922]). *Ulysses*. Oxford: Oxford University Press.

Lawtoo, Nidesh (2022). *Homo Mimeticus: A New Theory of Imitation*. Leuven: Leuven University Press.

—— (2023a). *Violence and the Oedipal Unconscious: vol. 1, The Catharsis Hypothesis*. East Lansing: Michigan State University Press.

—— (2023b). *Violence and the Mimetic Unconscious: vol. 2, The Affective Hypothesis*. East Lansing: Michigan State University Press.

Mills, C. Wright (1959). *The Sociological Imagination*. London: Oxford University Press.

Morin, Edgar (2008). *On Complexity: Advances in Systems Theory, Complexity, and the Human Sciences*. New York: Hampton Press.

Nietzsche, Friedrich (1989). *Beyond Good and Evil: Prelude to a Philosophy of the Future*. New York: Vintage.

Pessoa, Fernando (1998). *The Keeper of Sheep. Fernando Pessoa & Co: Selected Poems*, ed. and trans. Richard Zenith. New York: Grove Press.

(1988). *Always Astonished: Selected Prose*, ed. trans. and intro. Edwin Honig. San Francisco: City Lights Books.

—— (2002). *The Book of Disquiet*, ed. and trans. Richard Zenith. London: Penguin Classics.

—— (2010). *The Book of Disquiet*, ed. Maria Jose de Lancastre, trans. Margaret Jull Costa. London: Serpent's Tail/Profile Books.

—— (2018). "I See Boats Moving." *I Have More Souls Than One*. London: Penguin.

Rosa, Harmut (2013). *Social Acceleration: A New Theory of Modernity*. New York: Columbia University Press.

—— (2019). *Resonance: A Sociology of Our Relationship to the World*. Cambridge: Polity Press.

Shakespeare, William (1908). *The Tempest*. London: Cassell & Co.

—— (2008). *Hamlet*. Oxford: Oxford University Press.

Shay, J. (2002). *Odysseus in America: Combat Trauma and the Trials of Homecoming*. New York: Scribner.

Szakolczai, Árpád (2000). *Reflexive Historical Sociology*. London: Routledge.

van Gennep, Arnold (1960). *The Rites of Passage*. Chicago: University of Chicago Press.

Yeats, William Butler (1920). "The Second Coming," in *Michael Robartes and the Dancer*. Dublin: The Cuala Press, 19–20.

Zenith, Richard (2022). *Pessoa: An Experimental Life*. London: Penguin Books.

CHAPTER 13

LITERATURE, PEDAGOGY, AND THE POWER OF MIMESIS

On Teaching Maylis de Kerangal's *The Heart*

Evelyne Ender

> Things begin then—and this is what "imitation" is all about ... with the
> mark that language, "mythic discourses" ... discourses that are fictive
> originally inscribe in the malleable—plastic material of the infant soul."
>
> —Philippe Lacoue-Labarthe, "Typography"

In "The Mimetic Condition: Theory and Concepts," Nidesh Lawtoo tells us that
mimesis is consistently at play in our human existence. Inspired by Nietzsche, he
also establishes that the power of mimesis lies in its inherent ambivalence whose
effect is to render us vulnerable to "the inner experience of pathos" that "simultaneously [...] puts us in a position to set up a critical distance from such pathos"
(2022b, 11). Built on medical, psychological, and pedagogical premises, this
case-study presents findings that, culled from my seminars in the new domain
of *Medicine, Science, and the Humanities*, show that images and representations
embedded in fiction trigger a resistance that is nevertheless conducive to critical
thought, even among freshly minted college students.

I learned to measure the extent of mimetic power by teaching to my mostly
pre-med students at the Johns Hopkins University the novel devoted to a heart
transplant *Réparer les Vivants*, by Maylis de Kerangal.[1] This sustained reflection
on the pedagogical power of mimesis is driven by a questioning of a psychological and ethical nature whose significance is adumbrated in the epigraph to
this essay.[2] Its ancient source lies in Plato's *Republic* and the discussion about the

appropriateness and the nature of stories (*mythoi*) that should be told to children, with the warning that they might poison their minds rather than educate them (Book 2, 376a to 377b). But how, why would the pedagogue that I am subject my young students to inner experiences of a pathos susceptible of infecting their minds with a potentially poisonous *pharmakon*?

Theoretically and philosophically, a modern humanistic education relies on an ideal of boundless enlightenment. Given its pedagogical aspects, my case calls, however, for a more cautious approach. Indeed, as perceived in an august philosophical tradition that stretches from Plato to Derrida, writings all too easily lure us into images apt to contaminate the mind with dangerous fictions. This double textual genealogy gives the study of a fiction chosen for its exemplary mimetic power and its potentially medicinal properties its decisive inflection—in keeping with the ambivalent features of the *pharmakon*. Plato's *Phaedrus* (esp. 268c, 275a, 277a) and its modern re-appropriation by Derrida in "Plato's Pharmacy" (1981) thus undergird this exploration of a nearly contemporary novel whose mimetic representations call for a careful management of their effects and affects. The *logos* of philosophers has provided me the enhanced distance and lucidity needed to engage with a prose endowed with an unusual emotional charge and *pathos*. With its emblematic modern (because subjective) juxtaposition of the ills we owe to fictions and their contrary capacity to mend such ills, Rousseau's notion of *un remède dans le mal* also directs this inquiry.[3]

Given its inscription in a psycho-pathological field and the mimetic deployment of strong affects, the book *Mend the Living*, whose central theme is a premature death of young man, calls for a remediation that its title promises. Given its *mythos*, namely the accidental death of a young man about as old as my students, and its remarkably intelligent mimetic scenography, which involves a subtle meshing of medical and humanistic aspects of this story, its overt premise seems questionable. Granting this book redeeming therapeutic features has at times seemed unsustainable—even in light of the development, contemporary with it, of the domain of narrative medicine, which has shown that an informed relational "reading theory" connected to the clinic can exert its "transformative powers" and that reflecting on stories can be healing and propedeutic at the same time (Charon 2006, 108).

Why study it? For intellectual, academic reasons of a local kind. Many of our students at Johns Hopkins are drawn toward a medical vocation, and our hope has been, from 2015 onwards, that early exposure to history and the arts, to classical learning as well as to film and modern literature on illness, death, and dying could prepare them for later clinical encounters with patients and might inspire their research. This ideal finds its echo in the field of *mimetic studies*, when Nidesh Lawtoo identifies an *ethos* that tells us that an "immanent conception of mimesis" that "traverses the entire history of culture" can be a "*life-affirmative and future-oriented*" reparative social, relational force (2022b, 3; emphasis added). In "Viral mimesis," he exhorts us, researchers and teachers, to consider the need for "new mimetic gestures" and for "ethical care for others" so that *pathos* can turn "into a partially shared suffering (*sympathos*, feeling with)" (2021, 156). My wager has consisted in trusting that the teaching of *Mend the Living* would open up a *psycho-patho-logical* field of textual experiences that might insensibly guide my students toward an existential, though vicarious, apprehension of human tragedy of the kind found at a bedside. In addition, summoning up in their young minds intimations about mortality has seemed all the more urgent in the wake of a pandemic caused the SARS-CoV-2 virus, which has increased our awareness that "contagious pathologies …continue to cast a shadow on a … precarious world" in a world that is, moreover, rife with "toxic" mediatic chatter and disinformation (Lawtoo 2021, 155).

How can reading exert its mitigating medicinal faculties? How can we assume that fiction can teach us—grown-up and young minds alike—about our mortal condition? Though informed by classical sources, this study is inspired by modern conceptions of literature and especially by an ethics of reading that assumes exposure to what J. Hillis Miller called a "terrifying wisdom" (2013, 152). Another assumption is best exemplified in Rousseau's belief in literature's redeeming features as epitomized in the phrase *un remède dans le mal*, which grants fiction not only the power to enlighten us but also that of countering the ills of our condition through the judicious use of its therapeutic potential. The rise of the novel and its influence on our modern sensibilities involves indeed a historical as well as an epistemic shift that together open up the possibility that writing, which can spread the ills that plague us, provides its own antidotes and remedies. In this context, de Kerangal's work calls for a re-description of the stakes that her aesthetic choices define, namely a collective summons to respond to this death captured in a book with all the humanity at our disposal—as cognizant, responsible, compassionate subjects. Indeed, her book deploys its mimetic power not merely to teach us about *pathos*; it also induces—through its affecting images and verbal fabric—the kind of cognitive acuity that *logos* demands.

The Seminar: An Exercise in Medical Hermeneutics

What follows here is a double account, literary to the extent that it unpacks the grammar of this text to address its rhetorical force and pedagogical as it charts a progression from a naive to an informed reading of the text discussed in a seminar. Socratic promptings and questions find their counterparts in a text that incrementally subjects its readers to a hard-won knowingness and to a new wisdom. With a book and hermeneutics as my only instruments, we explore this story:

> On a starry night in Normandy, lured to the coast by the prospects of an exceptional swell, three young surfers pile into a small van with their surfboards for a moment of "extreme sport" and sheer physical exhilaration. On their way back at dawn to Le Havre, a skid on a slippery road, an obstacle on the way: two of them are badly hurt, the third one, Simon Limbres was not strapped up, and is now in deep coma, brain dead with a beating heart. What, in the French idiom, is called *un fait divers* becomes in the hands of Maylis de Kerangal an event of tragic scope—a kind of event easily "left in the cold," unrecorded except in police and hospital records. The setting is now a hospital: in limbo, inhabiting the borders between life and death, in what has been diagnosed as *coma dépassé*, the stilled body, its heart still beating and still symbolic of a life must enter "a grim machinery, the practiced choreography of a procedure, the surgical horse trading over inches of artery and vein" with, ultimately, the prospect of losing this heart to another body.[4]

The hero is in the flower of his youth on par with the students in a seminar room where a text exposes us to "the elemental and irreplaceable nature of narrative knowledge" (Charon 2006, 11). My role consists in planting questions into their minds, as a path toward better discernment, but decoding the text can be laborious, as it involves, for certain stretches, a reluctance to come too close to words on the page filled with intimations of a dark reality.

Edgy, contemporary in its style, *The Heart* seems in tune with the kinds of morbid and adrenaline filled dramas (some of them, such as "Six Feet Under," cited in the book) that have for a while now peopled the young imaginations of future doctors. At first blush, with its cast of astute, wise doctors, a sexy nurse, daring surgeons, as well as an attractively young patient, the scenario resembles familiar TV series widely watched for their distinctive medical types and the dramas that involves them. The thought process starts as "surface reading" prompted by a spontaneous natural identification with those who heroically and dramatically save lives in emergency rooms.[5] A young man is dying, he cannot be saved, his heart can, however. We follow the discussions leading to the parents' acceptance of a transplant, the peripeteia takes us into the operation room, where a woman in her fifties awaits the precious heart ferried in extreme haste, from Le Havre to a hospital in Paris. Dramatic representations of heroic medical procedures provide the thrilling materials that turned this book into a bestseller among *lycéens*. Translated into many languages, it also received an award from the Wellcome Institute, proof of its scientific intelligence and its capacity to communicate a medical *ethos*. Meanwhile, what could be our next steps? How to stage a more insightful coincidence between the object, the book, and the subjects that are holding it and reading it in ways that can probe deeper?

The process of mimetic imprinting starts seamlessly with the attentiveness we pay to Simon, as he lies dying and his body has become "mute, indecipherable, as impenetrable as a safe" (81). An image (replicated from different perspectives) exerts its emblematic mimetic power to the very end: Simon's dying, comatose body—*a beating heart and silent brain*—lies in state in a hospital ward, hooked up to machines and monitors, in an intensive care unit (ICU). The central figure of de Kerangal's *mythos*, Simon, is not extraordinary (he harks back to the kind of hearty fellow found in folk and fairy tales), but we watch him as he enters limbo, the dark space of an uncanny void of an absent, no longer visible consciousness. Lingering over these images seems crucial: it involves, to borrow her striking metaphor, listening to the "voice of a stethoscope" as it pulls us into the reality and mystery of what is a death.[6]

The novel is indeed not just medical. It is also, borrowing Thomas Mann's words for *The Magic Mountain*, "lyrical, medical, technical." Each connected to a distinct aspect of his medical fiction, these adjectives help identify the different strands of de Kerangal's modern version of a drama that involves the young, in a drama of collective magnitude played out, however, *not* on heroic battlefields, but in the ordinary, quasi domestic space of young people's adventures in living. The book is shorter and its style terse—at the other extreme of the meditative, lingering temporality that Mann experimented with. Its lessons are embedded in the compressed time of a tragic form and frame—the twenty-four hours of French classical tragedy, as marked in the book by clocks.[7] Constant, strongly marked changes in focalization jolt us in and outer of medical scenes that morph into introspective, intimate scenes that take us into the protagonists' consciousness. The best analogy to describe this stylistic choice lies with film and the possibilities it offers for fast paced rhythms and cuts. As with Mann, piecemeal descriptions lead to a panoramic vision of universe where death is a looming in the wings, but with a striking and meaningful difference, namely the absence of a palpable narrator. De Kerangal's panorama of hospital life comes to us through a single, "ego-less" lens that sedulously keeps its distances, so as to give way to sympathy.

The plot demands a precise documentation of medical procedures and with it, shifting experiential temporalities of waiting, attending, acting in urgency undertaken in the haze of warped diurnal and nocturnal cycles. The *pathos* is managed or dispensed through a subtle interlacing of dialogue, free indirect discourse, and flashbacks. Meanwhile, what in film might be seen as mere decor invades the space of the novel as, on par with phenomenologists, the author enlists words to evoke in the space of the hospital "qualities of feeling" imbued with the *inquiétante étrangeté* of the uncanny. In contrast with ancient Greek tragedies that delivered their share of terror and of pity in more obviously, visible theatrical ways, de Kerangal's aesthetics seems designed to lead us into a psycho-logical field that, with its subtly paced dispensation of pathetic representations, brings us, readers, closer to the unthinkable. This is how her literary sceno-graphy provides a space of *a transferential, psycho-analytic nature* that can be amenable, conducive to thought.[8]

Thus, narrative suspense, which in a "naive" reading focuses on a heart that must stay alive long enough to enable a transplant, gives way to a subliminal psychological registration of micro-events related to the time of Simon's dying. Insensibly, representations born from the necessity of a close up reading (how many words or sentences can be skipped before meaning disappears?) make way for another patho-logical scene: it spreads successive waves of pain on a canvas detailed enough to anchor affects in seemingly indifferent objects such as a glass of water, a paperweight, or a tattoo on a body laid out (Simon's) in imitation of a Mantegna or Holbein. An unbearable thought is what looms here—this one unteachable, I think—about what it must be like to face the death of one so young. Among the successive "takes" of Simon's death, some are highly descriptive, relying on visual allusions, as for example with Rembrandt's "Anatomy of Dr. Tulp;" others rely on literary allusions, as when de Kerangal cites Rimbaud's "Dormeur du Val," a poem often taught in French schools or when she draws for Simon's accident on the template provided by Racine's *Phaedra* (studied in many *lycées*), where a young Hippolytus is thrown off from his carriage by horses run wild. Together, these samples bank on forms of narrative knowledge—"elemental and irreplaceable"—that lie in literature's ability to summon up pictures, spun from words, that, nuanced, delicate, complex, transcend the ordinariness of a *fait divers*.[9]

Pain Management

In a section of his *Poetics* (1987, 58 ab), Aristotle engages in an extraordinary exercise of stylistic and poetic comparison to gauge what might be the aptest words for an appropriate dosage of tragic effects. In comparing versions of trag-edies, he sees that small amendments in the linguistic fabric of a tragedy might induce the right mimetic effects—the best fitted for the occasion. *Kekrasthai* is the word he uses; it means dosage.[10] My seminars with my young subjects de-manded, similarly, a process of titration and filtration applied to literary rep-resentations. Responding to de Kerangal's style involved minute adjustments applied to the verbal deployment of a tragedy that indeed invite a comparison with Aristotle's recipe toward the wise management of a relation between style and affect. What would be the impact of this or that scene? How would they respond to the volatile components of an "alchemy of art" so potently at work?

Meanwhile, from attunement to responsiveness, and in a dialogue, the sem-inar (an ancient pedagogical creation) offered itself as the ideal space for vicari-ous encounters with fictive pain—encounters that, instead of containment, de-manded articulation in conversations that could chart pathways between affect and cognition. Indeed, only with language and through attending to language can one begin to inhabit thought—as Ivan Callus aptly reminds us with this question, borrowed from another scholar: "Can one even think without the words of others?" (2015, 261). Unlike images, words can serve a double func-tion, representational and hermeneutic: language enables the creation of images while also providing us with the instrumentation to reflect on them.[11]

Remediation, as became clear, became a matter of trusting our book and its capacity to generate readerly experiences capable, perhaps of countering the existential(ist) burden of a narrative about death. Engaging with its tragic theme had to involve the subtle, patient forms of attunement with our book, with *its* words, and a gradual recognition of the tragedy but also of the vitality, the stirrings of desire, the celebration of "moments of being" that it dispenses in many places. Indeed, a persistent and delicately handled insertion of memories, desires, and gestures gives the book its life-affirming features. It seemed for a while that a balanced, careful dispensation of passages of the book, to be read closely in view of a discussion, would suffice when it came to warding off the perturbing effects and affects of its mimetic power. However, it soon became clear—sometimes through words, but most often in bodily attitudes, silences, and even an overt reluctance to look at the page we were reading in class—that I had underestimated the ambiguous, ambivalent potency of the medium at hand, namely of de Kerangal's writing.

When my pupils' studious and untutored minds reached shoals, not quite invisible to them though overtly conveyed in the fiction's tragic framing, of suffering affixed to mortality, their reluctance to speak or continue reading said "I cannot bear to think about it." Reaching this horizon, this *point limite* inevitably prompted a host of pedagogical interrogations but also converged with broader institutional concerns. In the *psychagogic* space that our affecting book defined, we faced the risk of deleterious, viral contamination of affects that through forms of identification or projection could become "toxic" or "traumatic" triggers.[12] Yet, the fictional stories bind us, and one cannot un-see or un-read, as Rousseau so presciently declares in his preface to his novel *La Nouvelle Héloïse*, in full awareness of his novel's ambiguous mimetic power, *le mal est déjà fait*.[13] Meanwhile, in his "Phenomenology of Reading," Poulet offers this perspective on a book's insidious capacity to colonize our minds, when he writes that, unlike what happens with other objects, "in the case of a book is the falling away of the barriers between you and it. You are inside it; it is inside you; there is no longer either inside or outside" (1969, 54).

Though transposed from their initial psychoanalytic context, Mikkel Borch-Jacobsen's words about the scene of reading and its unconscious dynamic seem even more prescient: "All in all, there will always be something or someone 'beneath' the representations, to which or to whom they will appear (in other words, there will always be an eye to see the spectacle that is offered on the stage)" (1991, 6).[14] If indeed, young souls are malleable and impressionable, while a mimetic image, though not fully registered, outlasts its initial presentation, there is no turning back. There is, instead, a need for philosophical wisdom that can help prepare pre-med students to face, in a not-so-distant future, an actual world, a real(ity) that the study of this fiction will have adumbrated.

An Apology for Literature

How then to teach this book *in* and *for* our changed times? The object, we know, is affectively charged with events calling for pity and terror as befits tragedy. The method involves the delicate, discriminating application of a hermeneutics, until obstructed, in the aesthetic realm, by a mimesis that suffuses the book with an excess of *pathos*. Granted that it might always be too early, why subject my students to these imaginings? As implied from the outset of this essay, a collective ethos can serve as a justification, as does the author's explicit commitment to representing in her recent novels self-generated communities related to individual actions.[15] Bemoaning the fact that "the conviction that everybody ought to read literature because it embodies the ethos of the citizens has almost vanished," Miller too calls for "an audacity of hope" ready to dispense critical thought through a collective alliance between literature and theory (2013, 145, 152–153), which in his last years delved also into mimetic studies. The book's promptings, the task of teaching a global ethics of care as implemented in the Medical Humanities, and Miller's belief (however cagily put) in literature's persistent potential for a dispensation of critical thought help contextualize my own pedagogical endeavors.

A historical context is needed, meanwhile, to address the question of *cui bono* and in terms of its genealogy, the answer lies as much with Aristotle as with Plato. Teaching a mode of critical distancing and transforming mimetic representations into objects for thought—as a way of dispelling their poisonous influence—is part of the founding gestures of western ideals of culture. As Aristotle argued, practically driven forms of education, in the guise of *phronesis*, will privilege intellect to prevent situations where emotions may take the upper hand. Indeed, his rich commentary on how to school the young seems to speak directly to the practical, pedagogical considerations I face when teaching *Mend the Living*. His "method" relies, for instance, on a formal preparation that, anticipating modern pedagogies, takes into account and works with the pupil's natural disposition and the pedagogue's craft lies in the choice and telling of a story.

A philosophical justification for our reliance on stories for schooling can be found, meanwhile, in an anthropological view laid out in the *Poetics* as *mythos*, an *histoire des origines* of how men came to create what we now call literature.

> Poetry in general can be seen to owe its existence to two causes, and these are rooted in nature. First, there is man's natural propensity, from childhood onwards, to engage in mimetic activity (and this distinguishes man from other creatures, that he is thoroughly mimetic and through mimesis takes his first steps in understanding). Second, there is pleasure which all men take in mimetic objects. (Aristotle 1987, Bk 4, 34)

This apology for *mimetic learning* and the implicit lure held by stories points at the educator's decisive contributions to the building of ethically and civically attuned cultures and societies. So does *hexis,* since it entails the management of affects *and* an inherent, namely "natural" early disposition or receptivity to lessons provided in a mimetic form. In his vision, good teaching relies on a gradual, habitual attunement of the emotions dispensed in "formal education" in which "stories enable children vicariously to inhabit multiple worlds beyond their horizons" (Steiner 2023, 112).[16]

The value of this model lies in its simplicity—especially when compared to the multipronged presence and impact of an exponential mimetic proliferation of stories that our mediatic digital universe has enabled. In my seminars, we *read* stories—under the assumption that my students' expertise as decoders of texts can, in that environment, prompt more advanced forms of critical thought. In terms of the phenomenology of mimesis, there is indeed a crucial difference between watching and reading: a book insulates my students from experiencing the ordinary whirlwind of sensory hyper-stimulations that their media offer, and it binds them collectively into a storytelling mode. Literature, in other words, offers its own distinctive propaedeutic instrument, that is, stories, for imparting a "cognitive acuity" that can inculcate virtues beneficial to a community.[17]

Such experiences constitute literature's unique purview and preserve. Enriched with phenomenological registrations (as is the case with *The Heart*), the mythos is part of a transformative process whereby receptive young minds are invited into a space of active exploration of new domains of experience. A seminar, with a book as its only accessory, defines then its own particular sphere for a lettered experience, which enables the imaginative deployment of new insights in "imperceptible ways." In this space, to be "affected" does not necessarily involve being "infected," exposure to the text can at the same time "animate" thought in a previously dormant soul (Lawtoo 2021, 156–157). Mimesis, in this model, obeys a principle of extension (creating as yet unimagined worlds in the reader's mind) and relies on literature's capacity to engender worlds and to effect what Jonathan Goldberg has called a "worlding." He writes: "the artists must 'see and feel,' and both capacities exceed the ordinary impercipience with which we think we grasp (or, more to the point, fail to grasp) the world" (Goldberg 2019, 103).

A Question of Dosage: A Deep Reading of de Kerangal's Style

The mimetic capacities given to stories have grown exponentially since Aristotle's days, as can be seen when probing the depths of de Kerangal's remedial fiction. Yet her craft still relies on the conjunction between modern representations and an older iconography. Repeated at intervals, inscribed in the fabric of her imagined world, these formal features yield their philosophical meanings in a subtle interplay between aesthetic and thematic features. Narratologically speaking, they involve the sporadic insertion of a descriptive *intaglio* that interrupts the story she is recounting. Far from being merely ornamental, these pictorial or lyrical scenes convoke representations of an allegorical kind and of a symbolic tenor. In such places, mimetic activity converges on what is both a "relational, embodied, and affective" *pathos and* a philosophical, allegorical, and rhetorical *logos* (Lawtoo 2022b, 7). De Kerangal's subtle scenography is in the service of thought and relies on a mimesis that, *in the slow time of reading,* can evoke feelings and insights very different from those produced by media and their multiplex, rapidly unfolding perceptually saturated frames.

More broadly even, where do we turn for wisdom when a perverse mediatic curiosity risks pulling us into a constant streaming of *faits divers*, with "fatalities," "morbidities," or "mortality" (as in "mortality rates" of our statistics) becoming a banality? De Kerangal provides her own answers when, in *The Heart,* she enlists a pictorial and textual imagery whose roots lie in the Renaissance. Eschewing clichés, she endows "her" *fait divers* with entirely different meanings through a stylistic, rhetorical performance that amounts to a *poiesis*. Two sources, namely Ivan Callus's essay on "Literature in Our Time" (2015) and Mitchell Merback's *Perfection's Therapy* (2017) —an art-historical inquiry into the visual/philosophical features of melancholia inspired by Dürer— are part of my demonstration. Together, they provide a genealogy for a decisive, scientifically driven, and thus inherently secular transformation in mimetic representations that involve the body. Just as meaningfully, they offered me—in that delicate journey toward greater wisdom about *thanatos* undertaken in my seminar—templates conducive to a reflection on the existential and philosophical aspects of the *mythos* dispensed by de Kerangal. Two seemingly innocuous passages (one at the beginning of the book, the other at its middle-point) brought us closest to that disturbing turning point at which representations that risk engulfing us in their *pathos* can be redeemed through a newly acquired intelligence.

At the outset of the *The Heart* we discover a *paean* to this organ. It relies on a cosmic perspective whose full significance only emerges when this initial poetic stasis gives way to the story that occasioned it and to its tragic *mythos*. Drawing on cosmopoetic images, the fiction begins by recounting the life of an organ that pulsates into a "night, that starless and bone-splittingly cold," and is born in synch with "a lightless swell roll[ing] along the cliffs" and with "the continental shelf [...] revealing its genealogical bands" (3–4).[18] But we are also drawn into a clinical-medical mapping of the heart's extraordinary physiological capacities and its biochemical tempering of our emotions when we learn that at rest Simon's young heart "pulses probably less than at fifty beats per minute" (4).

In a gesture evocative of a modern sublime, de Kerangal tells us that "Simon Limbres's heart, this human heart [is] too much even for the machines." Working by allusions, relying on tropes, and yet peppered with a technical vocabulary, her text thus inches its way toward the revelation of a "life of ebbs and flows, of gates and valves, a life of beats." The beating heart mirrors nature and turns into a symbol for the physicality and the meta-physical aspects of our human condition. This *incipit* then makes a first breach in anticipation of what is to come and invites us to think, proleptically about the unthinkable—namely *where is Simon's animating essence now, after the accident?* For that same body that experienced the thrill and the adrenaline of riding the waves now inhabits a natural biological, physiological condition of vulnerability and as part of its "fate" will soon become a case of life-in-death.

"The black box of [his] twenty-year old body": when de Kerangal stamps Simon's presence in this manner—with a metaphor that is also a synecdoche—she already outlines her book's morbid subject.[19] The metaphor denotes an impending death, connotes its mystery, and gives us the first lines of a dirge. Indeed, lying in rest (asleep or nearly dead?), Simon is enfolded and embraced into a cosmic order that outlasts the fragility of a human body. The book's prologue thus adumbrates the central quandary of its *mythos*: *Simon cannot think what his heart might feel; brain dead, Simon is alive in his heart.*[20]

Logic tells us that, applied to Simon's life and death, these two concurrent propositions amount to an *aporia*. From an existential perspective, this contradiction points at the scandal we *must* face with this book, that of mortality. The fact that Simon is young, almost still a child, only enhances the potentially terrifying knowledge this book portends.[21] In her poetic, lyrical prologue, de Kerangal dispenses the first elements of a philosophical wisdom about mortality, but it comes too early, as my student's body-language showed. This indirect plea to hold back from a "traumatic" knowledge is what prompted a more subtle pedagogical staging, for which I relied on the pages of Merback's *Perfection's Therapy* devoted to the *pharmakon* and a telling image (2017, 115–119).

"Therapies of the image," he explains, are part of a pharmacopeia that can be dispensed "at the point of convergence for both the representation of natural life and the presentation of charged matter" as is shown in the painting by Van Shriek, *Toad, Insects, and Morning Glory*, which became our prophylactic as we parsed together its luminous and shadowy zones. This Renaissance artwork belongs to an older spiritual *pharmacopeia* attentive to the natural, biological alchemy of life and death. In de Kerangal's novel, life and death are similarly intertwined at the border between nature (as a physical process, as *natura naturans*) and a vibrant, pulsing existence. This existence, in our case, involved a beauty that is not that of a flower—but instead, of the human body.

Framed by this meditation, the second intaglio that we studied involves a strikingly visual *scene* that, in the book, casts its light on the drama that is soon to follow, namely the accident. Its protagonists are Simon and the suggestively named Juliette.

> She smiles, and lifts her oilskin as high into the air as she can: [...] she stands on tiptoes to cover him with it—and herself too, the two of them contained inside the sweetish odor of the plastic, their faces reddened by the waxed fabric, their lashes dark blue, their lips purple, their mouths deep, and their tongues infinitely curious. They stand under the tarpaulin as in an echoing tent, the rattling rain above them forming the soundscape against which can be heard the breaths and hissings of saliva; they stand under the tarpaulin as if under the surface of the earth, submerged in a damp, humid space where toads croak, where snails crawl, where magnolias, brown leaves, linden blossoms, and pine needles rot into humus, where old bits of chewing gum and rain-soaked cigarette butts slowly molder, they are there as under a stained-glass window that recreates an earthly day, and the kiss doesn't end. (116–117)[22]

The bitter knowledge of "it is in the nature of life that we die" is indeed only palatable, my students have shown me, when perceived in counterpoint with Juliette and Simon's love—as imaged almost cinematographically by the author. So, reading *The Heart*, we take in first the sensuality, carnality, youthful desires it conveys, but then stumble, perplexed, over the detailed description of a descent into a different realm, of toads, flowers, detritus. We talk about the stained-glass window. Have they seen one? Only in a museum? Or perhaps in a church? But how do we read this symbolism? Is it religious?[23]

However challenging, the spelling out of the dark undertow of that seemingly romantic scene played an essential role in our search for greater cognitive acuity in matters of life and death. Experiencing the full mimetic power of *The Heart* has demanded this: not only the discovery of *eros*, but also fleeting encounters with the idea, the spirit of *thanatos*—as well as the dismantling of naïve impulses to merely garner from the book medical knowledge about the emergency room. On that cold winter day imagined in a fiction, someone's child meets death. A few of the images come to mind: here is Marianne, the mother, with whom we took in lessons about the unimaginable, while sharing little bits, here and there, of a "terrifying wisdom." Her mind in near terror, her body registering the blow, suddenly old, she is learning to act in a tragedy. Dim memories are there too, perhaps, of the author's distinctive style: "There is nothing to disturb Marianne's suffering as she moves forward like a robot, her movements mechanical, her expression vague. *On this fateful day.* She repeats these words to herself, under her breath, unsure where they came from [...] as if the words were lyrics accompanying her muffled footsteps" (67, italics in text).[24]

The Vigil

In the aftermath of the accident, Simon lies still in the intensive care unit (ICU)—in between worlds. He resembles a fallen Greek hero, as if struck by a bolt of lightning. But his body remains the same; it shows a marmoreal, sculptural beauty—it doesn't fade. Where to turn, however, for a philosophical description of this slow passing? In *Le temps et l'autre (Time and the Other)*, Levinas writes about dying in terms of a vigil, namely as involving a *veille* and the elements of an ethics that demands a "watching over" over an Other (Levinas 2014).[25] To name the event, the philosopher has recourse to a phenomenological description and relies on metaphors, telling us that "like the place of a radical foundering, like an atmospheric density, like the plenitude of a void or like the murmur of silence, there remains, after the destruction of things and beings, [only] the 'forcefield' of the existing, impersonal" (26; my translation, emphasis added).

Though clearly in tune with de Kerangal's *cosmopoiesis* in its outlining of a phenomenology of dying, Levinas's naming of death stands out in stark contrast with the physicality and the singularity shown in her text. In her poetic staging of Simon's vigil, his body looms and gloams, imprinting our imaginations with a vividness that tilts the balance toward a *remembering.* With her, the "forcefield" defined by Levinas is neither "void," nor "silent" nor "impersonal," but, on the contrary, filled with a presence. De Kerangal's mimetic construction is not merely about a remnant: it produces remanence. What remains is embodied, memorialized, encrypted in a name, symbolically: Simon-the-Limber.

In this way, a text reaches for *pathos* capable of retrieving forms of sympathy that, in a reading of her text, can become strikingly personal, intimate. This means that *The Heart* opens up a *psycho-logical* space and experiential universe that embraces the symbolic, the imaginary, *and* the real. A real of a kind that Bruno Schulz wanted us to acknowledge in his exhortation to find words toward the witnessing of "events that have been left in the cold, unregistered, hanging in the air, homeless and errant." His is a voice that, in 1937, admonishes us to make time for "all events," and to keep a trace.[26] Although de Kerangal's stage is much narrower and insistently local (and, of course, fictional), it too involves a use of language that gives a real presence to a death, and endows it with a moving, though unsentimental singularity. For this, her prose carves out interstitial spaces (in a tight, often paratactic diction) that read like dreamwork. The difference is striking between the bustling theater of epic medical feats, with its tight chronology, and those other momentary glimpses into the unbounded realm of anguish represented in the book that calls for a witnessing of human vulnerability and mortality.

The slowing of time that defines this other psychical stage enables a different *telling,* circumspect around death, stilled as if in awe of its mysterious darkness. In another *intaglio,* the author reaches for an image and its mimetic effects, in evoking Georges de Latour's gold suffused painting, "The Newborn" (ca 1648).[27] What illuminates this picture amidst the darkness is the candle: its light fragile, all too easily blown. Hence perhaps the stirring quality of a painting bleeds into that other story of vulnerability, namely Simon's, who seems asleep—his vital signs monitored by leads, wires, graphs. The picture, a familiar presence to the Breton author (who would have seen it in the museum at Rennes), serves as an allegory: in casting its light on a child's frail, miraculous life, it reprises that other scene, endowed with its own "atmospheric density," where in a hospital ward, on a starry night in Le Havre, a child called Simon lies dying. In the hospital, those "inside the book" and on a night shift watch over him and keep vigil—witnesses to these nocturnal, twilight hours of his passing. The contrast couldn't be stronger between the stillness and *aureatic* magic of that night hour spent with an infant and what was to happen—after a car leaves the road on that early morning of black ice when in twilight drowsiness, a child meets its fate. *Un fait divers*—not one of those colossal, collective fatalities of a historical/political, climatic, geological, or pandemic nature.

De Kerangal's mimetic staging of this moment calls for a momentary contemplation of the efficacy of representations that, in those nocturnal hours of the vigil, affect us with the power of a dream, and are yet all too real (a child lies dying, a child has died). Outside of time, Simon's body lies "mute, indecipherable, as impenetrable as a safe" in the penumbra. Next to that world where every minute counts and where chronological time seems to be the master, de Kerangal imitates the painters who can *still* the world. Reminded by Nidesh Lawtoo that for Plato/Socrates "it is necessary to be infected by pathos in order to develop a diagnostic logos (not from a detached clinical distance but from the perspective of an affected physician)," I must acknowledge here the affects summoned up by a "Real" that lingers, with full symbolic power, in the vigils staged in *The Heart*. They summon up, *in their mimetic power*, a transferential and intersubjective space of memory and desires attached to a dead child that lies beyond the pages of a book.[28]

The Heart owes its Barthesian *punctum* to de Kerangal's deployment of a *literary mimetic faculty* that brings to light, on the one hand, the mesh of relations among humans and, on the other, the relations humans have constructed with the universe they inhabit in order to ward off, *through mimesis,* nature's potentially terrifying designs upon us. But the *scandalon*, the stumbling block, cannot be removed: it is in the nature of things that we die. Symbols can only offer temporary mitigation for what remains otherwise unendurable. No *pharmacopeia* holds a cure for this tragedy, the pain endured by the mother, Marianne, and the father, Sean. He is the one who inspired his son to experience the bodily ecstasies provided by that small skiff—the surfboard that cut into the waves "in search for the most beautiful wave in oceanic history" (8).

What lessons can one teach about death and dying? One reads philosophers and psychoanalysts; they help paraphrase but, somehow, can only circumvent. In an older world, the story told here—a story for our time—would have been cast in the form of a *psychomachia*, namely as a conflict between the soul and the body. Instead, *The Heart* deploys a mimetic scenography whose weight and meanings lie with the body and its vulnerabilities. De Kerangal's greatest accomplishment lies, perhaps, in her distinctive style or stylizing of experience and in her faith in the regenerating power of verbal matter. In the wake of that legendary quarrel on display in Book 10 of *Republic*, which opposes philosophy and poetry, her writing prompts us to revisit this opposition. It reminds us that fiction, in the hands of a brilliant author, can indeed be *both* poetical *and* philosophical. Indeed, among all the mimetic arts, literature alone has a voice—a voice that, through its cries or whispers, can move us or carry us through collective tragedies while speaking to the *singularities of human experiences*. Thanks to her artistry, *pathos* seems to have found its *logos*. Accompanied by its subtle distillation of a *pharmakon*, *Mending the Living* provides us with an ethics for our fraught times—an ethics able to meld cognitive acuity and sympathy into newly imagined forms of *mimesis*.

Notes

1   *Mend the Living* (MacLehose Press, 2016) in the British translation and *The Heart* (Picador, 2017) in the American translation. *Heal the Living* is the English title of the film adaptation based on the book. My textual references are to Sam Taylor's translation, that is, to *The Heart*, chosen because of its greater immediacy.

2   My thanks go first to the students of "Heart Matters" and "Wired to Read"—for what they taught me—and to Nidesh Lawtoo, Mitchell Merback, David Steiner, as well as Clara Kheyrkhah, Louisa Benatovich, and Thomas D'Amato. I am deeply indebted to Shoshana Felman for the existential as well as pedagogical dimensions of this piece.

3   French allows for an ambiguity with the word "mal," which can mean suffering or evil, which leads us back to Socrates's question about the good of writing, and, for us, modern subjects, of books. Starobinski shows how writing is newly endowed with a therapeutic function in that inward turn taken by Rousseau in his autobiographical writings (Starobinski 1962).

4   Quoting from Schulz's words on witnessing that serve as an epigraph to Callus's article and from Priya Parmar's remarkably insightful review of de Kerangal's novel. "Coma dépassé" is the clinical word for the irreversible nature of the brain damage incurred by Simon.

5   A notion developed by Heather Love, in reaction partly to a hermeneutic or theory-driven tradition of textual criticism.

6   Recognizing and acknowledging the co-existence of these strands opens up, echoing Callus, what constitutes a "delicate" and "discerning" path towards a closer engagement with the variety of mimetic forms or genres that engage the reader's imagination.

7   In a foreshadowing of Simon's accident.

8   On par with what psychoanalysis has defined as a transferential space. Bellemin-Noël lays out with impressive clarity and concision different modalities of this relationship (Bellemin-Noël 2012).

9   "Fait divers," a common phrase that aptly labels Simon's accident, refers to "unimportant news items in a newspaper," the *Dictionnaire Robert* explains.

10   "Expressions must be the place of a dosage" (*kekrasthai*), the editors of *La Poétique* note in their commentary of section 58b of Aristotle's text (Aristote 1980, 360–363).

11   As Nelson Goodman reminds us, "We can have words without a world but no world without words or other symbols" (1978, 6).

12   The use of "scare quotes" seems necessary given the charged and controversial meanings associated to each of these adjectives. Every course I have taught that involves *Mend the Living* has carried a trigger warning. "Psychagogic" is Fortunoff's coinage (Fortunoff 1988).

13   In a literal translation: "the evil has already happened." Rousseau assumes that mimetic contagion will spread from the moment you open a book (including his).

14   Mikkel Borch-Jacobsen's *The Freudian Subject* (1991) occupies a decisive position in this piece's genealogy. The transferential stage explored in his early work provides an illuminating analogy for a "scene of reading" whose rational, beneficent effects, though desired, can never be guaranteed. His sustained critique, in later works, of the epistemologically problematic nature of the Freudian "psychoanalytic stage" has also guided me through this inquiry.

15   A collective ethos is a defining feature of de Kerangal's existentialist literary project, as discussed in her interview with Hannah Freed-Thall and Thangam Ravindranathan (2019).

16   For this incursion into the Aristotelian elements of a pedagogy related to stories and their conceptual and ethical significance, I am deeply indebted to the ideas that David M. Steiner developed in 2023, chapter 5.

17   Steiner shows that "cognitive acuity" and virtues go hand in hand in Aristotle's modeling of an education (2023, 108).

18   In his analysis of literature, Callus relies on Mazzotta's notion of a "cosmopoiesis" to respond to the need for "a literary renewal." The latter writes, "Only by drawing from [an] imaginative [...] reservoir will there be once again a rebirth of myths and memories for the future" (Callus 2015, 241).

19   "Morbid" as describing a state (as diseased) but also affects. See the chapter "Morbid Heart," in *The Sublime Engine*, for a history of how these two notions merged and imprinted the modern, romantic mind with the awareness of the heart's inherent organic vulnerability.

20   "Might feel," as the heart is medically and clinically speaking insensate, our perceptions about the heart are the effects of the vagus nerve's registration of interoceptive signals.

21   "Scandalous" as returning us to the Greek etymology of stumbling block and along the textual, philosophical, and literary path charted by Shoshana Felman (2002). "Death," she writes, "is the greatest scandal of all" (39). Patrick Blanchfield, her student, studies in his dissertation the ultimate scandal that the death of a child represents (Blanchfield 2015).

22   Claire Méjan, the recipient of Simon's heart, falls prey to images and to the fear of an "intrusion" that convokes a similarly morbid register of decay and dying (173). As a counterpart to the fiction, we study in the seminar Nancy's "L'intrus" (2022).

23   The parents' earlier beliefs are negated, voided in the face of Simon's demise, as shown when Marianne and Sean are asked to consider the transplant of their son's heart (98–99). However, the question of the fate of Simon's "soul" resonates across the whole novel, ending with Thomas Remige's patient "reconstructing" of Simon's mangled body accompanied, as if ritualistically, by the dirge of his "restrained song" (230–232).

24   Marianne's empty repetition of a common place phrase takes us to that place where, facing the un-thinkable, words fail us.

25   The original French word blends the two notions of "attending" and of staying awake. In American English, an "attending" is an advanced clinical practitioner in a hospital.

26   Taken from *Sanatorium under the Sign of the Hour Glass*, this statement is the first of three epigraphs in Callus's "Literature in Our Time."

27   The painting supports two concurrent interpretations, as a nativity scene and as a secular representation.

28   For further elucidation and exposure to "the art of psychic dissection" as practiced in mimetic studies, see Lawtoo 2013, 8. Jacques Lacan's interpretation of Freud's account of *The Dream of the Burning Child* provides me with another subtext: its overt theme is a vigil, and it offers a quasi-phenomenological exploration of the mimetic unconscious confronted with death (Lacan 1998).

Bibliography

Aristotle (1980). *La Poétique*, trans. Roselyne Dupont-Roc and Jean Lallot. Paris: Seuil.

—— (1987). *The* Poetics *of Aristotle*, trans. Stephen Halliwell. Chapel Hill: The University of North Carolina Press.

—— (2013). *Poetics*, trans. Anthony Kenny. Oxford: Oxford University Press.

Bellemin-Noël, Jean (2012). *Psychanalyse et littérature*. Paris: Presses Universitaires de France.

Blanchfield, Patrick (2015). "Paternity and Universality at the Grave of Schleiermacher's Son," in *Universalities in Crisis: Parenthood and Paternity at the End of the Line*, 113–196. PhD diss., Emory University.

Borch-Jacobsen, Mikkel (1991). *The Freudian Subject*. Stanford: Stanford University Press.

Callus, Ivan (2015). "Literature in Our Time, or, Loving Literature to Bits." *CounterText* 1.2, 232–269.

Charon, Rita (2006). *Narrative Medicine: Honoring the Stories of Illness*. Oxford: Oxford University Press.

De Kerangal, Maylis (2016). *Mend the Living*, trans. Jessica Moore. London: MacLehose Press.

—— (2017). *The Heart*, trans. Sam Taylor. New York: Farrar, Straus and Giroux.

Derrida, Jacques (1981). "Plato's Pharmacy," in *Dissemination*, trans. Barbara Johnson, Chicago: University of Chicago Press, 61–171.

Felman, Shoshana (2002). *The Scandal of the Speaking Body: Don Juan with J.L. Austin, or Seduction in Two Languages*, trans. Catherine Porter. Stanford: Stanford University Press.

Fortunoff, David (1998). "Dialogue, Dialectic, and Maieutic: Plato's Dialogues as Educational Models." *Ancient Philosophy* 3, 121–131.

Freed-Thall, Hannah, and Thangam Ravindranathan (2019). "'Le Monde relancé à chaque phrase': Entretien avec Maylis de Kerangal." *Contemporary French and Francophone Studies* 23.3, 263–272.

Goldberg, Jonathan (2019). "Stones (of Venice)," in *Saint Marks: Words, Images, and What Persists*. New York: Fordham University Press, 75–111.

Goodman, Nelson (1978). *Ways of Worldmaking*. Indiana: Hackett Publishing.

Lacan, Jacques (1998). "Tuché and Automaton," in *Four Fundamental Concepts of Psychoanalysis (Séminaire 11)*, ed. Jacques-Alain Miller, trans. Alan Sheridan. London: Vintage, 53–64.

Lacoue-Labarthe, Philippe (1998). *Typography: Mimesis, Philosophy, Politics*, ed. Christopher Fynsk. Stanford: Stanford University Press.

Lawtoo, Nidesh (2013) *The Phantom of the Ego. Modernism and the Mimetic Unconscious*. East Lansing: Michigan State University Press.

—— (2021). "Viral Mimesis: The Patho(-)Logies of the Coronavirus." *Paragrana: Internationale Zeitschrift für Historische Anthropologie* 30.2, 155–168.

—— (2022a). *Homo Mimeticus. A New Theory of Imitation*. Leuven: Leuven University Press.

—— (2022b). "The Mimetic Condition: Theory and Concepts." *CounterText* 8.1, 1–22.

Levinas, Emmanuel (2014). *Le temps et l'autre*. Paris: Presses Universitaires de France.

Merback, Mitchell B. (2017). *Perfection's Therapy: An Essay on Albrecht Dürer's Melencolia I*. New York: Zone Books.

Miller, J. Hillis (2013). "Cold Heaven, Cold Comfort: Should We Read or Teach Literature Now?" in *The Edge of the Precipice: Why Read Literature in the Digital Age?*, ed. Paul Socken, Montreal, Kingston: McGill-Queen's University Press, 140–155.

Nancy, Jean-Luc (2022). "L'Intrus," trans. Susan Hanson. *CR: The New Centennial Review* 2.3, 1–14.

Plato (1961). "Phaedrus" and "Republic" in *The Collected Dialogues of Plato*, eds. Edith Hamilton and Huntington Cairns. Princeton: Princeton University Press, 475–525, 575–844.

Poulet, Georges (1969). "Phenomenology of Reading." *New Literary History* 1.1, 53–68.

Starobinski, Jean (1962). "Lire Rousseau," in Jean-Jacques Rousseau, *Œuvres autobiographiques*. Lausanne: La Guilde du livre, vii–xxiii.

Steiner, David M. (2023). "Learning to Think," in *A Nation at Thought: Restoring Wisdom in America's Schools*. Lanham: Rowman & Littlefield Publishers, 105–133.

CHAPTER 14

THE BIOMIMICRY REVOLUTION

Contributions to Mimetic Studies

Henry Dicks

Introduction

The inspiring idea of a new research field engaged in the transdisciplinary study of mimesis—mimetic studies—has recently been put forward by Nidesh Lawtoo (2022). At the center of Lawtoo's vision for mimetic studies is the concept of *homo mimeticus*. Drawing on both ancient thinking of mimesis in the work of Plato and Aristotle, but also on more recent work on the concept, including Nietzsche's account of the role of "unconscious mimesis" in human evolution, René Girard's insight into the anthropological significance of the imitation of desire, and the recent discovery of mirror neurons, Lawtoo suggests that we see mimesis as the defining characteristic of human beings.

One topic that Lawtoo does not address in *Homo Mimeticus* is the imitation of nature in technology, that is, biomimicry (but also biomimetics, bioinspiration, and bionics), classic examples of which include self-cleaning surfaces modeled on the lotus plant, sewage treatment plants based on wetland ecosystems, and artificial neural networks inspired by the complex assemblies of neurons and synapses of the brain. Lawtoo is attentive to mimesis in the arts, especially literature and film, but, at least in *Homo Mimeticus*, he does not reflect on the idea of technology as mimetic, in the sense of being modeled on or inspired by nature.

This is not to say, of course, that Lawtoo excludes biomimicry from mimetic studies. Given the transdisciplinary nature of mimetic studies, it is open to other instances of mimesis that Lawtoo himself does not discuss. But the absence of biomimicry from Lawtoo's discussion may also give us pause for thought. Can we simply add in biomimicry to Lawtoo's foundational account of mimetic studies, as if it were simply another topic to which the theoretical framework developed in *Homo Mimeticus* might be applied, or could biomimicry make a more substantial contribution to mimetic studies than that, enabling us to extend and develop its theoretical basis?

With this question in mind, I will in what follows take Lawtoo's vision of mimetic studies as a starting point, before going on to show how what some have taken to calling the "biomimicry revolution"[1]—a radical historical shift from the dominant conception of the human-built world as a *creation of humans* to an emerging view of that world as an *imitation of nature*—can not only contribute additional content to this new field, but also help us further our understanding of its theoretical foundations, and in three main ways. First, the biomimicry revolution points to important new ways in which mimetic studies may engage with the natural sciences and technology, while also providing it with greater and more concrete scope for radical ecological activism. Second, whereas mimetic studies, as theorized by Lawtoo, is very attentive to the genealogy of the *concept* of mimesis, the very idea of a *bio*-mimicry revolution points to the importance of paying greater attention to thinking about the history or genealogy of the *objects* of mimesis. Third, anthropological insights relating to the underlying theory of the biomimicry revolution make it possible to extend and develop the anthropological theory underlying Lawtoo's concept of *homo mimeticus*.

Natural Science, Technology, and Ecological Activism

The three disciplines that receive the most attention in *Homo Mimeticus* are anthropology, literature, and philosophy. But this is not to say that it deals only with humanities subjects, paying little attention to the natural sciences and technology. The natural sciences—specifically neuroscience—play a large part in Lawtoo's conceptualization of *homo mimeticus*, for the discovery of mirror neurons, he contends, confirms the Nietzschean hypothesis of "unconscious mimesis" (2022, 54–55). Likewise, technology is also present in Lawtoo's understanding of contemporary mimesis, for it underpins his claim that we have entered an era of "hypermimesis"—an era in which increasing immersion in hyperreal simulations retroacts mimetically on the subject, leading them to experience much the same affects as those experienced by the characters in the on-screen simulations (2021; 2022, 287). Further, Lawtoo draws on Roger Caillois's theorization of mimicry in the context of biology to affirm, with Caillois himself, that mimicry is not specific to humans (2022, 157–189)—an insight that Lawtoo claims undermines the radical distinction often made between humans and non-humans, and that he thinks may potentially play a role in helping us overcome the anthropocentrism responsible for the ecological crisis. Indeed, for Lawtoo the entanglements between humans and non-humans that have led to the emergence of the Anthropocene are at least partly mimetic in character (2022, 161), in which case what many regard as the primary challenge of our time—avoiding environmental catastrophe—presumably requires us to rethink these mimetic entanglements.

Given Lawtoo's willingness to engage with the natural sciences, technology, and environmentalism, it is not unreasonable to wonder why biomimicry is not discussed. One possible explanation concerns his genealogy of the concept of mimesis. According to this genealogy, an initial concept of mimesis as representation arose in Ancient Greece, especially in the work of Plato and Aristotle, and then remained dominant until the nineteenth century, at which point alternative conceptions of mimesis began to emerge, including unconscious mimesis of bodily expressions and gestures (Nietzsche 1995 [1878]), mimesis of affects, initially desire (Girard 1978), and deconstructive interpretations of mimesis that question the straightforward precedence of models with respect to their copies (Derrida 1999). But this is to overlook the fact that already in Ancient Greece there existed an alternative way of conceptualizing mimesis, according to which mimesis was not reducible to (aesthetic) representation (in art), for it could also take the form of (functional) reproduction (in technology). Democritus, for example, claims that house building derived from observing the nest-building activity of swallows and weaving from observing the web-making activity of spiders (Freeman 1948, 154). In a similar vein, Aristotle (2000) did not restrict his understanding of *techne* as imitation of nature to the aesthetic representations typically associated with the fine arts, for the concept also applied to the functional reproductions of nature that we would today class as belonging to technology (as opposed to art).

If Lawtoo does not discuss this longstanding conception of mimesis as functional reproduction, it is perhaps not surprising; in focusing on mimesis as (aesthetic) representation (in art), he is simply following the mainstream western tradition. Plato's mimetic theory of art in the *Republic* and Aristotle's contrasting mimetic theory of art in the *Poetics* have undoubtedly attracted much greater attention than has Democritus's theory of the mimetic nature of technology. Further, while Aristotle's view of *techne* as imitation of nature put forward in the *Physics* covers both art and technology, both aesthetic representation and functional reproduction, it is nowhere near as developed as his theory of poetry put forward in the *Poetics*, and indeed is only even discussed because of its relevance to the understanding of *physis*. Had Aristotle written a *Technics* in addition to a *Physics* and a *Poetics*, it may have been much harder to limit the traditional understanding of *mimesis* to representation. Similarly, while, as we will see in the following section, the subsequent western tradition has not excluded the view of mimesis as (functional) reproduction, there can be little doubt that this alternative conception of mimesis has remained marginal with respect to the dominant conception of mimesis as (aesthetic) representation.

The fact that there is a strong tendency in western thought to ignore the view of mimesis as functional reproduction does not mean that we should continue to ignore it today. On the contrary, studying this parallel but marginal tradition could potentially play a major role in the development of mimetic studies. Not only does it bring a new dimension to Lawtoo's criticism of the traditional concept of mimesis as representation, but it allows for ways of engaging with natural science and technology that are broadly complementary with those put forward by Lawtoo, especially his concern with the mimetic entanglements between humans and non-humans characteristic of the Anthropocene, while at the same time opening up a more concrete vision of the ecological significance of post-human forms of mimesis. Indeed, it is important to realize that the fundamental motivation behind biomimicry, and what sets it apart from biomimetics and bio-inspiration, is the claim that imitating, emulating, and learning from nature provides a viable solution—perhaps even the only viable solution—to the ecological crisis. As Freya Mathews explains, the goal of biomimicry is nothing less than to: "model all our production (artefacts, the built environment) and the organization of all our systems (agriculture, forestry, mining, manufacturing, architecture, and urban planning) on nature" (2011, 366). There can be little doubt that this is a revolutionary proposal, and it is one that is already being implemented across a wide number of existing fields, including analogue forestry, permaculture, agroecology, industrial ecology, and the circular economy, not to mention bio-inspired and neuromorphic computing, biomimetic materials, biomimetic architecture, biomimetic urban design, and the like (Dicks 2023, 98–114). In view of this, there can be little doubt that expanding and developing mimetic studies in such a way that it may integrate and perhaps also help develop both the theoretical insights and the practical applications of biomimicry constitutes an exciting new direction for this nascent field of research.

The History or Genealogy of the Objects of Imitation

Lawtoo's theorization of mimetic studies focusses more on the genealogy of the *concept* of mimesis than on the genealogy of the *objects* of mimesis. The former genealogy begins with the broad affirmation that the concept of mimesis as representation was dominant "from classical antiquity to, say, the nineteenth century" (Lawtoo 2022, 95). It then affirms that, in the work of Nietzsche, there arose a vision of mimesis not as a deliberate attempt to represent reality, but rather as an unconscious process whereby human subjects instinctively, and largely unknowingly, reproduce the bodily expressions and gestures of others (Lawtoo 2022, 51–58). Perhaps the next key moment in Lawtoo's genealogy is René Girard's theory of mimetic desire, according to which the very reason we desire things is that others desire them—an insight that Lawtoo, drawing again on Nietzsche, extends beyond desire to other affects (2022, 37; 116). Likewise, Lawtoo also notes the importance of deconstructive analyses of mimesis put forward by the likes of Jacques Derrida and Philippe Lacoue-Labarthe, which challenge the traditional understanding of the relation between the model and its representation or copy (116). Just as writing, for Derrida (1967), is not just a representation of speech, for speech is always already imbued with traits traditionally considered characteristic of writing, so the same may be said of all models and their representations—an insight to which Lawtoo, drawing on Judith Butler and others, adds a performative and bodily dimension.

What underlies and holds together these more recent moments in Lawtoo's genealogy of mimesis—from Nietzsche to Derrida and beyond—is the fact that they all in one way or another undermine or challenge the traditional conception of mimesis as representation. When mimesis operates unconsciously, as occurs when we unthinkingly imitate bodily gestures or facial expressions, when it involves imitation of affect, or when it does not simply re-present something already fully present, the common denominator is the idea that mimesis cannot be understood—at least not only, not primarily, or not simply—as representation.

This is not to say that the objects of mimesis remain stable and unchanged throughout all these theoretical developments. On the contrary, Lawtoo's key idea of "mimetic pathos" (2022, 37), the imitation of affect, involves a significant shift in the object of mimesis. No longer is external reality the object of imitation; the object of imitation is an internal affect. But not only is this shift in the *object* of mimesis subordinated to an overarching narrative of the breakdown of the classical notion of mimesis as representation; there is also an important sense in which mimetic pathos *does not alter* the objects of mimesis. Since time immemorial, Lawtoo tells us, we have been unconsciously imitating the bodily gestures and expressions of others, and thereby also their affects. All that has changed is: first, that we are now aware that unconscious mimesis is occurring and have neurological evidence to back it up; and second, that new technologies—especially cinema, TV, and the like—make possible new ways in which unconscious mimesis may occur.

That biomimicry may point toward an alternative historical or genealogical perspective, focused less on the concept of mimesis than on its objects, is visible in the very term "*bio*-mimicry"; what we should be looking to imitate is nature, or, perhaps more precisely, life (*bios*). Further, if biomimicry is indeed "revolutionary," then it follows that imitating nature is not what we are for the most part currently doing (unlike unconscious mimesis, which goes on regardless of whether we are aware of it occurring). And this in turn raises several questions. What, if we are not imitating nature, are we doing? Are we imitating something else? Or are we not imitating at all, but creating new things from scratch? And if biomimicry is the hoped-for future, and something other than biomimicry the undesirable present, then what about the past? Is imitating nature something we used to do but have now stopped doing, or can we understand the past in terms of the imitation of things other than nature?

With a view to answering these questions, let us begin by noting that, before the advent of biomimicry or even biomimetics, Hans Blumenberg (2000) told a story of the "imitation of nature" that is in some respects comparable to Lawtoo's genealogy of mimesis. For more than two thousand years, Blumenberg tells us, it was believed that art, in the broad sense of *techne*—and so covering not just aesthetic representation but also functional reproduction—was imitation of nature. In more recent times, however, this ancient view of art has, Blumenberg argues, been replaced by another view: the view of art as human creation.

To say, however, that for two thousand years art was imitation of nature is, I believe, a major simplification. If it is true that it was not until the nineteenth century that the view of art as imitation of nature was explicitly rejected, it is also true that already in the Middle Ages a substantial shift in the understanding of nature imitation had occurred (Dicks 2023, 82–83). As soon as nature came to be viewed as the creation of God, to imitate nature was ultimately to imitate something created, in which case imitating nature ultimately becomes—albeit only indirectly—an imitation of the ideas underlying creation, and thus also of the mind of God.

That God was the ultimate object of medieval mimesis is also apparent in various other ways. Thomas Aquinas may have drawn on Aristotle to affirm that art is imitation of nature, but nature was thought of as animated by the creative power of God, in which case to imitate nature "in her manner of operation" was ultimately to imitate the divine power at work in nature. An even clearer testament to the foundational status of "theomimicry" in the medieval period is Nicholas of Cusa's character, the *Idiota*, who dares to reject—as only an "idiot" would[2]—the ancient principle of art as imitation of nature, advocating pure theomimicry in its place. What art imitates, the *idiota* tells us, are not God's creations, but rather God's *act* of creation; if human art creates new things not based on nature, it is because our art is an imitation of the "infinite art" of God (Cusa 1996). In keeping with this, it is also important to note the widespread belief that Man himself was created in God's image; it was not just human creations, but humanity itself that was theomimetic.

The next important shift with respect to the objects of imitation occurred with the Renaissance and remained dominant until the nineteenth century. During this period, the ancient view of art as imitation of nature was again upheld, at least superficially, and yet, in keeping with the transition from a theocentric worldview to an anthropocentric one, it was for the most part reduced to something quite different: the imitation of Man (Dicks 2023, 83–84). This shift is visible in the work of early Italian Renaissance architects, like Francisco di Giorgio Martini, Leon Battista Alberti, and Filarete (Choay 1974). Giorgio Martini reasons as follows. Human beings differ from other species in that they are free to make things however they choose. This raises the question of the best way to make things, and this question was answered by noting that, since humans contain within themselves the rest of creation—from the elements and metals they share with being in general, to the growth principle they share with plants, the sentience they share with animals, and even the understanding of disembodied angels—it follows that they are the most excellent thing in nature and there is thus no need to imitate non-human nature at all (Choay 1974, 247). The result of this sort of reasoning was an anthropomimetic tradition in architecture and urban design based on imitation of the human form.

A comparably anthropomimetic tradition also arose in modern political philosophy. Hobbes's *Leviathan* explicitly affirms the ancient view of art as imitation of nature, while also arguing that the state is the imitation of the "most excellent" being in nature, namely Man, and, as such, may be conceived as an "artificial man" (Hobbes 1967, 157). This view was then carried over into later political philosophy, an example being that of Rousseau, who based his central concept of the "general will" (*la volonté générale*) on the model of the individual will (Rousseau 2007).

Only in the nineteenth century was the longstanding view of art or *techne* as imitation of nature explicitly rejected (Dicks 2023, 84). A watershed moment was G. W. F. Hegel's lectures on aesthetics, in which the German philosopher rejects what he takes to be the "most common opinion" about art, namely, that it "aims to imitate nature," arguing that even the most insignificant of technical inventions—he gives the example of hammers and nails—are of greater value than the most accomplished of imitations (Hegel 1975, 41–42). It is also not a coincidence that it was in the wake of German idealism, especially Kant and Hegel, that there emerged the first explicit "philosophies of technology." Shorn of its traditional mimetic association with nature, technology could for the first time be considered as something in its own right—an object of study to be considered independently of the natural models on which it formerly rested.

If, as I have just suggested, it was the rejection of the principle of nature imitation that first made "philosophy of technology" possible, the first recognized work in this new branch of philosophy, Ernst Kapp's *Elements of a Philosophy of Technology* (Kapp 2018 [1877]), may at first sight appear to present us with a paradox. Indeed, in many respects this work represents the culmination of modern anthropomimicry (Dicks 2023, 85). The basic goal of technology, Kapp tells us, is to extend human power, and it does this through "morphological replication" of the human body. Simple hand tools, for example, are morphological replications of different configurations of the human arm and hand. A hammer replicates a forearm and clenched fist, a rake an arm and outstretched hand with fingers splayed, and a spade an outstretched arm and hand with the palm facing upwards and fingers held together. The same principle, Kapp claims, applies to more advanced technologies. Optical technologies replicate the forms of the human eye, musical instruments the forms of the human ear, the rail network the form of the sanguine system, and the state the form of the human organism in its entirety (as in Hobbes). Nevertheless, where Kapp breaks with the traditional view of *techne* as imitation of nature is in his claim that morphological replication operates *unconsciously*. Drawing on the newly forged concept of the unconscious found in the work of Carl Gustav Carus and others, Kapp argues that morphological replication occurs without us realizing it, which presumably explains why he prefers to speak of replication, rather than imitation. It is only after the fact, when we come to reflect on the technological objects we have created, that we may become conscious of their mimetic relation to the human body.

It would be remiss here not to mention a fascinating parallel between Kapp and Nietzsche. Just as Lawtoo claims that the traditional conception of mimesis as representation begins to break down with Nietzsche's hypothesis of the unconscious mimesis of bodily gestures and expressions put forward in *Human, All too Human* in 1878, so Kapp's hypothesis of technology as unconscious mimesis of bodily forms, put forward just one year earlier in 1877, marks a revolutionary break with traditional conceptions of *techne* as conscious imitation of nature. This parallel also allows us to see an important feature of Nietzsche's hypothesis of unconscious mimesis that is not emphasized by Lawtoo. Like Kapp's philosophy of technology, Nietzsche's social philosophy is anthropomimetic; it is the gestures and expressions of specifically *human* others to which we mimetically respond. When another human smiles, we unconsciously smile back. By contrast, while I may learn to imitate a cat in slowly closing my eyes when they do, this is clearly not an unconscious reflex.

Returning now to Kapp's place in the genealogy of the objects of mimesis, it is important also to note that it paved the way for more radical positions in philosophy of technology that rejected the very notion of mimesis altogether (Dicks 2023, 85). Max Eyth (1924 [1905]) rejected the traditional view of *techne* as imitation of nature, affirming instead the "spiritual autonomy" of technology, which he thought was born of the "pure life of spirit." Likewise, Friedrich Dessauer (1927) argued that technology arose not through imitating nature, but rather through the discovery of ideal technological solutions that were radically different from anything found in nature. Parallel conceptions of *techne* could also be found in the visual arts. Piet Mondrian (1995) argued that modern man was "turning away from natural things," and, in keeping with this, he thought art should no longer seek to represent concrete natural entities, and should instead become an abstract expression of the human mind. Implementing this theory in practice, his own grid-like compositions of the period in red, yellow, white, blue, and black deliberately avoid both natural forms (curves) and colors (green).

More recently, the high modernist rejection of mimesis has been challenged by postmodernism. If modernism in the field of art and technology embraced "anti-mimicry," postmodernism reacted by embracing "panto-mimicry": the imitation of anything and everything (Dicks 2023, 87). Originating first in the field of architecture, it is perhaps here that postmodern pantomimicry finds its simplest and clearest expressions. Famous works of postmodern architecture imitate all sorts of things, from cats to baskets, not to mention the works of other artists, styles, periods, and so on, which are often juxtaposed in playful and even contradictory ways—a famous example being Kengo Kuma's M2 building in Tokyo, which awkwardly juxtaposes modernist architectural elements with a towering ionic column. If the emerging biomimicry movement calls on us to "learn from nature," postmodern pantomimicry calls on us rather to "learn from

Las Vegas" (Venturi et al. 1972), with its replica Statue of Liberty, Eiffel Tower, venetian hotels, and the like, all lumped together in a fantastic pastiche.

Once again, there is a strong parallel here with an important moment in Lawtoo's genealogy of the concept of mimesis: deconstructive interpretations of mimesis put forward at around the same time. Deconstruction and postmodernism may have their differences, but there is clearly an affinity between the deconstruction of the model/copy binary and the pantomimetic ideal underlying postmodernism. If what we are imitating is not nature, but anything and everything, then we quickly find ourselves surrounded by imitations that are not of full presences, but of other entities that are already imitations. When we take Las Vegas as our model or source of inspiration, for example, it is not originals that are being imitated, but things that are themselves already replicas or reproductions of other things.

I have only provided a very brief sketch of the genealogy of the objects of mimesis. And yet even this very brief sketch indicates the significant contribution to mimetic studies that may be made by adding this genealogy to, and articulating it with, Lawtoo's parallel genealogy of the concept of mimesis. For a start, the concepts of theomimicry and anthropomimicry allow for a more nuanced analysis—albeit still tending toward generalization and simplification—of the long period from antiquity to the nineteenth century; the medieval and modern periods may have superficially upheld the view of art, in the broad sense of *techne*, as imitation of nature, and yet focusing on the objects of mimesis allows us to see that nature was not the true object of imitation, but rather God in the case of medieval theomimicry, and Man in the case of modern anthropomimicry. Likewise, the rise of antimimicry in the early twentieth century reveals another important dimension to the genealogy of mimesis. Lawtoo is certainly not unaware of moments of historical resistance to mimesis, but, since he is more concerned with social forms of mimicry—that is, humans imitating one another—his discussion of anti-mimicry tends to focus on what he calls the "anti-mimetic figure of the romantic genius," who creates new works through his own genius, rather than through imitating and learning from other artists.[3] To this, we may also add the various figures and movements in nineteenth- and twentieth-century art and technology that are anti-mimetic in the sense that they are openly critical of the attempt to represent or reproduce external nature or reality.

Another important way in which studying the genealogy of the objects of mimesis may contribute to mimetic studies concerns our understanding of the history (or genealogy) of art, as opposed to history (or genealogy) of technology. If I have thus far concentrated more on history of technology than on history of art, this is not to say that much the same story cannot be told with respect to the latter. Medieval art was theomimetic in the sense that what it represented were above all religious scenes, especially scenes from the Bible (the word of God) or those featuring saints and other holy figures. And art from the Renaissance onwards was anthropomimetic in the sense that the focus shifted to the representation of human beings. Michelangelo's David may be a character from the Bible, and yet the focus here is not on the religious message, but on the beauty of the human form.

As for the breakdown of the longstanding view of art as imitation of nature, which the medieval and modern periods continued superficially to uphold, there is another fascinating parallel that can be drawn here between, on the one hand, the rise of impressionism in the 1870s and 1880s, and on the other, Nietzsche and Kapp's theorizations of unconscious mimesis in the same period. What was represented in impressionism was no longer *external reality*, but rather the *internal impressions* of the human mind. So, just as Nietzsche saw the imitation of the bodily gestures and facial expressions of others as providing access to their internal affects, so impressionist painters like Monet and Renoir sought to represent their own internal impressions in such a way that the viewer could gain access to the artist's own fleeting internal impressions of beauty. Art here may still be imitative/representational, but the object of imitation/representation is an internal impression, not an external object. Further, as in the case of Kapp's philosophy of technology, there can be little doubt that impressionism's seminal break with the traditional view of mimesis paved the way for the many subsequent movements in the visual arts that, each in their own different ways, broke with the traditional view of art as the representation of external objects, including, to name just a few: expressionism, surrealism, abstract art, conceptual art, and found art.

The fact that art and technology have undergone a series of parallel changes—from ancient Greek imitation of nature, via medieval theomimicry, modern anthropomimicry, modernist antimimicry, and postmodern pantomimicry, to the emerging biomimicry movement—shows the importance of considering them together, as different aspects of a single history of mimesis. And yet this approach also raises an important question for mimetic studies. Is the history of mimesis the history of a concept that can mean either (aesthetic) representation or (functional) reproduction, or is it rather the case that there exists a standard history of the dominant concept of mimesis—mimesis as (aesthetic) representation—which an innovative genealogy of the marginal concept of mimesis as (functional) reproduction challenges, and in a comparable way to more recent concepts like unconscious mimesis, mimetic pathos, and deconstructive mimesis? To my mind, the truth lies closer to the former position. The view of mimesis as reproduction may be marginal as far as the history of western thought is concerned, but it has nevertheless remained operative throughout that history in the traditionally neglected field of technology, and, as such, relates to it in ways that are very different from the concepts of unconscious mimesis, mimetic pathos, and deconstructive mimesis, all of which arose at specific moments within a single overarching history of mimesis, understood in the sense of both representation and reproduction.

On Homo Mimeticus and Homo Sapiens

Lawtoo's main theoretical innovation is a new view of what humans are: *homo mimeticus*. This is not to say he rejects the view that we are *sapiens*; rather, his claim is that at a deeper level of our being we are *mimeticus*, and that it is this deeper level that enabled us also to become *sapiens*: "imitation turns out to be the source of human originality; *Homo sapiens* is born out of *homo mimeticus*" (Lawtoo 2022, 62). On closer inspection, however, the claim that we are *mimeticus* may be said to operate at two levels. The first level is that of unconscious imitation, with its neurological basis in mirror neurons. This, Lawtoo claims, plays an important role in anthropogenesis, because it provides us with a so-called "theory of mind" (122). When, through unconscious imitation of the gestures and expressions of others, we gain awareness of their underlying affects or experiences, we come to realize that they too possess minds. The second level at which we may be said to be *mimeticus* concerns conscious imitation, which Lawtoo thinks first arose in the form of pantomiming, a kind of bodily performance aimed at conveying meaning from one subject to another.

Between these two different forms of mimesis, unconscious mimesis of bodily expressions and conscious pantomiming, a bridge is required; how we get from unconscious to conscious imitation, pantomiming included, calls for theorization. With a view to providing this bridge, let us first note that Lawtoo approvingly refers to the work of the comparative anthropologist and primatologist, Michael Tomasello, and more specifically his "evolutionary hypothesis that the first uniquely human forms of communication were pointing and pantomiming" (Tomasello in Lawtoo 2022, 62). Unsurprisingly, what Lawtoo emphasizes in Tomasello's account is pantomiming. But what about pointing, a bodily gesture that is not mimetic? An important precondition of pointing is theory of mind (which Lawtoo, as we have seen, explains by unconscious imitation). If we are to point at something, we must think of other parties as possessing mind or intentionality, for the very purpose of pointing is to draw the attention of another mind toward the thing in question. Now, given that other species, such as chimpanzees, may be trained to point, it would seem to follow that they also possess a theory of mind, and, in keeping with this, chimpanzees possess a mirror neuron system (MNS) that is in some respects similar to that of humans (Hecht and Parr 2015). But Tomasello (2010, 116–125) also tells us that human pointing differs from that of chimpanzees, for humans alone point in a "declarative" manner, that is, simply to declare the presence of something worthy of interest. And the role that I suggest declarative pointing plays in making us *sapiens* is that, when we point at something, or more generally when we show something to one or more others, the thing in question may become *open with respect to its being*; it becomes, in other words, an open question as to what the thing is.

Let us imagine that the thing being pointed to is some sort of mark in the mud. Now, what may have been of interest to our ancestors in such a situation would have been to know whether or not the thing in question was an animal footprint. If one party thought that it was indeed an animal footprint, then, at least in the absence of spoken language, the obvious thing to do would be to mime the animal they thought produced it. This is of course just one simple scenario; but what I think it shows is that what makes pantomime possible, and later on also spoken language, is the *openness of being*, the fact that what things are becomes an open question (Dicks 2023, 73).

I would further suggest that, at the level of ontogeny, the well-known stage in which very young children begin to point is followed by another phase that one might call the "everything is everything else" phase characterized precisely by the discovery of the openness of being. Very often this discovery leads to play acting, as the child realizes that what they may be is endlessly open, and not limited even to specifically human roles. Lawtoo's quotation of Walter Benjamin is apposite in this context: "the child plays at being not only a shopkeeper or a teacher but also a windmill or a plane" (Benjamin in Lawtoo 2022, 166). And yet play acting, which does indeed involve a form of mimesis, is but one consequence among others of a deeper and more fundamental phenomenon: the openness of being, the fact that any entity can at least in principle "be" any other.

To illustrate this idea, let us consider a game that my son used to play at about the age of three with a family friend. This game consisted in taking it in turns to complete sentences of the form "I'm a…" with a multitude of different nonhuman objects. So, first the family friend would say something like, "I'm a table," at which point my son would roar with laughter, and then respond by saying, "I'm a lightbulb," and then it would be the turn of the family friend to say, "I'm a kitchen," and so on (often for much longer than others present might have wished). Now, an important feature of this game—let us call it "I'm a Table"—is that no mimesis was involved. The game did not involve miming or in any way pretending to be tables, lightbulbs, kitchens, and the like. Indeed, the comic element of "I'm a table" lay precisely in the absurdity of the predicate; and whether any given turn was comically successful would depend precisely on whether the predicate was more absurd or unexpected than the previous one. "I'm a kitchen," for example, would likely produce more laughter following "I'm a table" than would "I'm a chair," for a kitchen is an ensemble of objects that it is even more absurd and unexpected to imagine oneself being than a chair (which, though absurd, is not very different from a table). In view of this, what I suggest underpins this game is the discovery of the openness of being, the discovery that, in any conceived relation of the form "A is B" or "A as B," what A and B are is, at least in principle, entirely open. We can, at least in theory, take any entity and say of it that it is anything else, or see it as anything else.[4]

What makes us *sapiens*, I conclude, is neither unconscious imitation, which we share with other primates, nor miming, pantomiming, and other forms of conscious imitation, which, though unique to humans, are secondary phenomena, but rather something that both phylogenetically and ontogenetically lies in between the two, something that may well have been made possible by the former (unconscious imitation) and that I suggest makes possible the latter (conscious imitation): the discovery that anything may, in principle at least, be anything else.

But what, one might wonder, has this insertion of declarative pointing and the openness of being between unconscious and conscious mimesis got to do with the biomimicry revolution? The human condition, I suggest, may be defined as that condition in which humans must "speak (*dicere*) together (*con-*)" about "what's what." And among the almost infinite questions that this condition impels us to answer, lie the questions "what is mimesis" and, more importantly at the present juncture, "what is the proper object of mimesis?" And it is here that the biomimicry revolution comes in, for it affirms that what we should imitate is nature, for it is in nature that we can hope to obtain knowledge and wisdom. If *homo sapiens* is that being that, thanks to the openness of being, is capable of obtaining knowledge and wisdom, then perhaps it is only by turning to nature, by turning outside ourselves to the knowledge and wisdom already embedded in the natural world, that humanity's longstanding love of wisdom may finally be sated.

Conclusion

I have focused in this chapter on how the concept of a "biomimicry revolution" may contribute to mimetic studies, in particular by arguing that it may help mimetic studies: i) realize its environmental ambitions; ii) add a genealogy of the *objects* of mimesis to a genealogy of the *concept* of mimesis; and iii) further develop its underlying anthropology in a way that articulates a Heidegger-inspired approach, focused on the openness of being, with Lawtoo's Nietzsche-inspired one, focusing on unconscious mimesis.

Beyond developing these contributions and elaborating others, another research avenue opened up by the present chapter would be the converse one of considering how mimetic studies might contribute to thinking and realizing the biomimicry revolution. While this research avenue would no doubt merit development in a separate study, there is one notion present in mimetic studies that seems to me particularly promising: Lawtoo's twin concepts of "mimetic pathologies" (when mimesis leads to pathological results, such as "mimetic contagion") and "mimetic patho-*logies*" (logics of mimetic pathos, which are not necessarily pathological).

The first of these concepts is of potential importance to biomimicry, for it may help us better understand both the hidden dangers it harbors and the logics that govern them. As theorized by Benyus and others, the biomimicry movement may be motivated by the noble intention of "creating conditions conducive to life" and yet, as Benyus is also aware, the danger remains that it may also lead us to "steal nature's thunder and use it in the ongoing campaign against life" (Benyus 1997, 8), whether through military applications, ill-considered applications of artificial intelligence, indifference to the environmental impacts of biomimetic innovations, or something else again. In this context, the concept of mimetic pathology, and more specifically *bio*-mimetic pathology, may help us better understand and theorize the logics underlying problematic theorizations and applications of biomimicry and thus also how they may be countered effectively.

As for the concept of mimetic patho-*logy*, it may potentially contribute to biomimicry by calling attention to an important feature of contemporary discourses surrounding biomimicry: its general lack of engagement with questions of affect (*pathos*), that is, how nature makes us feel, including how such feelings might serve as models or sources of inspiration. Indeed, even when biomimicry moves beyond a focus on just technological effectiveness to consider issues relating to sustainability, the question of how remodeling the world based on natural models might make us feel—its impact on our sensory experience, our emotions, our moods—has yet to be taken up as an explicit theme. When researchers explore the concept of biomimetic cities, for example, the focus is traditionally on how this approach might allow cities to put in place more ecological and sustainable systems of energy generation and storage, water management, food production, and so on (Pedersen Zari 2015; Dicks et al. 2020). But the possibility that cities modeled on, say, forests might capture something of the experience we have of being in a forest, or that they may make manifest and realize a *love* of nature, has yet to be integrated into these debates. Understanding how biomimicry may not just be techno-logical and eco-logical, but also patho-*logical*, in Lawtoo's positive sense, could potentially revolutionize our understanding of biomimicry.

Notes

1   The notion of a "biomimicry revolution" was first put forward by Benyus (1997, 2), but has recently been developed in considerably more detail by Dicks (2023).

2   Etymologically, the word "*idiota*" refers not to someone stupid or unintelligent, but rather to someone who has a "private" vision of their own, which is not shared by others (Douglas 2022).

3   These anti-mimetic tendencies are also central to the modernist foundations of mimetic studies and are expressed in the Nietzschean concept of "pathos of distance," understood as a critical distance from mimetic pathos (see Lawtoo 2013, 3–83) [editors' note].

4   It is often said that philosophy begins in wonder, as we stop taking for granted the being and existence of all things, and begin to marvel at and question them instead. What "I'm a table" suggests is that the openness of being does not *only* give rise to philosophy, the love of wisdom (*sophia*), and therewith also our sense of profundity, but *also* to what one might call *philohilaros*, the love of merriment (*hilaros* in Greek), and therewith also our sense of humor. Hilarity and comedy, from this perspective, are grounded above all in the openness of being, in the fact that one thing may be another thing. Shakespeare's *Twelfth Night*, in which the comic elements derive from characters, objects, or situations being other than they appear, is a classic example.

Bibliography

Aristotle (2000). *Physics,* trans. Robin Waterfield. Oxford: Oxford University Press.

Benyus, Janine (1997). *Biomimicry: Innovation Inspired by Nature.* New York: Harper Perennial.

Blumenberg, Hans (2000 [1957]). "Imitation of Nature: Toward a Prehistory of the Idea of the Creative Being." *Qui parle?* 12.1, 17–54.

Choay, Françoise (1974). "La ville et le domaine bâti comme corps dans les textes des architectes-théoriciens de la première renaissance italienne." *Nouvelle revue de psychanalyse* 9, 239–251.

Cusa, Nicholas of (1996). "Idiota da Mente," in *Nicholas of Cusa on Wisdom and Knowledge*, trans. Jasper Hopkins. Minneapolis: Arthur J. Banning, 528–601.

Derrida, Jacques (1967). *De la Grammatologie.* Paris: Les Éditions de Minuit.

—— (1999). "Introduction: Desistance," in *Typography: Mimesis, Philosophy, Politics.* Stanford: Stanford University Press, 1–42.

Dessauer, Friedrich (1927). *Philosophie der Technik: Das Problem der Realisierung.* Bonn: Cohen.

Dicks, Henry (2023). *The Biomimicry Revolution: Learning from Nature how to Inhabit the Earth.* New York: Columbia University Press.

Dicks, Henry, Jean-Luc Bertrand-Krajewski, Christophe Ménézo, Yvan Rahbé, Jean Philippe Pierron, and Claire Harpet (2020). "Applying Biomimicry to Cities: The Forest as Model for the City," in *Technology and the City: Towards a Philosophy of Urban Technologies*, ed. M. Nagenborg. Cham: Springer, 271–288.

Douglas, Harper (2022). "Etymology of Idiot," Online Etymology Dictionary, accessed 21 December 2022, www.etymonline.com/search?q=idiot

Eyth, Max. (1924 [1905]). *Lebendige Kräfte: Sieben Vorträge aus dem Gebiete der Technik.* 4th ed. Berlin: J. Springer.

Freeman, Kathleen (1948). *Ancilla to the Pre-Socratic Philosophers (A Complete Translation of the Fragments in Diels, Fragmente der Vorsokratiker).* Cambridge, MA: Harvard University Press.

Girard, René (1978). *Des choses cachées depuis la fondation du monde.* Paris: Éditions Grasset et Fasquelle.

Hecht, Erin E., and Lisa Parr (2015). "The Chimpanzee Mirror System and the Evolution of Frontoparietal Circuits for Action Observation and Social Learning," in *New Frontiers in Mirror Neurons Research*, eds. Pier Francesco Ferrari and Giacomo Rizzolatti. Oxford: Oxford Academic, 153–181.

Hegel, Georg Wilhelm Friedrich (1975). *Hegel's Aesthetics, Lectures on Fine Art, vol. 1*, trans. T. M. Knox. Oxford: Clarendon.

Hobbes, Thomas (1967). "Selections from the Leviathan," in *Philosophers Speak for Themselves: from Descartes to Locke*, eds. T. Smith and M. Grene. Chicago: University of Chicago Press, 157–229.

Kapp, Ernst (2018 [1877]). *Elements of a Philosophy of Technology: On the Evolutionary History of Culture*, trans. L. K. Wolfe. Minneapolis: University of Minnesota Press.

Lawtoo, Nidesh (2013). *The Phantom of the Ego: Modernism and the Mimetic Unconscious.* East Lansing: Michigan State University Press.

—— (2021). "Black Mirrors: Reflecting (on) Hypermimesis." *Philosophy Today* 65.3, 523–547.

—— (2022). *Homo Mimeticus: A New Theory of Imitation.* Leuven: Leuven University Press.

322 Henry Dicks

Mathews, Freya (2011). "Towards a Deeper Philosophy of Biomimicry." *Organization & Environment* 24.4, 364–387.

Mondrian, Piet (1995). *Natural Reality and Abstract Reality: An Essay in Trilogue Form 1919-1920.* New York: George Braziller.

Nietzsche, Friedrich (1995 [1878]). *Human, All too Human*, trans. Gary Handwerk. Stanford: Stanford University Press.

Pedersen Zari, Maibritt (2015). "Ecosystem Services Analysis: Mimicking Ecosystem Services for Regenerative Urban Design." *International Journal of Sustainable Built Environment* 4.1, 145–157.

Rousseau, Jean-Jacques (2007). *Du Contrat social.* Paris: Gallimard.

Tomasello, Michael (2010). *Origins of Human Communication.* Cambridge, MA: MIT Press.

Venturi, Robert, Denise Scott Brown, and Steven Izenour (1972). *Learning from Las Vegas.* Cambridge, MA: MIT Press.

CHAPTER 15

ARKS AT SEA AND ARCS OF TIME

William E. Connolly

I

"Yahweh looked upon the human, saw him growing monstrous in the land—desire created only bad thoughts, spreading into his acts. Now Yahweh's pain was hard… 'I will erase the earthlings I have created from the face of the earth,' said Yahweh, 'from human creature to wild beast, to bird in the air—it chills me to have made them.' But innocent Noah warmed Yahweh's heart" (Rosenberg and Bloom 1990, 69).[1]

The story of innocent Noah, and the ark he built amidst the corruption surrounding him, is familiar to everyone touched by Jewish, Muslim, or Christian religions. Similar stories of Great Floods populated several faiths in Greece, Rome, India, Mesopotamia, and the Americas. The Ovid story, for instance, clearly insists that Jove had overreached himself in punishing humans for insufficient reasons. And Ovid may have had the same flood in mind. The above formulation is taken from *The Book of J*, an attempt to capture and translate the earliest version—the J version—of Genesis by Harold Bloom and David Rosenberg in 1990. Their translation—itself an event—became controversial, even though most scholars had already agreed that there had been indeed a J version of Genesis and many thought it important to try to distill it from the fragmented materials of the familiar Genesis stories from different times now crunched together in one text. Those debates are not my top concern at this moment, though they reveal how contemporary debates about a putative event thousands of years ago still arouse passions in those imbued with diverse faiths.

Yahweh, in a fit of righteous anger, decides to punish errant humans and other earthlings by drowning all of them, except the innocent Noah, his partner, and the crew of gendered couples from several species collected on the capacious ark. Does the inclusion of animals and plants imply that he is not only dissatisfied with the humans he created but with his own bungling in the creation of other creatures? Then: "The water overcame everything, overran the land; the ark made its way over a face of water" (J, 70). The crimes the errant ones committed must have been monstrous, for if you assess it in per capita terms, the story reports the largest holocaust in the history of the planet, one committed this time by an angry God. The survivors may have been burdened with a collective ambivalence that sunk at once into their guts, into both the more coarse and more refined brain regions, and into the bumpy modes of communication between these tiers within individuals and across cultural practices. Mimesis. Here we have both vertical and horizontal modes of transmission, with more elementary tiers projecting coarse prompts to future action communicated through bodily signs of anxiety, facial demeanor, and verbal intonations. The more refined responses take the form of stories connected to these prompts.

After the Great Flood, memorializations of it were loaded with affectively imbued prompts and premonitions toward divine obedience and, perhaps, subtexts of ambivalence toward an unsteady Being who could be both so powerful and so punitive:

> All living spirit on dry land—the wind of life in its nostrils—died. Erased: all that arose from the earth, earthlings from man to beast, creatures that crawl and creatures that fly. They ceased to exist, all but Noah, left alone in the ark with his company. (J, 70)

As the torturous forty days floating above drowned siblings, parents, and friends drew to a close, when the dove Noah released returned with a twig showing that there was now indeed land ahead, the crew prepared to start life again, this time more corporeally imbued than heretofore with prompts to divine obeisance and existential debt. After all, they had been exempted from a watery holocaust—an event that rattled confidence in the stability of the world. Noah builds an altar to Yahweh and makes it clear that all creatures below humanity are subordinated to both Yahweh and humanity. Human exceptionalism is born again.

The story of Noah reverberates with the biblical story of the earlier disobedience of Hava (or Eve in other translations) and Adam; the two stories together sink a profound sense of sin and indebtedness to God deeply into the collective psyche. After all, neither Noah nor his progeny would now walk upon the earth unless Yahweh had chosen them. Now "man," the progeny of Noah, "spreads over the earth" (*J*, 72). A new world is born with memories of the old floating around in it. Augustine later transfigures it into the story of original sin followed by God's punishment of later sinners in the Great Flood. Does that combination, perhaps, sow seeds—not necessities but seeds—for, first, the colonization of Europe by Christianity and, second, the later conquest of the Americas by a Christian/imperial/capitalizing Europe? We can note that Ovid also had reported a Great Flood, refusing however to read it as something profoundly deserved by those who drowned or fled during it. You might even fabulate a few stragglers to complicate the Noah story—survivors grabbing onto loose timbers to float to a safe, dry place over a few harrowing weeks. The premonitions of these stragglers may have contested those filling the soul of the cleansed, innocent Noah. "Did all living beings, except Noah, really deserve this?" they might ask. They might have vindicated those who died in that holocaust, though perhaps not too vocally. The first holocaust was not existentially deserved, they might say; neither is the Christian/evangelical anticipation growing out of it in a younger faith of a Second Return of Christ accompanied by the Final Judgment. The next time the Flood is to be replaced by Fire.

Some constituencies today take the story of Noah literally; others treat it as a symbol of the proper relation between God and humanity; others yet as a fiction that it is important to outgrow and replace. Some of the latter secularists, in making this break, however, themselves underrate how visceral modes of cultural communication—that is mimesis consisting of affectively dense, cloudy prompts below the threshold of refined conceptual communication—participate in the transmission of cultural commonalities and struggles. They overlook, as Talal Asad shows, how culturally implanted precursors to interpretation and judgment in the public sphere are already shaped in the private sphere (Asad 2003). They ignore how engrained prompts formed in families, churches, playgrounds, neighborhoods, media experience and work life fold into the discourses of "the public sphere." They may also, therefore, miss how conventional pre-orientations to the earth are inscribed on the visceral register of life as well as more refined registers connected to it.

I share with such secularists a desire to escape the *singular* province of both Yahweh and the Christian God, seeking societies of deep pluralism where several faiths contest and collude peacefully in the public realm. But I resist the tendency of many secularists to overlook or downplay both the periodic volatility of planetary processes and the significant role of mimesis in the consolidations and struggles of cultural life. These cultural deposits of often nonlinguistic modes of communication feel unreal to them, even though they participate in both too. They focus on collective practices of argument, deliberation, and rationality, only meagerly alert to the bodily prompts, proclivities, predispositions, and tremors that are absorbed and then in-form cultural life. Are other responses to the Noah story possible, then, irreducible simultaneously to the Noah version, the ambivalence of unnoted survivors, or the dismissals by secularists?

II

Lo! It now appears that something close to the Noah event indeed occurred in historical time, about seven thousand years or so ago, if not necessarily in a way consonant with the story of monstrosity, guilt, redemption, honor and obedience folded into the guts of Noah and his progeny and repeatedly regenerated through collective ritual enactments. The recent geological story, as with the older theological one, is contested, and it too has more than one variant. One version reports rapid flooding into the basin now forming the Black Sea; another contends that the flooding was less rapid but still extensive. The first identifies circumstantial evidence that many terrorized by the rapid flood into the Black Sea basin fled to Europe and others to Mesopotamia.

Indeed, the old theological story had until recently found a kissing cousin in the vintage geological myth of planetary gradualism, advanced authoritatively by Charles Lyell and Charles Darwin and confessed by most geologists for more than two centuries. That story insisted that geological, oceanic, climate, glacial and evolutionary change always and only occur on long, slow time. Such a myth discouraged geological investigations of ancient floods in Sumeria, the Black Sea, India, and the Grand Canyon until recently. Scientists who professed "catastrophism"—the periodic interruption of slow geo and species changes by large cataclysms of numerous sorts—were defined to be geological heretics. Such a myth/science distinction was drilled into the bellies and brains of geologists. That problematic pattern of insistence was finally broken in the 1980s, when several radical geo-events were uncovered, the rapid extinction of dinosaurs and much other land life 66 million years ago merely being one such event. An old myth/science distinction now faced a new challenge and then underwent a rapid reversal. So, let's pursue the new geological story to offer another possible reading of Noah, one itself infused with appreciation of mimesis.[2]

Until about seven thousand or so years ago, what is now the straits of Bosporus linking the Mediterranean to the Black Sea, was blocked.[3] A large fresh water lake occupied a chunk of the basin where the Black Sea now resides. Farmers and merchants lived on fertile land around that lake, a land refreshed by seasonal floods fed by rivers flowing into it. But then, suddenly, as the Mediterranean rose rapidly, the Bosporus block shattered, and vast amounts of water flooded into the basin over a short period. The Black Sea was formed quickly. Residents who had clustered around the old lake were forced to flee with their families, cattle and implements. Some headed south. An event, shattering confidence in the beneficence of the world.

There must have been incredible grief and gnashing of teeth after that event. "What did we do to deserve this? How come so many loved ones had to die so young?" There was no geological theory or compilation of evidence to mediate the responses. What, then, might be a nontheistic reading of it today, one that appreciates, against many secularists, the layering of culture without embracing a divinity in it to whom humans are indebted for their very existence? One that appreciates evil as radical, undeserved suffering, but does not automatically equate every act of evil to a singular agent responsible for it. Why? Because we think such a view underplays our shaky relation to the bumpy world itself and because we fear that the equation of evil with responsibility provides one of the sources of a conspiratorial view of the world. Perhaps with respect to the flood, because the punishment of Adam and Eve was already stored in sacred lore of the day, the stage was set for the survivors to blame the victims for the Flood that drowned them, while treating themselves to be purified survivors of it. The event, after the fact, summoned a story of guilt and existential debt, one that impugned those who had drowned and warned the progeny of those who survived. A calamity turned, retrospectively, into a story of desert, an infinite human debt to divinity, and humble obedience deeply into the pores of cultural life. Folding repentance and obedience to priests, after the event, into corporeal receptors. A story of desert, burned into the bones of survivors, and recorded in sacred texts for the faithful to recount on ritual occasions.

For we humans, among other things, are absorbent machines. Even bodily prompts engrained in skilled spectators at a tennis event, recall, are activated as they watch an accomplished star make a brilliant shot. The body simulates and memorializes the actions it observes, differently for those with which it already

resonates sympathetically from those against which it has built up visceral resistances. Such a reading of the Flood, then, offers a third option, dropping
divine vengeance from it, repudiating secular denial that such an event could
have occurred, and exploring relations between dramatic events and corporeal
absorption of cultural prompts and premonitions. What would they have been
like, what would we be like, if we acknowledged close relations between event
and mimesis, while cultivating modes of mimesis that drain such a deep sense
of primordial indebtedness and guilt from it? What if we retained the sense of
primordial incompletion in those stories and sought to attach it to a joyousness
in an exploratory life? What modified image of time might emerge from such
explorations? I will leave the first, nearly intractable questions, in abeyance while
pursuing more closely the relations between event, memory and mimesis. Except
to suggest that a new catastrophism appropriate to today needs to be matched
by concerted individual and constituency strategies to fold love of the grandeur
of the earth and the fragility of life into the collective sensorium.[4] No easy task.

To be clear, evidence in favor of rapid formation of the Black Sea through
surges from the Mediterranean is impressive. It remains less certain, however,
whether that event provided the basis for the Noah fabulation. An event at least
seven thousand years ago providing the basis for a story in the *Book of J* that was
written about three thousand years ago, after a long period persisting as a verbal
legend? It is uncertain. But let's persist, as if it did happen that way. Another set
of planetary scientists, for instance, suggest that the story of Eden in the same
Book may reflect dim cultural memories, carried orally in liturgical practices for
centuries, of a period 5,500 years ago when Northern Africa and the middle east
were fertile, luxuriant zones. And then desert time arrived.[5]

III

An event, a sacred text, a layered culture with pains, responsibilities, exclusions,
hopes and guilt sunk with different degrees of complexity into several layers
of embodied interpretation and communication. A hegemonic interpretation
emerges, sunk into multiple layers of embodied life. We don't only communicate
through words, recall, but wordy communications touch premonitions, prompts,
inclusions, and exclusions distributed among recipients. These prompts, too, are
culturally burned into life. They are burned in by surprising events, by parental

caresses and punishments, by priestly warnings and injunctions, by ritual performances, by habitual practices, and by several of these folded into one another.
Such inductions are then communicated authoritatively through characteristic
facial expressions, rhythms of emphasis and intonation, bodily demeanor, disciplinary actions, and inspiring or disapproving looks by authorities; the latter
both accentuate the words spoken and themselves in-form affective layers of
constituency life. These inductions, corporeal punishments, bodily disciplines,
inspirations, and injunctions to devout confession are brought to those who have
inadequately internalized, or who even doubt, the pertinence of divine stories.
Do you recall parents or elders staring down at you when your attention strayed
during a sermon or secular political speech? Innumerable stories and injunctions
slide and bump into preliminary orientations to meaning, obedience and doubt
woven deeply into cultural/bodily conjunctions. Affective absorption, communication, and enforcements. Mimesis, partly as embodied *imitation* of the demeanor of authoritative adults and partly as authoritative *disciplines* burned into
encultured bodies. Who would want to experience that Flood again?

New events can intensify the politics of contagion. Depending in part on the
prompts, priests, media organizations and politicians already there, they can propel
it in some directions rather than others. What if the sea had expanded more slowly
and opened up new ports of trade for farmers who had previously been marooned
on the shores of a lake, however large and fertile? Or what if new generations,
upon hearing the story of those very first two youngsters punished for a crime that
was at best hazy to them until after the punishment was invoked, receive that story
as credible because they, too, are often surprised by media insistences joined to
parental, priestly and professorial disciplines? Because they have been chastised for
crimes, they did not know they had committed until *after* the disciplines had been
imposed. Doesn't childhood knowledge of crime often occur after the punishment
for it? How does the experience of existential debt become molded into cultural
and political life? Events provide catalysts, but they are not enough.

IV

The uncanny involves a response by adults to a new event that both rattles them
in its irregularity and unconsciously taps into childhood events that resonate
with it. The uncanny thus moves on two modes of depth and two temporal

registers at once. Connecting them through resonance. Unfamiliar, but also strangely familiar, (the *unheimlich*) the story of Noah taps unconscious childhood memories, say, of being punished for a crime you were surprised to learn you had committed before the punishment. Without mimesis there would be neither cultural complexity nor experience of the uncanny. Without the layering of memory there would not be either.

Event, layered memories, affective consolidations, cultural meaning and action. By layered cultural memories I mean those that include and exceed recollection. People discuss and debate common or contested recollections, for instance. Did your mother stand up to that racist when you were a child, or not? Siblings debate the issue. Did Donald Trump lose the 2020 election or was it stolen from him? Did Putin invade Chechnya or did a majority of residents invite him in? Memory as recollection, both within individuals and circulating through constituencies who re-enforce and debate recollections among themselves. Below constituency recollection, however, exceeding and feeding into it, are two additional layers of constituency memory.

The first layer of memory below recollection takes the shape of shared dispositions, that is shared drives, prompts, insistences and premonitions digested through previous tokens of experience, affection, and discipline, all flowing toward interpretation and action and operating below the register of recollection. A selection of such purposive drives is pulled up to coalesce in the face of a new event; such coalescences help to bind a constituency together. A drive or a disposition, on this reading, is a consolidated, purposive tendency to response that faces in at least three directions: toward the event that activates it; toward other drives activated by the event, and toward a constituency that has gone through similar bouts of induction, reward, punishment and ritual performance. Different constituencies may well respond in radically different ways, then, to the same event. As those clustered respectively around Noah and Ovid did in responding to the story of a great flood. Or as white evangelicals and the professoriate do today in the face of wildfires, increasingly extreme storms, and glacier melts. A specific cohort may not be entirely reducible to a set of class, gender, race, and creedal positions. The cohort is also drawn together by the distinctive visceral dispositions called up by the event in relation to its previous subliminal experiences. There are, then, spiritual constituencies, haunting, inflecting, and sometimes stretching beyond those time-honored constituencies of class, creed, race, gender, and sexuality. Politics sometimes involves charismatic efforts to pull a visceral constituency into an operative actuality.

To be a self with a mass of internalized drives of various shapes and power circulating around it is to be a multiplicity marked by unevenly distributed dimensions that help to constitute it and its ties to larger constituencies. A new constituency, again, is sometimes pulled together by the conjunction of a new event, spiritual elements previously floating loosely, and the rhetorical creativity of leaders. Often such a formation surprises those sociologists who are more tethered to fixed categories. How many theorists, for instance, were surprised in the States by formation of a white evangelical/neoliberal resonance machine in the nineteen eighties? And then surprised again when a section of Black and Latino males migrated toward the Trump variation of that machine in 2020? Constituencies formed in part as prior spiritual dispositions face the shock of new events.

So, recollections and drives organized from past incorporations form the first two strata of collective memory. The third layer, both for individuals and constituencies, comprises remains, loose ends, scars, or memory traces that are important enough to float around and too incomplete to be recollected or to form definite drives. They can be *activated* by a new event in ways that may resonate with both it and other layers of memory. It would be surprising, knowing what we do about memory and entangled body/brain processes, if we too were not loaded with affect-imbued remainders that carry strange efficacies of their own. Maybe, in the midst of the Anthropocene, you recently outgrew an old belief on the refined register of articulation about human exceptionalism or planetary gradualism, now being more alert to rapid planetary disruptions than heretofore. Nonetheless, vague remainders or tremors from old beliefs poured and drummed into us as children continue to rumble around on a lower frequency register of being. Just because something is not known or represented does not mean that it can carry no efficacy under the pressure of new events. Maybe a gifted orator taps some of those remains after a new event rattles life, helping to pull them in a new direction. Or a gifted writer does so, as Nietzsche did when he sounded out the old European idols of God, time and reason in *Twilight of the idols,* trying to pull those remains in new directions. Because he thought the old ones were dangerous. Were there, too, vague premonitions in *J* that drew a certain wariness of Yahweh into her own prose, casting subliminal doubts upon his most grandiose actions, judgments, punishments, and pronouncements? Harold Bloom and David Rosenberg thought so. The very sparseness and distancing mechanisms of the J prose suggested that to them. Perhaps they themselves were already imbued with underground doubts and premonitions that resonated with the sparse text in new ways.

V

What, then, is an event? As a first cut—and only that—an event is an unexpected happening that interrupts tacit or explicit extrapolations into the future that had informed a constituency's conduct before its arrival. A jolt or shock occurs, an inspirational opening unfolds, or a prior confidence is shattered. A constituency is now pressed either to change its previous extrapolations, or to stick to them by calling up more strident pattern of insistence, or to save the old image by pretending that this is what they expected all along. An event thus rattles or disrupts the visceral register of expectation, more explicit expectations, loose pluri-potentialities on the way, or all three at once. Doing so, it sets up the constituency or culture in question to register new turns in its old creed or to hold onto it via more concerted work upon the visceral register of culture. Delays in the Second Coming formed the sort of event I have in mind. So was the rapid Bosporus flooding of the Black Sea. So was that double viral crossing from, say, a bat to a pangolin and from a pangolin to humans that spawned Covid-19. And so too was the rise of the Anthropocene, as it increasingly rattled old debates between those who believed capitalism promotes indefinite progress to master the earth, those who contest that with a future model of communist mastery, and those who contested both visions with a more organic image of the human relation to the earth. All three visions are disrupted by the event of the Anthropocene, perhaps helping to explain why so many residing in temperate zone, capitalist states remain frozen in place as the world melts down.

Some events fall within the parameters of sociocentrism—the quaint, Eurocentric, modern idea that the causes or sources of social change are always internal to social structures themselves. Many intrusions, though, actually burst into a regime or people from outside, as the Great Flood of the Bosporus, the Roman Climate Optimum, the Medieval Warming Period, and the 2020 pandemic all did. Such events, you might say, spawn bends, bumps or turns of time itself, suggesting once again how the idea that time is either cyclical or linear/progressive may both provide inadequate guides to experience. Indeed, how both notions—and the debates between them—provide reassuring images of time that have once again become dangerous to a world periodically marked by turning or accelerating events of multifarious sorts. For time itself may be a multiplicity, composed of multiple temporalities moving on different vectors, speeds and capacities. Showing us how events often find us before we find them, rattling modernist images of progressive mastery over society and nature as they also disturb the sufficiency of cyclical images.

Time is composed of diverse temporalities, as they bump and slide into one another. The rapid closing of the ocean conveyor system 12,700 years ago was an event that altered the trajectory of climate and eventually changed extrapolations into the future by populations in Europe and the Americas. So, too, was the stuttering into being of the Holocene, over perhaps a mere ten-year period. And the rapid emergence of the Medieval Warming Period, with its different consequences for Europe, the Mongols, the Inuit, Amerindians in the southwest of the current United States, and the Mayan Empire. Or take the emergence of Hitler through the confluence of at least five temporalities: the German loss of a war, defeated, trained veterans wandering around without a purpose, massive inflation, the overconfidence of communists and social democrats that they could take charge of things, and the charismatic power of a crazy, ruthless man. Or consider the shock faced by people in the Kongo when the first Portuguese slave traders captured and shipped many of their youth off to the "New World." They now extrapolated new dangers into the future.

Okay, events occur, you may say. But time itself is not anchored in such nonhuman shifts and human experiences. Experience may be jolted and turned by events. But time rolls on, unperturbed by those turns, like old man river who just keeps rolling along. Time sets a homogeneous container in which diverse experiences occur, you say. We will turn to that issue in a moment, Einstein. In the meantime, don't forget that the Mississippi river is itself a historical formation. So are the Black Sea and the ocean conveyor system.

An event may have been explicable in principle; or it may involve creativities that exceed any such account; or it may reside in a more indefinite zone that escapes current capacities to anticipate it. It is an event if it surprises key constituencies disrupted by it and presses them to alter previous extrapolations, in painful or inspiring ways—whether they actually do so or not. Typically, an event involves the crossing of two or more diverse temporalities moving at different speeds and on different vectors. As when the trajectory of that asteroid 66 million years ago intersected with the evolutionary trajectory of Dinosaurs. They had survived for 130 million years, and before that event it made sense to add millions of years more onto their calendar. Or when an intense El-Nino on one trajectory intersects with trade winds on another to fashion the monsoon interruption that devastated the African Horn, India, and parts of China at the end of the nineteenth century. That event may well happen again, with new twists.

The very diversity and frequency of events may teach us that time itself is not composed of any single dimension—even though Descartes, Newton, and Einstein have all taught the converse in insistent but different ways. It may be time to question, for instance, whether time is anchored only in the stable, rapid speed of light rays hurtling in separable instants (photons) to the earth, bending on the way as they encounter planetary bodies with different gravitational pulls. That conjunction, however, already involves the encounter of two temporalities—light rays and gravitational pulls. Einstein, for instance, had no clue about the Anthropocene rolling along beneath and above his gaze, or about numerous other bumpy periods on the face of the earth preceding it. His time was a homogeneous time, even if it could bend. Time itself, though, may twist and bend, accelerate and stall. Time, too, may be a bumpy multiplicity, as Michel Serres (2004) proposes. Perhaps that is a conjecture to pursue during the era of climate wreckage.

Albert Einstein's old chestnut that he had captured objective time through precise logical analysis and impersonal observation, while Henri Bergson—himself an accomplished mathematician—was floundering in fuzzy logic and subjective human experiences of time, does not cut the mustard anymore.[6] Einstein and Bergson in fact invested authority in different logics and features of human subjectivity: a human mathematization of experience by the first figure and experiences of duration by the second. Neither the physicist nor the philosopher, however, was yet prepared to delineate what might be called the eventual register of time. Even though Bergson set one preliminary for later attempts to do so by exploring multiple modes of duration, extending through and beyond human cultures. This plurality of temporalities—durations—would soon (in clock time) come to include viral durations, bacterial durations, whale durations, and extinction durations, with each periodically bouncing or inserting itself into others. Let alone glacier durations, climate durations, ocean current durations, drought durations, and volcano durations. Einstein's world, whenever he extends it to time itself, is dead and timeless. He could not render intelligible within his theory his own projections into the future. That issue may well have been on the horizon when Einstein confidently told the great quantum theorist, Hans Bohr, that God does not play dice with the world. Bohr is said to have replied, "Stop telling God what to do." The need is not to overturn key aspects of the special theory of relativity, but to resist allowing that experience of temporality, a temporality that indeed bends, to encompass or eliminate all others. The objective is not to eliminate clock time either, since some events happened in deep clock time while others have occurred recently. It is to suggest that the invention of clocks and clock time, while useful to set an alarm, eat breakfast and chart flight patterns in today's world, do not suffice to guarantee that time itself is uniform, linear and/or progressive. Tick, tock. Time, though, is tied to multiform experiences.

Another way to make this point, perhaps, is to say that time is composed neither by a single experience (the human experience of duration) nor a single measure (say, the speed of light). It is composed of multiple measures and trajectories, moving at different speeds, on different vectors, and carrying different capacities; temporalities that occasionally intersect. Time, multiplicity, and event now become woven together.

VI

Visceral experiences of climate wreckage today rattle and distress neoliberal capitalists, white evangelicals, classical communist idealists, classical physicists, and political liberals, albeit on a variety of chords and registers. But all are touched existentially by wildfires, droughts, and new storm intensities. This may be in part because the experience of accelerating climate change, itself composed through bumpy conjunctions between several glacial, capitalist, ocean, forest, fungal, monsoon, sunspot, secular, viral and theological temporalities, upsets both old projections into the future and old European images of time. Neoliberal capitalists purport to know that capitalism, once its social democratic tendencies are checked, is on a track of reliable material progress; neoliberals adopt any number of ideological, technological and institutional ploys to keep that temporal projection (or ruse?) alive as long as possible. White evangelical Christians obstinately insist that God would not allow human beings to shape something like climate or to influence, even unconsciously, the pace of time. Time, they say, steadily heads toward a Second Coming and the Final Judgment. Replete with a new holocaust for billions of non-believers. The forty-year long alliance in the States between these two predominantly white constituencies—evangelicals and neoliberals—is grounded in part in visceral affinities between them about time and the earth. The one seeks to master the earth; the other to leave it behind after a Second Coming. Classical communists previously projected dialectical progress toward a more abundant and egalitarian order. They are today, however, often more open to change, as the recent work by Mike Davis (2015), Jason Moore (2015), and Kohei Saito (2022) illustrates.[7] Classical physicists have found Einstein's image of time, governed by a single measure, to open the door to the precise and unified science to which they aspire. But quantum theory throws monkey wrenches into that very image. A battle also rages within the soul of Einsteinian physics on one side and numerous other sciences such as virology, evolutionary biology, climatology, oceanography, and glaciology on the other. The latter edge closer to an image of time as the composition of multiple temporalities of different sorts. Political Liberals traditionally aligned themselves with an image of linear time, too. They/we too may feel existential anxiety when confronted with other images; an image suggested by close attention to episodic events that interrupt or turn previous trajectories and speeds. That rattles many modernists almost as much as it does white evangelicals. Perhaps it rattles all of us.

Each time a major event bumps into the world, some old extrapolations into future probability and possibility either bite the dust or must be recalibrated. For that very reason, new events often tempt many, on several registers of being, into denialism to secure confidence in the old extrapolations. The Anthropocene, a new pandemic, a dogmatic return to correspondence models of truth, election result denials, and the danger of fascism merely present a few recent examples.

So, to dramatize the condition in which we are caught, you can say that the evangelical/neoliberal machine is inhabited by visceral dispositions to deny accelerated climate change, while its leaders work belligerently through the media to intensify embodied cultural prompts that re-enforce that conclusion. Liberals are too often pulled toward climate casualism, perhaps in part to sustain an image of time that has become wobbly to them? The first constellation is obdurate, and its belligerence poses the biggest danger. It must be opposed. The second, however, can be worked upon. Multiple experiences—including more intense storms, the expansion of wildfires, more extreme flooding, accelerating glacier melts, and the rapid growth of migration drives into temperate zones from the south due in part to climate change—pose counterevidence to those dispositions and prompts. Denialists become more susceptible to fascist, white nationalist drives that work on all three registers of fascist culture at the same time. Liberal casualists may be faced with a decision either to accept a new politics of urgency or themselves to slide toward the old right to maintain their place in the middle. Time moves fast today, as it has amidst other tipping points in lived experiences of geo-history.

VII

Nidesh Lawtoo is attuned to how mimesis works on multiple registers of culture. Attending to neuroscience research on mirror neurons, he explores how the choreographed rhythms, countenances, tonalities, and gaits of leaders become injected into the sensorium of followers. And how, when the prompts already installed experience new potential modes of ingression to be repugnant, a series of embodied resistances and exclusions are intensified even before more reflective registers of culture are engaged. If you add coarse brain regions such as the amygdala, olfactory sensors, and gut-brain relays to Lawtoo's attention to mirror neurons, you identify a whole battery of low frequency modes of ingression that help to compose cultural drives, prompts, and precursors below the attention of refined reflection and collective discourse. These deposits may contain some innate elements, but to a considerable degree they embody cultural deposits from the past. These cloudy and coarse deposits, once received and synthesized unconsciously, percolate—and sometimes rush—into more complex registers of deliberation and discourse, inflecting them. So, they perform double duty: influencing conduct on their own and flowing into higher registers to do additional work. There are also proteins such as irisin and clusterin that, when activated through aerobic and weight exercises, flow into refined registers and help to support the suppleness of cognitive life. Ingressions into the sensorium of cultural life, received and worked upon by it.

Keeping in mind that the low frequency register of constituency life memorializes coarse versions of past ingressions in ways not easily susceptible to the routines of reflexive recall and intellectual reworking (the magical dialectic of self-consciousness), we now see how new work in neuroscience and cultural theories of mimesis can help to sustain and inform one another. Together they teach about how unconscious ingressions become synthesized below consciousness, how experiences of the uncanny work, how old traumas become re-enacted, how denialism becomes encoded, and how fascist movements can acquire initial purchase below the attention of liberal elites focused only on refined discourses, deliberations, debates, and cultural arguments. Never forget the latter, but do not focus exclusively on them either if you seek to address the dangers and possibilities of today. Critical intellectuals must work tactically upon some visceral codes installed in us (such as our too singular images of time) and support reworking the visceral politics of church, corporate, family, and electoral life to open doors for a more pluralistic, democratic, egalitarian, ecological politics.

In *Conrad's Shadow: Catastrophe, Mimesis, Theory*, Lawtoo (2016) turns to Joseph Conrad, the sometime racist author with previous experience as a sailor on the high seas, doing so to explore how fast, intense mimetic circuits amid a ship emergency at sea bounce from nonhuman forces to the crew and into the relations between crew and captain. In a way reminiscent of Noah—without the

insistent theo-imprint attached to that story—Conrad addresses together the
sea, the planetary, and subterranean affective currents of being.[8]

A storm, a rocky sea, a tsunami, a rogue wave, a viral infection, a prolonged
lull, a shortage of water, a splintered mast, a hurricane—such planetary, nonhuman disruptions disrupt delicately organized balances of life on board a small
ark tossing around on an open sea; a panic may erupt just when close collaboration between captain and crew is most urgently needed, and indeed, when the
inner balance of the captain is most needed. Suddenly a ship seems small, at the
mercy of the seas it traverses. Here are a few things Lawtoo and Conrad say:

> Time and again, we have seen that a nonhuman, often unrecognized,
> yet always menacing shadow lurks in the background of Conrad's fic-
> tions of the homo-duplex. (Lawtoo 2016, 92)

> [A] mimetic approach requires a specific foreground to environmental
> forces first, in order to subsequently trace the complex interplay of hu-
> man and nonhuman forces. (93)

> [I]t also opens up channels for contagious infections that can poten-
> tially penetrate, contaminate, and eventually undermine the authori-
> tarian power structure of on which the body-politic of the ship qua
> "state" rests. (97).

> Panic is a mimetic reaction par excellence insofar as it spreads conta-
> giously from subject to subject, overtaking like a wave the entire social
> body and generating a type of horror that introduces sameness where
> difference should be preserved. (69)

During his engagement with Conrad on life at sea Lawtoo invokes the notions
of duplex-selves and duplex communities, in which mimesis plays a prominent
role; he then moves to multiplex-selves and a multiplicitous social order in
which diverse regions of past experience installed on different registers are activated to respond to new situations. A captain might recall an earlier incident at
one moment and enact a purposive instinct absorbed from the past at another.
Something like a point guard does at a key moment when allowing finely honed
and now unconscious instincts to take over. Why? Consciousness is slow and
reveals tells. The self itself is a social structure with each voice operating on a
distinctive level of refinement and affective energy. So say Nietzsche, Conrad,

Proust, and Lawtoo; hundreds of threads of different strength and tendency jostle around ready to be called up during a crisis at sea, particularly when the sea is stormy and decisive coordination is needed. Those old debates between the singular individual and the collective order now bite the dust; so do the dichotomies between innate instinct and detached reason. Life at sea throws them overboard. Thus Spoke Zarathustra and Nidesh Lawtoo.

When at their best during an emergency the captain and crew become simultaneously attuned to each other and to shifting situational challenges facing the ship. They often do not have much time to ponder. But such arrangements and prompts to collective improvisation are also fragile. Emergency, the possibility of catastrophe—indeed the very type of event for which the multiplicitous order has been forged—show how fragile the complex can become, how susceptible it is to breakdown, to panic, to rebellion at discordant moments. One guy goes berserk in a Conrad scene; his panic then followed by a captain's order drowned out by the raging sounds of a storm. Other crew members now become unhinged. A new contagion races through the ship, like a viral infection, only faster. The ship may falter. Or perhaps the captain himself, a denialist incapable of acknowledging how fragile things can be, panics under pressure. The possibility of a coherent response to emergency then collapses. Of course, things may hold together. But the probability of that happening improves if you have already acknowledged the fragility of a world in which affective contagion does not merely flow through crews but also bounces from rocky planetary events into and across affective contagions. Mimesis.

The fragility at the heart of a city-state, as exposed by Sophocles, the precarity of a ship (or Ark)) at sea, as shown by Conrad and Lawtoo, and the double planetary/imperial crunch faced by racialized, postcolonial non-temperate regions today have also infiltrated into the conditions of large states and imperial global orders. We—the latter—are now cast onto open seas, rocking along in wooden arks, during a volatile planetary period that invades and jolts various geo-capitalized regions and constituencies in diverse ways. Entire ways of life are at stake. And the ensemble of constituency denials, evasions, casualisms, and belligerent nihilisms infecting the first world—meaning the diverse, collective prompts to panic and denial in play today—carry tragic potentialities for hegemonic regimes in temperate zones who pull the most climate triggers and, above all, for regions in non-temperate zones that have pulled the fewest triggers and feel the worst immediate effects of the impersonal planetary circuits triggered by imperialists. The capitalist triggers activate planetary amplifiers of various sorts, which then recoil back upon diverse regions in different ways to be absorbed into cultural modes of embodiment. For example, capitalist carbon emissions spawn more intense El Niños, which in turn slow down and decrease the absorption capacities of trade winds heading east, carrying the potential to interrupt monsoon seasons in West Africa and India, as happened rather recently in 1897, creating a devastating famine. Impersonal circuits of imperial power, creating huge gaps between the source of emissions and the planetary distribution of enlarged effects. Or, accumulating emissions in large capitalist states may well release methane sediments in the polar regions, with this secondary planetary amplifier then fomenting a degree of climate warming that is much higher than that provoked by the initial emissions alone. Inducing a series of amplifiers, which means that a later reduction in capitalist emissions would not be matched by a corollary reduction in temperatures, storm severity, wildfires, glacier melts, hurricane intensities, drought retraction, algae blooms, and sea level rises.

We are today all in open seas bouncing around in "sovereign" arks of different sizes and resources, facing a series of tsunamis, primed to enact a series of panic responses ill-suited to the situation. This is not a call to pessimism—which is a spectatorial view set into competition to its twin, optimism; it is a call to develop a more radical politics on both the visceral and refined registers of being, a politics appropriate to a new, previously unexpected, era.[9] It is, above all, a call to overcome the climate casualism—with its implicit sense of parallelism between climate triggers and climate results—that still haunts too many humanists and citizens.

Notes

1   Hereafter quoted as *J*.

2   For an account of the history of these debates, first, within geology and, second, between geologists and Christian theologians about Noah and the Black Sea Deluge, see Montgomery. This book not only reviews the back and forth between geologists and Christians; it also records how a series of earlier geological claims about this and other great floods were first condemned as heresy by geologists upholding the geo-dogma of planetary gradualism. It also compares the history of contested findings with respect to the Noah flood to several other flooding events, each with both a geo-history of its own and accompanied between the 1920s and now by a series of debates between those geologists defending the dictum of gradualism and those pressed to call it into question. I am particularly taken with his account of a geologist named Harlem Bretz was long treated as a heretic for contending that the east Washington area of the United States had been hit by a huge flood until considerable evidence showed that Lake Missoula had indeed erupted into an overwhelming flood. When Betz was finally recognized in his nineties he said, "we are all now catastrophists."

3   This version of the story is supported by Ryan and Pitman 1998. Their claim requires the assumption that the event was later set in Mesopotamia by refugees from the Black Sea Del-

uge. Its support is the lack of evidence of any such major conflagration in Mesopotamia itself, even though notable floods did occur in the Tigris and Euphrates rivers.

4   It is notable that the nineteenth-century European philosopher who *emphasized* how rocky planetary processes could be at times is also one who emphasized the need to fold existential affirmation into the soft tissues of life. If you advance the first view about the planet the second infusions are needed to fend off *ressentiment*. See Nietzsche 1978. René Girard argues that Job was the scapegoat of a people seeking to unite themselves around punishment of him (1987). I find such a reading to be at least incomplete. The Theophany in Job teaches him that the earth is a grand repository of numerous species and powerful forces, and it may well not place humanity at the highest pinnacle of divine concern. Both the friends of Job and Girard seem to miss the key point of that story. A discussion of the *Book of Job* can be found in Connolly 2017, 1–9.

5   For a discussion of his event see Pearce 2007, ch. 26, "The Fall."

6   For a superb review of this century long debate between Einstein and Bergson, continued today by the followers of each, see Canales 2015.

7   The latter, exploring unpublished late manuscripts by Marx, shows how he became very ecological and also rejected the idea that capitalism sets a solid precursor to communism. He began to accept a "multi-linear and non-reductionist theory of history" (Saito 2022, 191).

8   For a discussion on the relevance of Conrad's narratives of the sea for navigating the Anthropocene, see also Connolly and Lawtoo 2021 [editors' note].

9   Those who wish to consider the "improbable necessity" of the politics of swarming can consult Connolly 2017, chapter 5. Such a politics consists of multiple sites of action, each with some potential to magnify the effects of the others. The various modes are to be capped by a series of cross-regional general strikes by citizens of the earth demanding remedial action by companies, states, churches, consumers, universities, and international organizations. You probably cannot hope to foment the latter strikes unless the lower case operations help to set them up.

Bibliography

Asad, Talal (2003). *Formations of the Secular: Christianity, Islam, Modernity*. Stanford: Stanford University Press.

Canales, Jimena (2015). *The Physicist and the Philosopher*. Princeton: Princeton University Press.

Connolly, William, E. (2017). *Facing the Planetary*. Durham, NC: Duke University Press.

Connolly, William E., and Nidesh Lawtoo (2021). "Planetary Conrad: William Connolly and Nidesh Lawtoo in Dialogue." *The Conradian* 46.2, 144–171.

Davis, Mike (2017). *Late Victorian Holocausts*. New York: Verso.

Girard, René (1987). *Job, The Victim of His People*, trans by Yvonne Frecerro. Stanford: Stanford University Press.

Lawtoo, Nidesh (2016). *Conrad's Shadow: Catastrophe, Mimesis, Theory*. East Lansing: Michigan State University Press.

Montgomery, David (2012). *The Rocks Don't Lie: A Geologist Investigates Noah's Flood*. New York: W.W. Norton & Company.

Moore, Jason (2015). *Capitalism in the Web of Life*. New York: Verso.

Nietzsche, Friedrich (1978). *Thus Spoke Zarathustra*, trans. Walter Kaufmann. New York: Penguin.

Pearce, Fred (2007). *With Speed and Violence: Why Scientists Fear Tipping Points in Climate Change*. Boston: Beacon Press.

Rosenberg, David, and Harold Bloom (1990). *The Book of J*. New York: Grove Weidenfeld.

Ryan, William, and Walter Pitman (1998). *Noah's Flood: The New Scientific Evidence about the Event that Changed History*. New York: Simon and Schuster.

Saito, Kohei (2022). *Marx and the Anthropocene*. Cambridge: Cambridge University Press.

Serres, Michel (2004). *Branches*, trans. Randolph Burks. New York: Bloomsbury.

BEYOND BRAIN AND BODY

A Dialogue with Vittorio Gallese

Vittorio Gallese and Nidesh Lawtoo

I think that a dialogue between cognitive neuroscience
and philosophy is not only desirable but necessary.

—Vittorio Gallese, "The Two Sides of Mimesis"

The genealogical orientation of mimetic studies led us to repeatedly look back
to the ancient philosophical realization that humans are imitative animals to
account for the protean transformations of homo mimetics in the present and
future. This entailed, among other things, operating a paradigm shift of emphasis in contemporary discussions of mimesis that can no longer be restricted to
realism but benefit from recognizing the imitative foundations of embodied
subjectivity. The genealogy of mimesis we have traced in the first two volumes of
Homo Mimeticus is of ancient origins; it finds in modernist philosophical physicians powerful advocates of the laws of imitation that flow contagiously between
self to others, stretching across the body politic. The untimeliness of a long genealogy in mimetic studies is now confirmed by the fact that the mimetic turn
found in contemporary neuroscience a timely empirical supplement to promote
multiple *re*-turns to homo mimeticus that cut across the brain/body divide.

    As is by now well-known, in the early 1990s a team of neuroscientists led
by Giacomo Rizzolatti working at the University of Parma made an astonishing
discovery. Like many important discoveries, it was accidental, unintentional,
and thus unforeseen; yet it will turn out to have a major impact that will go
well beyond the neurosciences, informing and transforming the human sciences

as well—if only because it both confirms and deepens our understanding of humans' all too mimetic behavior. The discovery itself didn't directly concern *Homo sapiens* at first but, rather, our close primate cousins, macaque monkeys in particular. Electrodes were in fact implanted in the premotor cortex area of the macaque's brain to measure motor actions, or movements. What surprised the Parma team was that an activation occurred not only when there was direct movement but also at the sight of movement, as the macaque saw the experimenter move the arm to reach for an object, for instance. Whether that object was a banana, an Italian *cornetto,* a peanut, or a gelato, is not essential and might belong to the register of myth—as Newton's famous apple.

Crucial for the humanities was the hypothesis that if motor neurons activate at the mere sight of movements in monkeys, evolutionary theory would suggest that these neurons should be present in humans as well. This is, indeed, what later experiments with single-neurons recordings in epileptic patients confirmed, leading to the discovery of a mirror neuron system (MNS) in humans. Why is this discovery important for the humanities in general and mimetic studies in particular? Because if neurons in the human brain activate not only at the sight of movements but also of facial expressions and images thereof, then, the ideal of an autonomous, fully rational, and solipsistic subject central to a dominant (read idealist) philosophical tradition reveals itself to be a myth. If we look in the empirical mirror, what appears instead is what mimetic studies has been arguing all along: namely, that *Homo sapiens* is also a homo mimeticus that is embodied, intersubjectively attuned to the mind of others since birth (actually, even prior to it), and open to unconscious forms of affective mimesis with the potential to give us a more or less direct intuitive access to what others may feel and think.

Skeptics might be tempted to retort: What now? Are complex human processes such as imitation, empathy, sympathy, and even something as complex as understanding the minds of others the simple product of neurons activated at the sight of gestures and facial expressions? How can something as concrete as physiological movements be linked to something as abstract as mental thoughts? And are empathy and understanding the only functions of mirror neurons anyway? What about the misunderstandings triggered by automatic mirroring reactions that, especially in a crowd but not only, can lead to antipathy, resentment, and violence?

These are valid objections that raise the double phantom of reductionism and scientific optimism. It is thus crucial to immediately qualify at least three points: first, neuroscientists are often the first to stress that "neurons are not epistemic agents" (Gallese 2011, 92) and thus emphasize that intersubjective phenomena cannot be "reduced" (92) to electric discharges in the brain; second, there is still debate about the specific role the MNS plays in theory of mind, imitation, and empathy (Hickok 2014); third, "situational" and cultural approaches attentive to experiential differences (in terms of gender, race, sexuality, life-experience and other categories) are needed to supplement the neurosciences (Pitts-Taylor 2013). Last but not least, a long genealogy in the humanities warns us that mimetic processes do not only generate rational understanding and empathy based on patho-*logies* but also irrational misunderstandings and violence generative of cultural pathologies. And yet, precisely for these and other reasons productive dialogues across nature/culture binaries are urgently called for—a transdisciplinary move that is all the more relevant as it is part of the entangled genealogies of mirror neuron theory and mimetic studies.

Before launching into such a dialogue with one of the originary members of the Parma team, and one of the most outspoken advocates of the centrality of mirror neurons for aesthetic, cultural and philosophical debates, let me briefly consider both sides. On the side of the neurosciences, it is worth recalling that Rizzolatti and Sinigaglia open *Mirrors in the Brain* (2008) with an affirmation by the theater and film director Peter Brook who claimed that "the neurosciences had finally started to understand what was common knowledge in the theater" (2008, 1). Early on, then, neuroscientists encouraged scholars to situate the discovery of mirror neurons in a broader genealogy in the humanities that finds in performance, and thus mimesis (from *mîmos*, actor or performance), a privileged starting point. Conversely, on the mirroring side of mimetic studies, a genealogy of thinkers has long been sensitive to the mirroring properties of the human mind, if not brain. As we have seen in both volumes of *Homo Mimeticus*, already Plato had expressed the fear that actors' impersonating a role via mimetic "speech or bodily bearing" (1963, 393c) would spread a contagious pathos from the stage to the audience spell-bound by those mirroring gestures. Closer to us, but still a century before the discovery of mirror neurons, Friedrich Nietzsche put forward the diagnostic that there is an "ancient association between movement and speech" (1982, 142:89). And, a few years later, Gabriel Tarde argued that "there is in the nervous system an innate tendency to imitation" (2001, 148; my trans.), among other precursors I discussed elsewhere.[1]

Notice that these advocates of an unconscious that has embodied mimesis more than dreams as a via regia are emphatically non-reductionist thinkers; and yet, their theory of imitation suggests that a dialogue cutting across old-fashioned "two cultures" divides should emerge naturally between exploratory advocates of both traditions. We could even go further and say that if our genealogy of *homo mimeticus* is correct, then the discovery of mirror neurons would provide an empirical confirmation, re-discovery, and extension of a long tradition in mimetic studies that was marginalized for a long time but is now *re*-turning to the forefront of the theoretical scene.

It is thus with great pleasure that we conclude *Homo Mimeticus II* by engaging in a dialogue with Vittorio Gallese.[2] Part of the original Parma team led by Rizzolatti, Gallese not only contributed to the (re)discovery that humans are imitative animals; he is also a philosophically-oriented thinker, or, to inverse a Nietzschean appellation, a physician-philosopher with a refined artistic sensibility. A strong ally for the mimetic turn, Gallese will help us articulate the theoretical implications of what he calls "embodied simulation" relevant for imitation, but also empathy, theory of mind, aesthetics, cinema and emerging hypermimetic subjects in the digital age as well.

I. Genealogical Connections: Mirror Neurons Now and Then

Nidesh Lawtoo (NL): In many ways, the discovery of mirror neurons lends empirical support to the hypothesis of homo mimeticus: namely, that humans are not autonomous creatures but are relational, embodied creatures wired to respond to the emotions of others, for good and ill. When mirror neurons were first discovered they generated a lot of debate within and beyond the neurosciences. For an idealist tradition in the humanities, they challenged a certain idea of what *Homo sapiens* should be: solipsistic, fully autonomous, rational, and disembodied. Debates are still ongoing concerning the specific role the MNS actually plays in complex emotions like empathy or sympathy. Thirty years later, what can you say that is neurologically certain about mirror neurons and what more has been learned since?

Vittorio Gallese (VG): First of all, we can say a lot more about mirror neurons in living animals at large. Our discovery was based on recordings of mirror neurons in macaque monkeys; it happened in 1991 with the first paper appearing in 1992. In the last thirty years, this neurophysiological mechanism has been revealed in singing birds, rodents, mice and rats, bats, marmosets, and even at the subcortical location: a very recent paper by our colleagues at Stanford University shows evidence of mirroring mechanism in the hypothalamus, dealing with aggressive behavior. So, the very same neurons that are active during the expression of antagonistic behavior also fire when the animals witness the aggressive behavior displayed by another animal. Evolutionary speaking, it is thus most likely a very old mechanism. Nevertheless, it subserves different adaptive roles in different species that have different lifestyles and have been adapting into different ecological niches.

That said, the most exciting part of the story, at least for me and I suppose for you too, consists in the fact that we as humans have mirror neurons as well. Since the original discovery and very early on there was a strong surge for empirical evidence in favor of a similar mechanism in humans. The first empirical evidence came from a transcranial magnetic stimulation (TMS) study, performed in Parma; the leading scientist was Luciano Fadiga. It showed that there is a motor facilitation in the corticospinal pathway when you observe someone performing a movement. So, you have an increase of the motor-evoked potential if you stimulate the motor cortex while participants are looking at someone grasping an object with a hand. Then there was brain imaging evidence that demonstrated that the very same somatotopic arrangement that controls the execution of different body movements can also be activated by the observation of similar body movements performed by someone else.

Around 2000, together with the American philosopher Alvin Goldman, we then went out on a limb so to speak: we speculated that the same logic in the human brain perhaps could be uncovered also in the domain of sensation and emotions.[3] A few years later our group was the first to empirically demonstrate that this hypothesis was correct. The first evidence came from an experiment on physical disgust where we showed that the anterior insula can be activated both by the subjective experience of physical disgust but also when witnessing the facial expression of disgust displayed by another human being. One year later came the evidence about visuotactile mirroring: the second somatosensory area is a part of the cortical network that maps our tactile experiences distributed in different parts of the body that can also be driven by the observation of the tactile experience on the body of someone else.

That was the major trigger for me to part from the traditional simulation theory as put forward by Goldman, which I thought was too cognitive and dependent on introspection, on putting yourself voluntarily into the mental shoes of someone else.[4] Instead, I proposed the idea of *embodied simulation*, which constitutes an attempt to provide a unitary theoretical framework for a variety of phenomena.[5] Some deal with social cognition: empathy, intersubjective relation, mapping the actual motion sensation of others. Yet, it is not confined to the social domain because it also applies to our relation to manipulable objects or to the way our brain-body maps space. Embodied simulation is thus a more general account of perception and imagination.

NL: Starting from the discovery of mirror neurons, then, the ramifications stretch well into problems central to the human sciences as well. To further the bridge between mirror neuron theory and mimetic studies, can you specify how embodied simulation helps us account for mirroring phenomena that operate not at the subpersonal but at the personal and interpersonal level? I am thinking of course of imitation, but also empathy and sympathy.

VG: I think that our discovery of mirror neurons was instrumental in creating, or at the very least greatly boosting, a particular aspect of cognitive neuroscience, which we now designate as social neuroscience: namely, the idea that we should map the brain and the body of individuals particularly when they relate to others. Embodied simulation provides a very parsimonious functional mechanism that shows how all these different aspects that characterize our social cognition rely on a very limited neurophysiological toolkit: namely, the reuse of a variety of brain circuits that serve different purposes to guide our navigation in the world and make us experience our relation to the world while simultaneously enabling us to imitate others, to understand others, to empathize with others.

You mentioned both empathy and sympathy. From an historical point of view, you can see why things got complicated because the Scottish enlightenment, specifically Adam Smith, in *The Theory of Moral Sentiments* (1759) spoke of empathy describing it as sympathy. In my account, empathy and sympathy are two different phenomena. I don't think you can be sympathetic without being emphatic, but you can be empathetic without necessarily being sympathetic. Being empathetic means to feel *with* the other; being sympathetic means to feel *for* the other. So, empathy has nothing to do with the Good Samaritan: that is, being naturally good, or showing the inbound proclivity to do good to others. I think that you can use empathy to manipulate others or commit evil acts. We should keep these two aspects of our sociality separate.

NL: Since you define empathy as a form of feeling with, which is the etymological meaning of *sym-pathos* that got lost in the wake of moralistic accounts of sympathy, maybe this already a good moment to go beyond good and evil and tell you why, as someone trained in the humanities, I got interest in mirror neurons in the first place. Two decades ago, I was working on a PhD on the centrality of unconscious imitation in subject formation in modernist philosophical and literary authors. The thesis was titled *The Phantom of the Ego*, which is a phrase Nietzsche uses in *Daybreak* (1881). He does so to account for an affective permeability between self and others that is not moralistic but troubles the boundaries of individuation while also opening up a mimetic hypothesis on how we understand the feelings of others. In the same book, I was struck by the following diagnostic of what you call empathy and Nietzsche calls *Mitempfindung* in order to designate a shared pathos or *sym-pathos*:

> To understand another person, that is, to *imitate his feelings in ourselves*, we do indeed often go back to the *reason* for his feeling thus or thus and ask for example: *why* is he troubled?—so as then for the same reason to become troubled ourselves. (1982, 142:89)

This is the theory of mind that philosophers to this day have tended to privilege, the so-called "theory theory." But then Nietzsche opens up the following, more embodied perspective:

> it is much more usual to omit to do this [that is, consider the reasons of suffering] and instead to produce the feeling in ourselves after the *effects* it exerts and displays on the other person by imitating [*nachbilden*] with our own body the expression of his eyes, his voice, his walk, his bearing (or even their reflection in word, picture, music). Then a similar feeling arises in us in consequence of an ancient association between movement and sensation (142: 89).[6]

You told me after "The Mimetic Turn" conference that you were familiar with this quote. Could you now specify the ways in which this passage resonates with what you call "embodied simulation" and the "shared manifold of subjectivity" it entails?

VG: I was pointed to this quote in *Daybreak* by Nick Humphrey a long time ago. Since then, I kept quoting it because, on the one hand, it shows how poorly original we are. In a way, we keep reinventing the wheel. Although, at every turn of scientific or technological theoretical development you have a new perspective, a new angle. Through the discovery of mirror neurons, we can now back up this genial intuition of Nietzsche with empirical evidence. But the same applies to a variety of other intuitions that you can trace back throughout the history of human thought and speculation about who we are and how we function in the world.

The recurrence of this intuition sometimes becomes obscured by subsequent theoretical developments. For example, this Nietzschean insight is coherent with the *Einfühlung* aesthetic that was blooming in the German speaking world at the end of the nineteenth century and in the early decades of the twentieth century. Thinkers like Robert Vischer, Heinrich Wölfflin, Theodor Lipps, Aby Warburg, and others became completely obscured in the first half of the twentieth century until today in many quarters of aesthetics and art history. Why? Because the body completely disappeared. Or rather, the body itself is turned into a text, while I would like to hold the opposite perspective: that any text is a body—and literally so. In fact, we embody words and sentences by means of mechanisms that are not very different from those that kick in when we relate with others through our body expression gestures, vocalization, and the like, which, in my view, is by the way where human language originated.

Being acquainted with this aspect of Nietzsche's thought and of similar views in a way reassured me about the theoretical validity of our empirical discovery. As a scientist you're always wondering whether the way you are interpreting your data is correct, whether your data can be replicated. In the background, there is always a lot of anxiety related to what you discovered and most importantly, what is the data supposed to mean: what can you do with those data? What is its heuristic power?

NL: Yes, interpretation is an art, as Nietzsche used to say; it also opens up competing perspectives and evaluations that sometimes, or rather often, generate disagreement. For instance, Gregory Hickok in *The Myth of Mirror Neurons* (2014) convokes the oldest trick in the philosophical handbook as he dismisses (at least in the title, the argument is more nuanced) mirror neurons—or the neurological mask of mimesis—as a "myth," appearance, or illusion. The rhetorical move is as old as Plato.

VG: Yes. In the opening you were mentioning the controversies revolving around our discovery of mirror neurons. In that respect, I like to quote a joke put forward by V. S. Ramachandran many years ago. Whenever you come up with something very new, the first reaction is: "it can't possibly be true." The second reaction after a few years is: "OK it's true but it doesn't explain anything." And finally, and we are not there yet: "Oh yes, it's true; it explains a lot, but we always knew it." [laughs]

In a sense, we are in the middle of the second phase. There are many colleagues who don't want to hear about it to the point that in many papers there are people discussing results that are not only coherent with the framework of mirror neurons but really deal with the very same mirroring mechanism in the human brain. Still, they don't dare to bring up mirror neurons because they are afraid of rejection. So, they come up with the alternative way of designating this mechanism like "action observation network" even if we are dealing with motor areas.

Finally, there is another element that probably didn't help in having a more coherent reaction with respect to the heuristic power of mirror neurons: it is the quantity of bullshit in the public media that revolves around mirror neurons. They became an idiomatic jargon to designate phenomena that, as I mentioned, cannot be directly linked to mirroring, like being sympathetic, being altruistic, being good, etc. This hyper-mediatic attention on this neurophysiological mechanism probably wasn't helpful in convincing many colleagues. Besides the fact that controversy is, of course, a common ingredient of science. So, I'm neither surprised nor bothered about the fact that we cannot all converge on the relevance of this mechanism in explaining social cognition.

NL: On the affirmative side, I mentioned Nietzsche for two related reasons: first because the passage in *Daybreak* among many others was the starting point for me to develop a theory of the mimetic unconscious that is embodied since, for Nietzsche, "the body is a great reason." And second because the theory of homo mimeticus is not only in line with Nietzsche's theory of unconscious imitation; it also inherits from him a genealogical perspectivism that recuperates untimely thinkers who were neglected in their times because they were perhaps ahead of their time.

You mentioned earlier that perceptive theories are sometimes overshadowed by other, more dominant theories. The mimetic unconscious is a case in point: it is not based on a repressive, Oedipal hypothesis that is accessed via the interpretation of dreams; nor does it emerge in imaginary identifications with mirror images, or *imagos*. Rather, it is manifest in everyday life in mirroring intersubjective reactions. Nietzsche, in fact, was an avid reader of theories of hypnosis and suggestion that were entangled with the theorists of *Einfühlung* you mentioned and were left in the shadow in the past century. My genealogical sense is that this neglect is at least partially due to the Freudian "discovery" of the Oedipal unconscious. It left in the shadow the pre-Freudian tradition of an embodied unconscious that was sensitive to unconscious imitation.

VG: Yes, in your book you discuss the tradition of thought of the unconscious preceding Freud.

NL: Right. Along with Mikkel Borch-Jacobsen and others in this volume, I find it important to recuperate this genealogical tradition to further mimetic studies. To give you another example as to how close the tradition of the mimetic unconscious comes to your account of embodied simulation, let me quote an untimely physiologist that inspired Nietzsche's theory of a type of embodied suggestion he called "psycho-motor induction." His name was Charles Féré, a physiologist working under Jean-Martin-Charcot at the Salpêtrière in the 1880s. He wrote a book titled *Sensation and Movement* (1887) where he says:

> It is possible that certain subjects who are particularly sensitive to the phenomenon of induction imitate unconsciously [*imitent inconsciemment*] the movements that necessarily accompany the idea of the one in his presence, and will consequently be led to feel the same emotion, the same thought, in a word, to obey what we call *mental suggestion.* (1900, 16; my translation)

Would you agree that this pre-Freudian physio-psychological tradition that has mental suggestion as a main trigger is in line with the theory of embodied simulation?

VG: Yes, indeed. Thanks to the progress of neuroscience also in psychoanalysis nowadays people speak of the unrepressed unconscious, or implicit memory, a sort of background knowledge, resulting from our constant encounter with the world. The dynamic outcome of this encounter affects the plasticity of the brain-body.

NL: If we move genealogically from the late nineteenth century to the dawn of the twentieth century, in your work you paid specific attention to phenomenology. The focus on lived experience and sensitivity to embodied forms of perception, especially central to Maurice Merleau-Ponty but also Edmund Husserl, Michel Henry and others, can indeed be aligned with both the pre-Freudian tradition of the mimetic unconscious and the aesthetic tradition of *Einfühlung* that were neglected in the past century but are now re-turning to the foreground in the present century, also thanks to the confirmation provided by the discovery

of mirror neurons. What led you back to phenomenology? And what genealogical connections are worth stressing to promote what we call a mimetic turn?

VG: The first attention directed to philosophical speculation in relation to mirror neurons was toward phenomenology. Many years ago, I think it was 2004,
after Marc Jeannerod published a paper on motor simulation, a French philosopher, Jean-Luc Petit wrote a letter to us, saying: "I'm flabbergasted! You should
turn to Husserl! You should read the *Fifth Cartesian Meditation*." So, we invited
him, and he gave a talk at our Institute of Physiology, as it was called back then.
I was already familiar with the phenomenological tradition, particularly with
Merleau-Ponty's *Phenomenology of Perception* in relation to my research on the
way we map space, specifically peripersonal space. I was thus already attuned to
phenomenology, but there was an incredible boost after the discovery of mirror neurons. I started reading Husserl, Edith Stein, the second book of *Ideas*.
Then I dug deeper into Merleau-Ponty. I even approached, although more shily,
Heidegger, Michel Henry, in short, many phenomenological thinkers.

I am not a philosopher, but as a neuroscientist what is central for phenomenology is also central for where I think cognitive neuroscience should head to:
namely, the notion of experience. But as we speak, most of our colleagues are
totally focused on the relationship between the brain and the way we explain
the world away, the way we cognize the world. Very few neuroscientists are interested in the notion of experience, while experience is of course central for
phenomenology.

More recently I also found very interesting to have a dialogue with American
pragmatism, particularly with John Dewey in relation to aesthetics. Although it
was written almost a hundred years ago, *Art as Experience* (1934) is a book that
is still very useful to understand our relationship with cultural artifacts. I would
say that phenomenology on the one hand and pragmatism on the other, as we
speak, are two important aspects of philosophy that I am finding highly relevant
for my work as a cognitive social neuroscientist.

NL: Closer to us and changing perspective, another transdisciplinary theorist
in the humanities who is relevant to discuss the psychological, but also aesthetic, social and anthropological implications of mirror neurons is René Girard.
Girard's mimetic theory tends to be exclusively focused on mimetic desire and
the violence that ensues, which is an important side of imitation. But as you also
point out in an article titled "The Two Sides of Imitation" (Gallese 2011) it is

not the only side, for imitation goes beyond good and evil. In this article you credit Girard's theory of desire as being in line with the intersubjective dynamic of the MNS that opens up the subject to the other—a point also shared by mimetic studies. At the same time, you also balance Girard's unilateral focus on violence with good forms of intersubjective mimesis central to the genealogical tradition we have been tracing.

VG: I had the opportunity and the privilege of becoming personally acquainted with Girard. He organized a seminar that lasted four years: we had two years in Stanford and one year in the Austrian Alps and the final conference in Paris where Girard couldn't attend because he was already ill. In this multidisciplinary seminar on mimesis there were people from many different traditions. One key protagonist beside Girard himself was Andrew Meltzoff, who discovered neonatal imitation. I found Girard's thought fascinating and thought-provoking, particularly if you think where he moved from. He was a comparatist who started from literary criticism and started discussing mimesis in Shakespeare, the double in Dostoevsky, and to build around this literary core a more comprehensive theory of mankind building upon anthropology, psychoanalysis, psychiatry, history, and the like. In a way, he was a man of the Renaissance, a polymath.

And yet, at the same time, the more I delved into his writings and became more acquainted with his model, the more I realized that his idea about mimesis was—in my opinion, and you agree with that, actually you build a well-developed criticism—too one-sided. The mimetic rivalry, which stems from mimetic desire leads to violence that in turn produces the phenomenon of scapegoating upon which the rites and religions are built. This is a possible theory, but reading your last book, *Homo Mimeticus*, it is clear that there are other paths for mimetic studies. With Edgar Morin, for instance, you speak about the likely shamanic origins of paleolithic art in the caves of Chauvet and Lascaux. In our book about the *Empathic Screen* (Gallese and Guerra 2015) with Michele Guerra we do the same: we start with Werner Herzog's documentary, *Cave of Forgotten Dreams* (2010). We both agree that mimesis leads to creativity, social practices, and to the creation of cultural artifacts, which are a trademark of our species. So, I'm totally with you when you pinpoint the one-sidedness of the theory of mimesis put forward by Girard.

NL: Good to hear. Indeed, one of the aims of mimetic studies is to go beyond Girard's theory of violence by considering that not only desire but all affects are imitative. If mimetic desire is the starting point of a quasi-Oedipal triangular structure of ambivalence and rivalry with a model, I introduce the concept of mimetic pathos to stress the centrality of intersubjective flows of sym-pathos from self to other that are in line with a tradition of the mimetic unconscious, find origins in ancient and modern thinkers, and reach up to mirror neurons.

From different angles we reach similar conclusions. In fact, your claim that "prior to any triangular mimetic relationship, the main object of infants' mimesis is the affective behavior of the 'other'" (Gallese 2011, 97) also seems to entail a distance from universalizing triangular structures. The idea that desire leads to an ambivalent and violent relation with a model, culminating with the hypothesis of a founding murder at the origins of culture is as Girardian as it is Freudian, as I tried to show (Lawtoo 2023). Your theory of the shared manifold of intersubjectivity, on the other hand, is much closer to the dynamic of mimetic pathos. This mirroring pathos ties self to others in intersubjective bonds of affective communication that start with a dyadic relation and tend to generate a network that does not fit a triangular structure.

VG: Yes. Not coincidentally, in *Violence and the Sacred* (1972) Girard stresses that the thinker that came closest to the theory of mimetic desire with the original herd, is the Freud of *Totem and Taboo* (1913). The Oedipal origin of this theory, as you pinpoint in *Violence and the Oedipal Unconscious* (2023), is very clear. I think that one of the more neglected aspects that make *Homo sapiens sapiens* who we are, is our neotenic nature: namely, we are born immature. Consider that our brain at birth weighs a few hundred grams as it reaches the completion of its maturation at the end of adolescence, and in adulthood the final weight is 1300–1400 grams. I do not want to reduce human culture to the weight of the brain; but since I think the brain is necessary, although not sufficient, to understand who we are that tells you a lot. The vast part of the development and maturation of this crucial part of our body happens after birth. And happening after birth also means that it happens within a network of social relations. So, in order to become who we are, we need the other.

NL: Indeed, the other as a condition for survival and communal cooperation rather than of mimetic rivalry seems central to both the development of the child and of the species. Any parent can witness the former, but we shall have to return to the latter in the second part.

II. Shared Subjects: Birth of Homo Mimeticus

NL: The mimetic turn aims to operate a paradigmatic shift of emphasis in discussions about mimesis from representing the world toward the subject, ego, or self and its imitative relations to others. It's a complex subject so apologies for the directness of the question but to get us restarted: how would you define the self?

VG: The notion of the self is a contrastive notion: there is no self without the other, and vice versa. I think that the beginning of our development as selves predates the moment of our birth but starts already in the womb. The first relation we experience is with our mother within whose body we grow and develop. This becomes even more evident if we enjoy the company of someone else in the womb, as in the case of twins. More than ten years ago, with Umberto Castiello we published a study that we entitled "Wired to Be Social."[7] We were able to show that the kinematics of the arm movements of the twins were quantitatively different from the kinematics of the movement that were self-directed or from the exploratory movement where the twins explore the inner walls of the womb. The kinematic features of the movements when they were targeting the other member of the couple had features that when transposed to adulthood suggested that those were the mostly carefully controlled movements. Put differently, when I move my arm toward another human being like me, I need more control with respect to when I touch my body or when I touch an external object, like the inner wall of the womb. And right after birth, we are wired to imitate the adult that we immediately encounter, which most of the time, if we are lucky enough, is the face of our mother.

NL: Interesting. This relational insight entails a reframing of the subject in line with what we propose as well. For a long time, in fact, a western patriarchal tradition also prevalent in ancient and modern aesthetics equated twins with loss of identity and children with phantasies of Oedipal murders of parental figures; the focus of neurosciences, instead, tends to favor life, intersubjective relations based on "'contagious' mimicking" and is sensitive to maternal bonds based on "empathic awareness" (Ammaniti and Gallese 2014, 27, 28). This binary is of course not stable and mimetic studies is currently engaging the problematic of gendered mimesis via feminist philosophers like Adriana Cavarero who also foregrounds "mimetic inclinations" (Cavarero and Lawtoo 2021) tying the mother the child and vice versa. For the moment, it seems mimesis plays a key role in the birth of the subject.

VG: These results on neonatal imitation cause a problem for some of the most vocal opposers of mirror neurons. For example, the cognitive psychologist Cecilia Heyes tried to reduce the impact and heuristic value of mirror neurons by equating the mechanism of mirroring as one of the many associative mechanisms we can find in our brain. In talks she introduces mirror neurons by showing one of Pavlov's salivating dogs. Heyes has a big problem with neonatal imitation: since there are no mirrors in the womb this seems to suggest that there is a rudimentary form of mirroring that is innate. And being innate defies the idea that all mirroring is simply one of the many associative brain mechanisms. Heyes published papers where she denies the existence of neonatal imitation, which instead is a very solid and empirically documented phenomenon not only in humans but also in non-human primates: it has been shown in chimpanzees, even in macaque monkeys. A colleague, Pier Francesco Ferrari was able to demonstrate not only that neonate macaque monkeys exhibit neonatal imitation but also that when they do so, you see a de-synchronization of the motor part of their brain very similar to the de-synchronization that we spot in human adults' brain when witnessing the action of others.

In sum, mimesis is one of the key ingredients; and it is not coincidental if mimesis is developed to the most extreme level in us humans. In common parlance we say that apes imitate—in Italian we say *scimmiottare*, to ape—but apes and monkeys are very poor imitators in comparison with humans. We are the truly mimetic species, or homo mimeticus, as you say.

Most likely, one possible answer for this discrepancy between human and nonhuman imitation consists in the fact that the "resonating palette," if you allow me the metaphor, in our brain is much wider than in the case of nonhuman primates. As far as we understand, in monkeys mirroring occurs mostly, if not exclusively, for goal-related motor actions. Whereas in the case of the human brain, mirroring also applies to apparently gratuitous movements like raising your arm, jumping, raising your finger. In order to imitate what others are doing you need to copy not only the goal but also the means required to accomplish that very same goal, or final outcome. To do so, you need a mechanism that can replicate not just the goal but also the movements. Apparently, such a mechanism is particularly present in the human brain and less so in the brain of non-human primates.

NL: It's very useful that you go back to development of the child, or ontogenesis, as Andrew Meltzoff's experiments provide a confirmation that at the beginning of a species born too soon, as Nietzsche also foresaw, is indeed mimesis. In the *Gay Science,* he also posited a mimetic communication of gestures and facial expressions at the origins of language and consciousness at the level of the development of the species, or phylogenesis. Both hypotheses have been marginalized in the last linguist-oriented century, but the mimetic turn developed in the present, more embodied and affectively oriented century, is currently reevaluating them. Does neuroscience provide any confirmation on those two fronts?

VG: Yes, the standard mainstream cognitive take on what makes us different from other primates, or mammals, is the fact that we have language. This leads some scholars even to imagine, or dream of a *deus ex machina* biological phenomenon like a genetic mutation. Steven Pinker even defined the Foxp2 gene as the gene of syntax. I think we should bring in a psychoanalyst here to explain why we need to sanitize the body and explain who we are exclusively in logocentric terms. Language, of course, is an ineludible part of who we are. You can't get away from language because we grow into language and, in a way, language deeply affects all the embodied mechanisms that lead us to language. But both from an ontogenetic and from a phylogenetic point of view, you can have cognition without language. And language is an expression or exaltation of mechanisms that are not strictly speaking linguistic. You note that in *Homo Mimeticus*, when you say it's a long story that begins with *Homo ergaster, Homo habilis, Homo erectus* where most likely language as we think of it, was not yet in place. And yet, these hominins were able to build tools. So, they had a social structure; they most likely were imitating others; they had cultural practices that were passed from generation to generation.

NL: Do you also think that mirror neurons played a role in the development of language then?

VG: Yes, I think so. One part of my research and of other colleagues of mine specifically deals with the relationship between the body and language. For example, years ago with George Lakoff, we put forward the idea that concepts can be embodied. The title of the paper was "The Brain's Concepts." And as we speak, we are investigating an apparently very abstract aspect of human language, which is negation: a logical operator that apparently has nothing to do with the body. We are exploring the possible relationship between linguistic negation and motor inhibition. This tells you how closely related I think embodiment, mirroring, embodied simulation, and language are.

NL: Both your theory of embodied simulation and mimetic studies stress humans' ontological openness to the other: namely, the fact that the subject comes into being in a shared experience of mimetic communication with privileged others, the mother *in primis*—what the philosopher and psychologist Pierre Janet called a *socius*. Before Meltzoff, Janet argued late in his career that psychologists focus too much on the individual and should pay more attention to intersubjective relations between self and others—what he also calls "psychology of the socius."[8] In a diagnostic evaluation of this psychology for the future that ties the newborn relation to the mother via imitation, he writes almost a century ago:

> The two personalities, the one of the subject and the one of the socius, emerge together in a confused matter. . . Here we come to what may seem to be a paradoxical idea. Namely, that the distinction between persons, between myself and the socius, is not as fundamental and primitive as we thought it was, and that there was a period, of which there are still traces, where my person and my acts were confused with the person and the acts of others. (Janet 1938, 145)

Does this mimetic hypothesis now find support in contemporary neurosciences?

VG: Yes, of course. A figure that influenced me a lot and that pointed me toward developmental psychology and infant research was Daniel Stern, particularly his book *The Interpersonal World of the Infant* (1985). Together with other psychologists like Edward Tronick or Colwin Trevarthen, for instance, Stern was fundamental to understanding what being human really means. The title of his book betrays the crucial importance of relations in developing our own personal identity, which is not a given. There is no box in the brain where the self sits. If you ask me what the self is about, in the first place, I see the self as a dynamic process. That is, a dynamic process of constant molding and remodeling through the variety of social relations we entertain with others. This is one of the few things I have no doubts about.

NL: It's reassuring to know. In fact, one of the fundamental hypotheses of homo mimeticus is that intersubjectivity is not added to the self or ego but is constitutive from birth onward. There is an ontological openness toward the other, as you also emphasize. This openness is as present in the phenomenological tradition as in thinkers and writers in touch with the body more generally. That is why I appreciate your focus on "intercorporeity" as foundational.

VG: Think about the experiment of Ed Tronick about the still face. Take a video footage of a couple: a neonate and her mother. They are cheerfully playing, exchanging vocalization, making smiles, and gestures. Then, suddenly, the mother is instructed to stop moving, to freeze and to keep an amimic facial expression. You see then that at first the neonate is very surprised about this sudden change in the behavior of the mother. He or she tries with all their means to reengage the mother into the dialogue. When the neonate realizes that all these attempts do not produce any results, he or she starts displaying a stressful reaction, starts crying etc. Many mothers are incapable of remaining still for three minutes, as required by the experimental protocol. This tells us how naturally attuned to the other we are, from very early on. As Max Scheler wrote in *The Nature of Sympathy* (1923), also the way we read our own emotions greatly benefits from the relation we have to other human beings. We literally learn to understand our inner state by interfacing with the other.

NL: Yes, indeed, this constitutive openness to mimetic pathos is *the* fundamental aspect of homo mimeticus. At the same time, as we develop, we also learn to put ourselves at a distance from the pathos of the other via what I call, echoing Nietzsche again, "pathos of distance." In the most acute thinkers and writers of imitation I studied over the years, I found a tension or oscillation between on the one hand, an openness to pathos that favors the sharing of affects, and, on the other, a critical distance that preserves individuality. This double movement of "attraction and repulsion," as Georges Bataille called it, seems fundamental for the emergence of a mimetic yet distinctly unique subject. If mirror neurons contribute to making us unconsciously feel the pathos of the other, I was wondering, then, at the neurological level, what mechanisms allow for the emergence of a more conscious distance? Is there a neurological support to account for this double movement of pathos of distance, mimetic and anti-mimetic tendencies that provides a palpitating heart to mimetic studies?

VG: This is one of the aspects of our research which I find the most difficult to communicate. It is difficult in itself and there are some paradoxical aspects to it. I don't like this spatial metaphor but since everybody uses it, I will use it to facilitate understanding. On the one hand, we have a bottom-up proclivity to simulate, responsible for the immediacy of this mirroring mechanism, of the unconscious nature of the embodied simulation in our brain and in our body when we are confronting the behavior of others; on the other hand, there is a top-down braking system that prevents you to be turned into an echopractic individual who involuntary mimics others. If you display echopraxia you're a patient. Often described by neurologists, echopraxia stems from a degeneration of the most anterior part of the frontal lobe. The idea is that this mechanism stops being subjected to the top-down gating.

One area where this top-down gating inhibition becomes less successful concerns the domain of emotions. If I see you grasping that sheet of paper on the table, unless I'm an echopractic patient, I won't immediately imitate what I see you doing. But if you start laughing, there are very good chances that my zygomaticus major muscle will start to activate in a way which is beyond my control and of which I'm most of the time totally unaware. Mirroring comes in degrees. The results of my empirical investigation suggest that the aspect of behavior where this inhibitory control is less effective is the one of emotions. In the domain of action, we do not automatically imitate unless we do it for the purpose of learning some skill. In that case we are instructed to reproduce exactly what we see. Where are we to locate this control mechanism? Most likely, in the prefrontal cortex: through its connections with the basal ganglia it plays a major role in restraining us from automatically imitating whatever we see.

The same applies to our relation to manipulable objects. Before mirror neurons we discovered a class of premotor neurons we later designated as "canonical neurons" that control the execution of goal-directed grasping behavior: grasping, manipulating, or placing objects. It was discovered that the very same neurons that control the grasping of the object can be activated also by the mere observation of that object; even when you don't have any purpose of actually interacting with the object. So, this activity is a simulation of the movement that you do not perform. The movement is inhibited, but this motor simulation is part of the neural mechanisms that contribute to giving meaning to that object. Hence, that object is the object that it is—be it a glass, a fork, hammer or whatever—not just because of its size or shape but also for its pragmatic intrinsic value. The pragmatic meaning of the object is the outcome of a motor simulation. There are neurological diseases in which if you put a comb in front of the patient the patient will automatically grab it and start combing his or her hair. It's called "utilization behavior." Again, you see a motor simulation that is no longer inhibited that is turned into ostensive behavior. But it's a pathology; we normally don't do that.

NL: Interesting. There is then a neurological top-down/bottom-up mechanism responsible for the oscillation or double-movement between pathos and distance, mimetic and anti-mimetic behavior. Your empirical findings support my hypothesis that it is indeed the sphere of pathos or emotions that is less under the control of top-down, more cognitive, critical distancing.

VG: Right. There are also social influences that are all funneled into our brain. So certain types of behavior are perfectly legitimate in certain cultures. Like making noises with your mouth when you eat noodles in a Japanese restaurant, for instance. I lived in Tokyo for two years and at first, I was a bit surprised to hear these noises. Japanese often don't refrain from it because they claim that by making this noise, you're in a better position to appreciate the taste of the soup. On the other hand, I immediately realized that you don't want to blow your nose with a tissue on the subway because immediately everybody will stare at you!

We are social creatures. Much of our behavior is shaped by mimesis that enables you to perform like the others do. But this mimetic behavior is in turn the outcome of cultural habits and social practices. The body is always the protagonist. But what the body expresses is in turn governed by rules dictated by what the bodies of others are doing. What we call social practices. It is a sort of chiasmatic relationship between my body and the body of others. As for the mirroring mechanism we have been discussing so far, in my opinion, you can't get away without it if you want to understand the social dimension of human beings.

NL: This is exactly the focus of mimetic studies. You also provided the perfect transition to my next question for the third and last part of this dialogue.

III. Reflecting on the Brain-Body: Interdisciplinarity, Experience, Hypermimesis

NL: When it comes to engaging with the neurosciences, one of the fears of scholars in the humanities concerns the double phantom of reductionism and essentialism. From different perspectives, whenever philosophers, anthropologists, historians, or literary theorists address a cultural phenomenon, we argue for the importance of contextualization, specific technical and cultural competences, and sensitivity to social differences in terms of gender, race, class, sex, nationality, and other social categories. In your work, you are mindful of the trap of reductionism. You have, time and again, stressed that neurons are not epistemic or cognitive agents and do not answer all questions operating at the personal and intersubjective rather than subpersonal level. Still, as disciplinary suspicions tend to operate not only consciously but also at the level of the mimetic unconscious, a repetition might help further interdisciplinary exchanges.

VG: Indeed. Well, let me first make this statement, which at first might sound a bit rude. For many years, we have both been engaged in a multidisciplinary take on our specific field of investigation: in your case, it is literature, cinema, philosophy; in my case, it is the brain and the body. In order to do so we had to study a lot. We had to become acquainted with traditions of thought that are not naturally part of our original background: you studied mirror neurons; I studied Girard, Merleau-Ponty and many others. This enterprise takes a lot of time and effort. The majority of our colleagues don't want to do this—perhaps out of laziness, perhaps out of territorial reasons. But dealing with complex questions like "who are we? What does it mean to be human?" encourages us to try hard to see things from a variety of perspectives, moving from the conviction that each singular perspective adds to the picture. Still, when confronting scholars in the humanities, I often happened to be addressed with sentences like: "Oh you're mechanistic! You are a reductionist! These reflexes have nothing to do with culture" etc. These are shortcuts. What really surprises me is the fact that most of these scholars have a very superficial knowledge of what we are talking about. At best, they read the titles or the abstracts most of the time misunderstanding the content. They're talking about something they really don't know. It's easier to wipe off the table a cognitive neuroscientist by saying: "It's mechanistic. It's reductionist."

Of course, we are reductionists, but in methodological sense and not in an ontological sense. I owe this distinction to my friend philosopher Thomas Metzinger. I think it's a very useful distinction between methodological and ontological reduction. I *cannot* be an ontological reductionist because as a neuroscientist I'm the first to know that what's going on inside my brain is just spiking neurons, electricity phenomena. Neurons don't think, don't imagine, don't experience emotions. Nothing of this vocabulary can be attributed to neurons. Neurons either fire or do not fire. And when they fire, they can modulate the frequency at which they produce spikes. Period. All this vocabulary, as you said, refers to the personal level of description, which includes the neurons, the liver, the heart, breathing, the world to which we adapted. We have the force of gravity, for instance, and it's not coincidental that we developed spatial meta-phors, so up is good, down is bad, and I could continue.

In sum, the first element to retain is that we are embedded in the physical world that provides a series of constraints on the way life developed on our plan-et. The second element is that the brain is fully integrated within the entirety of our body. The more we study the brain, the more we discover how this inter-twining affects the way the brain reacts to what we designate as external stimuli. There are now more and more neuroscientists, me included, that are studying the interplay between the heart and the brain, between the brain, the heart and the breathing system. Even within the West, almost a century ago, neurologists like Kurt Goldstein—not coincidentally very influential to Merleau-Ponty—presented this more holistic scenario. If you move to the oriental tradition, ho-lism is the rule of the game. And I think that moving from a completely differ-ent background with completely different tools and ways of asking questions to human beings, we will converge with the oriental tradition. We don't speak of chakra or meridians. We have a totally different cartography, so to speak. But the more we investigate the brain in relation to the body, the more we envisage the brain not as a magic box in which all kinds of wonders happen but how fully integrated the brain is with the rest of the body. This is one of the reasons why I don't speak of the brain anymore, but I always speak of the brain-body as a unity.

NL: In the context of this brain-body unity then, experience, as you already mentioned, plays a key role in shaping the plasticity of the MNS. Could you then address the relation between the evolutionary foundation of mirror neu-rons that are supposedly present from birth and the socio-cultural role of senso-rimotor experience in the development of what philosophers call consciousness, or self.

VG: In that respect, recently in the media you could read that twenty-five years later, philosophy beats science one to zero. In 1998, there was a bet in Tucson, and I was there. It was an international conference titled "Towards the Science of Consciousness." The philosopher was David Chalmers, and the neuroscientist was Christoph Koch. Koch said that in twenty-five years I'm pretty sure that we will solve what Chalmers defined as the "hard problem:" namely, how out of this billions of spiking neurons experience is generated. Well, twenty-five years later, we don't know yet. This still remains an unsolved mystery. It is not foreseeable whether and when this mystery will be solved. That's the reason I think that tackling human behavior from the vantage point of experience is so important. It has been done for another apparent transcendental entity, which is space. Space is by no means transcendental. It's the outcome of the relation of our bodies to the world. We don't speak of space anymore, but we speak of peripersonal space, extrapersonal, space being mapped by the brain in egocentric coordinates, in allocentric coordinates, etc. I always resisted to deal with consciousness with a capital C.[9] I would rather unpack or reduce the complexity of the term into methodologically more manageable entities. To come back to your question, this methodological reduction is the only possible strategy for someone who wants to do empirical science. The trick, then, is to go back to the personal level of description and see what we have learned about the question that we formulated, going through this methodological reduction. This entails asking questions of the brain to the heart, or to the brain-body.

NL: For instance, it has been shown that experience, let's say in playing sports has an impact on the activation of mirror neurons. Say, if somebody is a dancer or a soccer player, their MNS will activate more significantly if they see, respectively, a dance or a game of soccer. There is thus not only a genetic but an epigenetic development that molds the receptivity of the MNS.

VG: Yes, of course. There's plenty of evidence that mirroring mechanisms are the outcome of who you are, which in turn can be translated into the type of experiences that you have had in your life. If you are trained as a classic ballet dancer, the mirroring mechanism responds more vigorously to classic ballet than to capoeira; and vice versa if you are a professional capoeira dancer you see the reversal of the intensity of the activation; and both respond more heavily than a naïve observer who doesn't know how to dance. It's the life experience that literally carves molds in a plastic way the way these mirroring mechanisms are functioning.

NL: So, it's the opposite of essentialism.

VG: Of course. To me the only essential thing that I cannot reduce to something simpler is the body. I don't think I will give up the body. I can give up a more traditional notion of representation, although I resist the idea that we can entirely get away with something that in another domain can be defined as a representation. For example, I think you can speak of representation not just in linguistic terms but also in bodily format. You don't want to call it representation? OK, let's call it mapping. You can come up with different terms. But there must be something that kicks in also when there's nothing out there, for example when you imagine something: so imagination is another form of simulation.

NL: Mapping or simulation are indeed a better alternative to representation that in its multiple meanings (metaphysical, imaginary, or artistic) privileges vision over all the other, more bodily senses—a problem internal also to the trope of the "mirror" once central to Jacques Lacan's mirror stage and now at play in mirror neurons, which are not restricted to vision, as you explained. To continue the discussion on experience and simulation: since so far mimetic studies and embodied simulation provide two faces of the same Janus-faced homo mimeticus, let me try to anticipate some agonistic questions that might emerge in the future, as we continue to further the mimetic turn across body-brain binaries.

The tradition of hypnosis I mentioned early on reminded me of the risk of simulation emerging from intersubjective mimetic experiences. At the end of the nineteenth century there was a debate between Jean-Martin Charcot at the Salpêtrière in Paris, who argued that hypnosis was restricted to hysterical patients who displayed stereotypical symptoms like somnambulism or catalepsy, whereas Hippolyte Bernheim of the School of Nancy argued that Charcot's patients were simply simulating, like mimetic actors, the symptoms Charcot's theory expected them to display. I am not implying that the same type of simulation is at play when the activation of mirror neurons is measured for this occurs at the subpersonal, unconscious level, as you explained very clearly. However, given your phenomenological emphasis on the body and the fact that you have yourself been critical of the imprecise measurements of fMRI scans that only measure the MNS' activation via the presence of oxygen in relatively large areas of the brain, I was wondering: could the specific *bodily* position of a subject within a fMRI [functional magnetic resonance imaging] scanner—the horizontal position, focus on specific images or sounds, isolation from others, and thus brain-bodies not in a natural, or rather natural-cultural interpersonal relation— doesn't somehow all this artificial context operating on bodily dispositions have the potential to amplify (or diminish) mirror neuron activation?

VG: Well, as I always keep telling my students, when we want to understand something of the human condition by relying on a neuroscientific approach— which boils down to putting people into a fMRI scanner, so lying down or recording the electrical activity of the brain by means of the MEG or magnetoencephalography, which means sitting on a chair—it is like looking at the world through a peeping hole. It's an incredibly artificial situation, which only vaguely resembles real life situations. This is the best we can do with the current technological limitations. For example, nowadays in the case of the neuroscience of non-human primates there are chronically implanted recording devices that enable you to record brain activity wirelessly from macaques when they are freely able to behave in a room like this one: with no constraints, not sitting on a chair, not with the head fixed but behaving, well, not entirely as they would do in the wild, but still with a much higher degree of ecological plausibility. This type of solution is not yet available in the case of humans, but I'm quite optimistic. When I started this career there were no such things as fMRI or MEG, TMS [transcranial magnetic stimulation], there was nothing, just single-neurons electrophysiology in experimental animals and a very crude type of electroencephalography in humans. Now we have all this new technology. I think the ultimate goal is to test the brain-body in a situation that is more ecologically plausible.

That said, are we influenced by this technological apparatus? Well, there are studies that were able to demonstrate its reliability through repetitive recordings of brain activity at different times, and simultaneously mapping the plasticity of the response. In fact, we are having experiences that, in turn, affect the way our brain-body responds to what we are exposed to. In sum, even considering the artificiality and poor ecological plausibility of the approach, I think we still can understand a lot despite the present limitations.

NL: I have another, perhaps provocative, question on the discovery of mirror neurons, which was purely accidental...

VG: Absolutely serendipitous.

NL: At the same time, you also said somewhere that the Parma team was ready for this discovery, asking the right questions, so to speak.

VG: Oh yes, by all means.

NL: So, here comes the provocative, culturally oriented question: is it a coincidence that this important discovery took place in Italy first, and that some of the most important mirror neuron theorists often come from oral cultures that rely more on embodied forms of communication? It's a stereotype but there is some truth in it: as an Italian speaker myself who then moved to Nordic countries, I can certify from experience that Italians communicate a lot more via gestures and facial expressions than, say, British, Scandinavian, or even North American people. Could it be that a culture that is more immersed in embodied modes of non-verbal communication helped to put the brain-bodies of the Parma team in a position to be more sensitive, attuned, or ready to discover this phenomenon, which after all, implicates the scientific observer in what is observed?

VG: This is indeed a rather provocative question. Rizzolatti was born in Kiev from a second-generation Italian father and a Russian mother. We are still within the realm of continental Europe in that respect. I think that more than national-ity what makes the difference is the scientific cultural tradition and the method put forward by Rizzolatti. I started working as an intern in his lab in 1979, so we go way back. His method was revolutionary. The standard methodology was to train the monkey to perform a given task, while recording simultaneously the single neural electrical activity, and correlating the two off-line. Our approach was completely different due to our training. Rizzolatti came from neurology and neuropsychology, the study of human patients, so he tried to apply the same methodology to neuroscience. In the lab jargon, what we were doing was apply-ing a 'clinical study' of the neurons. This entailed not just asking one question and seeing how many of the neurons correlated or not with their responses to their single question. Rather, we were trying to ask as many questions as possible.

For instance, while testing motor properties in the motor part of the brain we were also testing sensory properties, tactile properties, auditory properties, visual properties, etc. Of course, you cannot ask all the possible questions, which are potentially infinite. Still, we did our best to ask as many questions as possible to the neuron we were recording from, to fully understand the functionality going on in that part of the brain. And it was by applying this methodology that motor neurons guiding, orienting or reaching movements turned out to be re-sponsive also to touch and to visual stimuli, moving around the same body part. This led to the discovery that vision can be mapped in the brain not only in a reti-no-centric or oculo-centric frame of reference but also in a body-centered frame of reference. A few years later, this then led neuropsychologists like Marshall and Halligan to test hemi-spatial neglect in human patients asking questions that were never asked before. For instance, can this neglect be dissociated for perip-ersonal and extrapersonal space, as Rizzolatti had demonstrated experimentally in nonhuman primates—and they discovered that also in humans.

If you don't ask, of course, you don't have answers. So this methodology is the outcome of a particular way of doing neuroscience that is related to the fact that most of us were Doctors of Medicine (M.D.s) and trained as neurolo-gists: Massimo Matelli was a neurologist, Giovanni Pavesi was a M.D., Rizzolatti was a M.D. trained as a neurologist, Luciano Fadiga was an M.D., Giuseppe di Pellegrino who's the first author of the first paper on mirror neurons was himself a M.D and a neurologist, so am I. In sum, you look at the brain very differently with the medical background with respect to if you come from computer science, psychology, or other disciplines. You ask different questions, and it's a pity that fewer and fewer M.D.s dedicate themselves to neuroscience.

NL: Thanks for this important methodological clarification. A side of me—probably the Nietzschean one—continues to suspect that culture might be operative in unconscious ways in the body-brains of perfectly trained, well-rounded M.Ds., generating *patho*-logies in which the bodily pathos helps inform or direct the scientific logos and techne of medical doctors. But I might myself have been biased by philosophical physicians here. Your mirroring point as a physician-philosopher is well-taken and equally in line with mimetic studies: namely, that depending on the scientific training and formation thinkers and scientists develop a different diagnostic logos on mimetic pathos, or patho-*logies*. From either side of the brain-body, pathos-logos, connection we have indeed a mirroring diagnostic that informs bodies and minds, individually but also collectively, in a scientific team or at the broader social level.

To now shift perspective from the individual to the collective level, another major context that reveals with striking clarity the all too human tendency to imitate, often unconsciously, is what was once called mass or crowd (*foule, folla, Masse*). In the late nineteenth century, across Europe there was a discipline that emerged to study crowd behavior, namely crowd psychology, and mimetic studies is currently revisiting this tradition. Still today, in fact, immersion in a crowd seems to have a physio-psychological effect on our bodies and brains that make us more vulnerable, often unconsciously, to what an entire tradition in crowd psychology, drawing on a medical terminology, called "contagion." Obviously, it's more difficult to measure empirically the activity of the MNS in a crowd, so most neuroscientific experiments tend to focus on individuals. At the same time, I have read that you recently developed an experiment on the role of emotions in cinema.[10] What were the findings?

VG: Now a hot topic in social neuroscience is synchronization not just of brain activity but also of heart activity, when for instance, a group of people behaves in a similar way, or are exposed to similar stimuli. A couple of years ago we recorded heart activity in a group of spectators that were looking at an actor-based performance and published a paper about it. We were able to show that there was a significant correlation between the way these people aesthetically evaluated the performance they attended to, and the way their heartbeats synchronized. The more the heart synchronized during the performance, the more they later evaluated aesthetically the performance in a similar way.

A colleague of mine, Luciano Fadiga, is now studying the reception of music in an audience by monitoring with an infrared thermal camera the variation of the skin temperature of the faces of the spectators. What you see is that in topic moments of the musical performance they synchronize: the color of their skin changes simultaneously, which means they are most likely undergoing similar emotions. I would definitely say that living an experience as a member of a crowd amplifies the experience. I mean if you watch a football game alone sitting on your couch or sharing the experience in the stadium, there's no match. It's completely different. Similarly, watching a movie in a movie theater when it was still fashionable clearly amplifies your reaction. I remember when I was a kid seeing a funny movie in a movie theater sometimes meant you had to go twice. In fact, the first time you couldn't hear the sentences that were crowded by the laughter spreading all over the audience. The same occurs with other emotions like fear. There is thus a multiplying factor that stems from the fact that a given experience is shared by many others.

The neuroscience of this sharing of experience is moving its first steps, mainly for technological reasons. If you ask me, I would like to record simultaneously from fifty people in a movie theater or in a concert hall, but I do not have the means to purchase fifty EEG [electroencephalogram] caps. It's very expensive and it requires a lot of people, but it's technically already feasible in principle. I think that the more noninvasive methodologies will be developed, the more we are going to see neuroscientists investigating what interests you—a very important aspect of mimesis—which is the added value of the people with whom you shared the experience.

NL: I look forward to that! To move toward a conclusion, this leads directly to your work on cinema. You have written a beautiful book with film scholar Michele Guerra titled *The Empathic Screen* (2015) that draws on both mirror neuron theory and film theory to open up what you call "experimental aesthetics" (2015, xviii). This is a promising area for further dialogues with mimetic studies. Cinema is, of course, a mimetic medium in the sense that it represents reality, but cinematic mimesis also operates on the body-brains of homo mimeticus. What are the main insights that emerge from this book? And can you explain how cinematic techniques like camera movement, angles, sound etc.

generate an embodied simulation that chains us to screens and leads to sharing emotions with fictional characters?

VG: One of the many aspects that I really enjoyed in *Homo Mimeticus* is when you underline several times that when we speak of mimesis we should leave behind the stereotypical account of mimesis of a passive and mechanistic reproduction of what is being imitated. Instead, you underline the creative, and active aspect of mimesis that sets into motion practically all parts of our brain and of our body. Of course, the same occurs when we experience movies. This, again, has been intuited a long time ago. With the guidance of Michele Guerra, who is a film theorist, I discovered how early on psychologists were interested in the impact that the cinema had on spectators. Hugo Munsterberg is one of the most interesting examples. Already in 1916, a few years after cinema was invented, he writes *The Photoplay*, where he asks himself: "why is cinema so powerful? why is cinema driving so many people going to the movies? why it's so effective?" Because it pulls the very same strings that are pulled by reality. However, just because cinema is a cultural artifact with all the technicalities like editing, camera movements, the use of sound, editing, close-ups, it reconfigures reality through mimesis—in cinema but also in literature or in painting—we acquire new knowledge about the world and about ourselves.

So that's why I think that you properly stress that mimesis cannot be reduced to a mere passive replica of what is already out there. Art and cinema are artistic forms of expression. They are artistic specifically because they reconfigure vision, hearing, in such a way that enables us to approach both reality and us in a different way. It tells us something prosaic reality cannot tell us. It makes visible the invisible to paraphrase Paul Klee in a different artistic domain. But the way it works is always through the very same mimetic mechanism that enabled us to relate to prosaic reality; it is the very same palette, which is being put into action, although differently because the context in which we watch a movie is completely different from the way we relate to emotions and actions in our daily activities; we are still; we are in a dark room; we share the experience with others. All these elements most likely potentiate embodied simulation, the mimetic mechanism that is at the core of the way we relate to feature films. It turns embodied simulation into "liberated embodied simulation."

NL: In fine, let me ask you a future oriented question concerning technology, which is changing very quickly and calls for additional interdisciplinary bridges between the humanities and the neurosciences I foresee will animate new mimetic studies in the years to come. In many ways, cinema is an art that culminated in the past century, just like the novel culminated in the nineteenth century. After the digital revolution and the spread of the Internet in the present century, other new media are now omnipresent and literally at hand. I am thinking of hand-held devices like the smartphone that accompanies homo mimeticus on an everyday basis and amplifies our mimetic dispositions, rendering us hypermimetic. New media do not connect us via traditional face to face embodied interactions but via the mediation of online simulations that may be hyperreal, as Jean Baudrillard stated. I prefer to call it hypermimesis for these simulations retroact on the still embodied nature of human brain-bodies, for good and ill. We are actually generating this double strategy right now for good reasons, via an embodied conversation captured on camera by a digital medium that will create both a written and an online simulacrum that, in turn, will hopefully reach other embodied subjects on the other side of the page-screen. Can you comment on both sides of hypermimesis and perhaps link it to your most recent book project?

VG: I think postmodern thinkers like Guy Debord and Baudrillard were foreseeing something that is now our common experience on a daily basis. In a way, they were prescient. I think they correctly pointed out that with the development of a certain technology or within a particular economy—financial capitalism we would designate it today—it is possible to build a replica of reality that becomes more real than reality. You point out, however, that this doesn't mean that these simulacra are not mediated by the very same mechanisms of mimesis affecting homo mimeticus, and I think you're totally right. Just because I fully agree with you on this point, this opens up a lot of questions about what we know about how this new technological *dispositif* works.

You were mentioning the smartphone. Well, the smartphone introduces at least two novelties with respect to more traditional technological devices that mediated our experience of audiovisual content: first, it's held by our hands, which means the experience occurs systematically within our peripersonal space. This is the space of proxemics; it is the space we were defending from the intrusion of the virus during the climax of the COVID-19 pandemics. It is thus a space that is mapped differently by our brain-body with respect to the far space where we normally have most of our audiovisual experience, be it a big screen in a movie theater or the TV set when we watch TV sitting on the couch. We don't know anything about this new form of mediation. To which extent does the experience of audio-visual contents when it occurs within this peripersonal space produce a different emotional impact with respect to experiences occurring far away from our body?

Second, we need to consider the new performativity of vision. With the TV set we have a control of the content by using the remote control, which is a technological device; in cinema we are totally passive, we see what's going on the screen and have no control; with the smartphone the control is represented by a part of our body. That's the reason I coined the term "the skin-screen:" the screen of the smartphone is like a skin that we touch with a part of our body, our fingers. All the haptic metaphors that were introduced in the aesthetic debate become literal. Bernard Berenson, for example, speaks of the haptic quality of Giotto, which makes Giotto a better painter than his master Cimabue. Or within film theory the phenomenology-inspired theories of scholars who speak of the haptic quality of cinema. Now these haptic qualities become literal because we literally touch the screen.

So, does this periodic performativity of vision have an impact with the way we understand and experience the content we behold through the touch-screen, or not? We don't know. On these topics I wrote an entire ERC project that failed; they didn't like it, so I didn't get the grant, but I will unpack it in in separate different projects. We started already with the part on the impact of auditory immersion in modulating the response of the brain to audiovisual content; the next step will be specifically to investigate this new quality of audio-visual experience mediated by mobile touch-screens as techno-prosthesis of our body to see whether they introduce modulation and of what kind. This is what's coming next in our lab. I'm also writing a book on the impact of digital technologies on subjectivity and on who we are becoming. It will be an exercise of balance, trying not to be too apocalyptic—although it's quite difficult.

NL: Thank you. Cutting across brain-body-cultures divides, we will certainly have to keep thinking about the two patho(-)logical sides of hypermimesis at play on a variety of touch-screens. I very much look forward to your book that will help us in *Homo Mimeticus III*, provisionally subtitled, *Plasticity, Mimesis and Metamorphosis*.

Notes

1   See, for instance, Lawtoo 2019.

2   This interview was originally conducted in July 2023 in Parma as ep. 9 of HOM Videos available here: https://www.youtube.com/watch?v=zmb52PNtrF0. It was subsequently transcribed and revised for written publication. I would like to thank Vittorio Gallese for

his hospitality on a warm summer day, for the inspiring discussion, and for joining forces with mimetic studies, both at the conference and in Parma.

3   See Gallese and Goldman 1998.
4   See Gallese 2001, 42–43.
5   See Gallese 2007.
6   For a more detailed discussion of this passage see Lawtoo 2013, 38–45.
7   Castiello et al. 2010.
8   On Janet's "psychology of the socius" see Lawtoo 2013, 266–280.
9   For a recent account of the "social bodily self" and its relation to "peripersonal space" see Ferroni and Gallese 2023.
10   See Kaltwasser et al. 2019.

Bibliography

Ammaniti, Massimo, and Vittorio Gallese (2014). *The Birth of Intersubjectivity: Psychodynamics, Neurobiology, and the Self.* New York: W. W. Norton & Company.

Castiello, Umberto, Cristina Becchio, Stefania Zoia, Cristian Nelini, Luisa Sartori, Laura Blason, Giuseppina D'Ottavio, Maria Bulgheroni, and Vittorio Gallese (2010). "Wired to Be Social: The Ontogeny of Human Interaction." *PLoS ONE* 5.10, e13199.

Cavarero, Adriana, and Nidesh Lawtoo (2021). "Mimetic Inclinations: A Dialogue with Adriana Cavarero," in *Contemporary Italian Women Philosophes: Stretching the Art of Thinking,* eds. Silvia Benso and Elvira Roncalli. Albany: State University of New York Press, 183–199.

Féré, Charles (1900). *Sensation et mouvement: études expérimentales de psycho-méchanique.* 2nd ed. Paris: Félix Alcan.

Ferroni, Francesca, and Vittorio Gallese (2023). "Social and Bodily Self: Conceptual and Psychopathological Considerations," in *The Routledge Handbook of Bodily Awareness,* eds. Adrian J. T. Alsmith and Matthew R. Longo. New York: Routledge, 522–541.

Gallese, Vittorio (2001). "The 'Shared Manifold' Hypothesis: From Mirror Neurons to Empathy." *Journal of Consciousness Studies* 8.5–7, 33–50.

—— (2007). "Embodied Simulation: From Mirror Neuron Systems to Interpersonal Relations." *Novartis Found Symp.* 278, 3–12.

—— (2011). "The Two Sides of Mimesis: Mimetic Theory, Embodied Simulation, and Social Identification," in *Mimesis and Science: Empirical Research on Imitation and the Mimetic Theory of Culture and Religion,* ed. Scott R. Garrels. East Lansing: Michigan State University Press, 87-108.

Gallese, Vittorio, and Alvin Goldman (1998). "Mirror Neurons and the Simulation Theory of Mind-Reading." *Trends in Cognitive Science* 2.12, 493–500.

Gallese, Vittorio, and Michele Guerra (2015). *The Empathic Screen: Cinema and Neuroscience,* trans. Frances Anderson. Oxford: Oxford University Press.

Hickok, Gregory (2014). *The Myth of Mirror Neurons: The Real Neuroscience of Communication and Cognition.* New York: W. W. Norton & Company.

Janet, Pierre (1938). "Les conduites sociales, " in *Onzième Congrès International de Psychologie,* eds. H. Pieron and I. Meyerson. Paris: Alcan, 138-149.

Kaltwasser, Laura, Nicolas Rost, Martina Ardizzi, Marta Calbi, Luca Settembrino, Joerg Fingerhut, Michael Pauen, and Vittorio Gallese (2019). "Sharing the Filmic Experience: The Physiology of Socioemotional Processes in the Cinema." *PLoS ONE* 14.10: 1–19.

Lawtoo, Nidesh (2013). *The Phantom of the Ego: Modernism and the Mimetic Unconscious*. East Lansing. Michigan State University Press.

—— (2019). "The Mimetic Unconscious: A Mirror for Genealogical Reflections," in *Imitation, Contagion, Suggestion: On Mimesis and Society*, ed. Christian Borch. New York: Routledge, 37–53.

—— (2023). *Violence and the Oedipal Unconscious: vol. 1, The Catharsis Hypothesis*. East Lansing: Michigan State University Press.

Nietzsche, Friedrich (1982). *Daybreak*, trans. R. J. Hollingdale. Cambridge: Cambridge University Press.

Pitts-Tylor, Victoria (2013). "I Feel Your Pain: Embodied Knowledges and Situated Neurons." *Hypatia* 22.4, 853–868.

Plato (1963). "*Republic*," trans. Paul Shorey, in *The Collected Dialogues of Plato,* eds. E. Hamilton and H. Cairns. Princeton: Princeton University Press, 575–853.

Rizzolatti, Giacomo, and Corrado Sinigaglia (2008). *Mirrors in the Brain: How Our Minds Share Actions and Emotions*. Oxford: Oxford University Press.

Tarde, Gabriel (2001). *Les lois de l'imitation*. Paris: Seuil.

NOTES ON CONTRIBUTORS

Nidesh Lawtoo is Professor of Modern and European Literature and Culture at Leiden University and principal investigator (PI) of the *Homo Mimeticus* project. Located at the juncture of philosophy, literature, and political theory his work opens up the field of mimetic studies via a series of books including *The Phantom of the Ego* (2013), *Conrad's Shadow* (2016, Adam Gillon Award), *(New) Fascism* (2019), *Homo Mimeticus* (2022), and a diptych on *Violence and the Unconscious* (2023). He is currently co-editing a trilogy on *Homo Mimeticus* forthcoming with Leuven University Press.

Marina Garcia-Granero is an Assistant Professor of Moral Philosophy at the University of Valencia. She is a former postdoc from the Institute of Philosophy at KU Leuven in Belgium, where she worked in 2022 as an Associate Member of the ERC Project "Homo Mimeticus." She is a Nietzsche scholar currently working on mimesis and nihilism as well as ethics and feminist philosophy. She is a member of multiple Nietzsche societies, including the Friedrich Nietzsche Society (United Kingdom), the HyperNietzsche International Research Group, and the Spanish Society for Nietzsche Studies (SEDEN).

Carmen Bonasera holds a PhD in Theory of Literature and Comparative Literature from the University of Pisa (Italy). She has held positions as postdoc researcher at Ca' Foscari University of Venice and at the University of Bologna, and she is currently a postdoc at the University of Turin. In her monograph, *Aporie dell'Io. Identità e trasfigurazione nella poesia femminile contemporanea* (2023), she investigated the relationship between poetry and life writing in modern female authors. Her current research interests revolve around the dynamics of narrative and negative empathy, which she is studying with theoretical, stylistic, and empirical approaches.

Mikkel Borch-Jacobsen is Emeritus Professor of French and Comparative Literature at the University of Washington. He is the author of numerous books on the centrality of mimesis in the philosophy and history of psychoanalysis, including *The Freudian Subject* (1988), *Lacan: The Absolute Master* (1991), *The Emotional Tie* (1993), *The Freud Files* (with Sonu Shamdasani, 2006), *Making Minds and Madness* (2009), and *Freud's Patients* (2021). He now lives and writes in Dordogne, France.

Carlos Carvalhar is a Brazilian researcher who focuses on Plato but is also interested in other Ancient Philosophies. Carvalhar holds a Ph.D. in Philosophy (Universidade Federal da Bahia), in which he studied the political figure of Plato, a master's degree in Philosophy (Universidade Federal do Rio de Janeiro), and two bachelor's degrees, one in Philosophy (Universidade de São Paulo) and another in Ancient Greek and Latin Languages (Universidade Federal da Bahia).

Teresa Casas Hernández holds a PhD in Philosophy from the New School for Social Research. She is currently an Adjunct Professor at Universidad Carlos III de Madrid and splits her time between academia and cultural projects on performing arts. Her research takes place at the crossroads between theater and philosophy. She researches the ideology behind the different transformations of the concept of "theater" with a special focus on the concept of mimesis. Through the analysis of contemporary theater she explores the potentiality of theater for an epistemology of resistance.

William E. Connolly is Krieger-Eisenhower Professor Emeritus at Johns Hopkins. His recent books include *Facing the Planetary: Entangled Humanism and the Politics of Swarming* (2017), *Aspirational Fascism* (2017), *Climate Machines, Fascist Drives and Truth* (2019), and *Resounding Events* (2022). His new book, *Stormy Weather: Pagan Cosmologies, Christian Times, Climate Wreckage*, is forthcoming with Fordham University Press in 2024.

Henry Dicks is an environmental philosopher, specializing in the philosophy of biomimicry. He is the author of *The Biomimicry Revolution: Learning from Nature how to Inhabit the Earth* (2023), the co-author of a special issue of *Environmental Values* on the philosophy of biomimicry, and has published articles on this topic in such journals as *Philosophy of Science*, *Philosophy and Technology*, *Environmental Ethics*, *Journal of Agricultural and Environmental Ethics*, *Ethics & the Environment*, and *Environmental Philosophy*.

Evelyne Ender, *docteur ès lettres* from the University of Geneva, teaches in the Department of Comparative Thought and Literature at the Johns Hopkins University. She is the author of *Sexing the Mind: Nineteenth-Century of Hysteria* (1995) and of *ArchiTexts of Memory: Literature, Science, and Autobiography* (2005). Body/Mind and narrative issues are central to her research. Her publications, in English and French, include articles and chapters on major authors and on poetics, trauma, illness, and literature, déjà-vu as well as reading. She coordinated with Deidre Lynch on two *PMLA* special issues on *Cultures of Reading*. She is finishing a book on *HandWriting: an Inner History*.

Vittorio Gallese, MD, is a Full Professor of Psychobiology and Cognitive Neuroscience at the University of Parma. Among his main contributions are the discovery, together with colleagues from Parma, of mirror neurons, and the development of the Theory of Embodied Simulation. He won numerous prizes including, most recently, the Humboldt Forschung Preis from the Alexander von Humboldt Stiftung, Germany (2019). He is the author of more than 300 scientific publications and three books: *The Birth of Intersubjectivity* (2014; with Massimo Ammaniti), *The Empathic Screen* (2015, with Michele Guerra), and *Embodying the Self* (2018).

Niki Hadikoesoemo is Lecturer of Philosophy of Art and Culture at the University of Amsterdam. She obtained her PhD in philosophy at KU Leuven as part of the *Homo Mimeticus* project, in which she focused on the theatrical dimension of mimesis in Derrida, Lacoue-Labarthe, and Irigaray. Her research is situated at the intersection of twentieth-century French thought, feminist philosophy, and broader philosophical investigations into the material, affective, nonrepresentational manifestations of mimetic behavior, such as mimetism and (human and non-human animal) mimicry.

William A. Johnsen is Professor of English at Michigan State University, author of *Violence and Modernism: Ibsen, Joyce and Woolf* (2003) as well as numerous essays in modern European literature and theory. He edits the journal *Contagion* and two book series at MSU Press, *Studies in Violence, Mimesis, and Culture*, as well as *Breakthroughs in Mimetic Theory*, all devoted to the work of René Girard and new developments in mimetic theory.

Kieran Keohane is a Professor in Sociology and Criminology at University College Cork, Ireland. **Carmen Kuhling** is a Psychotherapist, and Associate

Professor in Sociology at the University of Limerick, Ireland. Graduates of York University, Toronto, influenced by cultural sociology in the interpretive tradition, critical theory, continental philosophy, political anthropology, feminist theory, and psychoanalysis, Keohane and Kuhling are interested in individual and collective experiences of crisis and transition, and social pathologies of contemporary civilization.

María del Carmen Molina Barea is Lecturer at the University of Córdoba, Spain. She holds an International PhD. in Aesthetics and an MA in Contemporary Art Theory from Goldsmiths College. She spent several research stays at the Università degli Studi di Firenze, Warburg Institute, and École des Hautes Études en Sciences Sociales. She is the author of numerous academic papers published in international journals on topics such as avant-garde aesthetics, postmodern ontology, gender theory, film philosophy, and visual cultures.

Mark Pizzato, MFA, PhD, is Professor of Theater and Film at the University of North Carolina at Charlotte (USA). His books include *European Churches and Chinese Temples as Neuro-Theatrical Sites* (2024), *Mapping Global Theatre Histories* (2019), *Beast-People Onscreen and in Your Brain* (2016), *Inner Theatres of Good and Evil* (2011), *Ghosts of Theatre and Cinema in the Brain* (2006), *Theatres of Human Sacrifice* (2005), and *Edges of Loss* (1998). He also co-edited, with Lisa K. Perdigao, *Death in American Texts and Performances* (2010).

Henry Staten is Lockwood Professor of Humanities at the University of Washington. His acclaimed first book, *Wittgenstein and Derrida* (1984), was one of the first philosophical commentaries on deconstruction. Since then his work has ranged widely across literature and philosophy and includes *Nietzsche's Voice* (1990), *Eros in Mourning* (1995), *Spirit Becomes Matter* (2014), *The Craft of Poetry* (with Derek Attridge, 2015), and *Techne Theory* (2019).